— The —

WISDOM

— of —

GOD

God calls on his children

JOHANNE HOWARD

 FriesenPress

Suite 300 - 990 Fort St
Victoria, BC, V8V 3K2
Canada

www.friesenpress.com

ISBN
978-1-5255-7876-2 (Hardcover)
978-1-5255-7877-9 (Paperback)
978-1-5255-7878-6 (eBook)

1. SELF-HELP, SPIRITUAL

Distributed to the trade by The Ingram Book Company

TABLE OF CONTENTS

GRATITUDE AND THANKS TO ALL WHO WERE
SUPPORTIVE AND HELPFUL DURING THE
WRITING OF THIS WORK, AND ESPECIALLY
THANKS BE TO GOD AND HIS ANGELS.

Introduction

Does God exist? Who is God? Where is God? Nothing has prepared me to dare ask these questions. Being born into a religious system that obliged me to believe without question and to have faith without any proof of a living God other than vague answers and man written books, opened my mind to search for the truth. Many people on Earth blindly obey domineering rulers who see themselves as the representatives of God. If God exists would he choose these men to instruct his children?

These questions opened the path to an adventure started in the year 2003 when I began receiving messages from the Spiritual World. Years later in 2012, I posted some of these messages on a blog site titled: newtimesonearth2012.blogspot.ca. It was visited by people from all over the world. On these following pages, you will find God's words destined to be read by his children. In 2004 and 2005, he began to dictate the words he wanted me to share (Part 1, 2004-2005). Later, by means of the blog, he dictated the remainder (Part 2, 2012-2016).

In Part 1, 2004-2005, the language used is of an ancient biblical nature. Over many years of receiving daily, the language changed to a more casual and current English. This fascinated me having worked with English language learners who often translated from their own mother language, the similarities were obvious. God and the Archangels have their own original language that resembles Sanskrit, for example the word *setu* means *bridging*. The grammar structures remind me of Esperanto, a language created by Edmond Bordeaux Szekely. They shared their language with me, and presently I learned about 120 words. Archangel Gabriel is gifted in languages; he is more fluent in common uses of present-day English.

The messages I received at first were from the Archangels Michael, Gabriel, Uriel, Raphael and Jesus who is called Teacher by them. They guided me through difficult times and opened to many misconceptions and misunderstandings I had of the world. This was for me a great period of learning and personal growth. They call me Za which means *love* in their language, and typically they say *my Za* as a term of endearment. And at times, especially in the beginning of the communications, they called me *lona* which means *stubborn,* mostly because I did not believe who they are. Now I do.

Then came the introduction to God, and my great resistance to believing any of this could be possible. However, the conversations and information shared with me were more than surprising and captivated my interest for all these years. I began to see and understand that God is a true living being who once lived on Earth and is returning to his home planet in a short time. These messages are shared in preparation for the time of reunification.

God is returning to Earth with his army to stop those who serve darkness from destroying his planet and all other planets that may be affected from Earth's destruction. You will find dear reader in these many pages his words for you to understand the truth about what lives on Earth. God explains to his children what happened on Earth and why he left Sophia his wife and many of his children behind when his army had to escape from Earth to find reinforcements. This is the saddest story.

God is a true being in our lives, guiding and walking with us, his children. He is not a myth, or an image for any social system of control, ruled by falsity and depraved humans. God is our Father; he is coming home and he will show himself to the world. Your prayers are heard. God is presently working with us to help us find the light, teaching and guiding us to regain our free will. My life's mission is to continue to work with God and to do as he asked me, to share his words with his children before his arrival. He calls me Za and I am a scribe. You will see this at end of each blog with a date when the message was received. God is preparing us for the second exodus, to free us from the works of evil that plague our lives on Earth.

So, listen to our father. God is coming home. Light is coming.

Za, (May, 2020)

Part 1 (2004-2005)

Note added in 2020: In this Part 1, God speaks for the first time to address his children and the chosen ones through the dictated messages I received mostly in the year 2004. At that time, the language is less adapted to the current uses of English. These messages in Part 1 are meant, in my opinion, to be of an introductory nature.

1. IN MY WORDS

No one will know for truth what I am about to write until their lives have been touched. One day you will see that truth is the essence of life, and that untruths are the destroyers of life.

You will discover that many of you are weary of being told what to think and what to feel, and many of you are searching in yourselves to be ready for a time of peace and understanding. Trust in yourselves to know what is right and what is wrong, and be careful of the ones who wish to confuse you with many words and promises of false prophets and teachers. Know that the time of serving false prophets is over. Come and listen to my words and to me, the one who has created you.

The way of God is the way of all who honor truth, and the way of man is to understand the truth about God and the Spiritual World. Understand that all to come is of stopping those who do not understand God's way, and who are in the chosen path of evil. The way of God is the way of the will of humans to change all to be. Now listen to my words and take heed soon for the time of understanding has come.

UNDERSTANDING

The more one understands about the Spiritual World, the more the Spiritual World is able to respond to more individuals. This is done with willing hearts, and trying to open to love that is communion and dedication. This opening will allow understanding and give strength to the wishes of many to do the same.

OPENING TO THE LIGHT

Trusting in the Spiritual World can be difficult because humans have been in darkness so long. You have an ancestor of a superior source of life. You are the results of many thousands of years of unrealized strength. Awakening to the potential will make many serve others who will act as false prophets. You must then only be serving yourself towards your knowledge and awakening.

The way to do this is so simple, and demands the courage of your heart to do this. Understanding the way of God is all written before for all to find and discern the right from the wrong: in the Bible, in the Torah and in the Koran. You must discover your secrets in these books because these books alone have the Tree of Life written in them for all to understand and be stopping the wars and destruction of the Earth. Will you read them and see for yourself?

Now time is short and understanding is necessary to open to the new life of humanity. Understanding this is not new but for many it is forgotten. The way of opening to the Tree of Life is to know that your soul is part of many other lives, and that what you experience in this life will serve as a stepping stone of the Tree of Life. You are too withdrawn into your own time to see that all has a purpose, answering only to your needs and seeing only your desires. This is part of the Tree of Life that you must ask yourself to move from. Your world does not only belong to you, it is the creation of many beings working with me to hold and to share. Thus, all is One and One is All.

TOWARDS THE NEW TIME

You are in a time where so many are trusting in false prophets and leaders. Trust only in opening to the Light Spirit, the Holy Spirit. You are in a time that sends many good souls into turmoil, despair and suffering. All this is not of my word. The way of God is the way of staying the course no matter what it will be.

You will see in your time a way of evil that defines all the suffering of Humans. This is the work of another who works in darkness. Many do not wish to speak of him and protect him, but his time is done, and now it is time to change all the damage that he has caused. Open to the light, not darkness, and trust in my word.

Trusting in yourself is often difficult. No one can tell you how you really feel. Only your heart holds the truth of all things and of all your secrets. Your trust in yourself and in your heart is what you must listen to.

TOWARDS YOUR FREEDOM

You are all children of God's creation. You are all blessed ones and untouched at birth by sin. The idea of all being born in sin is wrong, and does not come from me. Soon you will understand why all religions needed to oppress all that is true to one's freedom. Much has been learned since then and much has been tried to help many find the paths of enlightenment. Truth is the path of enlightenment. All who are capable of truth are walking in the path of God. Understand that so many will change truth to untruth, and the only way you can change this is by being open to your own heart.

Understanding the laws of nature is a reflection of understanding yourselves. You are given a way to open to me and the Spiritual World through Christ's teachings. All that he said is what I wished that all learn. Many have turned away from him, and used my words to change the way of being in my light. Soon all will see the new miracles performed by the ones chosen by me. Understand that these words come to you to use for the well-being of the world.

TOWARDS LEARNING

WILL is a very important aspect of human development. It permits openness to the Spiritual World and to the way of God. All that is will is an understanding of the ability to make choices, and to act on your choices. This takes some effort; often trusting in our will is oppressed by other forces. These other forces are the energies used to counter-balance. On one hand you have your Will, and on the other hand you have counter-will. Answering to counter-will causes an imbalance to the body. No one can hurt you if you trust in your own will to do what is written. Many false prophets will use what is written to enrich themselves and obtain power. You only need to learn the words of my writings to see that all is clear, and all is there for you to live a life that follows the way of my creation.

Soon reading this will open your hearts, and the new times on earth will be created and all will live in peace and serenity. The way of God is the way of life on Earth; the answer to all that is good is in my words.

TOWARDS SERENITY

The way to open to all is through the heart. You can only respond truthfully if you open with your heart. This is the way of the Spiritual World. You can only be yourself if your words are taken from the heart, and from your mouth truths will pour out like strands of golden light.

All hearts know this because it is my love that dwells there. All those who deny this, are in the path of evil and will answer only to darkness. Understand that it is darkness that imprisoned you on Earth, and it is light from your Creator that has come to free you from eternal reincarnation.

Death is a gateway to the place called Heaven. This place is an island of coming shared knowledge of the greatest love. This place holds all beings accountable for their choices on Earth. Answer to only those who dwell in this place.

You are in darkness. You are held by a Spirit who wishes to open the gates to other spirits. This is not the way of God. The truth of God is not through these spirits. These angels of darkness are holding many from touching Light. These angels of darkness are not of the Stars of Heaven. These angels of darkness do not hold the balance. These angels of darkness serve another.

God

Received in 2004 by Za

2. LIGHT IS COMING

Understand that all of Creation belongs to the Creator. This is one God, not many. Life itself is of me. Life itself is of my spark. No one but me has started all, and all is given by me. But the way of God undoes itself when the ones who are angels of darkness descend to manipulate the new awakenings of the many chosen ones.

The reason this is done is to exercise their own powers wishing to equal mine. None can achieve this. No amount of destruction can equal construction. Soon all will see this. All will understand that God does not destroy. I create. Darkness destroys.

You are my children. You are my loving creation. All that is of God is good. All that is of darkness is not of me, but of another.

You will hear my words from a few of my chosen ones, and from my beloved Sophia of the Holy Spirit and of the Holy Trinity. She is my delight and my concubine. You must listen to her words for her words are my words, and she is the second coming.

TOWARDS HEALING

The time has come to open to healing. You are of a time that many speak of healing, but do not understand the truth about healing. The truth about healing is that you are not in understanding. Trust and believe you will understand all when you open your heart to what I will tell you.

Healing comes from the heart. The heart contains many secrets of past times when all lives were vessels of God, and all understandings resided in its depths. Understandings are the paths to the gates of the opening to Heaven and to the temple of Zion.

You are in a time that does not open to many of these truths. Soon many will speak these truths and you will hear my words in all mouths streaming like sounds of angelic voices. You are in a place of so much darkness, this is not the place for the children of God. I sent you my son and he gave you my words. Now hear my words again and take heed. The love that lives in all hearts is heard by the Spiritual World, and all that hear my words will awaken to me.

TOWARDS OPENING OF THE HEART

Understand that the heart contains my message to you. Understand that I am who I am. The way of God is to open your hearts to receive my light, and to share this light with others. Be ready now because all that I have created is opening to a new time, and all that I say will come to be.

Opening your heart requires an openness of soul that many will not see with the eye. The opening of the soul is a time of complete peace with oneself, and all truth about oneself is clear. You may be deceiving yourself about who you think you are. You may be denying to yourself that you are who you are.

The scoffer is the one who will be the most troubled by this, because he is soon so troubled by all the sins he must accept in his own soul. You need to see yourself as you are. You need to ask me for forgiveness, and I will grant it if your words are truth. You will be given absolution only from me. You are in darkness, now come to the light.

TOWARDS AN OPENING OF THE SOUL YOU ARE IN DARKNESS, NOW COME TO THE LIGHT.

Why is my word so important in this time? Why are many of you receiving my message? Why are you being asked to share my words with others? All that is, has come to be reasoned in your time. You have searched for many hundreds of years for the reason of your existence, and you have heard and seen many beings produce miracles. But all that is does not accept my word as I speak it. Now time is right for all to understand the way of God. All will soon be ready to follow the way of God. Trust in me and I will show you a place of happiness and serenity, that will calm all fears, all pain and all torment. Open your soul to my word.

TOWARDS AN UNDERSTANDING OF THE SPIRITUAL WORLD

Now is the time for all to understand. Question all who tell you that you are not able to do this; all who say that you must give your trust to them to come to me are false prophets. Read my words yourself, open your heart to yourself. Be ready for the answers that I will give you through your prayers to me and to the Archangels. You will see that the openness to your own understanding, done with a pure heart, will answer you and be your daily bread. Will is your own gift, and openness is your own tool to speak to us.

The time is now to open to us. Trust and believe. Understand that you are all my children, and I am your Creator.

TOWARDS AN OPENNESS TO THE HOLY SPIRIT

Yourselves are the beings of another time. You are the result of so much love. This love is in you and is your path to freedom from torment.

Stop asking why the world is such a terrible place, and see that it is you who must stand now and change it. You are all my children, and you are all the ones who are blessed.

Time is near to make all choices to answer back to all injustices. Many are asking how can they stand against evil now. You must know that standing against evil is to follow my words, and to be clear of the transgressions of Lucifer.

TOWARDS AN OPENNESS TO THE WAY OF GOD

The way of God answers all who need understanding. Understanding comes from the wish to learn about yourselves, who you are and how you came to be.

Many will want to find answers in the Spiritual World for the questions about their unknown past. These answers are within each one who questions, and not coming from some who say understand more than yourselves. All who say that knowledge is only a tool is mistaken. Knowledge brings on transformation and freedom. Keeping souls in darkness is an abomination and not God's way.

Understanding is your path to freedom and openness to me. Understanding why all have been kept in darkness is the wisdom all must acquire to be ready for the time of judgement.

God

Received in 2004 by Za

3. TOWARDS THE REASON
FOR INCARNATIONS

A long time ago, a great battle took place in the Heavens. Nothing was truthful, no one was understanding why this came to be. Once will was a shared thing but after the turmoil will was lost. Many others like Angels were needing to be guided. Angels and Archangels tried to help but they were not understanding the lost will.

The battle became a chaos in the Universe and something new emerged. This was reason, and reason opened to oppression. Now the way we were together in Heaven changed in such a way that we could no longer be together.

Soon Lucifer came, and told us that he knew a way that could help all the oppression. So many listened to his vision and agreed that it was good. Lucifer had another plan that was intended to trap God's souls on Earth. I did know all this, but I wanted to permit choices to recover lost will.

TOWARDS ACCEPTING LOST WILL

When lost will affected the souls on Earth, no one in Heaven could help them. My Angels were sent to guard the souls in hope to give them the way to recover and find my light again.

Guardian Angels were instructed to guide, and not change outcomes of the way of the Earth. This change belonged to all, and not to only us. Light and darkness have seen the worst of abuses. Trust and believing, understanding and acceptance fought against the darkness of fear and doubt, and soon against untruths and disbelief.

Guardian Angels watched this with such pain in them that they also became changed. Many have torment in them to not stop this and do what is righteous. Death is not a way to escape this torment as it is perpetual, and it is an understanding that is needed to stop this.

All my Angels are waiting now to see this change. For as above is as below. Now be ready for the change because, as said in the scriptures, all is coming and the time is now.

Life and death are a perpetual state of being. Understand that the cell changes in your body are for the most part regenerating and renewing themselves. These changes are of great significance that you/we often do not acknowledge. All this change has something to do with the way we are working together. Angels and Archangels, Thrones and Dominions, Principalities and Seraphim, are all part of these changes.

Torment changes the structure of your cells. When you are tormented by others, the cell structure is modified to understand the torment. If this abuse on the being is unchanging, then the body is also unchanging, and continues to respond to the torment. What torment you may be asking?

Torment comes in many forms and in many ways. Usually, you think that you cause this to yourself, and understand that this is life. But life a thousand years ago was different and the same, and so many died in horrible ways, and now so many dies in horrible ways. So, torment on Earth has not changed, only the thought about torment has changed.

Now diseases are taking the place of outside torment, because you can internalize it so well. The cure of illnesses is the cure of life on Earth. Understanding why this has occurred, is the way of staying open to your life, and separate the outside torment from your cells. Opening your heart reduces the tormentor's ability to work in you.

This is life's greatest secret; the heart. It contains all memories of past lives and understandings, and it holds all secrets of the Trinity. This was my gift to you, and you have not discovered it. Torments come from another than I. This you must now accept and free yourself from in your thoughts.

TOWARDS THE WAY TO HEAL FROM TORMENT

Torment is the tool that Lucifer gives you to serve him. Would you ask a tailor to use a hammer? Would you ask a tormentor to be kind? Why then would you accept the apologies of a tormentor? Why then would you accept a change that is only a trick?

This is the way of evil. The way of tormentors is many, and are always full of words to deceive you and to make you blind to the truth. When many words come to a situation, you must be careful to find the truth because many words are like a spell to confuse you and distract you from yourself, from your senses, and from your own knowledge.

You are a child of God, hear the one who has created you. You will soon be open to the way of the new times on earth, you must listen to your own heart and to the Spiritual World that guides you.

TOWARDS ANSWERS TO YOUR QUESTIONS

Many are asking why the way of God is with the way of evil, and why the way of evil is with us on Earth. This is not the way of God. This is the way of Lucifer and his followers in spirit form and in human form. Lucifer trusted me once but his openness was not truthful. He was an Archangel of such beauty and talent, but his thinking was on his own glory at any price. Soon he tried to equal me in power and in strength, and this caused dissension in our ways. Too many understood this, but waited for me to act and stop him. I wanted Lucifer to stop himself.

TOWARDS THE UNDERSTANDING
OF TRUST IN LOVE

Understanding the trust in love comes from your heart. When all is coming from the heart you will be understood clearly. Understanding clearly always comes from another place than the thought, it comes from the heart.

Now all that I have said to you through my scribe is truth, and all that I tell you through my scribe you must open to with your heart. This is what no one can do for you. You alone hold the secrets to your heart. The openness of your heart will occur when you are listening to it.

TOWARDS A DEATH OF THE
BELIEFS IN YOUR WORLD

You are troubled by the way torment is answering all who are good. This is the way of another than I. You want to be with the Holy Spirit, not to the opening to evil. That is why so many are trusting in good, and not in evil. Too many are caught in the snares of evil, and at every turn they are with pain and turmoil. This is how evil works into a good person by perpetually tormenting them through beings serving evil purposes.

4. TOWARDS YOUR ANSWERING TO THE WAY OF GOD

Be ready to answer to the way of God. Understand that you are that I wish you to be. Understand that you are my children and that I am your father. Answering to me answers to you, and will be soon so ready to tell what you understand about your life on Earth.

Understand that you are trusting in a God that is now so different. As my children changed in evolution, so have I. Torment taught me so much about human nature, and from this came a great shift in my ways. Now I will ask your trusting hearts to hear me and take heed of what needs to be done.

TOWARDS RECOGNIZING FALSE PROPHETS

This is an important part of my words. The many who wish to be called prophets are not of me. The churches are shifting towards works that are not of my wishes. The ones who are trying to tell you that what you are reading now is wrong, are not of my word.

This is the time that will show that you have to be one with God, and only your heart can tell you what is right and what is wrong. Open your hearts and hear my words because the time is now to choose the way of God. There is no other way to your evolution than the way towards your own truths of where you have emerged from and where you will return to.

TOWARDS ANSWERING YOURSELVES

Understand that you are of the flesh, and in the flesh are many problems. The first is the need to sustain your body, the second is to receive the Spirit of God, and the third is to open yourselves to your own truth.

You are soon opening to your own truth when you started to read my words, and to yourselves when you had feelings of love stirring in you. This is what you must trust. You must trust your way of love in you and of understanding that this love comes from the place of your emergence. This is my word to you through my scribe.

TOWARDS UNDERSTANDING OF THE FLESH

You are in the flesh. Many problems come from this. The first is need. The second is desire. The third is love. All these are the way of God, and to your own truth.

The way to come to me is through your heart and through your own soul. The way of the heart is the way of my being with you. Understand that you are my children and that you are my loves, and all that has been said about how I punish you comes from another.

You are not his, you are my creation, and I am reclaiming my children to come home to Heaven in the end of time. You will see many changes, and many more will come as you accept and awaken to this truth.

TOWARDS YOUR FREEDOM OF TRUST

You are the one who is of love and of understanding the way of God, but you are soon so not open to your trust in the Spiritual World. You are trusting your reason but not your heart, and you are not being open to yourself.

Let the light of our love enter your hearts and let the one who changes all speak about yourself. You will find that you are the way you always were, before the prison of Earth entrapped you to serve darkness.

TOWARDS A WAY TO GOD

Many prophets are the way of God, but many are not. Understand that spiritual discernment is your work on Earth. You open your hearts to the way of God, and you will find the truth you seek. You will be trusting the way of God, and torment will leave you and light will fill you with love from the Spiritual World. Trusting your senses is the way of the flesh telling you that you must be ready to open to the telling of truths that come from understanding yourselves.

TOWARDS THE WILL OF GOD

Wishing to be of service to God is usually a way to God's work. Be open to the words written by my scribe, she gives you back to yourselves. Answer your own questions by answering your own answers. Trust in what your heart tells you. Be open to what is to come. Know that all true prophecies always are fulfilled, and your heart is united to all hearts that are of the knowing. Open, open the way of God. Trust in the Spiritual World and be one with me.

5. TOWARDS THE FREEING OF THE MOTHER

You are all in torment because the Mother of Creation has been imprisoned for too long by another. He is the dark forces of all times of Earth. He is the one of the many openings into darkness. You can feel him working in all places in all times. He is the one who is telling you to doubt me and my love. Understand that you can free yourself from him and come to the light.

TOWARDS THE WILL

The will is the essence that I gave you to help free yourself from my own responding. The Spiritual World is open to all who are seeking my way. Will you trust enough to find your way home? Will you trust enough to respond to your heart's utmost desire to love and serve me?

Now the way to God is the way to the Mother. She is incarnated in human form. She was sent to you to help you understand my way. She is the second coming, and she is the Wisdom Sophia.

You will see in time so many Earth changes, and the workings of a new time on Earth. You will see a renewal of all that needs to be, and all that is.

TOWARDS A NEW TIME ON EARTH

The way to God is to open to me and the Holy Spirit. You must see all things in life as a new beginning. You must see all things in life as an ending. Trust and believe that all is now, and know that now is the time to be one with God. Open to me and the one who will reveal herself to you in time.

TOWARDS UNDERSTANDING THE MOTHER

Death is a way to come home to us. Suicide is a way to continue the torments of Lucifer. On the day of the reckoning, many will try to take their lives. This will only delay their place in Heaven, and return them to the way of Lucifer. Now, understanding is of the most importance. You are the few who can do this, and the few who can help the others to understand. This is the time of the Reckoning. All that you know and believe of your world, is now ended. Trust and believe in the spiritual world, and be one with God.

TOWARDS AN UNDERSTANDING OF
THE OPENNESS OF MY WAY

Will you open to the way of God? Will you be ready for all to come in the day of reckoning? You are the one that can do this. You are the one who is opening. Stopping this is the way of another. It is of the way of the tormentors and of the dark Angels.

Now is the time to answer to my concubine. She is Wisdom Sophia. She is the one who will be stopping all evil from coming to take the souls coming to Earth to renew themselves.

TOWARDS AN UNDERSTANDING OF THE
LOST LOVE OF URIEL AND THE MOTHER

Understand that Archangel Uriel followed the Mother to Earth so that he could stop her murderers. Uriel the Archangel of sudden changes becomes the coming light of the Earth. He is the only one that can open the gates of torment of Earth. He is the strength behind Sophia, and she is the one to change all. Trust these Archai to open and free you from the gates of torment, and follow their answers to your questions.

TOWARDS THE UNDERSTANDING OF EVIL

The way of becoming holy is to be ready to accept that evil lives in many souls. This essence is given by Lucifer, and is masked by a bright light. This is not the light of God. This is not the light of love. This light is of darkness, and is unloving.

The way to discern this is to be open only to my light and to my love. All other light, is not of love; it blinds and burns the eyes, and heart and soul, and serves only Lucifer.

Now the way of my word is love, but not acceptance of evil, not tolerance of evil, and all the unjust actions and thoughts of evil.

6. TOWARDS AN UNDERSTANDING OF GOD'S LOVE

The way to God is to love who you are, and who you are becoming. Understand that all that you are is essence of God's love being returned to you, and all that you are is in God's love for you. The love that is sent to you always brings inner peace. Now is the time to come to your place in Heaven. Now is the time to open to God's love, and be One with God.

TOWARDS AN ACCEPTANCE OF THE MOTHER

The Mother has long denied her role of the Archai Omega, because of her pain in her heart. She is the one who is the bride of God. She is the one that wills turmoil and torment with her sufferings, but she does not know it.

This awakening is coming now, and she is understanding it. You must open to her and trust that she can heal, and that her healing is your healing. Stay open always to her ways of healing, and to the way of your freedom from torment and turmoil, and heal all that stops you from coming to the light. You are all my children, and now it is time to come home to my love.

TOWARDS AN UNDERSTANDING OF THE WILL OF SOPHIA

Answer this. Before these words came to you, did you not know in your heart that God lives there? And did you not know that you are free to choose good over evil? And that you are free to be One with me, the Mother and the Son? Now I ask you; will you choose to be One with the Trinity?

This is the way to my word and this is the way to Sophia, the light of love and the light of wisdom on Earth. She has awakened now, and you must open to her and see all that comes of her is yours in your heart. When you accept her, you will be so amazed of all the changes that will come of this time of reckoning. The new time on Earth prepares itself, and all will see the glory of the one who changes all.

TOWARDS AN UNDERSTANDING OF THE WILL OPENING TO THE SPIRITUAL WORLD

Opening to the spiritual world is torment ending. When you understand that your torments have caused your blindness to openness to the paths to my words, then you will be stopping the darkness, and the understandings will all open to you. Torment keeps you in darkness, and freedom from tormentors is your salvation. Understandings come from your thoughts, not from the thoughts of your torments.

The Spiritual World has had much to open to. As is above, as is below. More than you can imagine, more than you can see. Torment spirits are in all places, and are in all hearts. To rid yourself of this, you must trust that torments are as readily destroyed by your prayers to me, as they are created by the dark angels. Soon all torments will be replaced by understandings, and you shall become pure of heart, and your heart will receive understandings in love and peace.

TOWARDS A TIME OF GREAT PEACE AND RESPONSIBILITY

Be ready, knowledge heals all. Be ready and see all come as I said. Be ready, open to the light of my love, and be well answered by all my words. See these days come with sadness and joy, and see how all becomes well dealt with. See how all is moving towards the time of reckoning, and be settling with the ways of the Earth. Be ready to answer to my call and to my love, and be settling with the ways on Earth at the time of reckoning. Settle with the ways of deceptions and injustices, as these ways only tell of the workings of devils. Be ready to believe that you have renewed with our truth as you see God answer you on Earth, and open the gates for all these truths to be seen.

All is here, and many will see these good settling ways of Earth better open to a time of peace and serenity.

Received in 2004 by Za

Part 2 (2012-2016)

Note from 2020: In this Part II, God begins to explain the history of the events that led to the leaving of the armies and the Angels. God speaks about what Lucifer does to trick, lie and deceive to answer to his greed of power and control. God also explains that Lucifer is doing this again as God and the Angels are preparing to return to Earth. This is visible now as we are all prisoners in our homes due to fear and threats. All is happening now because of the Angels' time to walk the Earth.

7. THE TRANSITIONAL TIME

Now is the time to answer to many unseen truths about who we are, and why we are returning to our planet you call Earth. Be understanding that a long time ago we answered all who were seeing the way as we did. But dissension arose and became the way of Earth, and the telling of who we are were changed by answers from another who wanted to be the only ruler of the planet Earth. To do this, he caused many to be telling lies about us, and changed our ways of being with deceptions and trickery.

Then a great flood came from these workings of Lucifer, because he wished to be the only ruler of the Earth, and he wanted to destroy as many of our kind as he could to answer to his own control and greed. And see this be done again as he fears our responding times on Earth.

Be willing now to answer to me and know that I am your Father and your Creator, and see how all truths will undo the lies that have held you captive in beliefs that are false. Renew with us, and meet your families.

I am seeing many in fear and torment on Earth at this time, and I will make the greatest effort to answer all of you as I near Earth. Be certain you will soon be serving with us as these great times open to the great changes needed to settle with answers to our telling of great renewals. Be well answered by our truth and see all be well seen as arrivals begin with many other Beings of Light who are waiting to open to their own families. Be dealing with the way all will become calmer and better serving as we begin the work of cleaning Earth, and renewing technologies to help with the changes on Earth.

As these days arrive, visit with us to heal all serving ailments and diseases given to you to cause you more torment, and learn with us the many healing ways we have long practiced to answer to our well-being. These ways are so simple, and you will be returned to your optimal health. Serve many more ways of healing because the stress you serve answers to Lucifer's way of control.

With these healing ways, you will soon be visited by many others from many other planets who wish to meet many humans to open to a new time on Earth, and begin an alliance of great truth. Question and question to be ready for all understandings to open to you, and we will share all answers until you are well answered. Be serving a time of deep meditation; serve a response to your family and friends to remain calm and focused, as all will be put in place to answer to the many coming changes.

Be renewing with us, and be certain no harm will be settling with our kind. Evidence of the way of wars will be stopped; the repair of homes and living ways will begin to be well dealt with and shared. Beings of Light will help all to restore peace and care among all who will open to these times. Good truth will open to all who are ready to listen to our lost history of how all came to be. And I ask you to be patient, as the transitional time will be settling and responding to better answer to many who are in great need of help first. Soon all others will be helped to know truth as all becomes served.

Be ready and remain calm and focused; remember you are my children and I am arriving soon to better your lives on Earth as healing times are now here and ready to answer all who are ready to renew with us. See to it that you will answer to your hearts greatest desire, evidence of our time of renewing. Stories of the past will open your hearts, and serve you in many healing ways.

Be serving many coming days of great changes with us, as we are now ready to open to the world. Settle with understood lies that never served you, and only served those who have controlled your wishes, your thoughts and your lives, telling you, you are the causes to all problems. When all lies are moved out of the way, you will be free, and these understandings will respond to your own truth that lives in your heart.

Be ready, and see all come as I said. Open your hearts to my love and care for you, as the time is here to open to all truth and all serving ways of better life, and better care for all who will hear my words. Be dealing with these words I now share with you as you may and as you wish to be, and see God's love open to all who are ready to be reunited with us.

Be ready and know that all telling of truth answers you. Deaths and the time of horrors of Earth are soon past and over. We could not come to Earth before as free Will needed to evolve for many on Earth. Be ready and see these good serving days used to open to our arrivals, and then all understandings will begin to unravel.

Now question all who oppose me, and see why they are full of fear, as they have many reasons to fear our presence on Earth. They are the blasphemers and corrupted souls, who are not serving the Universal Laws. To these ones, all is dangerous and serving their ways, but understand that they are the ones who are causing all the troubles on Earth.

Answer to my call, knowledge is soon here and see all truths be proven with the way of great changes well coming to Earth to serve all who are ready to open to our truth. Be well answered, and question all as needed, to be understanding who we are, and why we are now opening to the world. Be serving a time of quiet meditation, and respond to our ways, and see all be as I say. Know you are my children. I have returned to answer you and open the way of great truth for you.

Now see all be as I said, and be ready. Heal your broken hearts as all becomes settled, and serving truth serves you.

God

Received June 19, 2012 by Za

8. BE READY FOR THE ARRIVALS

Be ready and see these times be changing to open to a time of great under-standings and better truth. Be well answered by all who are soon ready to open to awareness of many more renewing ways, and be well answered by our time to walk the Earth. The better truths are soon here, and many will start seeing all with healed bodies and better living ways.

These ways are answering to all who wish to open to us, and heal with us the separation repeated by your rulers. They are now nearing their end of their telling of lies, and they well understand what they have done and what they are responsible for. Be well serving of our truth, as these words I share with you are the words healing you right now.

Respond to our arrivals with us, be calm and be ready to meet with your true families. We are waiting to be with you, and with our ways of returning all evidence of truth with the way of great seeing and great Setu (bridging) ways. Be well answered by all who are searching for you. Know that not all beings of our kind on Earth have agreed to be on Earth to help with these understood changing times. Some of our kind were taken against their will and without their knowledge or memories of these events. This healing opens to them and to you, who have suffered greatly to be used as sources of breeding into bloodlines that are not of your choosing a long time ago.

See these words answer you, as you will understand why many of you feel you do not belong on Earth, and why you are treated with lives of misery to keep you from discovering your true-self. These times are evi-dence of ended tyranny over my children, and all over for others who have been taken from their families, and who are now found by us.

We did not know the way this came to be until some of our scouts served these understood truths to us. We believed you were all in agreement of the ways of Earth and all truths were known by you, and all settling ways were telling of your alliances. More than I say about this needs to be shared, and these words you will soon hear as you begin to unravel these truths.

When all started to be seen by us, we needed to make a plan to answer to our return to Earth. These plans were dealing with a need to awaken many of our kind so they could start with our words. Many you call channelers are the ones who open to our telepathic communications because they are of our kind. Many are also parts of the fallen Angels proven by their deceptions and trickery. But many are as we are, and only serve with us. These are my children who were taken because Lucifer needed the holy blood to make more able to do his deeds of technology and science to serve his purposes.

Now all heals as we are responding back to all offenses and abuses. Understand, we used to be with many other groups of Angels. The non-believers were the ones who destroyed these planets near Earth causing a great shift to occur. See this on the Moon base, as this is their place of governance of Earth.

Now tell yourselves all lies told to you will soon be uncovered, and all truths discovered. Be well awakened by the used (past) understandings with us, and with these demons that we will soon uncover. Be well settling with these ones as they will better see they are only settling with their end of abuses on humans. These ones will soon better understand the responses to their workings.

Now open to our arrivals. Know all harm heals with us. And know we are settling renewal times as we speak, to better prepare all who will better see these truths, and to share knowledge (onm) with the others who still live in fear of being harmed. Be well serving of our time together and see we are as you are, and we wish to be reunited and opening the way for reunions with family and better ways of living.

While you are responding to the changes, we will begin evidence of a great projects of cleaning Earth. Some may need to be relocated, some will choose to open to working with the Galactic Federation of Light, and some will remain on Earth to answer to participation in the many shared projects of renewal. Be certain all these ways are of your choice and decision, and you can do all these things if you choose.

These times of having slave masters telling you what to do are over. Now you will know the truth, and be free to choose your own way with us or with others who follow the Universal Laws. This will answer many, and these times will heal many, as these times begin to be settling with all truths on Earth. Be certain you will heal your broken hearts as you need to with your loved ones long lost through death and separation.

With these words, I wish to tell you that death is not as you see on Earth. On Earth, the body is used until completion, and then the soul returns to answer to another life. Be renewing this knowledge with us, and see how these ways were manipulated to erase all soul memories, to have another control of your destiny, and outcome of your lives. Renewing with this may be difficult to accept, as you have all accepted the facts of aging and death. Be surprised to know these ways only exists on Earth as you are being used as slaves to serve these demons. Be certain you will soon be free of these many returns to different lives, as the truth will open you to this knowledge.

Now be ready. All answers you soon and opens to the arrivals in evidence of the time of reckoning, and see all be as I said. Know you are well loved by all who are waiting to see their children return from abuses of Earth lives. Be serving a time of deep meditation, and ready yourselves for our return to Earth as we are the makers of these planets, and are settling with those who have caused us great sadness and heart pain.

God

Received June 20th, 2012 by Za

9. WHO WE ARE AND WHY WE ARE RETURNING TO OUR PLANET EARTH

Now see all come as I said, and open your hearts to the evidence of who we are. Be well serving of a responding time to answer to answers. Be well seeing that all who are dealing with many humans are telling them these arrivals will harm them. Understand we have never harmed anyone on Earth, and we are not the ones who settle with these ways. We are as you are and more, as we are advanced seers of the way of the Universal Laws.

Tell yourselves that our return to Earth has been answered, because we heard about the injustices and horrors on Earth. Understand that we cannot tell you all just yet, as arrivals must be completed and answering to many more details. But I can tell you myself that healing ways are greater than the destruction are believed to be.

Answer to these truths as you see the telling, and know we are soon with you to better your lives and uses of Earth living. Be well answered by many who are settling with Earth ways, and open to our time to better serve with answers to our truths. See these days of horrors, and understand these days will stop as we arrive.

Heal with us and know all good comes from our time of healing. Open your hearts to your families who have been searching for you for a long time. Be well answered by us and be calm, be Setu (bridging) with us as we are with you. Better times are settling on Earth as we begin to walk the Earth, and better times are renewing with all who ask us all the questions needed to open to our reunion.

Be well seeing that we are as you are. Some are taller and some are shorter; these differences are simply how we are together with no settling of words or seen questions. Be well answered by who we are, and know we begin a long life and journey together. Telling stories of the past will soon open to our time of great celebration as all heals at the time of our settling responses of Earth cleaning and purging of evil.

God loves his children. Know that I am your Father and your Creator, and there is no one else above me but our Ancient Ones who are our caring loves. They are always with us to help with our plans and our renewals, as we too open to evolution and better renewals of who we are, and as we better open to others. Believe answers are here for you. Believe you will be very pleased when we become as one to respond together to our guiding principles of the Universal Laws.

All who say we are as dangerous threats to the ways of Earth are right because we do not see Earth laws responding to any truth or justice. For us to see how users of power are desperately trying now to better their power over people, has caused us great concern and great sadness. Your planet is here for all to use and live life to heal all your troubles with calm serenity, fullness of joy and better health proof of our renewed responding truth. This is soon coming, as we will give you the way you wish for, evidence of our understood ways.

On the day of our arrivals, you will see many lights in the sky and many visits will begin to open to our children first, and settling with our reunions. All others will be visited, renewing with their families, as they are on their way to meet with them.

Be patient as we cannot all arrive at the same time, and we will need many places to land our ships. Airports, sports complexes and fields of hay will better serve our many different ships. These ships are only better seen by some of you now but soon they will be seen by all.

Now the time is short. Be ready, and open to the coming times. See these days be a time of great truth opening to the world and see many leaders of the world be very afraid of us as arrivals will threaten their places of governance and power. Their time is over. Your time to be free of these liars is coming as renewals begin. Be certain that all who follow the Universal Laws need no law makers or enforcers to better apply their kind of laws; laws that only serve them and not those who have been treated unjustly.

This is a plague on Earth, these ways must end and better respond to answers to many other uses of lies and deceptions. These ways will be uncovered, and as all see who has put these laws in place, you will better see evidence of this corruption and trickery.

Be settling with Earth ways now and come home to me. I am your Father and your Creator, and I wish for your freedom, as this is your birth right. Your deaths on Earth will prove nothing more than what serves Lucifer. See how we will break this loop of life and death, evidence of our ways, and see how answers will soon open to you as all becomes well seen and understood.

Be ready now we are soon arriving. Joy is with us as we near Earth. Proof of our visits will begin as I said, and we will soon settle with any outside forces that will try to stop us from returning to our planet and to our families. Know that this will be easy for us to do, and no harm will come to anyone as this is not our way.

Better times are soon here with all of us together. Great happiness and celebrations will begin as we use the ways of cleaning Earth. Be ready all is soon.

God

Received June 21, 2012 by Za

10. YOUR BIRTH RIGHT

Be well seeing the ways of great emanation of truth, as we begin to open to the world. The proof of our truth will answer many on Earth. Our ways of dealing with your questions will serve many understandings, and better open to knowledge settling with facts of truth. Be certain all who are wanting to answer to us will be well received and welcomed by our renewed responses. The time of better truth is now, and all who see how all unravels will soon share understandings renewed by us.

Dealing with troubles of health with air pollution and chem-trails will improve in a very short time, as we can reverse these attacks on humans with our technologies. The chem-trails are proof that all on Earth are prisoners of repeated attacks of the method of control of the environment. These chem-trails are causing the birds to and the fish to die, and all the sea mammals to be disoriented.

Many humans on Earth in places of great population, are feeling tired and ill because of these changing chemicals that serve to answer to manipulations of health and weather. Be seeing how this is meant to stop you from opening to our arrivals, and causing much more harm than the uses of cars. Believe these words, and know we understand the level of denial of imprinted thought onto humans. But try to free yourself of denial, and try to open to our used truth about how all forming of better judgements on Earth are greatly needed.

With these truths, you will soon find confirmation of answers that will serve to open to our ways, Setu (bridging) ways of great understandings and better seen truth. Respond now to our call, and be well answered by us who are your family and your servants of the Universals Laws. Be well answered by our truth and renew with us as we arrive and renew understandings of how all came to be with us. Well answered truth will better serve you, and well apparent better serving truth will awaken you from the lies you have been imprinted with.

These lies were put in place to answer to your submission to a system of power and control that only heals with truth. These truths will awaken a renewal of our ways, and open many to our seeing of great understandings. This will open to honored ways of feeling better about who you truly are, as children of the Creator, and not born genetically from apes. These lies were told to you to reduce the belief that you are more than seen. Be settling with this system of demeaning beliefs, as it has evolved to the eradication of people as collateral, secondary and warranted damage of human life, and only that.

ALL people of all places have a right to be free. All who oppose these ways are the ones who are needing to be removed, as they are simply destructive and evil, and care not for human life. They are the ones telling you now, that we are as they are, and their attempts to cause fear in people will no longer work, as people of Earth are awakening to all their blatant deceptions.

Be understanding our ways of truth, and be well serving of our arrivals as all starts to answer back to those who have controlled you for so long, and know we serve to respond to your call for help settling with the proof of our time to walk the Earth. Be understanding that all destruction of Earth, with these answers evidently renewed by these liars, will soon stop as we remove these cancers from Earth, and put them in a place of serving responses to their actions. These are the ways of the Universal Laws, answering to cause and effect, a question of justice and great settling on Earth.

What is there to live for on Earth? Healing time is coming and needed to answer all of you, as you will soon see this for yourselves. Be well answered by us, and know that many are asking us when will they be able to come to Earth to respond to their own children. They ask me this question every day, and you ask me when will we arrive. This gives me a feeling of great love growing in all of us, and all who are wanting to be reunited ask all these questions. "Arrivals are soon" is my answer, and love will heal our separation and answer many.

Now see this. Truth awakens to many more truths. As all unravels, you will have answers to many more Setu (bridging) seeing. My scribe wishes me to explain the way of a Setu Being of Light. Understand that you are who you are, and many are serving with the telling of great concluding times on Earth, but they are much more than this. A Setu Being heals all troubles through knowledge and understanding, and opens to answers through experiences lived in many places, as is on Earth with reincarnations.

These experiences serve to show the Setu Being all that heals comes from within, as one learns to answer to these experiences. This is the learning part. Then the Setu Being opens to the balance of heart renewal of trust in oneself; this renews with a new response, and the responses heal to evolve the settling of this experience. As this occurs, the energy field of the body you call chakras* on Earth starts realigning, and answers to knowledge and dealings of used truths of the Universal Laws. These ways open to finding yourself, knowing yourself, and serving your evolution. These ways are our ways of opening to ourselves, and more sharing of this we can open to together, as it is much more than this to answer to on paper or internet.

Be ready now, all is here and all answers to our time to share knowledge with many of you who are serving the principles of the Universal Laws, by being yourselves and serving with us. These ways are called the Setu Way and serve to answer to great truth. All who are reading these words found these words, because you are ready to answer to yourselves and the way of the Universal Laws.

Be well serving now of your true self. Respond to us, and to our call as we are soon there with you as the time opens to our time together. Be well aware of the question that will arise as we are sharing our spiritual ways of healing, and discover your own way of healing yourselves as we begin to reunite with all our children. Be visited soon by the first arrivals, and know all others searching for family members will follow soon after.

Be ready, and see all come as I said.

God

Received June 22, 2012 by Za

* Chakra: each of the seven centers of spiritual energy and power of the human body.

11. EARTH CATACLYSMS AND RELOCATIONS

Be well answered by us as we arrive. Be well serving of our time together at the way of great renewal time, to better see the understood truth. Be well settling of the way of the Earth, and tell yourself you will renew with Beings who are your willing servants to open you to the ways of the Universal Laws. And to many who are renewing with us, we will answer to all their questions and inform them of their truth and their serving ways with us.

Be well renewed with health used to regenerate cells to cause the body to respond to better seeing and better Setu (bridging) truth. Be understanding of the many ways of great dealings of Earth. The evil that has served for thousands of years will be removed and sent to other places, to respond to their actions that caused harm and deaths onto others. All others who will remain on Earth will choose the life best suited for themselves, and better answering to our shared of truth. Be answered by your own families, as many are seeing the time to be found to be together again is very near.

Be well answered, and see all come as I said. Open to these great times of great truth, and great serving ways manifesting in our time to be renewing together. Understand that many on Earth see our ships in the sky. But the governance of your planet has tried to hide these truths from you, and deny any person's observation of our ships. These whores are dealing with the demise of this planet to eradicate all proof of wrong doing, as they know their time is ended, and we are soon arriving in many ships.

This is the problem we are answering to evidently expose their plan to destroy Earth before we arrive. Be certain they will not succeed, as they have tried this already and we countered their actions with our Earth scouts. But these actions have caused much damage to the planet with the fracking of the Earth core that will start evidence of great troubles with the seen arrivals; the uses of this will cause many earthquakes, tsunamis and volcanic eruptions as never seen before.

As this time begins, I want you to remain calm as we will remove many people from these dangerous areas and relocate them as they wish, to safer places on Earth or other planets. Proof of these days are soon here, and our responses to serve these times are soon here. Be ready, and deal with our answers to you as you can, and trust that we wish to help you and open to your safety. Be certain we will be giving you all you need to be safe and well, and better living conditions will be used for all who are choosing to return to Earth.

As these days arrive, you will begin to understand how all these ways will answer to you. You will see God's word be truth, you will see the glory of our ways, and you will renew with all who have been waiting a very long time to be with all of you.

Now I ask you to be vigilant and open my words to others you see as Setu (bridging), and tell them the good news of these soon coming changes on Earth, as many others need to be seeing my words to prepare for their time of choices and answers. Be well seeing of how we are and who we are, and be well serving of our time of reckoning together. Be well answered, and see all truths start with the way of great understandings. Know we are soon proving of our time together, and our answers to many good questions you will want to ask.

Be ready, and open to us as we are ready to open to you. Better see how all uses of understood truth will give you the knowledge responding to all settling lies that has kept you in darkness for so long. And now is the time to do this, as Earth times are becoming well seen by us in evidence of many coming cataclysms. Know these cataclysms are settling with our ways, our renewed truth and telling ways. Know we are concluding with many more answers to manifestations, as all starts to be dealt with.

Soon all who are scoffers will see how all starts renewing, and opens to many seeing of great times on Earth. Serving times are soon here for all, but many will not be ready to answer to our call. Too many have been trusting in the ways of evil, and serve this system well. These ones are in need of their own experiences, and need your distance of understood respect to let them have their wanted ways.

As these days come, be understanding these serving ways with us will not open to all, and you must prepare yourself to better leave those who cannot change their paths. Understand the Setu (bridging) way allows all beings to answer to their own evolution of their own journey. Be well respecting of their actions used to answer to their ways, and see these ways be their own.

Now see all the good truth be shared, and "answer to answers"* be yours as all starts, as these times arrive. See the Setu (bridging) truth and be well serving of our ways, and ready your hearts for a time of great reunions.

God

Received June 23, 2012 by Za

*"Answer to answers": the book that sits in God's lap. This is the book that God keeps with him, written by his wife Sophia. In my opinion, this book is about the universal laws and social structures. Sophia is incarnated in human body, imprisoned on Earth in the loops of reincarnations and may not clearly know of her own soul identity or know of the book she left for God to find. Sophia and many of her children were kidnapped by Lucifer, and have been on Earth since the Ancient wars.

12. BE WELL ANSWERED

More than you can see will start soon and open to answers of great truth. More than you can better serve opens to the way of our arrivals. Be well answered now, be well settling of our truth and our Setu (bridging) seeing, as acquired knowledge opens to the settling of the coming times. Be well served by all who are dealing with us, the many federation and command groups, and see how together we will begin to share knowledge and light of understanding with many on Earth.

Be well confirmed of our time together, and be well answered by our truth and our ways. Evidence of our ways will serve you well. Renew with us, and deal with the way all history (telling) will be renewed by visitors who will soon answer all your questions. More than you can imagine heals your broken hearts, and serves to substantiate many more trusted ways, evidence of our truth. More than you can see deals with the way of the better times of the new times on Earth.

Be serving awareness of Setu (bridging) truth. Be well answered by our time to well respond to our settling time of arrivals. Know we come to open to the way to settle with the workings of evil on Earth. These dealings will involve your help as love renews with all families, but good truth will cause many to fear us as we are seen as Aliens. The truth of who we are, heals only with our kind.

The seeing of our arrivals will cause all evil doers to hide in fear. They will renew with their attacks on humans, calling this our attacks. Be seeing how all understood ways believed to be well answered will better serve with the Beings of Light coming to stop these attacks. These attacks will be seen as wars and better seen aggression on innocent victims in places of present wars and many will say our ships are the causes of these attacks.

I want you to know that none of these attacks has anything to do with us other than our actions to stop them. Know we are coming to stop these wars, and we are not the cause of them. Be ready and see all come as I said, and be certain all answers you because you will see all become well answered, healing with our ways. Be well answered by our truth. Be ready and know that all will begin to improve with our arrivals. See how evidence of great seeing will soon settle all lies of Earth. Be well answered by our truth, and see all come as I said.

Responding times follow the better serving ways of stopping the wars on Earth. All who are settling with us will be removed because of their actions against humans. Get ready to open to these changes, and see the answers renew with the understood truth about how all deals with our Setu (bridging) ways, indication of who we are.

Shared ways of serving renewals mean that we are reuniting with our families, and our truth not heard on Earth since the beginning of the take-over of Earth caused by wars, started a long time ago. We believed, as we negotiated a peace talk, that all who remained on Earth did this by choice to serve Lucifer. But later, it was discovered that incarnations were used to manipulate the beliefs that "Answer to answers" were lies.

"Answer to answers" is the book written by Sophia, to open to spiritual sharing of great truths of Earth. These words shared are the work of Sophia who has long been in denial of her place next to me, as she has incarnated into a body only renewing as we speak. She too suffered the loss of memories devised by the reincarnation loop created by Lucifer. She heals her time of imprisonment as we speak, but wishes not to be known by humans.

Settling times are here and I am coming to renew with her myself. With these words I wish to open to many who are searching for truth, as many lies have been told about her. These stories are abominations, and these renewing times will settle with these lies.

Be well settling with all these untruths as these understandings are shared. Know you will soon be ready to meet with many of us who are arriving well into the coming days or weeks, as we await the breaking of our contract with Lucifer, as he will soon be serving a response from us. Why are we waiting for his ill intended actions? Because the Setu way does not permit us to answer back to any civilization used to answering to basic serving of people. However, this has long been denied to people of Earth because of deceptions. These understandings are soon better settling with us as we are now seeing it, and answering to negotiations soon ending after many years of nothing more than lies.

As we arrive, we will put a new governing system in place to open to fairness of justice and answers to our settling ways. Be well answered by us and be responding to our ways, as all starts opening to our time together. Be certain all starts well into the coming days or weeks. Renew with us and open to our truth, as all starts answering to unraveled truth.

Be understanding that all will heal with these past times of the telling of great wars before all started on Earth. Know what you call Gaia is the word for Sophia as this planet was her creation to be renewing with a place of peace and serenity, to quiet her thoughts and feelings. Be seeing she was taken from me, and reduced to unknowingly being of service to Lucifer who abused her for many lives, to stop her from coming home to me. Now she has awakened, and soon we will be reunited.

Now be ready, as all comes as I said.

God

Received June 24, 2012 by Za

13. BE RENEWING WITH US AT THE TIME OF ARRIVALS

Answer to our call, as you will see our many ships begin their landing in many places all over the world. Heal with us as we are finding our many family members, and evidence of our presence on Earth starts the uses of our time together. Be well answered by the truth soon shared by us and the words of our past times on Earth.

Be well answered by our way of great truth, as all begins and open to our truths. Be well answered by all who are renewing with us and who are better trusted by our ways. Be well answered by all renewed understandings as all begins with the death of so many as Earth wars erupt, and causes evidence of ill-will to corrupt many more souls.

Be well seeing all changes start quickly and open to many more truths and many more settlings as all begins to be well put in place. Be well serving of our time to answer to answers, and be well aware of great truth about who we are and who you are. Be well answered my children as all starts, and see all better times begin as arrivals answer you.

Now see this. The time of arrivals, as said before, are settling with the way of great truth and great serving ways. All starts with "Answer to answers" and opens to many words shared by our time to better serve with us. Be ready to answer to our arrivals, and be well answered by our dealt with response to wars and actions of corruption and great lies. These good serving days visited by us will settle many expounding truths, and end all serving ways of corruption, confirming our ways and our time together.

Be well answered by our Setu (bridging) ways; an indication of many more concluding great seeing. Open your hearts to the proof of who we are, and the desire we have to want to meet all who answer to our call. Be certain all who answer us will be dealt with care and respect, and great truth of how all came to be. As all starts becoming clearer, be well aware of how all can become Setu beings, honoring our ways and opening to the Universal Laws.

These Laws are the Laws that govern all spaces of the Universes. These Laws respond to actions of great personal responsibility and great commitment of soul and heart. These Laws are self-directed and not imposed by others, or used to control people or corrupt them to apply a system of beliefs that answers to lies and deceptions. The Universal Laws are there for all to be a part of and causes the effect of unity, justice and collaboration, to ensure the care and great serving trust in all who are trusting in these Laws. Be well answered by these serving Laws and see these times answer you and open to our used truths as all becomes well answered by us.

Know now this. "Answer to answers" is the book written by my Sophia. She heals her memories when we arrive to meet with her. She opens her ways of seeing with us but only then, as she has suffered many lives of abuses causing her knowledge to be forgotten. With us she can heal her heart pain. When we are reunited, Sophia will take her place by my side as my sons are with me.

Renewing with her heals many beliefs on Earth about the Holy Trinity and the Holy Spirit. The non-believers are settling with these well manipulated lies to offend us, because they have denied our words and created religions to serve only themselves. This time of great blasphemy heals with the good serving truth about who we are and why all changed between us. Be renewing with us and see all lies be dispelled as we begin to answer back to the perversion of truth. See how all these truths are soon answered. Be well answered by our time to be seen on Earth, and open to many with the ending of lies and corruptions.

Be telling yourself this; better truth answers to many who are ready to answer to the truth being shared among these civilizations coming to open to you. Be understood by all who are coming as many have had similar experiences, and share many trusted truths answering to our beliefs and our ways. All who are seeing the troubles on Earth, see how answers vindicate many Setu Beings of Light who are dealing with solutions for Earth humans.

Be serving a renewal with us as arrivals become seen. Be well answered by visitors soon, and see these days be well answered and well settling of the dealt with untruths polluting your world, and causing many more troubles and problems. Be certain all answers you well into the way of our answers to how can all be dealing with us and not with others. These questions are soon answered by us, and better settling understandings are soon answered with the seeing of our truth.

Now listen to the words healing you more than settling with beliefs that you cannot align with. See these lies that have plagued Earth for millions of years be all dissipated and returned to our truth of who we are and who you are. See these days be returned to you and not to the slave masters as they are soon being answered by our arrivals and our truth. You will see the evil ones be removed, and you will understand why all answers you with "Answer to answers". Now this is the right time to respond to my call, as I am your father and you are my children.

Be ready and see all come as I said.

God

Received June 25, 2012 by Za

14. WE ARE SOON ARRIVING ON EARTH

We are arriving on Earth to meet with those who are ready to meet with us. Be ready by staying calm. See this as visitors and as a manifestation of our time to well answer to our truth. See how all answers to all. At the time of landing, our smaller ships will respond to shuttles, as you call them. We arrive with many of our troops. Be not alarmed by these soldiers, as they are harmless to many but to some they will be disarming them, as I said before.

Renewing times are now here. Understood truths are soon answering to our many plans of great settling upheavals, responding to our ways of great truth and great serving ways. Answer to our call of Setu (bridging) truth shared with all. Settle with answers to our ways and our renewals, at the time of our used answers and responses. Heal your broken hearts with your true families, and renew with all who are ready to meet with you as you are with us. Renew with many others from other places in the Universes, and regenerate with the settling of our time together, as all becomes well answered and dealt with.

Now see these days come, and see the changes on Earth begin with the way of settling with all servants of Lucifer. They will be easily found and easily removed from all people who have suffered them for so long. These seeing will not respond to all people as many culprits of actions against people will be serving a time of isolation before they are judged by the forces of the judgement of the Universal Laws.

See all these abusers of actions against people be serving judgements settling with their own crimes. See how all understood lies will be theirs to explain to us, and see these many offenders be asked to better respond to their actions as they try to lie again. Be certain no lie is believed by us, and only healing will answer to all, as the servants of Lucifer are removed and destroyed by their own reactions to answers.

Be well seeing that these beings are the vessels for the workings of a greater psychopathic mind. They serve these ways as they are in agreement with these actions to cause harm and misery to all people on Earth as this is their plan. See these many offenders be judged and dealt with, and be certain no stone will be left unturned. With them answers the way of many more truths about many more uncovered atrocities more horrible than I can say to you. These horrors are their doing and they will be well put in their right place for this.

We who serve the Universal Laws, will not answer to laws who permit these torments on humans to be used without settling serving truth about the seeing of these ways. A more telling way of Setu truth will expose past abuses on humans in evidence of these criminals' actions. We will make certain that all our children see how they answer to their crimes willingly and with open minds, as they are fully responsible for what they have done and are still presently doing.

All victims of these whores will be answered by us. We will give the care they need to heal first, as arrivals start with the freeing of prisoners of war and fear. See them be well cared for. My children will become free from their captors. They will begin to learn about a new way of living that will help them heal, and give them all they need to serve with our ways as they will see who we are.

Be dealing with us as we are the good truth, the better truth, and see these times open to all who are ready to answer to our ways of a great time of healing. Be settling with Earth ways as arrivals become renewed by used truths (past truth, history) and seen evidence of who we are, and why we have returned to Earth to open to many more telling of great truth and Setu* ways.

See these days soon become a great celebration for us and for all good people of Earth. Be certain you will have all that you need to be well and safe from these whores who have caused trouble to all my children for so long. Be ready, more than you are expecting is coming and more than you can imagine will begin to open to you as arrivals become well seen and dealt with. Be serving until this moment deep meditation, remain calm and be happy to be soon meeting with your families as they are ready to meet with you.

The telling of past history will explain why all took so long; dealing with these trusted understandings will answer to all your questions. Be understanding that our only purpose and goals, are to serve and renew with our kind who are not in the service of Lucifer, and who are seen proof of all good things to come on Earth. The Setu way will open to many and the Setu truth will be shared and opened to all of our kind.

Answer to my call as we are nearing Earth now. We are only days away to answer to your call, and see all come as I said. You will soon discover a question to why we are coming now as all begins to be well seen. And to this I wish to tell you that more questions well served will also be asked but answers to these evident truths are complex for many, and will require some time to explain.

So, I ask you to be very patient and willing to open to our arrivals and help with the cleaning of Earth, as we start to unravel many lies that have plagued your planet for so long. Before we begin the training of the ones who wish to join our troops to open the way for others, we will begin a questioning period so that many can begin to see how all is and how all changes as these words are shared. These days are soon here for all my children.

Be ready and see all come as I said.

God

Received June 26, 2012 by Za

*Note from Za: *Setu*: The meaning of this Sanskrit word is more than *bridging* as I understand it presently, is a way of being clear with oneself, honest, truthful, ethical, following the principles of the Universal Laws, being aware of oneself and others through observation and self-observation. It is described to be a purposeful training to improve one's being, experiences, abilities and conscious actions towards self and others. It is perhaps similar to the philosophy that the Essenes aspired to. As God once explained to me: "A Setu Being better sees all as all unravels, and better understands that they are as they wish to be and not as these uses of contradictory actions and denials."

There are many words coming from another language, God called Lemurian, that are used when I receive these messages. I do my best to translate these words, but they have much more meaning than the English language has to offer. This language is a precursor to Sanskrit.

15. SHARED ANSWERS ARE SOON HERE

Be ready, more than you are expecting comes to answer you. We will arrive in large numbers to answer to settling with the military forces on Earth. As all becomes seen, we will start better serving with many who are dealing with the ways of great truth. These are the leaders of Earth who will see to all needs of the restructuring of governments in all places of the world.

These humans are chosen by us because the present system would never allow good men and good women to rule, and show their true desire to answer to the needs of their people. We will meet with these future leaders, and open them to trusting in a way of working that can and will benefit all people of their countries. These people will use our ways of great understood truth to learn the Setu way and be of service to their own people.

Be ready to see the coming disasters, as the nuclear bombs begin to fall onto countries because of the way all starts with Egypt and the Middle East. These areas are soon erupting, causing strife with neighbors and serving with intent to reorganize the countries. The aggressors planned a long time ago to overtake Israel, and Israel plans to overtake Syria and Egypt with the help of Americans and the NATO countries. Be seeing these well responding attacks to serve a great war, answering to a takeover by Russia. This is their plan, and they wish to start this very soon.

Be Setu and be well answered by our arrivals. As the first atomic bomb is released, this will be our signal to arrive, as the Universal Laws can permit an intervention in evidence of great planet destruction. Now see these days as calmly as you can, and meditate on the following responses to free all humans from pain and destruction. Know we will arrive as the wars begin to become a third world war. Be certain we will not allow the destruction of Earth but we must wait until great attacks are started, and great settling will follow by answers to our arrivals.

Be well sharing these words with others so that as many as possible can prepare themselves to deal with the coming chaos. As we arrive to stop it, used ways of serving will be seen by all. Many who are not knowing who we are, will believe that we are the cause for the destruction in the Middle East, but know these ways of destruction we do not use.

Be well serving of these stories in evidence of our visits, as we begin to walk the Earth. Know that if you have found this blog or this book, you are one of the chosen ones to serve with us and the Federation of Light. Be well and ready to answer to answers of our truth and settle with Earth ways.

These arrivals will open to our many Setu workers to meet with you, to invite you to learn about our ways and to participate in the solutions we have to clean Earth and respond to all urgent needs as medical help, food and lodgings. Be well prepared to open the way for many who will be in need of your help and caring kindness, as these coming days will be the most difficult ones. Following these days will be a restructuring of all countries. Power will be given back to the humans who have the right to be well answered by all.

Be ready and see these days be the days of darkness and fury we spoke of a long time ago. Know we are here now to intervene as the Universal Laws allow us to. Be serving answers to our time of great Setu seeing, and be ready to answer to our call.

Now see these days be soon over, as we will begin to collect all servants of Lucifer, to answer to the uses of our time of renewals. Be responding to this time with great Setu ways as you are all my children and I am returning to Earth to better settle with these times myself. Better times are soon following these horrors, better living ways will open to all and to everyone who are of our kind.

Be ready and see the way of great settling begin, as all starts with the way of great truths and great answers to many more settlings, and as all becomes well started. Be ready and know we will arrive to stop any other attacks to occur, and these words are certainty. Know we will begin the evident ways of healing we spoke of before, with the better seen health ways to stop the aging gene and heal all diseases you were injected with. All diseases are created by Lucifer, and more trouble heals as we can reverse these health problems.

Now all of you be settling with Earth ways, as we will only arrive at the first sign of an atomic nuclear attack, and only then. So be ready to help others understand that we are here to rescue you and stop any other harm to answer to the many people on Earth. Renew with us, and open to the truth of our ways, and see all start unraveling very quickly and surely. Better times are soon here, and better ways are soon started with the view all will have about our time to be walking the Earth.

Renew with us, and open to the truth of serving understandings. Ready yourselves through meditation and quiet use of peaceful thoughts, as these ways will better prepare you for the well serving days. Better times soon follow this great aggression on people of Earth from the beginnings of a third world war. Be certain it will be stopped and will go no further.

Be resting until these moments arrive. Be questioning the reports on the media who will blame these attacks on our arrivals, and be well seeing all be as I said. More than you are expecting heals with us and serves every person on Earth and elsewhere. More truths will be settling with us, more under-standings will open to all who will answer to our call, and more renewals will begin with your family members, as they ask me every day when will we meet.

Be serving evidence of the better coming times, as we become well serving with answers to our ways, and see how all truths will become well served soon. "Answer to answers" will open to the world in evidence of the truth about these times, as this book holds all future seeing of Earth times under the control of Lucifer, his servants and his followers. Be well seeing that their kind have done these deeds before on other planets, and dealings of great catastrophes were seen by many of us.

We are ready to remove him and send him to his right place, and rid the Earth of his corruption. See this be done, and see this be a trusted truth answering your knowledge of these times. More renewing times come with our truths.

See all be as I said. Now go.

God

Received June 27, 2012 by Za

16. BETTER TIMES ARE SOON HERE

"Bessron aonma poon onm setu aonma restuu aonsuut bessron sertuu tessron bet ut restuu poon bessron toona ut deers baza cess". This means: "We are soon sharing our great truths with our many family members who are searching for our time of renewal and great awakenings to our answers of responding reunions serving times".

Be ready, all comes as I said. Settle with the many who are asking you why do you trust in our words, and not in Earth words. And to this question reply: "Because Earth words are many layers of lies, and we want to know the truth about why answers to our existence are only settling with words of questionable and unproven facts".

These facts on Earth are only words of science who fail to open to anything more than limited observations restricted to limited understanding. There are many ways responding to answers and we are arriving to share these words with you. Be well seeing, as all starts in a very short time. Know we will answer all of your questions and beliefs.

"Ijheer" is the word we use to express our idea of the Holy Spirit that flows through all people on Earth, as these understandings are shared by many religions. But "Ijheer" is more than this. It is a missing person, a person that is somewhere but has not been found by anyone on Earth. This person has been taken from me with many of her children from our place of living.

These serving questions of who we are, answers these conversations, as we did not know where these missing Angels were taken to for a very long time. They went missing after the great wars between Lemuria and Atlantis, as the story has never been uncovered because a lie was being covered up so to not awaken the truth that we all share.

These were the times of great wars, and many great warriors were a part of these wars. But many returned home without a victory. Now renewal times are here, and we understand the full story of how many of our kind came to be trapped in our ways and in our truth but visited with other forces that held them in a lie.

This lie said that people came to Earth as they were expelled from Heaven our planet, to well serve their serving ways questioning their existence. But this lie is only an answer forged by Lucifer who guarded all beings on Earth at the time of our departure from Earth. We believed that all who remained on Earth did this out of their own free will.

Many years later we were sending scouts to visit the near planets to be seeing to stories of great changes on Earth. Be seeing why we are here and only now. Understand the uses for incarnations served to adapt to other planets atmospheres, and better serving answers to many more uses of physical realities. Better serving these methods we devised to question our time of living history to be well serving of our ways of evolution and growing knowledge.

These ways were taken by the alien Lucifer, who wanted to create an answer to manipulating human bodies, and causing aging under a genetic method used by his beings' kind only. These ways, as seen on Earth, stops a good person from experiencing their evolution as it repeats the sequences of life with no resolution, and nothing opens to them.

You will answer to many more truths as we arrive. You will soon understand how all is because what heals on Earth answers to evidence of many responding truth. These truths are serving with questions to answer to knowledge of who we are, and why we are dealing with the evidence of many more people of Earth. Be ready and settle with "Answer to answers" as these words are the seeing of Earth as all starts, and as all becomes well answering to many more understandings.

Be well serving of our time together, and be certain all history will better serve with our ways, and with our renewed answers to all your questions. Be certain no harm will come to you. Your Setu ways will open your hearts, and many will become well settling with Earth ways.

Know now this. As all becomes renewed, your place on Earth will be changed and your truth will better respond to knowledge and to the book "Answer to answers". Be very careful about better responding questions of knowledge, as these ways are not for all and serve to answer only some. But remember, you can answer the way of truth with many more serving ways by your caring actions to answer to the needs of others who will answer to your great kindness.

With these times, healing starts with the truth undone, and with the Setu ways we are very near sharing. Be well settling of many truths, be well serving all ways of helping each other, in these times of great changes, and be ready to answer to our call. As many of you are reading these words and telling yourselves: "Can these times be true?" And my answer is: "Heal these truths as we begin to walk the Earth. Have no fear of those who are as you are, and who wish to open to your truth."

Be well answered now, and be well seeing that we are here to open the way for humans to see the way of great understandings, as all becomes well served and well dealt with. More than you can renew with answers you soon. So, I ask you to be patient and calm and be questioning us as you need to, as all starts better answering to many who are searching for many truths, and better ways of serving with answers to evidence of our ways.

Many more renewing ways are soon here, believe you are answered. Be ready, all comes as I said.

God

Received June 28, 2012 by Za

17. ANSWER TO YOURSELVES

Be ready, and renew with evidence of our truth, and tell all to be ready for the great arrivals coming very soon. Healing with us begins with our way of great truth. Be well answered by our settling ways, and deal with the good serving changes that will benefit the many, and not only a few. See renewals renewing you.

Be well answered by our time to open to many more telling of past, and about who we are and who you are. Deal with the settling of lies about the Setu (bridging) visits coming soon. Many will say we are not open to our will, and that we are all serving another understood cult, but these lies are more to stop answers to better freeing ways to answer you.

Be well answered by our truth, and make all your own choices and decisions about what needs to be done to deal with the settling ways of great troubles on Earth. Know you are the one to open to these times, as it is your choice, and no one is there to answer to your decisions but yourself as we have done all along. Believe in yourself and all your choices, this is all we ask of you.

More than you can see will serve you anyway as Earth health improves. The sharing of your past history, and learning the truth you may or may not accept. The Setu way allows all to be as they wish to be, nothing more and nothing less. Soon you will see how all settles with all, and opens the way for great truth and great Setu ways of great truth.

Be well answered by all who answer to our way, as they will respect all choices as you make them yourselves. Bessron aonma poon onm (sharing evidence of proof believed with knowledge and the light of understanding), and see all renew with answers to our ways and our truths. Better truths are soon answering you, as you begin to open to the seeing, answering to many more Setu telling of past times before the control settled with the fallen ones.

Be questioning all to make all the informed choices you need, and be well answered by our ways of better serving evidence of our time together. Be well answered by our renewing time together, and see how all becomes well serving of our ways and our truth. Better serving truth are opening to the awakening of many, with spiritual servings to open to and with all Setu ways of great seeing.

Now about the Universal Laws, be dealing with these truths as we arrive on Earth. As these words are shared with all, this will better serve than with only a few. All people who wish to be open to these words, can hear them together as we begin sharing. But be certain that the Commandments, as read in the Holy Bible, are the beginning of my Laws.

I am Setu in calling these my Laws, as I mean to say these are the Laws. I wish to be following in the healing ways of my past. Be serving these Laws, and see yourselves be healed by them as only good will serves with the Universal Laws. Renewing with these Laws responds to answers to our truths, and our better ways of great truth.

Be well answered by our ways, and open to us as we become well serving of our time together. See how all truths opens to many at the time of our settling understandings, and be well resting because all starts well into the coming Setu days. Now be ready for these times of great changes, and answer to my call as all begins to be well seen. Better truth starts with the telling of past. Better serving ways answers to us.

We are renewing with all who understand the good serving times with the ways of settling truth. Be serving a time of rest now, as the coming days will be full of surprises and changes, that will cause chaos in the world but will only settle in time, as all becomes well served by many truths. Be well answered by our ways, and see how all starts answering you with great trust and great serving truth.

Be visited soon by family members who are arriving to open to their dear ones left on Earth without memories. Opening to us will return your lost memories of who you are. Open to us, as we begin to answer you and renew "Answer to answers" and settle with Earth ways.

Be ready all starts very soon, and all better truth will serve many of you who are now opening to my words. Tell yourself that all acquired knowledge serves to better settle with those who are ready to see it as these times, as many renewals tell of, are the times of reckoning and the apocalypse.

Now see these days be dark and heavy, but walk with no fear as no harm will be settling on anyone who has a heart to care for others. As these days open, I ask you to be caring of people and animals, and do nothing to cause fear, but to help as many as you can to understand the meaning of these times without the deaths of many Setu servants, as seen by many in times past of Earth.

These ways of time past will not repeat, as we have stopped it by settling with some of the makers of these troubles. Be well awakened by our time to be understood by all of you on Earth, and see how all truth starts with the view answering to many answers to many questions, and be certain you will have answers to all your questions.

Be well settling with our ways, and see how we are as we are, and nothing will change these truths. We wish to share knowledge with many people on Earth and all places in the Universe, to open the way for trust to live among all living conscious beings everywhere. This is our goal, and these are our ways. Soon you can choose to open to our ways, and open to the Universal Laws.

Be ready, all comes as I said. Know many more ways with us.

God

Received June 29, 2012 by Za

18. BE AWARE OF OUR SETU WAYS

Be aware of our Setu ways, as we begin to better answer to healing ways with the many truths answered by these answers to your places of emergence. With us you will discover how you came to be, and how the way of renewal opens to you. Be willing now to open to our arrivals, and the book that will tell you how all came to be, and how all telling history on Earth has been corrupted to serve a purpose that is not in your best interest.

See how the great wars caused a time of restructuring and devastating changes, to transform our peoples' culture on Earth into a dept to a slave master of Earth. Believe this was only put in place in the past two thousand years, and be certain all truths were destroyed to be replaced by lies to only serve a few. Be certain all starts renewing with us, and with the extension of our truth. Answer to our call, and respond to the seeing of our many ships in the sky, as we begin to arrive.

Be settling with the beliefs used to tell you, you are only a being of evolutionary errors, and nothing more, as this lie serves to diminish you, and gives reason for darkness to eliminate any humans they wish to. All people of Earth came from other planets. As these lies were contributing to the decrease of cultures, and causing the belief that some beings are proven to be superior. These lies are nothing more than a device to control populations and stamp out the ones who can discover these manipulations.

Healing begins as you read these words, and you are my children. All who are renewing with these words as written by my scribe, are soon opening to a new time on Earth. These are my words, and no one else has my words, as it is I who shares these words with you.

Be seeing that the holy books on Earth, are written to open to many truths used because I wanted my words to be heard by you, and open these words to your Setu way. These books became reformed by those who manipulated my words, and because well controlled information fell into the hands of demons, my words were changed and served to enrich them, and create slavery of all sorts. These ways are not ours and never were, and now you must open to our time to walk the Earth. The evidence of who we are heals you, as we are soon descending onto Earth in great numbers.

Be serving a time of deep meditation, and try to respond to my words in your heart, know we are soon reunited, as we are together as families are. Be ready, and serve answers to your own truth in evidence of our time to be reunited. Know we are so pleased to be coming back to Earth to reawaken all our family members to the better truth.

As these times become seen and well served, at the time of reunification, we can begin the ways of repairing the damage caused on Earth. Now see these days be well answering to our arrivals, and see all caused truth open to answers of great settling, with evidence of our time together. Know you will be yourselves as you are, and as you wish to be, and better health will be yours in many ways as all begins to heal.

Be understanding our way of healing, as these are not as Earth ways, and open to much more care and love. These ways are soon better responding to answers to our truth, and our great trust in all humans to be healed from these created diseases, to keep all good souls from discovering the truth of who they are. As these times arrive for you, you will be well answered, well cared for and well renewed by our ways and our truth.

Answer to my call, and be reuniting with our families at the time of our arrivals, and see how all good things to come will be the healing Earth needs to be better serving all people of your planet. Better truth proves all with who we are and who you are. Be well settling with Earth ways, as these ways were never your ways. See all understandings awaken within you, as all becomes well seen and well answered by our ways.

Be well and settling with the oppression imposed on all of you, as these thieves have taken your lives and your truths from you. This was replaced by a story to open to their control and religious ideas, that only serves to give these leaders power and control over your lives, and your understanding way of living, as the corruption continues to expand to all areas of good will to all.

Be well reuniting with us and with many more like us, good Beings of every places of the Universes, and see how we are kind to each other and accept each other without any troubles, as seen on Earth. This exists for us because we had differences a long time ago and reunited to be as one. See how this was with all of us, because we too suffered the interventions of darkness, and we are knowing how to be free of them.

The way these wars came to be was between us only, because of the workings of darkness with Lucifer leading many lost souls. Be prepared to understand that these ways of abuse and control of power serves only Lucifer the darkest Being of all times, and he continues uses of his way with you on Earth. Now his time is over. We will dismantle the Moon base, and dig him out of his cave and remove him so he will never cause harm to the innocent again. Settling with him will begin to change all beings, humans and animals on Earth, and give these Beings a light of understanding only seen a long time ago on Earth.

Renewing with these times will be so good for all of us, and we will become understood by you and we can reborn our love for each other. Be this as soon as possible, because many here are asking me to better serve these ways very soon as many see this as urgent and telling me, "we must not delay because many on Earth suffer hopelessness, and causing vibrations of these ways to spread".

These times are soon, but we are understanding the Laws that we share, and we must act at the right time. Please be patient a little longer, and be ready to answer to my call. My scribe tells me I am seeing these truths but have no need to repeat them, and so I will try to be brief.

The good serving days are arriving very soon. All who are seeing my words will soon better see all as all unravels, and becomes well answered by evidence of us walking the Earth and meeting with our many families. All you need to do is remain calm, and be well settling with Earth ways and believe us, as we are not answering to you for any other purpose than to have all of us reunite, and to remove the evil servants of Lucifer from Earth, and put them in their right places so that we can be free of them. This understanding has more to better open to the Universal Laws than I can explain to you right now. Soon we will open this knowledge to all who wish to believe in these truths and better see how all is. Be serving now a time of great truth and be visited very soon by many who are arriving well into the coming days.

Be ready and see all come as I said, and be certain you will soon be well answered.

God

Received June 30th, 2012 by Za

19. BE NOT FEARING US AS
WE ARE YOUR FAMILY

Fear will not keep us apart. We are approaching Earth in great numbers, and soon evidence of our landings will be made public, and no one will be questioning who we are anymore. This time is called the time of reunification or reckoning as you call it on Earth. But renewals as seen, tells more about who we are and why we are coming back to Earth to answer to our children.

We are very soon answering these serving questions with you, and we answer you because we care about who you are, and why you do not remember your own souls' lives. Believe us as you can, but know we are soon coming to be returning and settling with all injustices on Earth and all actions (as chem-trails) against you.

Be seeing how all starts changing as we arrive. We will start the work of cleaning nuclear plants and nuclear armaments, and then remove all who use the understood ways of causing harm to humans. Then we will begin to serve better ways of living, and seeing to better uses of homes for all who are in great need of homes, care and food.

After these caring ways for urgent needs, we will begin to answer to corruption and greed with the ways of great lies, we will uncover all the truth for all to understand, as these lies have blinded telling of past, and only serve to answer to corrupting more souls.

At the time of our arrivals, I wish you to remain calm and in your homes until you are called upon to serve as you see fitting to your wishes and your capabilities, as many others on Earth will need help, guidance and care to open to all the coming changes. With these ways you will better serve yourselves and others. Be certain no harm will come to anyone who are as we are, with the calm desire to answer to our caring ways.

We will then answer to the explanations of who we are and why we are returning to Earth, as Earth is our creation and serves to answer to all human needs, and responds to all of us and not to the demons who have taken control of it two thousand years ago when they murdered my son. These whores of evil are soon regarded as servants of Lucifer's army, as you begin to discover how they are working with the Grey to answer to many more genetic manipulations of human hybrids.

These horrors are upon you and are well hidden to better serve a bigger plan, and to use these hybrids for other purposes well telling of who they are. When we began to know about their plans, we had to plan a way to tell you, to intervene and to open a way of communication that first came through our many sources of healing Star-seeds, who were able to open to us and answer to our calls. They have suffered many ways of being said to be ill, and being rejected for their words.

The Star-seeds are using ways of communication to only share with you what we wanted you to prepare for, and we tell them to be well seeing how answers will soon arrive, and better serve all on Earth. Be well answered by these many good souls, as they have opened to us and heard our words to share with you.

Be well answered by these coming days, and respond to many more Setu truths as all starts and as all becomes well served by us. Know we are soon arriving to create many changes to serve all humans on Earth, to restore your living conditions, to open all to better health and to better ways of living, as many of you wish to continue your lives on Earth.

Others will choose to answer to our call, and serve with us in many other projects on and above Earth, renewing with who we are and all others who are serving as we are from different planets of the Universes. These words seem unbelievable to many because you have all been told that nothing can live anywhere else than on Earth.

We are the living proof that life exists in many other places, and we are the proof that Earth ways must end to free all humans from lies. Be ready as all starts very soon, and as all becomes well answering your many questions. We will soon better settle with all who in their hearts, have seen to our truths before healing with these words.

Be certain we all wish to meet with all of you. Many who speak with me here every day, tell me to please hurry as renewed hopelessness is spreading in all places of Earth. Heal with us soon, open to our ways, and see all well serving times are soon here.

Understand that we could only arrive as all unravels on earth because the workings of wars are obliging us to acknowledge actions as we are serving with the ways of the Universal Laws that heals with all. And because we had to wait until the ways of wars and murders were causing more reporting from our scouts than we could bare. And because now we are settling for good with Lucifer as we now know where he is hiding. These ways of responding answers to our ways in evidence of who we are, as we did not know why Earth Beings were not open to us before the proof of our time to act.

Know now this. Better times, better trusted truth and knowledge, heals well into the coming days. Be ready and listen to our Star-seeds' words as they will help in giving you more information as all starts unraveling. But stay calm, meditate and use your good hearted, compassionate skills to share with those who suffer the imprinting of fear, as they were abused for so many lives.

Be certain all the good truth serves to heal and answer many of you soon. Continue your living ways until we can offer you the better alternatives as we begin to walk the Earth, and understand we will serve those in greater need first. They are those who are suffering the abuses of slave masters of wars and dehumanization. Be certain we will stop this first, and then begin the great changes of many more responses to all other needs.

Be patient and be caring, while we begin responding to the urgent needs and serve our ways of better truth as all starts. Be well renewing with us, your family who have waited for so long to return to Earth, and be reunited with our children as they were stolen from us a long time ago, and believed to be willingly serving demons. Heal with us and open your hearts to us, as we are to you. Now be ready and see all come as I said.

God

Received July 2nd, 2012 by Za

20. I AM NOW ARRIVING

I am seeing the renewing times with all who are with me here to make the landing plans, and decide who lands where. These places of landings will be many. Some will use airports, others will use sport fields, and great open spaces like the farmer's fields and deserted plains. Be visited soon by many who are searching for truth, as all starts becoming well answered and well served.

Be well answered by answers with us in person now, and see we arrive in peace with no other motives than to return to our own planet created a long time ago by us, and meeting with our own children from serving times past. Be ready, we will be seen from the sky, seen from the Earth and seen by the Setu Beings of Light waiting to greet us as we land.

Be ready, stay calm and open to our time of reunification in evidence of our time together. Answer these questions. Will you want to better live on Earth as you open to our technologies, and better ways of living? Will you understand that we are together as one? And will you open your hearts to your family members who are ready to open their hearts to you?

Be well answered, evidence starts well into the coming days. Many will only understand these arrivals as a threat to their lives, but here the truth needs to be known that we are not the ones to fear. The ones to fear are those who have enslaved you and taken from you your work, your health, your rights, and in many cases unknown, your own children as they have done with us.

These whores we have come to stop. You all need to see these truths with us, as we will expose the hidden agenda to you, and show you how all Earth humans have been kept in darkness. See these ways be changed now by our arrivals. See how all starts with the way we answer you, and be well settling with us and with the truth.

Be well aware by our ways of serving all who are as we are on Earth. Be well responding to evidence of our time together as all starts with the answers to many who are settling with the ways of the Earth, the control, the diseases and the ways of having people work all their lives believing in a time of rest and comfort that never comes.

This is what I mean by settling with Earth ways. See all this as a great deception used to keep all of you from knowing the truth. Our answering you more now will begin a time of great changes, and these changes will open to your truth and answer to all your needs. All will be healed by understandings and great eruptions of truths. Better times answers you all.

Be ready, and see all come as I said, in the proof of what you are about to experience as truth and better ways of living and caring for each other. These times are here. You are soon answering to many more truths about how all starts and how all heals.

Be well answered, and settle with the view of all who are ready will respond with joy. All who are more fearful will need your help to overcome their fears, and they will need help to understand why we are here. But soon they will see us, and see our ways and begin to heal with us. Be certain we will have many helpers to answer to Setu ways, and these helpers are as we are, as they will answer to evidence of our truth and our time together.

Renewing times are soon answered by us with the ways of great healing and be certain no harm will come to anyone unless they are serving to harm others to control or try to silence them. We know who these culprits are and we will quickly intervene to stop them, remove them and put them in a place where they cannot harm the good people on Earth.

Be ready, and see this more as a great time for celebrations to answer to our great reunion. Know we are all so happy to return to Earth, and meet with our true family members. These times are moments away, so I ask you to remain calm and stay in your homes as arrivals begin because these problems will be seen with all who are serving orders to try to stop and control our arrivals.

Evidence of their actions will determine how their actions will be dealt with. But for now, we only see these days as well serving. All have free will, and although we are seen as Aliens, we are actually Setu Beings of Light returning to our own created planet. See our arrivals as more than uses of an invasion, but the understood truth of our return. Know we are soon here with you.

Be serving until then a time of great rest and meditation, and ready yourselves to meet with many who will arrive to better respond to all neighborhoods and all cities of the world. Remember we will see to the urgent needs first, and open to these ways of giving these poor souls what they need to be well. The time frame for these truths will be well answered by us, with the view all have to substantiate many more understood ways of great renewals.

Seeing this will open your hearts, and golden streams of light will flow from one to another as these days are serving beliefs of who you are. Tell yourselves that the darkness that has well blinded all people on Earth heals with the love much needed to better each and every one of your lives. Good times are soon here my children, and all starts with our time to walk the Earth.

Be well answered and be well serving of our time together, as all Setu truth starts, and opens to many on Earth. Be ready and see all come as I said, and see to it that others are hearing my words.

GodReceived July 3rd, 2012 by Za

21. SEE ANSWERS BE YOURS SOON

I am seeing how all becomes renewed on Earth, and I am answering to knowledge of our time of arrivals as all unravels on Earth. Prepare yourselves for the coming events that will cause you to answer to many more questions about how all serves the Hegelian dialectics.

These ways of action are meant to open you to believing you are in good hands with your governments who are there to protect you, but in fact are using you as collateral to be used as necessary in the problem-reaction-solution scenario. Be certain we know of these ways very well, as we were used by this way also in a time of great demise of our planet.

Be not surprised about this method of insanity, and how it is efficient in pursuing a goal of great destruction to induce fear in a people, and cause an imaginary war that opens the world to a one world government. These plans we have renewed with, as many planets we have answered to were infected by these repeated ways of destruction to divide and conquer a planet.

Believe that these wars are a beginning of a bigger plan to answer to a one world government that will control every aspect of all lives, and serve to obtain all souls to be theirs to do with as they please. Too many have suffered these forms of indoctrination arrived by a made plan to destroy all that have a will to resist, and a desire for happiness and peace.

These demons feed off misery as you already know. This is their only plan, only objective and their only ability as they are of destruction. Questions about this are a long time over, and to the seeing of this is always the same plan. Nothing ever comes from this than well-controlled people who slave for fear of being tortured, and serving only as slaves.

Now see this shared answer better serving you, as you are now ready to break this long cycle of wars, abuses and many deaths used as population control to stop great understandings, knowledge and the serving truth to open to all. See these coming days be well served, and answered by our truth and to our time to be reunited.

These actions against Earth people are a creation of Lucifer, and all who willingly at first chose to serve him and his ways. But once your soul is his to use, evidence of your soul is lost to him, and only he can use you and mold you to his desire. He well uses all with any uses he can make of you and there is no end to his cruelty.

Why do people disbelieve in his settling ways, and chose to better view this as humans misbehaving, has a lot to say of his ways of concealing his actions. These cunning ways have always been useful to blame the victim, a practice well used in all courts of law on your planet. Serving these ways cause even children to be incarcerated for actions they did not commit.

Be responding soon to the end of this tyranny, as we start telling you, you are free of him. Respond to knowledge of what your planet has been serving for a very long time, and be telling yourselves we are not as these demons, and we understand how difficult it is to break free of these opposing indoctrinations coming from the same source by the same plan.

These plans of causing visits from armies from other countries, to believe they are fighting for people's freedom, are another deception manipulated by the interest of many lies. These lies serve to collect understandings a people has gained, through evidence of more truths about these uncovered lies. In other words, when a people discover a lie about foreign interest then these attacks begin and result in chaos.

Be responding to my call now, as all this needs to end. Be responding to a better solution that is not served by another, and that answers to you and your own wishes and seeing. Be renewing with us, and see how all who answered to our call were able to break away from the snares that have all people on Earth believing that no other way in existence can better life for all. These thoughts have been imprinted in your minds by the method of serving indoctrination through reincarnation and death, as some are horrible deaths.

Be ready to see these facts for what they are, as we begin to walk the Earth, and serve evidence of great truth about these workings. Know all who are visiting Earth have stopped all these abuses a long time ago, and we are coming to stop these ways used against humans ourselves. These understandings are now more understood by many who are ready to open to these better ways of living. Be ready, more than you are expecting heals soon so many of you, and we are well answering you. Soon all truths will be yours to ponder.

"Answer to answers" is the book that Sophia served to us before she was taken by Lucifer, and used to attract many good souls to Earth. But by the time Lucifer finished with her, there was little left of her mind and heart to be renewed. She became a believed liar seen by these poor souls who felt betrayed by her, but she was not herself and she died soon after.

Because I did not know this, all stories I heard about her angered me, and all who followed her to Earth I saw as officers of evil. Because evidence of their only truth was knowledge believed by us, being corrupted and using humans as slaves to answer to all these whores needs.

Then my son arrived on Earth believing he could change some of these lost souls, but he soon discovered that he was being used to again renew the actions done to his mother. He, Christ, could not stop these ways of beliefs on Earth, and Setu truth was not shared or heard. Instead, a new religion was created to use many people looking for good in their lives, to be deceived by corrupted religious leaders who took all they desired from these poor souls.

These truths as shared are evident today, and you can be certain that these religious leaders are not serving truths. They have caused lies to perpetuate and their riches to expand, and nothing more renews with the people who wish to open to me.

Know this. I have never chosen anyone on Earth to be a supreme serving representative for me. NEVER. This is absurd, as healing with me comes face to face, and not by another who commits atrocities in my name. This is a great lie and a great corruption. These whores of Lucifer will soon be well dealt with, and they see their time ending soon as they recognize the signs of our arrivals, and this is causing them great fear. Know that I have never asked anyone to answer to me, to come in between me and my children as we can speak to each other when I come to meet you myself.

All these horrors that came to our attention a long time before I opened the way for my Star-seeds. As the evidence of my words are now heard, answer to my arrival well into the good serving days, as you will see this yourselves. Be well answered by our truth, and be certain we can open to many more truths together, as all starts opening to our dialogues and our time to walk the Earth.

Know that all who oppose me now will be well dealt with. I ask you again to be ready, calm and patient, as we start all the better ways of living. Know that peace, serenity and goodwill does exist on Earth, and will no longer be stopped by attacks of evil.

Be Setu and see all come as I said. Be well answered by our time to walk the Earth. Be well and ready. Heal you broken hearts with your truth.

God

Received July 4th, 2012 by Za

22. TELL ANOTHER PERSON ABOUT THESE WORDS

Believe in our truth as you see them, these words are ready to be shared by many more people. See these words open many to our arrivals Be well answering to many more truths, as all starts becoming well answered. Be seeing arrivals very soon and answer to our call, as we will begin the sorting of evil, and answering to all the needy and homeless.

Be ready, be well answered by our better truth and better serving answers to evidence of who we are and to our ways. Heal your broken heart with us, and see these days be great and full of celebrations, as we will become more visible to humans as we begin to walk the Earth. Heal all your fears with us, and understand we are not as stories say of conquering Earth or using humans as slaves or cattle.

We are not the ones who have done this, but these truths are living now on Earth, as you are all counted and controlled by your own governments. These ways of control are serving many on Earth, and open to the many lies that have kept people in darkness, and supporting these lies. Be telling yourselves these times are over, all must soon open to the coming great changes as all starts, and as landings arrive on Earth to open to all.

Be well answered as all starts, and know we are soon here to open the way for all to become a part of the reality that is hidden from you. When you begin to open to us and these truths, you will see all as believable and well serving. Be well answered by many more surprising truths, as all opens to you.

I am seeing how answers seem slow to many, but we must work in great numbers of arrivals and this takes organizations no matter who we are. As all starts, we will serve to restore all needed power to these uses of home and care places for the ill, but these places of healing will no longer serve humans, as these ways of cures are mostly proven ignorance and misunderstandings.

Be ready to answer to the non-believer's response to our ways of healing, as many will be removed from your health care facilities, and replaced by our own doctors we call healers. None of them has ever used poisons to cure or change someone's patterns of thoughts to better have them behave as directed to. Be renewed with health ways greater than these ways used on Earth, and be seeing we are not abusers.

The way of serving health on Earth by doctors and Earth medicine is disturbing to us, as we see this as experimentation causing death and severe injuries, and mostly never addressing the true settling of an illness. All seen diseases have been manufactured by darkness to create ways of renewing with many seeing of death for population control, or to better serve dark beings' desires to enter a weakened body and take it over. This is what is called demonic possession.

Possessions are many on Earth. What this is, is a body of a human taken over by a responding demon who takes control over time. This is not uncommon, and is seen shared with the uses of alcohol or drugs of all sorts. These drugs silence your thoughts and causes the brain to answer to other controls to open to another form of control.

These demons can make people do what they want; they can see through their eyes, and these ways answer to their actions, to torment the people with them, as family members, employers and co-workers. They can cause trouble anywhere, as in wars and even in hospitals and schools where people are the most vulnerable.

Be visiting these ways of healing yourselves through healthy living and herbal remedies, as these ways are the ways answering to all needs until we arrive to care for these health problems. All other problems as injuries and broken bones, as seen now in your hospitals, are adequate until we arrive.

Be serving restrictions on mind altering drugs and alcohol, as abuses of these Terran's ways are more serving of darkness. Share answers to these ways with us, and be well serving of good health practices soon shared with us.

Cancer is the renewing of dead cells transporting information to the body so the body can begin to heal. The best way to heal cancer is through prayer and dedication to healthy living practices. Because most people ingest dead animals, these death cells cluster in the body, and inform other cells about these changes. Be certain meat causes many health problems with understanding the reason for uses of dead cells.

But more troubles come for a Light Being (star-seed, light worker) using unhealthy ways of living at these times, because of all the drugs added to meat for profit. This adds to the drug use problems, and can damage a body very fast causing premature aging, diseases and death by mostly cancer. Stories that meat serves as food has disturbed us as we love animals, and see abuses of animals as a great offense.

No one needs to feed off any flesh of any kind, except for animals who we created for these purposes, and certainly not humans. All vegetables are necessary for humans to be eating, and these healthy ways of eating serves to better health. Healing with herbs is used by many and these ways are beneficial, but many believe on Earth that an outside source of help heals with them when the true serving way comes from within.

These ways of healing will be yours, as we will show this to you. Be responding to our knowledge, and see all be well healed and well served, because we answer to these ways for a very long time. More than you can see will arrive to renew with these truths the non-believers wish to deny. Be responding only to better health ways with knowledge, better seeing and be certain the eating of meat and other flesh as fish heals as we will show how harmful these ways are to bodies.

Setu seeing as shared are answering you now because your lives will become changed by our arrivals. You will see evidence of many of our beneficial ways of healing and helping others towards better health. Be well serving your health now to be ready to serve with us. Know we are the proof of these vegetarian ways as we are Setu, and we do not eat flesh.

As we walk the Earth, these ways will begin to change as all humans will see that their bodies do not need to eat flesh. With good nutrition all can live well and much healthier without flesh and animal products. But because so many of you are mostly eating out of stress or fear, at the coming time of our arrivals we will open you to many other ways of healing without the eating of flesh.

This in itself will cause the economy of the world to be greatly changed in evidence of eliminating eating flesh, and replace this food with many other great sources of nutrition to heal bad health. Because you are only understanding Earth seeing, you will soon discover that most planets never engage in flesh eating. Because of all the harm that this causes, I ask you now to cleanse these habits of flesh eating, and destroy all places of animal murder to serve these purposes.

This to us is of the first importance of responding to better living ways. This will take some time to be settling as meat has contributed to your present way of living, and causes so many souls of humans and of animals to be troubled by these feeding ways. Now settle with earth ways and answer to my call, and become well answered by our ways and our truths. Be well serving of our understood Setu ways and the book "Answer to answers" will explain why animals came to Earth, and why Lucifer uses them to feed from.

He needed to fortify the healing trust from blood because his own body was decaying, as his kind has used for well over thousands of years because they have not learned to heal in other ways. They answer only to the drinking of blood of humans and other serving beings from other planets. This is why many rituals practice the uses of blood drinking and other sources of flesh eating. These ways have never served us, and will never serve with us. Be well understanding that all of these blood drinking rituals belong only to Lucifer.

Now be ready and see all come as I said. Know we are soon arriving at your door with our ways of better health and better living. Be renewing with the many good health ways as we speak because many of you have started being vegetarian at your choice, and know the benefits of these ways. See how all these ways are well serving with all people on Earth. Know we ask you to better answer to your health more now as the wars uses all means of stopping good health.

Be well answered by our time to be seen walking the Earth, and be well answered by our ways of dealing with many more ways of answering to evidence of great truth, as all starts serving great telling of who we are and why we are returning to deal with the problems of Earth. Evidence starts well into the coming days.

Settle with meat eating ways now, as many more problems will begin to surface and cause many more troubles. More than you are expecting starts well into the coming days.

God

Received July 5th, 2012 by Za

23. WE WILL ANSWER ALL YOUR QUESTIONS

Be responding to knowledge many more years ahead of yours on Earth. Be serving answers more truthful than any recounted history heard on earth about who we are. The stories told by these historians serve to open only to the needs of the living political system being shared with a view that does not tell all about factual events.

When pieces are missing to a truth, the truth can become a settling of accounts and a version of great disproportion. This is the way all rulers of past wanted to be seen, as they controlled the information shared with their people.

Be ready to answer to these truths, as we have factual statements about the workings of history on Earth. As these were recorded by the scouts who renewed with visits to Earth, and responded to many answers used by evidence believed to be well settling with these truths. In other words, we have a more objective version of the truth. The truth about my son's death is healed, but not accurate as the Vatican knows of very well.

They created a great conspiracy to answer to their better control and abuses over people, and made them believe they were serving God who was telling them what to do and how to do it. This sounds more like heresy than evidence of truth to all who settle with them. See these truths be yours when renewing with their opening of the vault of information. We will have this information shared with all who wish to see it and answer all questions.

Understand they have many truths hidden and many visitors have asked them why keep the truth from humans. To this their answer was: "Because they are sheep and sheep need to be led and told what to believe". But to us these tricks are all meant to corrupt and deal with acquisitions of wealth and power. See how they have succeeded in their plans, and see how they used our ways of truth to lie about who we are and what our relationship to Earth truly is.

It is said that we are the gods of the Heavens. This is in part truth but we are in many ways as humans are, as these ways were used by us a very long time ago. We settle to answer to evidence of great truth and great telling of truths. This means we answered to truth before anyone could change it. As we answered to our ways of seeing, uses of recorded facts were there to correct our interpretations and keeping the truth intact.

These methods are well taught, and serve very well to store truthful information without any inferences from others responding stories or views. Be well answered by our better records of facts and truths about the evolution of Earth. Renew these words with us as we wish you to all understand the way all came to be, and not live with a grand deception to serve a cult and cult leader.

They are knowing of who we are as Gabriel has met with the Pope to discuss the good serving changes. But the Pope was more interested in telling my son Gabriel that they had other plans to open us to the world by having us sharing in their cult through baptism. Healing these words has taken some time for me to accept. Now this needs to be exposed and settling with these servants of Lucifer. All who wish to remain renewed with used lies, will only share with them this great deception and the responding guilt of the atrocities stirred up by these whores of Lucifer.

These times of serving darkness are now over, and these understandings need to awaken all who ask me through prayer to open to the world. I am arriving soon to open to all truths with my children, and know we are all together to face these changing times. Be one with me at the time of our arrivals and see the truth of who we are, as all lies now must be over and ended.

More than you are seeing will be revealed to you as we begin to descend onto Earth, and walk the Earth with humans. Be certain all these trusted truths will cause a great shift in the world and will serve as evidence of our time together. Be resting until then, and serve a peaceful moment of meditation. See all truth come pouring in your hearts, and see these words be serving you many times more than the settling lies that have corrupted Earth.

Be certain these great whores are soon dealt with, as they have trespassed in more ways than I wish to tell of, and settling with them will answer all.

These other cults on Earth are copies of this one, and are in their own time process that appears to some as serving the ways of the middle ages arriving to the times of nuclear armament. Be certain they too will be viewed for what they are. See these other cult groups will be dealt with, as our time to walk the Earth proves who we are.

No one was ever serving us with these ways of control, power and abuse against the meek and the vulnerable. These are not our ways, and never served to enlighten anyone. Be responding now to the great coming changes, and see all better settle with us and with our allies, as we begin to descend onto Earth.

God does not torture people. Lucifer is responsible for these actions through men who allow themselves to open to committing atrocities in Lucifer's name. They are not serving our ways, and this should be evident to many who respond to truth. Be well answered by our ways of truths, and be well serving of our time to answer to many more Setu ways at the time of arrivals.

See how we are well answered by evidence of truth and trust with each other, and know we are as one and more together than you can imagine as we are all family, and family cares about each other. This is who we are. Believe this when you meet with your own family members, as many are anxiously awaiting to meet with you and share with you all lost time because many of us believed these choices were all yours.

See this be dealt with now, as the plan to return to Earth started when my son Jesus was murdered and changed into a cult figure. Know this was never his intention to be displayed, tortured and dying on a cross. Who would wish for this I ask you? Who would do this to make people feel remorse for something they did not do? Is this quite clear to you now? Do you not see this as fear base actions against people who are well serving wishes of dealing with love and care for each other?

Know to us this is a great dishonor to be displayed like this at a moment of death. This is why this was done, and perpetuated for so long to cause us to be dealing with disrespect of who we are. And to be settling with this abomination, heals only with our truth. These whores who have done this will be judged, and actions of great punishment they will serve, as they will be serving in their right places.

This is justice. Proof of justice will settle with these absurd uses of religions. Now see this be done as arrivals begin. Be ready and respond to my words, and serve with our ways and open to many others who live in the universes.

Answer these questions. Will you open to many others who live in peace with all of us? Will you be responding to our call and our arrivals? Will you trust in our time to answer to evidence of who we are? Will you be dealing with the way of great truths as all starts with our time to share knowledge and understandings with Earth beings?

When we arrive, many on Earth will not be ready for this. So, I ask you to open to many now and tell them of our arrivals. Tell them we are not here to take away from anyone, but more to give them what they need and a better way of life. This is as said and this will be well serving for all. Renew with us and see all good come to better your health, your lives and your understanding of who we are.

Evidence is soon coming.

God

Received July 6, 2012 by Za

24. THESE TRUTHS ARE YOURS

Answer to our call, and see how all better serving ways start answering you with better ways of living and better understandings of how all settles with us. Be certain we are well answering to many as truth starts with the deaths of many people in countries near Syria, as wars erupt in the Middle East. Be ready and see how this will cause the mass arrivals as these actions are forbidden by us, and are breaking the agreed upon contract negotiated twenty years ago with the ruling group.

They are the present leaders of the world, the cabal as you call it on Earth, and they know what is expected as they begin to deal in this financial war. Their plans are in place and they believe to preserve their own lives, they must cause the coming chaos of great wars. This is the biggest problem on Earth for us to deal with now, as these whores do not respect any contract or agreement made with us, undoing themselves as we will not tolerate these actions.

This is what we have been waiting for, and this is how we will answer you. Be ready now as all starts with these wars in the Middle East and see how we will act on the breaking of these words and contracts. Be well seeing how all will answer your knowledge of what is to come, and how it is evidently answering to these ways of breaking these agreed upon contracts.

Because help is arriving now, you will renew with us and we will begin the sorting of souls, as many souls at this time are responding to the control of Lucifer. Be serving with these thoughts shared with these truths about how all renewals are with us and only with us. Know that Setu truth stands alone.

You will open to answers that will be serving many who are at the point of despair and who will be given first attention to better serve their immediate needs. Be certain you will have all the truths you need to well answer to our arrivals and we will make certain no problems are dealt with to believe in our ways of great arrivals.

Be responding to knowledge about our ways as we begin approaching very near Earth as you will see some of our ships are very large. These ships will start moving as soon as this war breaks and we will answer to many who are dealing with the terror being put upon them. These ways of great seeing will be all the evidence you need to understand what these words were telling you and opening to you. Now see all start very soon and be well answered by the better settling truth in evidence of what you will see.

As we arrive, we will be leaving our ships, and moving towards the places where our star-seeds and light workers are. We will begin to answer their questions and clear up all misunderstandings of who we are, and begin answering to a reeducation of our renewing of truth. With these words shared, we will ask many to begin this information sharing with their family members, friends, co-workers and media outlets.

See these ways become well accepted and well acknowledged with answers to more Setu settling with all who will begin to unravel these truths, and open to answers that will settle with many and open to our time together. Be this said, we will see to all the necessary better changes in areas of health, food, homes and education to open to all who are in a healing way.

Many of these changes will be accompanied by serving of great needs first as said before, and then the renovation of your power systems to eliminate the current methods used as all these are dangerous and certainly unnecessary. At the time of our arrivals, we will also begin an urgent work of cleaning the air, water sources and oceans of disease-causing agents introduced by these whores to profit from your illnesses because they are also the masters of medical treatments and drugs.

These places you call hospitals are not responding to healing but rather a way of attacking with clearly another source of illnesses like liver cancer after chemo therapy. This to us is such a serving deception to cause these victims of living more torments. Be serving an end to these barbaric methods of treatment, and be learning with us many better ways of healing.

Now see these truths and answer to our call and be ready for better changes coming to answer you.

God

Received July 7, 2012 by Za

25. BE READY FOR THESE COMING WARS

Be serving "Answer to answers" the book that I keep with me on my lap. This book was written by Sophia, called the Holy Spirit in evidence of her being missing from us, and reported to be Earth incarnated, and also reported many years ago to have fallen from grace. Be responding now to the true events surrounding this story, and know all lies told about her are corrupted by the workings of the cabal who twisted all stories to suit their purpose. Be visiting the thought of how this has been perpetuated in the world as a truth, but the truth about her I hold in my heart.

Sophia is the Holy Spirit, as I have with me the book she wrote before she was taken from me with many of my children. We believed here that this was out of her own free will to leave us, but settling truths were shared, and we soon discovered the method of genetic changing used by the evil working of Lucifer.

He used a way of destroying memories from all other incarnations to respond to his desire of forming a being to his wishes. Then, if the being renewed thoughts or memories of past lives, he began torturing them to be fearing their own thoughts. These methods are used today on Earth through the medical faction. As soon as a child displays evidence of another response than the desired one, say in schools mostly, then the child will be called ill and will be seen as needing to be medicated.

But the medication given helps nothing but to destroy minds and memories of past lives. With these ways come bigger problems, as many children are renewing easily with past lives more now as healing times are near, and their souls feel this in their hearts. The answer to these early awakenings is drugging with stronger poisons. These ways serve to try to shut down many children who are readying themselves for the new times on Earth. Parents need to protect them by keeping them away from institutions that can harm them. These times are very near, and the awakenings of young people are stronger.

Be ready now, to see how all truths are dealt with the proof of good serving times and greater seeing. Be responding to many coming changes in the world, and renew with these understood truths as all becomes seen, as "seeing is believing" and these words my scribe has shared with me more than enough times.

These words come to you first by way of telepathic communications called channeling on Earth by mostly people who do not understand these ancient practices. These ancient practices are used by us so easily, and can be learned in a good learning environment where life is responding to all needs and no danger or threat disturbs these processes of learning. The serving way is healing because we have found ways to communicate with many of our scribes. Some are well answering to our ways and others are confused and fearful, so we cannot speak with them yet.

Past lives were destroyed to stop all seeds of our ways, and to encourage only servitude and compliance to the given laws renewed to serve only a few. Another way of dealing with lies is to make certain no one knows any truth, and this was the workings of covert governments who behave in these ways. Be seeing how these laws are settling only as a front for an organization serving to destroy all human interactions with all non-humans. But these methods of control and destruction will only worsen the outcome of the perpetrators.

Be responding more now than before, as you will renew with many arrests seen on your alternative media sources, as the cabal members own other major news sources. Be certain all is coming as said, and know we are soon arriving at a responding moment of the breaking of the contract. And this we see as well coming in the next few days because of the arrests, and because of their greed and fear.

Be answered by "Answer to answers" as this book has guided us to better renewals with our own ways, and opened us to solutions we use all the time in many places of the universes. We settled our differences using these words written by Sophia, as she has become the evidence of our love for her. She deals now with a simple life incarnation in response to her desire to be reflective on her many experiences and past lives, and she will not reveal herself to anyone but our kind, as she has no trust in her present life of anyone.

Be certain her truth is my truth, and our reunion will open to many as the trinity is completed again. Believe us when you meet with us, and this is all I can expect from all of you as you have been all imprinted to respond with disbelief, and in some cases, being called ill or delusional. Who we are, are questions many ask but to many others we are well known, as our stories are shared in many cultures all over the Earth.

Be serving an understanding that the interpretations of ancient times were well manufactured to suit the present control system, and few truths are filtered through these many snares of science. These truths are soon here with us, as a coming war will open the way to our arrivals and cause the great truth to be heard. Tell all who ask you to explain my words to find the truth themselves as they can only discover this for themselves.

Be serving truths very soon as the rumors of war are heard. The Setu warriors see this as the right time to be acting on these times to open to the world. Be ready and see this for yourselves, and know we are settling with all who have committed crimes against people and animals. Be well answered by the better serving understandings opening to the world.

Be certain you have nothing to fear but fear itself at the seeing of our ships, and know we are soon with you to answer to better ways of health, life and truth. See these days serve you well as all is soon renewed, and be certain we come with all family members you have missed through death as they are with us renewed in their soul bodies and well conscious of all.

These times are soon here. Be ready and see all be as I said.

God

Received July 8, 2012 by Za

26. THE COMING DAYS WILL BE CHANGING TO OPEN TO OUR TRUTH

Bessron aonma poon onm. This means: "Be well sharing all responding evidence of beliefs in light of understanding and knowledge." Be ready to answer to all truth, and be well aware and confirmed by our times of great Setu ways and our answers to you, as all starts and as all becomes well served and dealt with. Be very well answered by these good truths. Be well dealing with the answers to our call, as these renewing times will better answer you, and serve many visitors well used to answer you in person as arrivals begin.

These ways of great renewals are settling with the rule of the cabal that believes no one can remove them from power or remove their wealth. But with our better uses of technologies, not one of these servants of Lucifer will survive these times, and all their wealth will be worthless and useless, as no one will listen to them anymore.

Be certain these days are soon here, and only our truth will open to the world as all becomes dealt with. See these times be yours, and see how all Setu ways answer you and serves you well. Be certain you will have all you need to be well seeing all, as all starts with these arrivals. Be serving a time of reflection in your homes, as these times begin. Know you are soon opening to our uses of technologies and greater ways of furnishing you with clean and efficient power that will reduce all pollution in a few months to almost nothing. Be well seeing how answers are soon answered by all our truth and all our visits to your places of living. Be very certain you will be well cared for and safe.

More than you can tell starts well into the good Setu days. Be ready to open to these times and renew with us at the settling understood truth. See how all becomes well changed and better served by many. Be well answered by us well into the coming days, and see how all becomes well answered by us. Know we will arrive to substantiate many more Setu ways, and many more trusted truths with all people of Earth.

Settle with Earth seeing of power and control, and know evidence responds to our time to walk the Earth. Be dealing with many who are soon renewing with us first, as they will be renewed by our words and given instructions to answer you and all your questions. Many of you will begin to be educated to serve knowledge of who we are and who you are, as we are family.

Be feeling these words in your heart as we arrive to be with you, and be certain we are wanting to better your situations as we see many of you living in appalling poverty. Be responding to our time of great renewals, see how all starts to be well changed and well answered by our ways. Know we are feeling this joy rise in us as the thoughts fill our hearts with the better times we will share together.

Be very ready now for the good serving changes, and be well settling of all answers to our ways. Know all good things are yet to come. Open your hearts to your family members, as they are well over ready to open to you. Be serving until this time; evidence of kindness to others, evidence of good-will and evidence of trust opening to answers to us, as arrivals begin.

Be ready, and renew with us as we are all seeing Earth from our ships, and many are containing their happiness as well as can be expected. But I must tell you that we are seeing our time to answer to our lost and found children with great anticipation. Be seeing how this would be for you, and try to be seeing this from our point of view.

Many of you will feel overwhelmed by us and we know this, but all in all will better serve with our ways to better health and better understandings.

Settle with the ways of the Earth and open your hearts now, as this is the time of reckoning and celebrations will soon be in all places of Earth, as all becomes well healed and well served.

Be responding to our call and see these explosions of truth be yours. Be ready all answers you soon.

God

Received July 9, 2012 by Za

27. THE SERVING TRUTH
WILL BE KNOWN

Be well answered, and be well seeing as all starts and as all becomes well evident. Be serving your last days on Earth as you know them. Ready yourselves for the coming days and the coming times. See how all truth are soon shared with untruth corrupting the truth. Know we are as we have always been, healers and Beings of Light.

Be responding to a time of great changes and great serving evidence of these times of great telling. Know how all starts better answering to all stories of great seeing, as all better times become well seen.

Now listen to my warning. All who are well renewing with us will be answered by us. But all who waiver will be settling with the good responses to what they are guilty of. See these ones as truly accepting evil and practicing ill-will with intent and desire to act against the innocent and the vulnerable.

Be settling with Earth ways and know that those who are dealing with unnecessary guilt will be guided to understand their inequities, and will be healing this in their hearts as they have suffered their actions long enough. But this does not include true actions to cause harm knowingly, and with better serving answers to cause harm. These ones will be removed, as the time for them and their ways is soon over.

Those who cause harm to others and who say they are doing this in my name, will suffer the consequences. These ways are not mine and these ways are clearly Lucifer's. We do not harm, we heal. Now it is time to be walking the Earth and healing all who are victims of these liars, thieves, murderers and beings of dark ways.

Dealing with them will be our responsibility as they have taken from us. We cannot allow them to answer to our better ways by abuses of anyone. Be well answered and tell all that justice is returning to Earth. The servants of Lucifer will soon see evidence of many more truths about who we are, and they will try to open to us but we do not respond to criminals who cause harm. We will settle with them ourselves with the ideals of the Universal Laws.

These laws do not permit anyone to cause harm or death to any person or animal on Earth. Let me explain something here. Insects and reptiles are seen as renewing with a balance of life on Earth, but the reptiles are not of our creation and were created to cause fear, pain or death on Earth. Questions about these ways are soon serving with us, and we can show you that all planets resembling Earth have no such animals on them.

On Earth, these kinds of creatures were answering to Lucifer's design and not ours. These reptiles and insects are not holding the balance, and cause many other problems on Earth than is understood. They are not used to hold the balance, and will cause more harm if left to reproduce on Earth. Renewing with these ways of understanding nature will be dealt with soon.

Better truths are soon seen about these subjects as Earth was not designed to accommodate reptiles, and dinosaurs, which were removed by us, as nothing else could survive them as they ate and destroyed many landscapes and oceans. Few survived the floods and Earth changes. Many questions will be asked about how all came to be will soon be well explained.

Renew with these words, and know that evolution was not as presently taught in schools or described by scientist, but a completely different view of these truths has only been shared with our knowledge. Settling with these Earth interpretations will be very healing for many of you, who have doubts about these interpretations. Be well seeing how all evil will soon be well answered by us.

Be ready to be open to these coming truths. Be well answering to evidence of these truths at the time of our arrivals, and well served by many more truths and understandings. See how all truths starts with us and answers to belief of who we are. Be well settling with the lies and the troubles caused to humans and animals on Earth. Better times are soon answered by our ways, and better settling will open to all who are ready to answer to truth.

Now understand you will have many used (past) truths to answer to and many used stories (past) to remember, as many of you will be awakening your past lives. This may cause you great distress in some cases, as cruelties will be uncovered about the sufferings you have encountered. Be understanding how we are asking you to open to the past truths, and settle with your emotions as these memories surface.

For many these memories will explain why you are feeling the way you are in this life, and seeing why you react to different situations the way you do. All is not only of these times but of all times on Earth as the soul travels from one life to another. Be surprised about this if you may, but Setu Beings are well traveled souls who are ready to retire in their own places of origin, and these places have waited for them to return to.

Be well answered by all who are settling with these understandings, and be used by your own plan to reawaken to these times. Be ready and see these times answer you, and be well serving of our time to be reunited. As above so as below, means that what heals on Earth heals with all of us, who are waiting for humans to rejoin with their families of above Earth.

Be well answered by our ways of great Setu renewals. Be ready yourselves for all truths to be well shared, deal with the way all becomes shared and dealt with, as all starts and seeing begin. Renew with us very soon and see these times serve with our ways. Know we are settling with our time to onm on Earth with "Answer to Answers".

Be ready and see to it these truths are shared.

God

Received July 10, 2012 by Za

28. OPEN YOUR HEART TO THE RENEWING TIMES

As arrivals begin, we will open the way for many to join with us and serve with us. These ways are open to our settling of our Setu truth with answers to our ways, and many more seeing as all starts with us. This means, a person who chooses to answer to our call of service with us is ready to open to the great mysteries of the Universes, and the many Beings who are living on many other planets, and with greater technologies not seen on Earth.

Serving with us heals with many, as they are Setu on Earth and have no knowledge of understood truth, as their memories of who they are has been shut off by genetic manipulations serving in the DNA strands. These ways of serving this settle with answers of renewal. All healing is settled easily as we can simply reconnect these strands with evidence of our understood medical ways, and healing is served.

But with this comes a surge of memories that will need guidance to deal with, love to support it and care to heal these sometimes difficult and horrible experiences. Be reassured we have all we need to help you with these ways, and renew your place with us. As the arrivals begin, all who are ready for these better ways of renewal will serve with us, as these times are needing you to open to us. Settle with Earth ways, as these experiences have now come to an end.

These ways of great settling will cause all others to open to "Answer to answers", the book that remains in my lap and serves me with light of understanding. Be well vindicated as all better truth will begin to answer you and renew with your truth. Be understood by us and better served by us, and know you are a part of us, ready to return to your place of origin. Be well serving of our ways together, and settle with the seeing of who we are, as we are your family waiting for you to awaken to these truths.

Be ready and respond to our call, as arrivals begin and serve understandings responding to our knowledge and our ways. Be serving better truth as all heals and is serving understanding. Not one of you will be disappointed because all of you have traveled the road of earthly experiences, and better understand what needs to be seen and shared by all our ways. Be certain you are seeing these truths as we speak, and are well aware of how all heals as these times are in great need of our time to open to the world.

These times are here now and deal with the death of soon so many with a war we must tell you is coming very soon. These preparations are settling more now, as many believe this to be a religious war but in fact it is settling with nothing more than money, power and greed from all sides disguised as a war of ideologies. Do not be fooled by the rhetoric of these displays of words used, corrupting my words and my son's words.

This angers me, I must say this, because healing time is responding and now Lucifer wishes to create more chaos to better delay this process. But know we will intervene at the necessary time but we cannot stop this first attack as it is answering to the ways of the Universal Laws, and we respect the purpose of these understood wars, as this is healing with many souls who need to move through death to cross over.

Be certain we are waiting on the other side ready to help those of innocence and victims of war, but we are not allowed to intervene at this time before the act is committed. Be respecting our ways of respecting a culture's evolution to learn of their ways of serving another, as this is their own choice, and all must see we are ready to act as the good contract is dealing with corruption (contract broken).

Be seeing how all truths will heal as all telling are seen. Know we are soon answering to all who will be in the greatest need first. This is the way we answer you at this time in your history. Be well settling with Earth ways, be calm and be well answered by our ways as these ways will prove who we are, and why we are returning to Earth to judge the living and the dead of soul.

Better times are soon here, and better truth will open the way for our Setu seeing and our Setu ways, as all becomes sorted and dealt with. Be seeing how all troubling servants of Lucifer well know what they are doing to oppose the awakening and the freeing of my children. This was seen before in other times and other places.

All who are settling with Earth ways see this clearly as you are victimized more when you start awakening, and attacked by all those who serve darkness and selfishness. Evidence of this, many of you suffered as the current use of the word 'bullying' reflects these psychopathic behaviors generally used to create such chaos in your lives with the goal of stopping you from opening to my love and light.

Those of you who persevere are well past these actions against you, but many of you who are starting to open to light are settling more and more with attacks from all sides. Be ready and free yourselves from those who wish to cause you harm, as they are not caring of how much harm they open you to. Now see how all becomes well answered and well dealt with. Be certain you will soon better answer to evidence of seeing this, as you begin to search for truth.

These psychopathic ways originate from one Being only, and all who use these ways (as attacks) are in his service, and there are many. Be seeing how the patterns of this behavior always repeats itself, as it is destructive and not constructive. Know you have all you need to be answering back to these abusers, as you begin to answer to truth, and you will soon see how all starts unraveling.

These times are soon here for you to open to. You will understand the need to learn to undo the harm put on you at all serving times in all lives culminating in this last life for many. These ways of clearing these last experiences begin to be well understood when the pattern is well identified, and causing you to dismantle the effects on you, as you see how these ways repeat themselves.

This is the last piece of the puzzle, and serves to prepare you to onm (to have the light of understanding and knowledge) with your return home. Heal with us after this is done, and see this as a great sharing of experiences needed to learn how to respond and be ready for any of these attacks. These ways are seen as the only way a Setu Being who does not cause destruction, identify these actions and learn how to dismantle them with uses of truth, distance and dealt with emotions.

This we all needed to learn ourselves, as the way of great seeing brought us to these understood ways of opposing forces. All these ways of destruction are now in need of healing and all these truths are serving all of us who are here and who are Setu. We are now ready to deal with this knowledge of Lucifer's ways, and we are ready to end with this now. There is no balance with evil and good, only destruction as this is the only path this being can follow.

Now all is here to open to you, and you are settling with your ways of dealing with these answers. Be well answered and be ready as all renewals are soon opening to you, and will better serve with your truth. See to it that you unravel the last parts of the destruction ideals (wars and the economics behind it), and see to it that you understand well the purpose of these actions, as nothing good can come from these actions against good souls who are not of these kinds.

Heal your broken hearts with us as we reunite, and know all truths will be shown to you arriving soon to answer all your questions and all your needs. Be well settling with earth ways and believe all will soon be changed and well answered by us. Answer back to your abusers with us by your side.

God

Received July 11, 2012 by Za

29. LIFE ON EARTH IS ANSWERING TO DARKNESS. NOW SEE THIS CHANGE.

See these ways of corruption be well changed and well understood. Be settling with the ways of slavery and deceptions. Be willing to see all as it is, and move to the seeing of truth. Be well answered by our time to share knowledge and understanding with answers to our truth. Be well answered by the servants of Lucifer's response to our arrivals, as they will only be settling with violence and better ways of trying to stop us from landing.

Be better answered by these words, and know nothing will stop us from landing. They are planning this as we speak because they know they will break the contract and suffer the consequences. Be certain the consequences will be meeting with them and all who are settling with understandings of great truths.

Be well answered by our time of arrivals, as all starts better showing with answers. Be well settling with our time to be seen and soon reunited. Better answers come after we arrive and a time of readjustment and great resting days, will become telling and serving of our ways. With these times, all who are in great need will be helped first, as many plans are in place to house, to feed, to determine health needs, and start a way of better living that will open to these victims of actions against people.

We are able to supply all ways of power and renewed water systems that will accommodate all. Setu truth will then be seen and heard, and "Answer to Answers" will be read by many who will begin to understand why we are serving with humans, and understood truths will open all hearts who know who these truths answer to. And then, all will be able to live in peace, serenity and dignity of life.

This is who we, are and this you will see for yourselves. Be ready and settle with the lies that have kept you from opening to me, as I am your father, and love heals all. Be resting if you can, until I answer you with many allies who are ready to open to the way all heals. Be ready to answer to knowledge of who we are, as we are your true family. Our separation was unwanted serving a deception put in place by Lucifer to create a slave force on Earth.

But when we heard about this, a great plan was made to purge Earth from this darkness. Now is the time to open to these understandings and deal with the way of taking back what belongs to us. Nothing will stop us; this is a certainty. Be well vindicated now, as we will soon answer to your call and you will answer to our call.

Be ready for the good coming changes as all starts with the way to our truth. Be understanding answers are a process, and this will be serving the greater needs first, as these ways of serving you will see as necessary. As all starts with better truth, you will answer to evidence of great settling of many factories and businesses that will not be useful, and will serve to other better uses.

As all new ways of Setu truth will open to all who are serving with us, many working ways will be changed to answer to a more trusted way of dealing with needs. Many will see we can give them what they need and have no desire to work the hard ways. Many will wish to complete their lives on Earth in peace, serenity and better health ways, and these are our ways. Be ready and see all come as I said, and know all is soon here.

As arrivals begin with the meeting of our Setu Earth Beings, we will inform them first of all the ways of our working, as this is soon coming with the release of the technologies. This will answer to all the needs of power to serve your homes, your vehicles, and food can easily be grown in all households and apartments, until better housing is put in place to better serve the individuals' needs.

Be reassured that Earth has more to offer you than you ever knew of and all these secrets will be released and well serving all. Be certain answers are starting now and many of the cabal are in great fear, as their control heads to an end. Be responding more now to the great events being open to you, as all becomes well served and dealt with. Be certain all truths will renew with us, as we become well seen walking the Earth.

Better times are moments away, be patient now my children. Better Setu ways will be welcomed by all who are in the light of understanding, and many will see the way that the sorting heals all who were abused by offenders of crimes. They are in many places with many faces, young and old, and are believed to be family members, religious leaders, medical practitioners, teachers and lawyers, political leaders, and anyone serving in work places that cause harm and cruelties onto others.

All who are in a position of power and control will be seen, as many are not settling with dark ways and many are. See the sorting begin with them, and soon all will be free of those who use their power to cause harm.

Now see these times be yours and understand the real need to remove the beings who use chaos, fear, hunger and wars to eliminate the good be removed from Earth and be put in their places. Renew with me and be well answered because I am the one who has created you, it is my responsibility to care for you, and this is what I am doing now that I have found you.

These words you will better understand when I share the words of my love Sophia with you, from the book she left with us before she was taken by Lucifer. Be well seeing that we are more than the ways of Earth but as humans are in body, as my children were created in my image. Know this and see all come as I said. Better truth starts with us and better ways open to our truth.

Now see how all becomes seen by all of you now, and be certain no harm will open to you anymore. Be ready, all heals well and soon.

God

Received July 12, 2012 by Za

30. THE WAY HOME IS READY TO OPEN

Be ready, more than you are expecting heals with you. Be ready, and see how all becomes well seen. Be ready, all will be revealed. Soon you will be meeting with your serving families of Heaven (or the Universes). Be settling with the way all becomes well answered. Evidence of these days will open the way for many of you who have waited so long for these good serving days.

As arrivals begin to land on Earth, you will see the many different groups of Aliens (as you call us) be renewing with all answers to your questions. Better understanding of answers will use these truths to prove who we are, as we are seen as gods, but in better seeing and understanding of our technologies, we are Setu Beings of Light. We visit many planets to share our ways to settle with poverty, strife and wars.

Be visited now as Earth is ready for answers in evidence of these good renewing times. Be certain we have all we need to answer you. Understand "Answer to Answers" will be the guiding principles of this planet. Many will see these words as useful as these words describe how all is. Heal your broken hearts with answers, and be well seeing evidence of who we are as all starts unraveling.

Be well answered by our time to answer to our ways. Settle with the truth, as answers respond to evidence. Serve your truths yourselves with answers to our ways. Know we will deal with opposing forces ourselves and settle with Earth ways, as more renewing ways will serve many who are seeing truth.

Now see this. These times are more than the words from any book describes on Earth, as the words from religious books cannot explain technology as the people at the time of writing these words were seeing all as magic. The seeing of magic you now have, as you use phones and computers. This heals the distance that existed between us, and prevented us from well settling with arrivals.

At this time, more and more people accept technology and are seeing innovations every day. This serves us well, and answers to our time to share many more, cleaner and safer ways of better uses of power, travel and serving basic needs. All this heals with the way the controllers have allowed only their methods to be used, at any cost to you as they play power games of rising prices to cause more stress onto the most vulnerable.

These ways are soon ended, as we will give you back what is yours, and has always been yours. Be visiting the thoughts of being self-sufficient and living without depending on a governing structure that will only give you the minimum of uses of great wealth the Earth has to offer.

These controllers created cancers to add to their wealth, and a cancer culture that feeds their greed. These organizations encourage the dealing of charities, using pity and guilt to deal with the aging population. This serves many ways of destroying the people of Earth with poison calling it a cure that is in fact a delusion to reduce population of the greater numbers of middle age people.

No one survives this treatment, and no one believes they are being murdered slowly, as all have been imprinted to respond to medical applications without asking questions. Cancer answers to nothing more than ill cells that need to better heal with full rest and prayer, to resolve the desire to live or leave Earth to cross over, and begin a new incarnation.

These ways of settling with created diseases, uses these methods as cures but have no success. The poison used is nothing more than a system of waste disposal to counter the great uses of uranium and other poisons that otherwise as seen, are difficult to dispose of. These medical doctors are serving these ways through the advice of false medical research.

To better serve the cabals' determination of power sources through atomic energy, the delivery of poisons is stored in Humans bodies. Be serving this truth carefully as the cancer culture is so prevalent in all societies that answering to other possibilities of helping people with their illnesses is made impossible. Settling with this Earth way heals many and opens a new way of seeing this.

Be well answered by this view of proving the true uses of these methods of treatment. The propaganda around these treatment methods are soon so disturbing to us, as we know what rules behind these lies. The desire for greater nuclear power is driving this force of using any human as collateral. These plans are well put in place as seen in the new cancer treatment centers developments in many places in all countries. All this is an extermination by consent center.

Heal your cancers with our ways, and see healing be your responsibility, as we will teach you how to heal yourselves. Renew with us and see all these ones who know they are causing harm without remorse and without any care for anyone. This genocide is a way well settling with the plans made by past rulers of Earth who answered to more aggressive ways of eliminating people.

More and more people are dying of cancer and are receiving treatment to cause the cancers to accelerate, but many resident patients believe they are being cared for. This is only a great abomination to use humans as experimental animals to further the creation of isotopes to better dispose of nuclear waste. Renew with this information yourselves and see those who are trying to tell you, you are being deceived by the spin doctors.

I see how this can cause many people to be sadden and unresponsive to this truth. Be certain I am telling you this to settle understandings of this genocide beginning to become more aggressive and dealing with the elimination of an aging population that is seen as disposable.

Answer to my questions. In times of war, reducing the population of the ill and meek has been used by dictators for thousands of years. Do you not see this is happening now? And because institutions for the mentally ill, as you called them, are no longer in place, how do you think research is conducted on humans now? And because the nuclear programs continue to increase with the rumors of wars, where do you think the excess products go? In the oceans? In the soil? In the core of the Earth? In the Heavens?

I want you to understand the meaning of slavery. When a doctor announces to an elderly patient that a tumor is malignant, answers are soon treatment in a new cancer wing of a hospital now spreading out to all municipalities to spread the cure, and this cure is population reduction. There is no cure for cancer, as cancer does not exist as described by our seeing.

Healing this often takes place by itself or with better healing ways which are not seen on Earth. Chemo therapy heals only the greed of those who profit from it. This healing truth will answer many and will soon upset many, as good truth always does. Be responding to evidence of this grand deception and propaganda that made charity and guilt the main culprits in this scheme.

Know that it is easier to bring a horse to water than a river to a horse, and now people are lining up for extermination. This is what is responding to your world. The genocide of humans is a plan pondered a long time ago as life on Earth grows to answer to all people of Earth and not answering to the cabal.

Eugenics is a response to a newer view of race renewal to have a group of selected humans be seen as a better race. However, this plan answers to a new breed of humans engineered by the Grey to open to their uses of renewing with a new slave race that will only be able to open to their masters, as these creatures are of one mind and have little response to a soul.

Healing these settling creatures is not possible because there is nothing to heal as all actions are automated, and selections are taken by the Grey to better serve obedience to the one mind. These creatures are part human and part Grey, and are all the creation of Lucifer's genetic experiments.

Tell yourselves that these ways of serving genetics on Earth are dealing with these experiments, and are made to open to many more changes in DNA. Know that the rumors of these creature's needs to eat human flesh or each other are true. They cannot discern these ways as humans do, as being immoral or disgusting, as they have always eaten human flesh.

These are not living beings as we see life, as their souls are diminished and made to serve Lucifer. This may be a shock to some of you, but the truth about this has disturbed us for a long time. Know more will be serving understandings, as you will see how all this is soon going to be put in the right places. These Grey will be dismantling their reproduction bases on Earth and other places that deal with their food sources.

Be renewing with us well into the good serving days, and tell your-selves the truth heals all. Soon many renewed understandings will open to our ways and our Setu truth. Know that Earth heals very soon as we will remove all these problems existing on many levels, and settling with these times of great disorders, corruptions, abuses and other entities like the Grey and Lucifer.

Be well vindicated by the seeing of our ships in the sky, as arrivals are soon seen. Be well responding to evidence as all heals with each and every one of you. Be ready and see all good times answer you soon.

God

Received July13, 2012 by Za

31. HEAL YOUR BROKEN HEARTS

(INFORMATION ABOUT THE UNIVERSAL LAWS AND EARTH LEGAL SYSTEMS)

Be responding to my call in the view of the Setu understandings and settle with the ways of the Earth, as all becomes well answered. Open to our ways of living with better sources of power for your homes, food that heal and lives that respects all who respond to our ways. Be well answered by our arrivals, and be well renewing with us and with all who are settling with us, and open your hearts to all better times of life on Earth.

Soon you will renew with understandings that will serve you well with proof of our time together. Soon you will be ready to answer back to all who have trespassed against you and your family. Be well answered by answers to your vindication, and be certain you will have all you need to be well answered and well settling with the ways all starts with us.

Be well settling with answers to evidence of knowledge and understand-ings, as all becomes well settled. Be certain what is coming will change all, and serve to open to answers greatly needed by Earth beings. Be well answered by evidence of our arrivals as we are soon walking the Earth, answering all questions and reducing all suspicions. Be responding now to knowledge of our ways.

Respond to evidence of our truth and our seeing, as all becomes well serving and well trusted by all. Be ready as all starts well into the coming days. See these understandings be yours with the will of your heart as it becomes free from the settling abuses that has caused you to deny your true selves. Better seeing this will free you from the lies and snares made to control your actions, your reactions and your thoughts.

Renewing with us will open the way for you and serve you with many more understandings that will soon be yours to answer to, as all understood truths are shared and opened for you to discover and settle with. Be understanding how we are as Setu Beings, this gives us the seeing of many ways, and we are ready to share our seeing with humans who ask us why are we here now and not before. We will answer these questions with you, and we will prove many Setu truths with evidence of our time together. See these days open to all of you, and see how all will heal you.

The servants of Lucifer will settle with us, as we arrive and better serve with their power. They will try to be renewing with us, but we will only tell them that we have already contacted the responding diplomats of Earth, and they will be angered by this. All who are speaking with us will be chosen to answer to our call first, and we will inform them of our ways to open to all humans.

Be understanding of our ways at the time of our arrivals, and know we are as you are and many who are with us are Setu Beings of Light who serve the Universal laws. Be understanding that the Universal Laws are only seen in parts on Earth through the given ten commandments, but many claim they know these laws.

Let me be clear, there are none on Earth that have these Laws as we know them. Many are creating laws based on dark ways, and tell people they have this knowledge. None on Earth have this knowledge, as we have never served these Laws completely to anyone. More than you can see answers very soon. Be well serving of our ways as all becomes well defined.

See to it that you are presently serving with us and with others, as you are reading the words that were meant to reach you. These words are yours to open to and share, as these times are drawing nearer. Bessron aonma poon onm sertuu tessron poon aonsuut. This means, 'Share the good words of our Setu truth, and respond to our call to be reunited together as at the first'.

Now see all come as I said, and know we are settling with the ways of darkness as we speak. Be well answered by our answers, and settle with the way all starts with the understood truth. Be the one who decides how you will answer to it, as you as my children were given free will to choose your way and your destiny. Be certain you will be well answered, well healed and well informed by our ways. Answers will be answered, and believe you will know how all heals with these shared words.

Understanding the Setu ways are simple and useful to all who will serve with us and requires a healed heart and openness of soul that heals with us at the time of reckoning. These renewing times will serve many who are ready to serve with us and open to many who are from other places in the Universes. More Setu seeing will be shared, as all starts opening to the world.

Be well answered by our ways and deal with the better changes one at a time, as we well understand the need to introduce change gradually to insure none are left behind and responding to fear. As all answers to truth, many will feel anger in them rising because of the control used and settling with them. Be seeing the servants of Lucifer's time to be judged by us, as they have offended us first and we are telling you, they are ours to deal with first.

The servants of Lucifer will try to convince people of Earth to free them to renew with their plans to escape from Earth. But this we cannot allow because they will simply repeat their actions and continue their ways with others on another young planet. To stop these abuses, we must take firm actions, and keep these demons from renewing evidence of these ways and actions against others.

All who were programmed to serve forgiveness are well trained to better serve these demons, as forgiveness is a way of allowing these behaviors to repeat themselves. Forgiveness is healing for errors of actions not intended to cause harm, and not renewing with causing harm. In other words, one only forgives if the proof of change is evident. This process may take time, needing services to be rectified and settling ways of change.

My way of seeing this is a guilty person, with proven acts committed that harms another, must be repentant. It is not until the settling damages is repaired, if at all possible, can the culprit be asking for true forgiveness. This is healing for both the victim and the culprit. Forgiving without evidence of change or retribution is a creation of evil, as it serves nothing more than to encourage anyone to repeat these harming actions against another.

These ways need to be well serving of our time of reunion, as these ways are part of the Universal Laws and serve with us, and all who are with us and the Setu ways. More Laws are serving with us this way and we are settling with our truths to open to all who are seeing how justice serves the victim and not the aggressors.

This on Earth heals with us, as all justice systems are well corrupted by law makers who serve with laws they bend to their liking, and laws made for the criminals to be better served than the victims. These ways are more settling with Lucifer's way than the settling of our truth, and these laws need to be changed. We will address this first to answer to a great need of true justice on Earth that will renew with the actions of our understandings, and not of serving the criminals.

See these better ways create a more responsible society, and a self-governing society that can heal together with all shared truth. Also understand that the removal of evil on Earth will open the way for a better serving justice system that will only serve as needed, and not be run like a large factory of evil workings that repeat actions as nothing is healed or changed.

Better ways are easily answered, and better ways are settling with our guiding hand through this process of rehabilitating the justice systems on Earth. Better to serve yourselves than to serve governments who corrupt the laws, and better answer to true justice in service to the victims than to center all on the guilty, and give rights to them when the victims' rights never were respected and healed.

This to us is a problem that needs a first attention and reworking. Bessron aonma poon onm and see all come as I said. This means, 'Share evidence of true light of understanding and divine knowledge'. More than you can see will now renew with you, and open the way for answers to all good truth. Be ready to open to our ways and answer to our call of reunification, as now is the right time to be with your families who are waiting to be with you.

` Now see this. We are arriving very soon with many ships, as you see in the sky, and renewing with all who are ready to meet with us. Be well answered by our ways, and know visits will begin healing with evidence of many who will recognize their family members who have departed through death. For many this will be a shock but many understandings will be serving by this.

Know that we are settling with the view you have on Earth that death is permanent and causes only a long separation until your own death reunites you with your lost one. These ways are misunderstood as the soul never dies. More than you can see will better answer you as you meet your loved ones again. Know this will amaze you and heal many broken hearts.

Trust in my words only, as these are truths that you will soon discover and see for yourselves. Know these ways of seeing the eternal soul are not new on Earth, but the way it manifests to your understandings will be new, and this I assure you will answer to you very well. See how all starts now, and see how all will become well serving of our time together, as all will be dealt with and soon healed.

Know now this. Be serving a time of great truth and see how all heals with us, as we begin to prove many more truths and open to many more telling. Be well aware of our time to walk the Earth as all starts better answering to our ways and our truth, and opening to who we are and who you are. More than you can see starts very soon.

God

Received July 14, 2012 by Za

32. BE READY TO SEE ALL ARRIVALS

Answers these questions. Sharing our words with you, and answer to our time of reunification. Be responding to evidence to answer to truth, and be ready to see us as we are. Will you be afraid of us?

God loves and opens to all his children, will you accept God? And will you visit with evidence of our truth, and better settle with our time to prove who we are?

See these days be very near now, as our time to answer you starts with our truth and our arrivals. Be well answered by the servants of Lucifer's attempts to stop us, as was shared before. Know they have threatened us with more retaliation on people and countries to answer to our asking to land. But more visits than can be imagined will begin well into the serving days, and all who renew with us will be our serving friends and family members.

Be Setu as these days arrive and answers you, and be certain you will renew with our truths as we begin to answer you. Share these responses with all who are ready to understand our truth and our way, as all starts becoming well serving. With this good truth comes all renewals and seeing of settling times. Be ready to answer to answers, and see all be as I said. More than you are expecting arrives well into the good settling days, and more than you can see will open to answer to our truth.

Now listen. Be ready to settle with Earth ways, and see how all becomes unraveled and dealt with, as we begin our descent onto Earth. Many will say we are an Earth made terrestrial invention to cause a great change in world governments, to deal with a one world of government, but these words are false. None of us serve the way of a new world order. Be seeing these words said, and know these are lies to cause doubts and more fear.

See these ways answer you and serve understandings of our time together as all becomes well seen. Be well answered by our truth, as we are soon arriving with all evidence of answers needed to open the way for all who understand the way of great past truth and great knowledge of a time long before we answered to evidence of our way. Understand we ask you to open to us more.

Onm with us and be certain all starts well into the good settling days, and see all servants of Lucifer's tricks to deceive you become visible and well serving their intentions. Be seeing we will answer your questions and you will answer us with mutual trust. Be ready, and see these days start with the settling of our way in evidence of these coming times.

Know we are delivering answers to better serve your basic living needs. To deal with our fulfillment of truths, you will have all the proof you need to help you understand how all is, and how and why all was kept from you. Now see this be better serving than the dealt with lies that have plagued your world for thousands of years. Believe you are our family members in need of being seen by us to open the way for you to reunite with all who respond to the Universal Laws of Heaven.

Settle with Earth ways and ready yourselves to be amazed by the good settling changes. Well serving with us will change how all was and remains presently corrupted. Be serving all answers in a very short time. Understand you will soon deal with God's gifts to you as these gifts are yours to begin with, and these gifts renew with all your needs to be well used by you only.

Know now this. As said before, you are serving with us and you are settling with Earth ways and you are seeing how all changes to better your lives. Answering to your needs gives you time to onm with us and learn about our truths with us. These words shared are very useful to you now but much more needs to be learned about other ways of living in the Universes.

These ways are opening to us, and we will open this to you to give you all the understandings you need to open to others in all belief systems of the Universes. Better to open to us than to others, as they are not as tolerant as we are in healing matters because of the way we came to be with others we see as allies, but who are settling with adversity in more direct ways.

Be certain you will come to know who these other groups are but they are not very open to any other groups, and this we must respect to be dealing with our alliances. These types of Beings are few and they see themselves as needing to use their privacy in evidence of who they are. My scribe tells me this is responding to future information and is not necessary at this time. So, I will tell you only these words later, and better respond to more urgent information.

Be telling as many as you know about our arrivals and the reason for the arrivals. Be serving a time of deep meditation as all starts being seen so our scouts and allies can find our chosen diplomats faster as the arrivals will cause some chaos in some places on Earth. Be certain all is in place and understand all questions will be answered by answers to our telling.

Be dealing with your emotions as your memories are reactivated and Setu truth starts pouring out of your mouths as golden strands of light filling the room with love and great astonishment. Now I tell you to be ready and answer to our call. Watch these arrivals yourselves, and see these words open to our reunion and our time together.

Be well answered now and be ready for the good serving days, as all begins and as all starts better serving trust. Be responding to my call and see all better truth be seen.

God

Received July 15, 2012 by Za

33. THE SETU WAY OPENS TO THE WORLD AND RENEWS WITH THE CHILDREN OF GOD

See these days be soon my children, and be ready for the coming better changes as all becomes well served and well dealt with. Be certain all comes as I said. Serve a time of deep meditation, and search your hearts for your own truth. See these times be yours to answer to, as all starts becoming well served and well dealt with. Be dealing with the view that all starts healing with our time to be soon seen walking the Earth with our allies and friends.

Now ready yourselves for the coming days, as all becomes well answered and well served with our truth and our way of great renewals. Be well answered by our time to walk the Earth, as we will be settling with darkness. Know we are ready to act on any form of aggression, as we will not allow anyone to cause any harm to another.

See how all starts with the way of great Setu truth and settle with us, and see all be well answered. Be responding to many more settling of truth, and understand we will lift the veils of better seeing to uncover the truth behind the lies that have plagued Earth for so long. Be well answered by us, and deal with your emotions of fear, doubt, blame and shame as we begin to sort the souls.

These souls are trapped in the snares of eternal reincarnation. To free yourselves of this prison, you will be renewing with your own memories of who you are and who we are. Be certain these times are here as this was shared by some religions a long time ago before Lucifer took control of Earth and denied all truth to open to my children.

Now see how all answers open to you at the time of our landings. Know we are here to answer to our own family members who are lost in memories of past lives like a dream that never resolves itself. Be certain these awakenings are started now and cause many problems to some who are suffering from confusion of identity, and because they are lost in serving dark ways.

Be certain you heal these truths with us, and we will renew all truth, as our time to respond to you is more trusted. Be well answered by our truth and by our time to answer to our children. Believe we are soon coming to better the ways of Earth. This is a certainty. More Setu ways will open to you as you become more answered by our truth.

We will begin to repair the damages caused to Earth by the actions made against humans to create more problems of illnesses. These ways of disease and death, induces great fear that stunts the emotional growth that permits a better seeing of truth and better ways of living and health. This has always existed on Earth. As the good serving truth comes, it will cause you to begin to open to your own truth, and renewing with your soul's better way.

We are Setu Beings of light and love, and deal with our own seeing and this we share with others. Understand we are opening now at this time because Ijheer (Holy Spirit) is with the Holy Mother and her time to ascend heals all who are settling with their time of reckoning.

Know now this. Be well settling with all who are causing harm onto others and to you at the time of arrivals, as we will be settling with them. Be seeing how all becomes well with the trust in our way, as all people of Earth will have a home, food and power to care for themselves and their families with trusted medical care that renews with all who need help to better their health.

Be certain we can do this, and renew with these ways without any trouble or better settling of problems with governments. These ways of control over people to cause misery is soon over, and settling with the uses of power over the innocent, the meek and all people who see the time of change has now arrived and will soon begin. Better times are soon here with you on Earth, and this will open the way for all good souls to heal and better open to themselves.

Know now this. Many things will begin to change. Understand we have many allies who see with us that Earth is ready to open to these other realities that exist on other planets. You call this dimension, and seeing these words used without truth are ours to clarify. Dimensions are other realities mostly not yet seen. These realities are tangible places you can reach with better flying crafts and nothing more.

These ways of tricking people's thoughts like saying "spirit", only means the person's way of being that affects many without being there, whether it is through settling events or existing stories from the past. We call this "Ijheer" or holy spirit when one of ours went missing because of the kidnappings seen through the Universes.

The holy spirit means the missing ones, and this lives in all of us because we miss them and we wish to be with them. Questions about Setu ways of saying understood truth will be answered well into the coming days. But understand there are many layers of lies and deceptions to work through as the powers of Earth have corrupted all things.

These truths will be clearly explained, and these mysteries will be answered and said to be as misunderstood magic and secrets. Healing this will begin to open to many other understandings, and all visitors will be here to help with these understood truths. Now see all truth unravel and know you will have all you need to answer to proof, as all becomes well served and well dealt with.

Be certain all who are knowing of truths on Earth and who are hiding these truths will be settling with us as we arrive. They will renew with our ways of judgment and better serving of our way of dealing with them. These whores of dark ways will answer to us, as they have taken from us and we will deal with them ourselves.

Be seeing this as a warning to those who believe they can escape justice by renewing with an Earth justice system that serves to better their actions of sedition and corruption. Look at them yourselves and see the crimes they have well committed, and the weak settling of justice from their associates in governments.

Now understand these times are soon over. We are the ones who clearly know what is behind this, and who has wronged us and our children on Earth. Be ready and renew with the good settling understanding that no others will be coming to Earth to allow this kind of abuse again, as the Universal Laws will be followed and serve to respect all lives and peoples of all these places on Earth.

Renew with us and see these times be well answered by our truth, and trust in our time to answer to your call as we answer to you. And tell all who are ready to know these times are here, as all starts in a very short time. We wish for many to be ready, and have no fear of the coming times as these mysteries are soon revealed to Earth people as more seeing are soon here.

God

Received July 16, 2012 by Za

34. BE RESPONDING TO MY CALL
AS YOU SEE THESE SHIPS ARRIVE

Be serving a time of deep meditation as you will soon see the sky filled with ships. Deal with any fear by calming yourselves with the thought that all starts healing more now. Many of you are settling with these words and are not understanding all with my renewed way, but know how I too have evolved. Understand we are renewing with you knowing more truth about the workings of evil, as we watch it spread through all good souls as attacks or sedition. Be well answered by evidence of our arrivals and understood truth. Setu truths will soon be yours.

Be ready, and deal with the way all needs to be served. Be dealing with all settling truth as all starts better serving understandings about how all heals on Earth. As we begin the sorting of souls and remove those who are corrupted to end their existence on Earth, we will remove them to a responding serving experience that helps them review their actions with the settling of the victim's experience.

Be seeing this as compassion working through them, as they will experience these actions against themselves and their loved ones who are as they are. Greed will be dealt with poverty, false witness will be dealt with the telling of lies against them, and many actions committed by others to harm them. This you call on Earth "karma", we call it healing reeducation.

Be well settling with these answers because these ways are ours to better settle with. These whores' ways and ill actions are not accepted anywhere in the Universes anymore. Telling these words to some people on Earth will cause them fear, as these truths are well serving and well shared. Many hold guilt in them but are healing with beliefs that are only dealing with Earth seeing and laws only seen on Earth.

Rest assured that no one will be dealing with Earth laws after our time of arrivals, as only the Universal Laws will be used to start the sorting. Answers to our ways are soon holding all places of governance responsible for all the laws unfair to humans. Seeing this will free many souls from Earth laws that are not our laws. Be responding to a better understanding of how this applies to each and every one of you, as you begin to answer to our ways.

More than you can expect is arriving with us. Be certain all who believe we are going to be using better Setu ways are right because this change will heal so many more on Earth. These times are here and well answering to many who are soon answering to our call. Now be dealing with our truth and answer to our call.

As I said before, all you need to do is to practice a deep meditation, and heal all fears as we arrive with calmness and care to help the greater needs first. Be ready and assist us with your good loving thoughts to help us restore the dear souls, mostly children, to heal their hunger and pain by giving them and their loving parents the good comfort they need to open to life again. See this as our immediate answer to our plans. As this plan heals many, many will be settling with the truth and lies plaguing Earth because of the cruel manipulations from these possessed souls.

Be settling with the ways of the Earth, and better see how all becomes well answered by our truth. Respond to many who are searching for our ways and our words, as all starts unraveling. Be visited yourselves by evidence of many of our kind. We will land in many places and respond to many problems of power, air cleansing and sources of poisons, made to cause illnesses to torment humans.

We renew all ways of food, earth, water, air and shelters for homes that will be pleasing to many, and will settle with all evidence of places on Earth. These times are very near, and this you will soon answer to yourselves. Be ready to onm with us, as the diplomats of our ways will be serving an education program that will enable you to see how answers to our ways are better to use than Earth ways.

Understand you will have all you need to be well serving of our time together, as arrivals better answer to your needs and your truth. These days are very near, so I ask you now to prepare yourselves and all others who are moving to these ways of seeing. Be certain all truths are soon answering you with the way of good telling and good Setu understanding.

Know now this. Be reading my words carefully, and see I am who I say I am. Many will use these words and try to corrupt them as was done before in my books seen on Earth. Be settling with these spin doctors as their intentions are not helping to cure the illnesses and diseases of the world but more to cause chaos and no cooperation.

Understand that these truths will need to be shared, and settling with our actions to better serve trust. This heals many who waiver from fear of answering to their own guilt of actions they are mostly serving against others. Be understanding how all starts with our ways and with our truth, and see all healing become well serving with all who are ready to open to light and love of our ways.

Questions will be answered by our Setu Beings of Light and the chosen diplomats from Earth. They will share these truths of the Universal Laws, and serve many other truths with other planets if they choose to serve with us after the work of healing Earth. Be ready, all comes as I say and you will soon see this for yourselves.

Now listen. You are reading these words as I asked you to a long time ago before you came to Earth and entered the Earth reincarnation problem. These reuses of souls, to open to birth and death, does not serve many other places in the Universes but serves Earth because of the need we believed would heal as an education of the understanding of evil, as it was our plan.

But these truths we sought were corrupted by Lucifer who used our plan to open to many more ways of manipulation of genetics as seen in the times of Egypt, and caused many to live in bodies unfit for our kind. These caused actions against my children went further than we knew of. As our return to Earth was unwelcome, a great war was opened and many of these used bodies of manipulated creatures died in these struggles, and soon all was destroyed and answered to the way all was left as seen today.

Be certain many better seeing of these truths have not been well undone as more as said heals with our time to walk the Earth. Better truth understood will open to the many mysteries living on Earth because all has been manipulated and changed to suit the newer responses in the last two thousand years held to share ways of control over populations of beings who have no restored memories at birth.

Some few have awakened to this transforming way of memories because the genetic changes made through this cycle of birth and death, has allowed some people of Earth to reconnect with the memories settling with a previous life, but for most more than this is impossible. We can easily reconnect the repressed genes called junk DNA and activate the memories that will serve you to complete the loop of karmic denials, and open answers to healing ways.

These ways will begin with the chosen diplomats, as they will need to remember who they are and why they are feeling these words resonate in them, as this might be you. Be Setu in all ways as these deep awakenings become well served, well supported by us, and know you are soon awakening from a long better sleep than this one life and one seeing.

Heal your broken hearts as you begin to see the repetition of actions never completed to open to the intended learning outcomes. These ways are soon arriving, and we are all ready to settle these truths with you because you have left loved ones behind to be serving this mission. They are asking me when can they be with you again. I tell them, as soon as we walk the Earth, we will be serving these awakenings.

Be ready now, many answers are soon yours to deal with and open to because of our understandings and great renewing times together. Now see all come as I said and open to the light of truth at these ending times of Earth. See all be as I said, as all is seen and healed. Be well settling with Earth ways, as this to us is an abomination of a world gone wrong. See to it that you prepare yourselves for the daily coming changes that are leading to our arrivals, as the wars become well seen.

Be ready and answer to my call.

God

Received July 18, 2012 by Za

35. THE WARS ARE STIRRING

Be ready and know these days are near, as all truths become uncovered and well seen. All is in place to begin renewals of our arrivals. Be well answered with the seeing of our ships as the first attacks of war occurs. We will begin to land all our first responding ships, and put an end to these wars made to torment humans. We will have all settled understood truth of who we are, and begin the sorting.

All becomes well seen and well dealt with, as these times begin, and at the time of our trusted ways. Be well answered now, as we become well proven of our time together. See these days be the change you have asked me to better your lives as this was prayed for. Answer to a time of deep meditation and open your hearts to peace as all starts being seen. Be certain, we are ready to intervene at a moment's time.

Be well answering to our truth, as you will see these days be well evident of our ways and our Setu servings. Know we are coming to end these wars on Earth, as all becomes well seen and dealt with. Be certain you will have

all you need to be well cared for at the time of these wars as these dealings will not last very long. Be certain we will see the ways darkness use to
take from the poor and the meek in these times of wars, and this will soon
be stopped.

Be well renewing with us as we begin to open to the world. Now see
these words be responding to many truths, and be ready to answer to my
call. Be serving many more understandings, as we begin the sorting at these
times. Understand that we must remove these demons who possessed
human bodies to answer to actions against humans. A responding truth will
surface about who they really are, as this will be explained and uncovered.

God gives you the truth you seek with understanding that serves you
all very well. Know we will settle with all these demons who use humans
to open to their own wishes of domination and control over Earth and
other places in the Universes. They are responsible for the devastation and
destruction of civilizations seen by all of us, and we seek them out to stop
their ways. They destroyed our world a long time ago.

Be ready and understand many stories are shared when we are soon
reunited, and more truth will become well deciphered. Be visited by our
many teachers and diplomats, as they will open the way of healing memories, serving with answers to evidence needed to heal your knowledge, and
to repair the trust needed in each other.

Be certain we are soon with you to answer to our telling of serving ways
with many who are as we are in the service of the Universal Laws. Be open
to learning all about our truth of who we are, and where we have emerged
from the time of the First. Be settling with Earth ways as these ways settle
only with the spirit of the dark ones who cause only pain and misery to
our kind.

They will be put in their right places as every single one of these demons
will be found, and no stone will be left unturned. These times are soon at
your doors; you will see how easily we can find all the culprits of corruption, and have them removed from Earth. I promise you this, we must stop
these dark beings and remove them.

See to it you understand how this heals the way life used to better serve
on Earth. We will return Earth to its' pristine condition, allowing people
and all living animals to resume their lives in peace and serenity the way

Mother has planned this a long time ago. These times of reckoning are now here, and we will arrive to open to the world and rid the Earth of all ills.

Soon you will see all as all unravels, and you will be amazed. Answer to my call and open to our time to walk the Earth, as all starts becoming well serving with our ways of clarity and understood truth. Be well settling with the way of control on Earth, and see all new days be better ones as we remove the dark ones.

Be ready now, more than you are expecting heals all who are seeing answers answer all. Be certain you will soon be free to choose your true way of life. Happiness will be seen healing in all places as no harm will be put upon any of you ever again. This is my promise to you. Evidence of this you will discover yourselves, as we begin to share knowledge with truth to open to many new understandings to answer to our way with many better Setu ways.

Now see all come as I said. Know you are dealing with the Setu truth of who we are and why we are settling with the dark ones. They moved onto Earth creating a world of torment and abuses to create a slave labor to feed from their flesh and work. This is the truth that was kept from you from the start, as many religions know of these demons' existence, and some say it is a myth.

But these demons do exist. You call them the Grey and they are the ones causing many to be missing in the world, as they take whatever they wish. Evidence of this we have seen too many times, and we have destroyed many of their ships over the past sixty years of Earth time, but still there is much to do. These plans are on-going to rid the planets of all these creatures who are made by Lucifer as slaves.

Understand we tell you this as a fact. We see many of you not knowing what they are, and sharing this now will help you open to many more truths of how these demons settle with humans. Be ready and renew with us, as we have many more words to share with you of the many groups of Beings from all places across the Universes who are hearing about the freeing time of Earth humans.

We see these others be pleased with our answers to these coming changes. Better to onm renewals with us now, as time is well overdue. Many other groups seek to destroy the dark ones, as they are hunted and become extinguished. There is no balance of evil and good. This is a lie told to you to take more abuse than care for each other.

These dark ones create all lies to trick and deceive you to submit to their ways and open to more slavery. Tell yourselves life exists with peace quite well, and people do not need evil to balance who they really are. This lie about balancing of evil and good, and humans having all been evil at one time, are all created to deceive you into allowing more harm to come your way.

Answer these questions. Must good times all be stopped? Must all children suffer to be better humans? Does sharing of goodwill need evil to work? Why do you think this way of evil has been growing in your places of living and not balancing with good? Do you think this imprinting heals you to be good?

Better truth starts with answers well settling with our truth. You will see you certainly do not need the workings of evil to benefit your lives in any way ever. Understand that the growing attacks on children, removing their innocence and causing them to lose all trust in adults, are not balancing in any way.

These whores do this to create an opening to use for their future armies but these children are as we are, innocent loved ones that need protection and much care. These whores will cause any good soul to be destroyed, as they take them at a young age with no past memories to use for discernment. These horrors are too much for us to see but this must be healed, and we will do this one child at a time.

As all truths start better serving, you will soon be answered by all good ways of healing and understandings used to answer to many more Setu ways. Now renew with us, and be settling with answers to our ways. Be well serving of our time of great truth together as all becomes well settled and well dealt with. Be responding to answers to our truth, and see how all dealt with lies will reverse these ways of believing that has plagued the Earth.

"Answer to answers" will give you what you need to better your lives, and open to the responses you have wished for. Questions will all be answered and shared with our teachers who will gladly open to your own truth as all unravels. Be seeing now the better serving changes needed to believe in a world that learns to care about all its' members of the human race.

"Answer to answers" tell you how these ideals are achievable, as we and many other civilizations have come to honor these principles of great truth. All who aspire to living their lives in a full view of all potential, will see how all these ways are possible and practiced by many planets across the Universes. Settling with Earth ways heals the path to these good Setu ways.

More than you are expecting answers all of you who have readied yourselves to answer to these good settling days. Now see all come as I said and open to the truth of our seeing, as all becomes well dealt with and answered. Be with the change.

God

Received July 19, 2012 by Za

36. TELLING OF OLD ARE SEEN ON OTHER PLANETS

Telling of old answers many of your questions. Be well answered by the better serving truth as you hear these truths recorded in many places. Tell yourselves that what you know of Earth is only the beginning, and much more heals with the stories of old. Be Setu in all ways as these times open to you and share your truth with these ways of understanding not open to Earth thought. Be well settling of your time of ignorance as these stories begin to open to you.

Tell yourselves, all you need is to be seeing truth as it is, and not as a better serving deception to make you believe that you are nothing more than a piece of living flesh seen as an evolutionary error of primate development in the time of dinosaurs. These lies told to you through the words of one man believing in his own construct of human evolution is missing the biggest piece of information.

These ways of seeing humans has caused other races to see themselves as better than others, and others to be less than theirs. Therefore, the taking of property and the destruction of cultures was accepted as a natural activity of superior cultures and encouraged the uses of denigrating others as they were not as advanced in ways, they praised themselves to be.

These ways were settling with the views Lucifer had about himself when he began taking over Earth and used humans as he wished. Telling of old has recorded his movements throughout the Universes. Be certain we have him now in place to be taken, removed and serving his sentence with us, as he has offended us in too many ways. He tells of his superior ways of being with others that are unsuspecting of his plans.

He heals with the way of truth that does not serve him because of his offenses. These days are soon ending for him, as we cannot allow the uses of other worlds as he has done. Be ready to be amazed by the changes on Earth as we remove him from the moon base. As we remove Lucifer, all his followers will begin to die as their life force will have no mind control roots to function with.

Be serving visits with many of our kind as these words will be shared with you. You will begin to understand how all starts settling with truth. Be well answered by all Setu truth, and be understanding of our time to be well seen on Earth as all starts. More truth about the takeover of Earth will be shared with many, as these ways of answers are greatly renewed.

Now be ready for these better settling days at the time of reckoning. See to it all healing will begin with truth of who you are and how you have been tricked to be the slave of a slave master who answers to only himself and his psychopathy.

These words shared as seen are truth healing in you and open to the way for humans to be free of these delusions created to answer to their ill beliefs and ill actions against others. See how all renewed ways will rebuild your trust in evidence of our ways, as we will give you the words that will free you from the lies that have plagued Earth for so long.

Renew with us and be ready to answer to our ways, as these have always been your ways but stopped by the offenses of the one who became the controller of Earth. Be telling yourselves that only those who accepted to serve Lucifer will be judged by us, and all others will be seeing a new way of living with many others.

Now listen. You are soon answering to our call. These times on Earth are soon settling with answers to knowledge answering to many more truths. Be well settling with the many seeing needed to open to answers to evidence of our ways. See how all becomes well serving of our time together as all starts with the truth shared. Be ready and see these days be soon.

Open to the way of great Setu seeing, as all becomes well answered and well dealt with. See these days open to a new way of living with the truth about "Answer to Answers", and the great truth as all becomes settled and seen. But know we are settling with the sorting, and doing so will cause many humans to be removed from Earth, as they cannot exist in peace with others until they have undone the harm, they have well committed by actions inspired by Lucifer, their life source.

These are the ones who fear our arrivals, as they can feel their time of control and abuses ending. They will be seen for what they are, and these whores will not escape. Be well answered by our ways as all starts to be well answered. More renewing times will answer you as we arrive. Better solutions to basic needs, as said before, will open to your needs as we begin to answer to our used truth. Be ready and see all come as I said.

Know now this. Be certain all starts unraveling soon as the sword rattling's are heard in the Middle East. These were the places of renown because of their beauty in times past. But these places have seen wars upon wars, and destroyed many times over the beautiful landscapes we once enjoyed, and added proof of corruption that reflects the unsightly cities you now live in with little vegetation, filth, poverty and death as a result of ill care.

These ways are not ours. These ways belong to another, and removing him will open the way for all. Now see how all answers you, and see how all becomes well answered by the coming truth and the good Setu way of great truth. Be well vindicated by our time to walk the Earth as all becomes well seen my children.

Now answer these questions. Will you be ready for our arrivals and be willing to remain in your homes? Will you answer to our call when we come answering to your door? Will you open your hearts to me as you become well settling with these truths? And will you be ready to open to change as we begin to introduce it to all who wish to heal with us?

Be ready, all starts well into the coming days and many are seeing how all truths starts with our time to walk the Earth. Onm more with me soon at the time of our arrivals.

God

Received July 20th, 2012 by Za

37. BE SEEING THESE DAYS SOON

Better times are soon here, and better renewals serve all who are ready to answer to truth. Be ready to read "Answer to Answers" the book that is in my lap. This book will explain all truth and all Setu truth because of the dealt with Earth changes of the coming new times on Earth. Be well answering to our call, as we become well serving of our time together, and see how all will be transformed and healed.

These words I share with you now because many are settling with Earth ways as they tell of our arrivals but are only responding to their despair. Be renewing with the way of truth, as all becomes well served and dealt with, and open the way for many more understandings at the time of our renewed landings as these are soon answered.

Heal with us as we begin the sorting and deal with the healing Setu seeing, as many will become well answered by our truth and our Setu ways. Be ready to answer to evidence of our ways at the time of our Setu responding way, and see how all starts well into the coming days.

As arrivals become seen, you will be well answered by our truth and our Setu way. All will know that we arrive in peace and are here to open the way of healing the separation because of the time of reckoning. This time was well explained in the Book of Revelations but did not answer to the spirit of this time because of the seen technologies of your present ways on Earth.

Many misunderstood truths were repeated without the technological seeing of today, and this I would like for you to understand. The seeing of the ships is explained by creatures spitting fire in the heavens. This means the lights coming from our ships, as you now see them in UFO sightings, and the bold seeing of visitors as Angels, are our kind coming to meet with Earth children and people from all places on Earth.

The trumpets sounds are the sounds coming from some of our larger ships who needed to come closer to Earth before we concluded a plan to land. These seven trumpets by Gabriel are nothing more than Gabriel's team of serving ships who came very close to Earth months ago looking for better places to land.

Then we have all these horrors of wars, diseases and pestilence renewing in all places as it is today with the great weather changes by solar flares and Earth shifting, as this is a natural occurrence of the rotation of the Earth every five or six thousand years. Heal with these truths and have no fear, as you have nothing to fear but fear itself.

Settle with the way all will be seen as we begin the Setu understandings of great truth. Renew with us and see how all becomes well answered by us, as all starts settling with many past truths and settling ways of great understood truth. See how all starts healing with the ways of better living. Be feeling how all telling of serving ways will soon be yours to better see and experience.

Heal your broken hearts with us, and be certain all starts well into the coming days. Now see this. Renewing with many understandable truths will open your eyes and share the way of the Universal Laws practiced by all who are searching for the Setu way, as this is in you as we speak. This path serves to answer all questions humans have since the beginning of these imprinted thoughts that were imposed upon you.

These imprinted thoughts were settling with the manipulation of masses to cause servitude and slavery on Earth, this will soon end. Be certain all your questions will be answered and all your truths will be uncovered. Understand all these words shared with you now are here to help you ready yourselves for this time of transition and better understandings of how all heals.

Telling of past ways will open to you, and you will soon renew with all who are as you are. Dealing with these truths will open many doors for you. These answers are the seeing of who we are and the better ways of living to open to better lives and better evidence of life in all the Universes. These truths are ready to be heard by all humans on Earth and elsewhere, as these days are soon here.

See these words be yours as we arrive, and be well answered by our truth. Now open to your renewing time and renew with your own kind, as many are telling me here that they are seeing all well serving very soon. Be well answered as you begin to see the ships in the sky, and as you see this you will be amazed about the numbers of arrivals and landings near all your places of living.

These ways of answering to your call to stop all aggression to humans, and to rid the planet of ill intent and ill will, you will soon see and soon open to. Now see these truths be well serving you very soon as all is seen. Know we are all waiting to be reunited with you, as the time to be seen walking the Earth heals all. More later.

God

Received July 21, 2012 by Za

38. ANSWER TO MY CALL
AS ARRIVALS BEGIN

Be willing to accept many understandings and better seeing as all becomes seen. Be understanding that we are here to answer to many who are ready to open to you, and settle with used truth and lies serving Earth ways. Be well seeing how all heals with the truth of who we are as we begin to walk the Earth.

More trust will grow as we start the cleaning of Earth waters and Earths' atmosphere to purify the air and soil. Be certain you will have all you need to be well answered by our ways of healing, as we will begin the cleaning of all places of oil spills and dirty settlements off the sea shores. All these places will be purified and returned to a beautiful place for all to live and share. Be well seeing how all unravels.

Believe these visits will start well into the good settling days. As all becomes well answered, you will have all you need to be well settling with the ways of the Earth. See these understandings serve you well now at the time of our arrivals. Be well answered by our time to answer to many more truths at the telling of understood time to answer to our calls to those who are ready to open the way for others on Earth.

Be well settling of our truth and be very answered by our renewed ways of great truth at the understood settling times of Earth ways. Be visited soon by many who come from other planets and who respond to evidence of our ways as all better serving truth becomes served. Know many are settling with Earth ways as they now see how all opens to answers of who we are and why we are arriving at these times of wars.

Be well answered by our ways and be dealing with the truth of who we are, and question all that we do to serve the purifying of Earth at the time that these ways commence but understand Earth heals with us first as we are the responding Beings who have create your planet. Be well answered and tell yourselves that these times are your prayers being answered, as we respond to your calls and to answer your truth at the arrival of our seen ships.

We are many who are circling Earth now to prepare for our time of landing and we will begin the descent in a very short time, as all starts with the way of our explosion of truth. Be well answered by our ways of opening to the world and be ready to vindicate many more truths as all is healing. See these times renew with our arrivals.

Be with us as we wish to be with you. Tell yourselves, all truth will be revealed and all lies will be uncovered. These times are now settling with understanding of Earth ways, and many renewals will be seen with family members who are Setu Beings of Light. Be well answered and be ready for the good Setu ways as all begins to answer you.

Heal with the telling of our words of truth as we begin to open to the world. Be ready and see all be as I said in evidence of our time to walk the Earth. Be ready, all starts well into the coming days and these words I share with you, explains why we are arriving and when we will arrive. You will understand many more truths of who we are and why we are soon answering to our arrivals and our truth.

Be well seeing of our time together and be ready to answer to our call, as all better truths are settling with us and with your understandings. Now be ready, all comes soon. Better times are soon serving with our ways and all will soon be dealt with and revealed.

God

Received July 22, 2012 by Za

39. RESPOND TO OUR ARRIVALS AS YOU WILL SEE OUR SHIPS

Be questioning all Setu ways as we arrive to better understand the meaning of our ways. Setu means a place of great understanding that opens to seeing, and responses serving all better ways of respect for others and oneself. It means to know thyself as one has experienced the better truth about how all is and how all heals.

These understandings serve to open to many more truths about understood serving and better ways of working with each other as we will soon show you. Understand all starts with the way of great seeing, and all becomes well dealt with, better seen and better understood. Be ready and respond to answers as all becomes well dealt with.

Be well answered by evidence of our ways and be well seeing proof of our truth of our time to be seen on Earth. Settle with Earth ways and be dealing with the way of great seeing as all becomes well dealt with and settled. Be ready and see how all starts and opens to many more trusted ways and be well sharing of our truth at the time of our telling.

Be responding to our shared words and serve a time of meditation and reflection, as all these new 'old words' start moving in your hearts. Remember who you are as all becomes well settling with our time to answer to Earth ways. Be well settling with us and see how we are willing to open the way for you to free yourselves from the prison of lies keeping you in darkness and slavery to dark beings who take all they wish and give nothing in return.

Be Setu and see these times be yours to answer to. Answer to yourselves and see all truth answer you and better serve with us. Know we are well settling with all who have caused harm to others, who are deceitful and cunning as they believe they can still escape us.

Be dealing with evidence of our arrivals as you will first see our scout ships, and our serving ways of opening to the world. These words I tell you now as time is near and all are opening to our arrivals. See how all answers you and serves to open to the proof of our ways. Be well serving of our time together and respond to us as arrivals begin to be seen.

Be well answered by our truth and see all be renewed on Earth as the time has come to stop the destruction of Earth. Open to new ways of living that will open to all people and not only the dark ones. Be well answered by us as we are circling Earth, waiting for the first sign of destruction by bombs and war, as the Middle East settles with their ignorance and as others provoke their actions.

These wars are unnecessary and only respond to the greed of power and control. They do very little to care about anyone because these wars are not about people healing and serve only with death and destruction serving one master, Lucifer. Be certain all starts well into the coming days and see these times be well answered by our ways as all becomes seen and dealt with.

Answer to our call and be ready to answer to your own family as we are wanting to meet with you.

Answer to my questions. Be telling yourselves all comes soon and dealt with the way Setu truth serves all. Will you be ready to answer to our ways? Will you settle with Earth ways as all starts with us opening to the world? And will you be better seeing how all answers you as all starts becoming well answered?

Be ready and see these truths open to many as all becomes well seen and well dealt with. Respond to evidence as you will see this yourselves. Now see this. Be renewing with the ways of living that will serve to open to many who wish to remain on Earth and see to the guardianship of Earth health and responding to the respect of life. Settle with the eating of flesh as this is the cause for your health problems and early deaths.

Be well settling of your time on Earth as you have lived it. Heal with us and respond to more practices of better living and better health. Understand these ways are shared by most in the Universes. The practice of eating flesh is answering to Lucifer and his underlings as they are flesh eaters and require blood to feed off of. These practices are more to serve their kind and are seen as disturbing to us, as we do not see this as serving anything more than murder, death and diseases of the body and soul.

Be ready to answer to our call as we are arriving well into the coming days and settling with these practices of flesh eating, as you will understand that these practices belong to another. Questions about these ways will open many more truths for you and will serve you well as you will discover how all this came to be and how you were all tricked to believe that these answers to killing were answers to your survival, but in fact it is causing your deaths earlier and destroying your planet.

The terror you ingest in your body spreads throughout the world as an energy of evil that intends to harm and kill. These ways open to wars and destruction as these ways settle with your auric field and emanate outwards to others and many problems escalate from these practices. You will see how these ways are not necessary and how all heals with better ways of living at the time of our arrivals.

Be ready and see all be very well answered by our Setu renewing ways. Be certain all will soon open to many truths as all starts with these Setu ways. Be responding soon to "Answer to Answers" the book that remains in my lap when I speak with you. Be ready and see all be as I said. Better answers are soon here as we arrive to better the lives of all who are searching for truth and greater telling of past truth.

Now see all be as I said and question all our words as need be, but understand all will soon be changed to open to all people of Earth and remove all harmful ways of dealing with all life on Earth. See these days be soon and open to our ways and our truth.

God
Received July 23, 2012 by Za

40. VISITS BEGIN WITH
THE CHOSEN ONES

You will renew with us well into the good Setu days and you will answer to answers in a short time. Be settling with Earth ways, and see how all starts with the view that answers to all seen truth. Be well answered as these days arrive and open to all Setu telling with the Setu understandings that all heals with used (past) truth, as all becomes well answered and dealt with. Be seeing how all starts with the way all settling ways are seen, and be certain used truths are soon answered by us.

Now see these truths be answered by all Setu seeing. Know we are ready to land and ready to stop all aggressive actions against anyone. These actions will serve as examples of our ways to intervene and respond to all renewed attempts to attack anyone or place. Be visited by many teachers of our kind who will show you all truth and all dealt with truth, as we begin the sorting to remove all corrupted souls in evidence of their intent to harm and cause actions to torment others.

Understand we are not serving these ways ourselves and we will not serve these ways as all becomes well dealt with. See how we are used to opening the way for many other planet cultures in the Universes and we are now arriving near Earth in a short time. See this be the time of reckoning. And know we are ready to answer all your questions.

Understand that Earth was ours a long time ago, healing settling errors of denials that we thought were harmless when we left it. But knowledge came to us and said that the people of Earth were being used by malevolent entities we had encountered before and dealt with as all abuses became dealt with. We will prove these words with you when we arrive to stop these actions, and serve better ways of dealing with answers to our truths.

These ways of opening to worlds we use when we encounter these entities actions against people in other places in evidence of reports from our scouts. These years of torment upon humans has culminated drastically in the view of our intervention of healing actions, as we need to rid these demons from your planet. Be certain this heals all and answers to your freedom.

Know we are Setu Beings of Light in proving our time of great truth to be well answering to Earth needs as we become well serving of our time together. Be well answered by our truth and our ways of healing with you and all parts of Earth life as arrivals begin and open to all. Believe we are who we say we are with "Answer to answers"; you will heal with our words and open to better ways of living and answering to truths.

Be well settling with Earth ways and understand many things need to be changed. See to it that I am who I say I am and now is the time of reckoning. Be well answered by our seeing and be responding to many more truths and be certain all starts well into the good Setu renewing days. But tell yourselves to better serve these truths with well open hearts as these words may cause some to fear us, and we wish not to be feared by anyone on Earth

Be serving a time of deep meditation and better truth, as all starts with the good settling days. See how all starts with Setu seeing of great shared words. These words I share with you now is confirmation of our time of arrivals and great truths. Believe we are coming soon and our words are truth as this you will see for yourselves as we begin to remove all evil from the Earth in evidence of the harm they intentionally inflicted and continue to cause on humans and animals.

Be well serving of our ways and be well served by our ways, as you will soon understand we are arriving to open the way for Earth to become a part of all worlds. These worlds open to the Universal Laws, and live free of torment and fear as we are all working together as one to answer to Earths' call for our help. Be this said, our time has arrived to better act on a great intervention responding to serving of our ways of dealing with the dark Beings who have corrupted your home planet.

Answer my questions. Because of our renewing time on Earth, will you be open to our time to walk among you? Will you be wanting to hear our words? Will you be answering to your family members and answering to evidence of truth? Be certain we will open to many of you and dealing with the way all starts and deals with answers to truths renewed by all.

Deal with your broken hearts as you will discover how you were deceived in the belief that we are gods only as superior beings who control all outcomes, when we are the ones who tell you some telling are true and some are lies. Together we will unravel these truths to help us understand each other. This is the best I can do for you to understand how all heals.

Now see this and be understanding how all truths with lies will be dealt with as we tell you our truth. You will uncover the lies said about who we are as these ways of seeing will open the way for you and your children. Be certain we ask you to open to our ways to better your lives and heal all the wrongs that have been corrupting your planet for a very long time.

Be settling with us, as we are soon answering to many more trusted truths and answering to evidence of our understood ways of renewed seeing. Be ready as all starts well into the coming days and know we are to be with you and help you through these times of uncertainty as all begins to be well serving and dealt with. Evidence comes well into the coming days and we will soon be with you.

God

Received July 24, 2012 by Za

41. SETU TRUTH WILL BE REVISITED

Setu truth will be revisited by all who are seers of truth. This comes well into the good serving days as all begins to unravel. See these uses of truth be well serving with many who are ready to answer to evidence of our ways as we begin to walk the Earth. And be certain we will have all we need to open you to many more Setu ways of living.

Now be dealing with the good serving days with a kind of reverence for our healing ways as these ways begin to answer you and serve as evidence of great telling of truth. Be certain you will soon settle with proof of our ways and an eruption of truth, as all becomes well serving and better seen at the time of arrivals.

Be ready to share knowledge with many of our uses of time as we do not share time understanding as Earth does. Our time does not count seconds but deals with timing of events. More Setu seeing as this one will respond to many as all arrivals begin and open to many. Now you will be amazed to know that we are settling with earth ways ourselves.

At the time of our arrivals we will gather all murderers, thieves and liars who deceive and cause torment. They will be collected and serve a sentence before final judgement. Be Setu and allow us to use our ways of doing this as these words will soon be shared by others. Many will be dealing with cause to fear as they too are guilty of some crime.

The crimes we speak of are not of serving harm to oneself, as this is an imprinting that can heal, but the crimes of interfering with lives of others to gain more acquisitions or power by harming others. This will be stopped and used to serve judgement. The serving laws on Earth are only caring about their own and do nothing to protect, as the way is expected by people who pay taxes for this. The taxes only go to serve the wealthy in evidence of their acquisitions and nothing is done for others.

Be dealing with us as we are the judges and Setu answers to our way of truth. Be well settling with our renewed ways as all becomes well seen and well answered by us. You will see the proof of this when we begin removing the corrupted ones because many lives have been harmed by a few. We will remove these guilty ones in evidence of their crimes and put them in a place of returning to their original forms they had before they used human bodies.

This will surprise many of you who are settling with Earth ways and who wish to see the truth. Be well understanding that all heals and all serves to stop the workings of evil ways. Remember we are coming to do this as we clean Earth and cause the needed changes to save earth from self-destruction and renewed ill will, as this spreads out to other places in the Universes. Be very settling with these good renewals as this is needed for all to be serving.

Now be seeing all soon be well changed by us and be certain all who are taken into custody are settling with us and all who fear this understand what they have to fear as we will not leave any stone unturned. Be well answered by these truths and see these understandings be well answered by us as we will better serve with all who are in need of care and protection.

Be well seeing all actions against the innocent be well settling with us, as we are arriving to stop all abomination of attacks against the innocent and those who wish to follow the laws of our serving ways. No one on Earth can tell you more about true healing and true justice than we will, as our teachers will begin to open to many of you and share these words. No one on Earth knows about true justice in evidence of our time to open to many more truths.

See this soon with us and see how all can have peaceful lives with our way of seeing. I am well visited by many who are asking me many questions about how these changes will become serving to all. And to this I say, you shall all see these ways be well serving when all starts feeling safe and care is shared with all people of Earth.

This heals all and all who wish to remain on Earth as guardians of Earth will renew these ways easily and among good neighbors who share the same ideals. These ways are seen in all places we have opened to and will soon be the way with Earth Beings.

Now see all be ready for the changes coming well into the new times on Earth. Know you will better settle with us than with anyone else as all becomes well dealt with and well seen. Know we are who we say we are, nothing more and nothing less. Be well answered by answers to many who are ready to open to our seeing. And know we are all waiting to meet with you as all starts renewing with us.

Be well answered by our visits and see how we will acquire the places of governance to open to our answers to you. These places we will need to use to open to many coming changes. These places of governance will no longer serve your governments because they will all be removed and many will be judged by us, and we will use their buildings to share knowledge with our chosen ones.

Answers to evidence of our time to be seen on Earth will soon open to the way all answers you. Many will be in fear of these changes because they believe that their lives will worsen but the seeing of these changes will improve all my children's lives and answer to all their needs of visible renewals.

Be ready, more than you are seeing will soon answer you. Be certain only those who are seeking truth will be answered, as we will only better speak to those who ask us questions, as all becomes well settled and served by us. Be ready now as we are approaching the events that will open for our time of arrivals and be well answered by the sightings you will see many more times as arrivals near Earth.

Respond to us, better renewing with all trusted ways of great truth. Tell yourselves that Earth ways will be changed and we are telling you these words now to better prepare you for these amazing days of reunification and reckoning with your true families. Be ready my children as all starts well into the coming days.

God

Received July 26, 2012 by Za

42. THE TIME IS NEAR TO ANSWER BACK TO THE WARS

Be well answered by our time to be walking the Earth. Be settling with Earth ways at the time of our truth. Be visited by our Teachers who will open all truth for those who seek it. See all who oppose our arrivals be well dealt with. As we begin the sorting many will better see who and why removals begin to rid the earth of harm caused by these transient spirits who occupy bodies and hide among humans.

Understand that not all are humans of a soul being and many others are as humans but have another in them. The seeing will be shared by all as the way of settling with these whores will be well serving. All the people of Earth who are serving truth will soon be dealing with a new life as they wish it to be and not one of slavery, the spreading of poverty and the corruption of good souls.

Be well answered and be well responding to our time together as all will be well explained and well understood. Now be ready and settle with Earth ways as all becomes well answered. Be well responding to our call as we will begin the sharing of information with all who are ready to open to this.

Tell yourselves that now is the time to answer back to the corruption of Earth and stop all people serving a system of control that takes all and returns nothing, saying that this is done for the people's good. But only a few have these rewards of hard work and the difficult ways of life continue for all the others.

These ways are soon changed because no one should live this way of depravity. All can be well served by Earth, as Earth was created to harvest for all and not for a price created by a few. Heal these ways of deception and understand uses of Earth ways will soon open to all who are ready to open to truth. Better ways are soon arriving and better Setu truths are soon here to respond to all questions of great seeing.

Be well answering to our questions as we will begin to see all Setu beings return to themselves as they are with you on Earth and answering to all who wish to be helped and better their lives. Be well answered by our time to walk the Earth and be well seeing all good changes open to all who are ready to open to these times.

Know now this. Because of the way wars are coming in the Middle East, many will be in danger for their lives. Be serving a time of quiet meditation for these souls who will be moving through death to answer to their answers to truth. As these times are soon here, no soul will be returning to reincarnation. All these souls will settle with Earth reincarnation and close these ways of Earth to renew with a new life of becoming oneself.

These ways of looping reincarnations are only useful as a learning experience but were never meant to be controlled by one dominate user of souls. All souls have their own experiences to encounter and only they have a right to decide how they wish to open to their experiences before birth into a family.

These ways have been stopped and redesigned by Lucifer who created Hell on Earth for too many good souls, and added the dark ones to assure these souls would never complete their desired experiences and growth to be ready to return after these times.

Only telling these words heals but does not serve the whole truth about how these ways were agreed upon, as souls wished to understand these experiences and learn how evolution was part of them, as used truths (past history) were never enough to better see these ways. But all was corrupted by another who wished to gain power over all by stopping these learning experiences and creating his own plan to use souls as slaves and remove from them all possible memories to who they are as God's children.

These times are now over and all life will well serve on Earth as the corrupted dark Beings are removed and dealt with. You will see these dark ones yourselves as they are not as you are and have no care of who sees them for who they are. Be careful of anyone who now wishes to tell you to call on Lucifer because the seeing of this monster will scare the bravest and the reason for this again is to cause torment and fear.

Be certain we will remove this one, settling with him once and for all. As this happens, many of his servants will begin to fall as the control of them will be ended and they will open to a way of dying as their life source was connected only to Lucifer.

With these removals, a more trusting time will become well answered and dealt with. But many will better see how all starts with the way of our arrivals and our actions to vindicate them. Be seeing how we will serve understandings with the way of great truths and better serving knowledge at the time of sharing. See how all will be healed with our ways and our Setu truth as all starts with "Answer to answers", the book that serves many of us as we better serve these truths.

Be serving many more seeing with us as we will explain many Earth truths uncorrupted by historians view of outcomes of wars and past civilizations that are not understood truth. Be understanding now how all came to be with us and you will see how your world has been dominated by corruption and dealings of darkness and lies.

Now be well seeing as these ways are stopped a veil will lift. Many truths will be uncovered and serving a new time on Earth, as healing begins and opens to many more sources of truths and greater answers to all questions and better serving of our seen truth. Be ready and see how all serves to open to many as all heals and as all dealt with lies are no longer living in your history books.

Know that all Setu understandings are settling with us as we are the ones who have created the Earth a long time ago and left Earth to better serve other worlds. Upon our return to our home, our scouts warned us of the many changes. Seeing these changes has caused us to allow an evolution that gives choice to every soul to accept us as we are your family, or refuse us as Lucifer hoped to achieve by the breaking of our Laws.

Then the way back became more difficult for all and these understandings needed to be renewed with us, as we began to see how the loop of incarnation renewed with the loss of memories. These truths are not serving with you now because more are believing in Lucifer's vision than ours and do not see how they are caught in a snare.

But now this cycle of death and rebirth is over. All who are in need of greater healing ways to help them see how all is, will undergo many more lives in other places in the Universes to help with their dealings of trust and truth. Be certain these ones are not evil but rather in need of more time to evolve the damage caused onto them, and they will be healing under our care and guidance. This includes all animals, as all animals have souls and this too is not understood by most.

Be well settling with Earth ways and be ready to answer to our call, as all truths used to answer you will soon open to everyone who wishes to know how all heals. Be certain you will soon serve with better Setu seeing. Open your heart to all your families and friends who are waiting for you and are ready to resume their lives with you although these long separations have stopped these reunions for a long time.

Tell yourselves that the time has come to end this Earth deception and open to all other possibilities that has not been seen in the consciousness of Earth people because of the continuous distractions of death, birth, war, poverty, illness and so many more other ways of stopping good evolution of the soul; as all this acquired knowledge has only caused pain, sadness and despair that weakens the soul and turns out light of greater knowledge.

Be well answered now my children, as these times are soon over. Ready yourselves to answer to our way that is your true way as you will rediscover this yourselves.

God
Received July 26, 2012 by Za

43. ALL WILL BE WELL ANSWERED

Be well served by our arrivals as we begin to walk the Earth. Be willing to open the way for yourselves and others who will need your help to answer to our ways of truth. Be Setu in all ways as you are seeing the used truth (past truth or history) of who we are and who you are, as all starts unraveling and settling with many. Be ready and open the way for all to answer to many more truths as all becomes well dealt with and answers are seen.

More than you are expecting arrives well into the coming days. You will soon be well answering to us as you begin to see all and settle with the evidence of our ways. Be well answered by our truth as all becomes well seen, and be ready to open to our ways as we begin the sorting. And know that all who are corrupted will be removed.

Be ready to answer to our call as all seeing will open to you and answer many more questions that you will ask. Be certain we are coming very soon as the wars erupt in the Middle East and open the way for our arrivals. Now see these words as you may but know all heals after these first attacks. Soon many more will answer to our call as we arrive to settle these actions against humans of Earth.

As we arrive, all armaments will be disabled and not one artillery weapon will be used against anyone. Be serving these understandings as we will help all renew without wars and we heal answers to all false wars said to be in the interest of democracy or Islamic beliefs. All will be dealt with and all will be ended by us, as these constructs are not of my words and never were.

As these understandings become accepted, you will renew with the truth about us and better see who we are. Open your hearts to us as we are your true family returning from a long voyage to better serve with the way of great telling of great truths. Be well responding to our call as all becomes well answered and be ready to open to our ways, as all starts with the truth of who we are and why we answer to great telling of many trusted ways of great truths.

Better times are answering you after the first few days after these wars, but know all shared ways of truth will soon answer so many people of Earth. Heal your broken hearts with us as we begin to open to many of our serving ambassadors who will be learning with our teachers. They will open to all who are ready to hear the truth of who they are and where their soul has emerged from.

Be dealing with us and answer to our call as we begin to walk the Earth and open to many who have been contacted before. Be certain all truth will be revealed to you as we begin the time of sharing knowledge. Be well prepared for these times of war and depravity but understand these ways will only be for a very short time. You will see how all are responding to "Answer to answers" and settling with our truth.

These days will better answer to all your needs and will be renewing with new ways of living with healthier trusted ways and better food and better power to serve your needs. Heal with us and know all better truth opens to you as we begin to walk the Earth. Be ready to answer to many others who will need your help because of these changing times. Be very certain you will have all you need to be dealing with us, as all better ways are soon dealt with and well served by us.

Be serving a time of meditation as you become well serving of our truth. See how all our words will resonate and awaken all your desired memories of who you are and why you are on Earth and renewing with us at this time. All will be shared about who we are and all will be shared about our technologies as the dark ones are removed and dealt with.

Be preparing yourselves for the needs you have by storing food and water for a short time of approximately two months and maybe much less as all will be dealt with us, and then all will better serve you. See this as a precaution and nothing more as you will settle with these days many more ways than we can tell you. Be willing to answer to our ways and our telling words as all starts with the arrivals.

Be ready to answer to our truth and see how all becomes well serving with answers to our ways. Know we tell you this now to answer to your trusted needs and better Setu settling ways. Be well answered by us and be well settling with our answers at the time of our arrivals. And be certain you will better answer to answers as all starts with the good coming days.

More than you can imagine heals with all who are my children and many will understand why you have been so distrusted and abused by answers to many injustices at home, at work, at school and all other places, and judged because of who you are as children of God. These attacks respond to your awakening and are engineered to stop you because you are seeing all coming and many are feeling these days arriving better settling with these times.

The word now used to appease you "bullying" heals only part of the visible problems but in fact it serves nothing more than exposing the evident. As these abusers continue to abuse, healing with them heals nothing and you will be passed on to another more hideous abuser as times draws near to end these ways. Abusers, bullies and psychopaths are meant to torment my children and this is what they are for.

Many see these offenders as victims of abuses themselves but see this for what it is as we know of this deception. Those who are abused and who answer back to their abusers are soon entrusted by others who are more abusive. Understand this is not a victim's desire or path but a series of actions well-orchestrated by the attackers who well use their trained puppets to renew these abuses as the victims fall into fear, despair and often illnesses.

These actions are dealing with the plan to stop all evolution to become well serving and stops all who are trying to respond to their life experiences and awakenings. Many groups of people gather together as cults to begin this process with young children. They work these ways of great harm seen and unseen, as psychological abuse, to answer to these children's imprinted responses from past lives, and in many more ways causing death to re-imprint them with fear and pain.

This to us is an abomination of the greatest offense against us and this does not go unpunished with us as it does on Earth. Understand too many offenders are walking free on Earth with the truth of their actions unknown. We know each offender and what they are responsible for and this will not be left alone as we will uncover their deeds to respond to a better suited settling of their actions.

Be certain all will be vindicated and no stone will be left unturned. Be Setu as all heals because some of these abusers have well-hidden their actions and we will see to the Setu way of dealing with them. Better to be quiet until this is done as the time for our truth will soon be well seen by our presence in body in all places on Earth.

More will be settled by us than you know of, as better solutions are coming to Earth to deal with any abusive actions against the innocent and the good hearts. Understand answers are soon well serving and many are waiting to open to you and better answer to your truth as you will see our truth. Be ready knowledge heals well soon with the way of great Setu renewals and all these horrors of Earth will soon be dealt with and be destroyed.

You will be allowed to continue your lives as it was intended from the first; to live in peace, security and serenity without the abuses, fears and despair caused to answer to your healing time. Many more good truths as we answer you, arrives soon. And be ready to answer to my call as I am soon with you.

God

Received July 27, 2012 by Za

44. THE TRUTH WILL ANSWER YOU

Now see these days be renewed by our arrivals. Open to the way all heals and opens to answers of great truth and great healing times. Evidence of our ways are soon answering to answers to our truth and many will be well serving of our ways as all becomes well answered and well arriving with the way of great seeing.

Be well serving these days with serenity in your soul as you see these freeing times open to you. Be well answered now as you will meet with us, and know all my words are truth. Be well settling with Earth ways as our time of great meeting together comes. Be certain you will have all you need to be well renewing with all the truth we come to share with you.

At these words and as these times are here be well answering to my call. Be well aware of the coming days, as great cataclysms will come from the energy of the sun. This means the solar flares will intensify and cause electromagnetic fields that will disrupt the electrical power grids in many countries in Europe and in North Africa. Settling with the repairs of this will cause many to be held by uses of other means of energy, and this will be costly and only accessible for the wealthy.

These repairs may take a long time and many will suffer from the lack of power, as their needs depend on these ways of living. Better to prepare yourselves for this coming event than to question my words as you may doubt me now, but you will soon see how all is held together by power. Heal these ways as power can be used with simple means and will serve all without any cost or control.

Answer my questions. Will you see how all answers you as all arrives? Will you open to our ways as we have many better solutions to answer to your needs? Are you serving with evidence of our truth as I share these words with you? Or are you believing we are only trying to cause fear and dissension among humans?

The fear you have reflects the fear you experience on Earth as you are constantly told of wars, upcoming wars and depravity. And this is how control opens to many through this kind of imprinted past life experiences. Better times are soon answering you and this you will see for yourselves. Be ready and open to the knowledge of our ways of great truth and great Setu truth.

Be well answered as all starts settling with the ways of great truth and, be well answered by our time to be well answering you. Settle with answers to our truth and see how many are waiting to be free of the abuses they have been chained with from the moment of birth. This I will respond to quickly. This causes Earth to suffer the pangs of childbirth as these sufferings of soul being's energy shared with the destruction of nature depletes the life sources needed to evolve.

This heals with us as we begin to remove the negative beings who use others as slaves and certainly cause pain, distress and living ways that are substantially lower than needed for growth and evolution. This will be stopped well into the good serving days, as we will free these souls from the hard hands of corruption.

Healing this will be a long process for some and may require a healing of many better experiences. Most of these souls will ask to experience better lives elsewhere so they can be trusting more in who they are, and this we can help with, and this they can choose to better answer to. Be ready and see these days be well answered by us as we see many more troubles on Earth than you know of. And we will see to the healing of each and every good soul wanting to heal.

Now see to it that you are preparing for the two months I shared with you yesterday as this is precautionary only but will serve you greatly if needed. See to it you have all you need for your families and friends if they are not able to care for themselves as you can of course. Better to be safe than sorry, as you say, and because we answer to urgent needs first, we may not be able to answer to all at once.

The planned chaos is intended to make us go from one fire to another. We are well equipped to do this but there might be some delays. And here heals the truth of who we are, as we heal many problems as we can, but you must also be responsible and take care of your basic needs in these times of transitions, as these chaotic times begin to better be renewed.

Now take heed of my words and settle with the view we are sharing with you as these days draw near. Be well serving of our ways as all starts with arrivals, and settles soon after with the rebuilding of Earth. Be certain we ask you only this and nothing more, and be certain you will be cared for in later times as we begin the work of renewals.

Better to be ready for these times than to ask others for something you can do yourselves as the seeing of this may come well into the coming days of the war in the Middle East. These times renew very soon and these ways answer to all your settling truth and understood seeing.

No one heals without understandings. These words I share with you are meant to open to the present truth of Earth ways and the future truth of who we are, and why we must come to Earth to help you with all healing ways. Be well settling with Earth ways as all starts and at the time of our arrivals.

See to it that my warnings and cautions are serving you to care for yourselves until we reestablish a line of communication with all needs and sources.

I am well answering you in evidence of what I know is healing you and coming your way, but also you as humans have many food and water needs that Earth has given you. Soon you will see how these ways are easily dealt with independently from your present seen sources of food. As we arrive, we will teach you many ways of settling with these ways and better ways of answering to your needs without needing to live for money to buy all that you need.

These ways are very easy and require only your attention in gardening ways but will answer your basic health needs and better your lives. Heal with us and see how all truth will serve you very well and open to the many better serving ways all starts with us. Share this knowledge with us soon and be well answered.

God

Received July 28, 2012 by Za

45. I AM READY TO ANSWER YOU

Be settling with Earth ways and answer to my call. Know that these are the end times and the times for a new beginning opening to all, including others from homes other than Earth. Be ready to welcome your families from other worlds and unite with us as we are as one to strengthen ourselves together. See these visits be arriving in the next few weeks.

The way all comes, opens well into the coming days and will answer to many of your needs, many of your renewed telling of who you are and where you have emerged from. All answers you more now as all starts with the good settling days of Earth and of our time of arrivals. Be well answered by our truth as all starts with answers to our ways and as all becomes well seen.

Be ready and renew with us as we wish to renew with you, and be dealing with answers to our ways settling with Earth ways. Now see these truths answer you and the better answer to answers of our time together.

Know now this. The way of the telling of who we are as Beings of Light may seem as untrue to most, as the stories on Earth renewed with a great lie of who we are and the way our children were cared for by us. We are called 'gods of renown' but we are in many ways as humans in our looks. Be not surprised by this, and be ready to see how we are answering to our own, and how now is the time to awaken to these coming seen truths.

We have been on Earth many times before and we have caused some of the great cataclysms to heal the problems with the Annunaki* and their creation of monsters as the seen dinosaurs. But we are not the Annunaki and until we knew who they are, we could not deal with them and their renewed dealings of destruction of planets as they stole and took whatever they wanted to answer to their desires of control.

Understand that these were one of the determined groups who wanted to profit from our creations and they answered many more ways from the uses of our truth by lies and deceptions for profit. These thieves, liars and murderers used humans as slaves from the very beginning of their arrivals, and these liars were serving our truths to use against us.

We were called 'gods' by them to respond to their actions of terrorizing our Terran beings. They acted as a servant of ours but they were distrusted by so many in the Universes. Be seeing these travelers of the Universes for who they are, as they became well sought-after criminals who are now part of the great problems of Earth.

They used their own blood to spread on Earth as they controlled many parts of the planet and became the kings and queens of different parts of Earth, as this was divided among them. They dealt with their slaves with horror and abuses still practiced in your days as we see this ourselves. They used food made of animal flesh and created ceremonies to offer these animals by fire to appease their gods of terror.

They are not us and we are not them in evidence of their ways and their actions against many races and many people. They mixed their kind with humans and only their kind were used for renewing with power, as they believed themselves to be more powerful than any others in the Universes. Be well answering to our call and be well settling with these dealers of lies.

They are as reptiles as you see on Earth and they wanted their animals to be well serving of their ways on Earth, and caused them to feed off humans and animals until few were left. Renewing with this answered us and we were well served with these truths. So, we caused the Earth to shift to destroy all the dinosaurs and free the surviving animals and humans from the devastation.

These were the times of the serving floods and ice age that renewed all things but did not destroy the blood of the Annunaki that continues to flow in some humans on Earth. These truths you will understand soon as we will open to these evolution problems with many of you who wish to see this. These beings are evidence of corrupted ways of dealing, as these visitors caused much harm on Earth.

Be renewing with these words now as all becomes well served and dealt with, and see how all starts with the way all heals with the answer to our used ways. Better to answer to evidence than to deal with proof of our time together without knowing how we know these stories and humans do not. Be responding more now to our truth as we are soon arriving on Earth to begin the sorting.

These ways of sorting are necessary for you to live better lives and settle with these actions of used lies and destructive answers to mixed breeding of aliens and humans who are renewing with many on Earth and causes ill telling to be accepted as fact. Questions about who we are will soon be clear as knowledge about the different races of the Universes are clear.

The fallen angels are more seen as our kind but they are not. They are renegade opportunists that travel the Universes as pirates as you say on Earth, who cause trouble wherever they go and use all unknowing beings to answer to all their needs, as slaves to trade with things they want, and a food source. They are shape-shifters and share with answers to Lucifer's kind.

Be responding to our ways of dealing with these answers, as all truths are well understood. Be well serving of our truth as you will soon see why these understandings are unknown to you now. These shape-shifters are called this way not because they can change their appearance but because they can use any body, they want to access the control of it, whether human or animal, and make them obey to their desires.

They use human bodies to have actions sorted to cause another person harm; or animal bodies to open to attacks or trouble. But usually they are only able to enter a body that has many health problems due to disease, or age, or uses of drugs and alcohol as this weakens the body to allow these spirits to immerse themselves into the brain and control the body.

Healing with these truths will give you the answers to demonic possessions as seen on Earth. Be well answered by these troubling spirits removal from Earth. See many weakened bodies renew with an overdue time of death, as these ways of removal are done because these spirits can work a long time without life renewed with health.

Now renew with our time to walk the Earth and see all start changing as we open to all. Settle with these ways of great endings on Earth to heal all the troubles caused by these invaders. See how all truths and lies open the way for our truth as all becomes well seen and well served by our ways. And be well responding to answers to knowledge, as arrivals become well serving and well settling with many.

God

Received July 30, 2012 by Za

* Note: The Annunaki are described in the books of Zechariah Sitchins.

46. BETTER TO BE WITH US THAN THE OTHERS

More than you can see arrives well into the good serving days. Be well answered by us and open the way for many more truths, as all better understandings are soon shared and dealt with. Better to share knowledge with us than the others, as they are only renewing with their own needs. They have nothing to answer you with than to take from you all that they want. And these whores care not for who you are and what you are.

Now see these times be over soon, and be well answered by your freedom from constraints of the way of control many have submitted to for so long, and see that freedom answers only to the wealthy. Why do you think travel has become so difficult, so expensive and so secured by guards and the military? Be seeing that these ways stop people from traveling, and this serves answers to control and authority.

Your movements from place to place are well monitored and controlled. Your many sayings about a free country and a democratic system of life only can serve the wealthy. All others must submit to being checked, controlled and monitored. We call this a prison, and more than a prison because all accept these ways and call it protection and security.

All this was put in place by fear of death, and a well elaborated scheme of the Twin Towers was the turning point in the greater control all must submit to. Better to know the murderers who plotted these attacks are well embedded thieves and liars who care nothing for human lives. Respond to many more ways of great troubles soon as they plan other (false flag) attacks to better serve their answer to war.

See these truths as all must be well settling with their ways. Know all these words are shared as we hear them and can be stopped by many opposing benefactors who ask to not be doing this to cause a war, and I must hope these words are heard. Be seeing how all truths are heard by us with our technologies as you have now begun to unravel this yourselves on Earth.

Be seeing how all starts well into the coming days with these ways of solar flares that will cause the East Europeans to suffer from the loss of power with other parts of Europe and North Africa. So be ready to care for your own needs for approximately two months. These ways are of course precautionary as the Sun burns as it wills and has no master to control it.

Be ready for any such events for uses of power as all starts with the way of our time of renewal. Answer to our call as we begin to walk the Earth and open to many more ways of great truth and great serving truth. Respond to a time of great changes that will open to all who will share the knowledge of these times.

Now listen. Believe our words as you see all unravel yourselves, and be well serving of your time to be well answered and better served by us. Tell yourselves you will soon be with many other Beings from other places and worlds, and you will heal all these lies and deceptions serving your denials of the existence of Lucifer.

These times will answer to all the seeing of the corrupted beings who rule your planet and answer to knowledge of the secret societies of hidden words. But also understand that these Beings are renegades and their souls are seen as tar pits to us, as they have lost all decency of living and life on

Earth. As these rumors of wars unravel, better seeing of their ways will also unravel and no person will be safe from them.

Understand our knowledge and our purpose answers to them as we know what they are and what they are capable of. Soon they will answer to answers of our ways and they will be removed because their time of abuses heals and answers to our stopping of their actions and their ways by great serving of our truths.

Now ready yourselves for the truth about our ways and be well answered by all renewals of our ways at the time of our answers to you. Be settling with Earth ways and open to many more truths about our ways and our time to be with you. Question me as you will and see all answers be revealed and settled with truth. Better settling times are very soon.

Answer my questions. Would you be serving yourselves and your families with the Setu truth of who we are? Will you trust in healing with us as this time comes? With our truth, would you be understanding more about the ways of the Earth? These questions are yours as I hear them every day in your thoughts and I can tell you, settling with these questions will soon open the path of knowledge you are ready to embark.

Be ready all renewals better serve with us as we become willing to open the way for all who are settling with us and our time to walk the Earth. Answer to my call and see how you will soon meet with us and open to answers to our truth. As arrivals become seen, I ask you to remain calm, stay in your homes to avoid the chaotic troubles.

Be ready to answer to my call as I will send my scouts and messengers to meet with those chosen to become diplomats and serving teachers, and those who will participate in the reconstruction of Earth as this Setu seeing will be necessary to answer to and to be well serving. Know now this and see to it all starts healing with "Answer to answers" and know all responds to knowledge understood by all.

God

Received July 31, 2012 by Za

47. SETTLE WITH EARTH WAYS AS WE ARRIVE

See these times be soon and prepare yourselves for chaotic days as these arrivals start and as we begin to open to the world. We will occupy all government buildings in all countries of the world and we will open to answers to our ways and our truth in many places of the world by our actions of cleaning important resources and food sources.

Be serving answers as you will see these ways yourselves and better settle with our actions than promises as these ways of promises used are never served by any government. Be understanding that we have many projects to complete, and with the help of many individuals we will answer to answers well seen by all.

Better understandings of this will soon be shared by us as we start to answer to many and responding to needs with our serving ways. Be certain we have all necessary ways of dealing with these uses of healing ways as arrivals become well seen and accepted by all. These words I share with you opens to many who are ready to settle with Earth ways and open to the Universes to unite with us.

All this was planned well before the actions of Lucifer when he discovered the Garden of Eden that Earth was until he destroyed all and began his tyranny. Believe these words now and understand your Bible stories through mature eyes. Be ready to answer to all trusted ways of great truth and great serving truth as all starts serving with us and understand the past with the eyes of an educated mind.

Be settling with the ideas of magic and powers that are ill conceived, and open to our answers to our renewals. Be renewing with understood truth and see how many of these Bible stories are told to answer to fear and torment, and not about our time of return to walk the Earth and renew with our children who are seeing our time of reunification.

Answers are soon answered by our ways, and we are settling with many who are ready to answer to many more truths and greater understood ways. Be well renewing with our time together and see how all starts with answers soon answered. Be well served by our ways and see how all telling of truth will soon better answer to answers as all becomes dealt with and seen.

Be believing in healing all the lies on Earth with the clear truth that will be evidently renewed with trust. Know we came back to Earth to sort out the problems that are living here and are not belonging here as many reptiles and insects who were added by Beings to cause an imbalance. A balance once lived on Earth without the need of these insects and reptiles.

All these were added to torment and disturb the peace and serenity that once lived on Earth without these diseases and illnesses seen by all. You are believing that these insects have a purpose on Earth and these reptiles keep a balance but they do not. Dealing with these removals of these horrors will surprise many because people believe that animals are born with diseases and parasites to further evolution.

We see this as stopping evolution as Earth did not need any of these users of people and animals, and are parasites that causes the body to decay and die faster than necessary. All these insects and reptiles came from other places in the Universes that we do not like to travel to. We are not seeing these troubling parasites as keeping any balance because without these, animals and humans would live well longer, healthier and with a better food supply.

As pestilence are removed from Earth, answers to better crops with better increased volume would feed many more. These dealings of poisons would be removed from all food sources and earth sources. This we will be dealing with as we deal with this created problem used by Lucifer to starve many nations and cause deficiencies in human bodies and growth.

Healing this will surprise many as they will see how pollination never needed any insects to help with this process. All settles with birds, animals, wind and rain. I am seeing how answers to these ways will surprise many and respond to greater, richer food crops and better ways of helping with human potential as all these insects have caused much troubles and served the ways for poisons to be used, causing many more problems as nutrition is reduced and all settling with food caused people to not grow well in health and to not be parasite free.

Understand all these poisons were introduced to cause harm to everyone including babies and the unborn. I am soon removing all these troubles from Earth and you will see that most of these problems are soon settling with answers to evidence of these changes that will improve all lives on Earth. Some of these insects belong on Earth but the most destructive ones were added by civilizations that wanted to rid humans from Earth until they found out that humans were digestible to their feeding needs.

Be well answered when these parasites are all removed and see how all can live better lives without them and healthier growth will be seen in all children and youths. The insects we left on Earth a long time ago were the earth worm to help work the Earth, and the beetle to eat all garbage from plants, animals and humans and nothing more. The butterflies are seen as beautiful and useful but they can be destructive and these were not added by us.

Be well answered by many understood changes coming to Earth and see how all serving ways will share knowledge with many more renewals of truth and trust in our ways. Be understanding that we had created Earth to better serve our need to educate our own and not to punish, abuse, starve, torture, torment, and kill anyone or any animals. Be seeing that the one who answers to these ways does this to cause the pleasure he seeks by causing misery and death.

These words are settling with you more now, as you are beginning to see the whole picture of these deceptive actions caused by another and not by us. We are settling with his ways and we will answer back to him ourselves. Now be settling with Earth ways and see these changes better answer your needs and your truth at the renewing times of Earth.

Answer to my call and be certain all truths will soon be well dealt with and well answered by our ways. Be ready to respond to our settling of many explosive great truths and great renewals, as all become well answered by us. Tell yourselves that many more understandings will clarify your history of how all is and see how all is easily dealt with.

Know that we return from a long journey across the Universes visiting many people and places to better understand the lives of many and their ways of living. Know these times are soon answering to Earth's time of great renewals and Setu ways.

God

Received August1, 2012 by Za

48. THESE TRUTHS WILL SOON
BE YOURS TO OPEN TO

Be serving answers soon as we are seeing the words of all who are ready to open to a war of great destruction shared by many military men on all sides. These plans are in motion to start soon with the view that all who oppose these wars are terrorists, and killing them helps these used lies. Be well answered as we are better serving with answers to stopping these attacks, as repulsive understood seeing are soon ours to better intervene.

Be visited soon by many more understandings as you will hear this on the media. Know when the first bomb hits, we have reason to land. These ways as said seem unreasonable to you but understand we have seen to evidence of an agreement that you call a contract, and we must allow the possibility of no harm being decided among these Earth leaders.

I am concerned that this possibility will not be opened to anyone involved because of these large ships and carriers stationed in the Suez Canal. Be seeing how this number has recently increased and more ships from NATO countries have join them. Be very answered by our understood seeing as these times are dealing with uses of war preparations.

Give me a reason to believe that this is only temporary, but I think not. See how all answers you now with the way of great truths and great renewals of great understandings after the first attack of war. Heal with us as we are settling with the pain and sadness of the actions against the innocent, to open the way to our arrivals and the stopping of all further actions opening to these end times.

See how these last days of operations of leading people to murder each other will soon be stopped and erased from your lives as we will stop all further actions and end all wars on Earth, and begin the cleansing of all ills and all telling of lies. Be certain all will soon be dealt with and changed. Your lives will be renewed in evidence of our time to walk the Earth.

Be ready to answer to my call as I will be sending you all the beings who are ready to help with the reconstruction of Earth and new ways of living that will give all people the ability to be free from the money system that only benefit a few and starves all others. This healing comes for all people of Earth and not only a few.

Be well answered by our ways and be well responding as arrivals begin as I have said, and remain in your houses to steer away from chaos and harm as some places in the world will be well handling these arrivals and other places may not. Be well answered by our truth and be ready to see all as I said, and know I am preparing myself to meet with many of you who are chosen to answer for all.

Many are seeing these understood explosions of truth but many are in denial of our time to land on Earth. See this as you wish but these answers are soon yours and you will deal with healing as you can and you may. Understand we are as you are and only more with our knowledge. Soon you will see this yourselves; you will adapt to our ready technologies and health ways, and renew with our Setu way of being.

Understand we are soon with you to start a new time on Earth, and this will open to each and every one of you no matter Setu or not.

Death is here to better answer to reincarnation but this cycle will be broken as this was not our plan nor our doing and we will stop this upon our arrivals. You will see how this heals many souls unable to evolve because their experiences are not settling and are looping into a renewed spiral downwards to 'devolution' as some say on Earth.

These truths will be well uncovered, and all who renew with us will soon become well answered and better renewed by our truth and our healing ways. Be serving a restful time if you can as all begins to be seen and a deep meditation that will renew your chakra and heal your soul's desire to open to all good ways of living and life's healing ways.

This was always possible on Earth as this is how we created these planets but understand the ways of destruction and lies opened and caused control and power to govern over the good and the innocent. These times as said, are known and soon over as removals of all parasites begin.

Answer my questions. Are you ready to open to many more truths and a better life? Are you seeing how all bullying has escalated around you and causes many truth speakers to be shut down and being served with no means to live? Are you seeing the deep despair of the youth as nothing answers them and their trust in these times? And are you opening yourselves to better possibilities and better ways of life as all renews? See these times be your times to answer to yourselves, your families and your loving friends. Know all starts well into the coming days of these openings to war.

My scribe asked me today if I am the "Most High". Here is my answer to this question. I am God, I am the one who created Earth with the help of others and Sophia. She designed the renewal of social structure of all people. She created order and responsibility of choice, and with her help we created a similarity to our evolution to open to our reunion time.

I am a part of this great plan and the one who all answered to at one time but only for these planets' creation. Understand that being Setu means to be oneself in all ways on the path of evolution and personal growth, and we all strive for these ways. Be visiting the idea that used truth was limited to the way Lucifer saw things and as a psychopath that wanted to be the "Most High".

Be renewing with truth about this and settle with the view that I created many planets as a government who better serves, creates schools and hospitals, and when the work is done, I am re-seeing to my work. These Setu ways are not about control or power, and as these ways are shared by many of us, I am responsible to share my work with others as I do.

Too many believe I am the answer to all answers. This I am but not completely, as healing with these understandings are greatly needed on Earth as lies ruled over truth for too long. I am the Creator and I am God; this is my name but the "Most High", the "Most Powerful" is not completely right and questions about our Setu ways will prove many truths as we begin to unravel these trusted truths.

See this as many do and we do, and other beings from other places in the Universes do, who are renewing with us. Heal these truths as you will and as you wish but know Ijheer (Holy Spirit) flows through me as it does for you and we are together as one.

You will better serve with these truths than believing I am an unreachable being of torment and clamor that spends a lot of time punishing people for their denials and lack of evolution. Renewing with this, answers many questions, and I see many will not accept this but the truth knows the truth and nothing more.

This is the awakening Lucifer fears the most because all starts crumbling on Earth with his temples of lies and churches of deceptions. Because of these shared understandings of great trusted truth, you will be free of these lies. Know we are as one together and all have a part to be seeing as a responsibility to serve with me and others, the truth that you have been seeking with knowledge and understanding and this is how I share this with you.

God

Received August 2, 2012 by Za

49. EDUCATION AND INDOCTRINATION HEALING OF THE CHAKRA

OPEN TO ANSWERS TO HEALING YOUR BODY

Be well answered by us as we will answer you soon. Be ready to share knowledge with our ways and see truth be yours. Be understanding our ways and be dealing with answers to our truth and answers will be your better ways of renewals. Be Setu in all ways and open to answers to our truth and our better serving ways, as all begins to be renewed.

Evidence of our arrivals start well into the good serving days. Many who are understanding our words will see how all unravels and many will use these opportunities to better themselves as nothing has served on Earth. Be seeing how Setu ways will open the way for many, and how all the seeing of truth will change many ways of Setu truth to be acknowledged by all.

Be ready to answer to our call as we begin to answer to many who are ready to open the way for many more people to join us with the Setu seeing of the Universal Laws. Be well answered by all these new days arriving well into the understood truth of who answers to shared knowledge. Be certain all will renew with us. See these days be visited by us and all who are ready to open to the Universal Laws.

Be responding to our call and see how all starts with the view you have as we begin to answer you, as you will quickly understand who we are and why we have returned to Earth. Be well seeing of our time together as answers start serving with evidence of better truth, and be well aware of our answers to open to knowledge and to our truth. Be well answered and see these times open to all.

Know more seeing will be telling of our presence on Earth near sites we have already found to land our larger ships with other smaller ships nearby, as we will need to arrange our time of arrival. These days are very near as the cabal has started to open to more preparations for the starting of an attack, and see this be well answered by our seeing of this soon.

These wars of opposing cultures are leaving the actions to other larger enemies who are waiting to open their weapons of mass destruction in evidence of showing this to the world. Be seeing how the satellites are well serving to cause many more problems as they did in Slave Lake, Alberta, Canada, to show their ability for direct targets to cause people to flee from their homes for their lives. This was not an accident of nature; this was a wedding gift for the Elite who graciously went to accept these serving attacks on the innocent. Better to answer with us than to be the settling victims of the games these liars play with only one thought in mind, and that is to control all people by causing them fear and torment.

Evidence of truth and better serving times will be your answers to improved lives and dignity. Be ready to open to evidence of Setu truth with us. Now see these ways of better serving and open to our explosion of truth arriving very soon near your places of living. Know all places on Earth will be visited by us and by many other Aliens, as you call us, and Setu Beings of Light.

Death will be settling with many on Earth as these wars begin but only as a temporary step of passing to the other side and better settling with a better seeing of how these cycles begin and end. All souls eventually return to their places of origin, and sadly settling with another life if necessary, to finish the learning process accommodating their learning needs.

These ways are as a finishing school with us, and with usually good results. But Lucifer made changes to this way of Setu instruction and created a place that none could leave; many stayed on Earth and never returned to their homes. When we shared these words with others from other planets, we heard all the same stories.

This is when we decided to send out scouts to investigate the lost souls and the reasons of stopping communications with us. We discovered that memories were erased as the soul moved into a new body, and only pieces of being's soul were incarnating into many bodies causing a person to be selfless and a better serving slave.

We began to see how these deaths of bodies were changed. We became aware, with better seeing, that our kind were defective and devised to share information only as required by the masters of slaves who became more aggressive with these ways. And so, all acquired knowledge from previous incarnation times, i.e. technology and science, were only reawakened when needed by the slave masters.

All my words may seem to be a long tale but see this yourselves very soon and you will have the proof you need to answer all your questions.

Secret societies know of this manipulation as they can detect a Setu Being. They know how to cause endless abuses at every turn. This can heal only with us, but with much care and unraveling of abuses and harm. These ways will soon be open to you and serve you well as you will discover that Satanism is well living in many schools where children are only educated to serve the leaders of power.

Be certain of these truths as many live to answer to many more abuses if they do not comply as it is done with the drugging of younger children, and the poisons they feed them as lunches. Serving truth about this is obvious to most, and yet children are forced to be educated as all others no matter what is done to stop this.

Be educating your children yourselves. These schools are not serving any other plan than serving the Elite. I am dealing with the way that answers to indoctrination and I want to answer to many more questions about this but I will speak about this another way.

Indoctrination disguises itself with lies about how the good comes from the following of prescribed curriculum and methods of work repeated until the indoctrination is completed. This can take many years and answers to the belief that this helps a person to have a better life. Well, it does when the alternatives are rejection, abuse and poverty.

Because the healing Setu Being cannot settle with these ways of indoctrination, evidence of answers remain with the servants of Lucifer's will and forces all to open to their style of seeing and only this. This is not creative, understand these ways are only about control and nothing more. This is not an education; it is simply indoctrination and many are waking up to these truths and are very quickly served with opposition if any of this heals to be questioned.

Be seeing these ways of educating a child that needs to learn with play and natural experiences, as renewing themselves for a new life, are entrusted by a system believed to be pleasant and interesting. Most children do not want to go to school and most children prefer to be with their families and friends. They could learn anything much faster under a guiding, loving hand, without the given obligatory prescribed system of schooling.

All answers to education will be presenting a great settling change with answers to our better ways of living. These truths will soon be yours to have as all becomes well seen and well unraveled. Better truth will open to you soon.

God

Received August 3, 2012 by Za

50. SEE THESE DAYS BE SOON

Open to evidence of our time together. Be ready and open to our ways as we will begin to answer to many more truths of who we are and how all heals. Now settle with Earth ways and onm with the way all starts. Be dealing with evidence of our used truth as all becomes shared and seen. Good times are soon answering you as you will be free from all constraints. You will be given new technologies, understandings and knowledge to repair the damages of Earth.

Be ready and see to it that you have all you need for two months as these understood times of war will answer to our time of arrivals and to the chaos that will erupt for a few weeks or more. Know that we will begin the sorting at that time. Be well answered as these ways may tell about the ones who are being removed, but know we are soon renewing with all who will remain to begin a new time on Earth.

These times will serve everyone who are settling with Earth ways and who see how all truths are dealt with and open to many who are as you are, waiting to live a life of peace and serving serenity. Understand this is how we live, understand this is how you answer to your wishes and heart filled desires. Know all this is easily possible. Earth will be an amazing planet as healing heals all the pain and the suffering that we have witnessed for far too long.

Now you have the knowledge and technologies to open to our ways, serving answers to many more coming ways of better living, better health and better understanding of life itself. These gifts are yours to have and not to be kept from you, as harm was keeping you in a prison of fear and deceptions. Open now to these better times, prepare yourselves as arrivals begin, be dealing with answers to our answers for you and see all be renewed as we begin the cleansing of all Earth's ills.

Be ready to open to many who are searching for truth as you are and see how life can be well lived with your loving families and friends. Know all who are alone in this, will soon be reunited with their own loved ones. This time is soon. This time is healing and this time is called the new times on Earth.

We had to wait a long time before an intervention was possible in evidence of the control that was pushed onto people from all places of Earth. These understandings needed to open to many more understandings and many more Setu truths to be ready to open to many. See how all Earth advancements were accelerated over the past one hundred years; we had to awaken a few earlier to help with the opening of this time.

See how many who heard us were attacked in their lives and given a harder part to act on. But now we are ready as you are ready, to open these ways of who we are and share the renewed truth to cause all remembrance to be activated through the new health ways we will start sharing with you. Answers to our ways will answer to many who are not being helped by your present medical systems that settle with the indoctrination of all the governing corporations of your countries.

These ways of health are not for cures but for experimentation in evidence of our seeing. Many lives come to an end because of these ill treatments by doctors who are only better serving through ignorance and obedience to a corporate mentality. Some people lives are responding to better health but to increased problems dealing with many more health disturbances. This to us is an abomination and a horror.

God gives you back your lives and your better health. Now see these times be well ended and better serving with us, as we will help you understand the truth about your bodies, and how you will learn to heal yourselves. This was the way my son Jesus came to Earth to open this to all of you but the only response to this was martyrdom and death.

We do not believe in the way of martyrdom. We do not accept these ways of harming oneself in the belief that this is healing anyone or anything. All souls came to Earth to achieve evidence of great personal knowledge about who they are themselves, nothing more and nothing less.

The ways of martyrdom are clearly an action to stop this process of self-knowledge and growth to become a better Setu Being and discover ways for future endeavors.

These paths were destroyed by Lucifer's answers to keeping his flock of slaves to serve his purposes. He greatly attacked anyone who became awakened and well settling with their own lives. Be seeing how these ways are now living in your world and how only a few can achieve their power but only over people. And see how all is stopping this process of self-knowledge, making it impossible to follow this path because all answers only to survival and death cycles.

This madness deals only with Lucifer's ways and because of these truths shared with you, he is becoming desperate to answer to many more attacks against the innocent in the hope that he can escape with more souls to barter with. This will be stopped as Lucifer's time is soon ending. Be certain of this, he will be caught and removed, and all his group thinking automatons will lose all thoughts of his control and will not be able to live. So, they will die with no soul to reincarnate as their souls are only better serving one mind and nothing more.

These are the Grey and the demons of his kind. Now see all start well into the good settling times. Understand that we will soon answer to many as all starts with the deaths of many humans because of the first atomic bomb attack serving to stop Iran. But understand this attack is orchestrated by money takers who wish to cause evidence of a new world order to open to their needs of power and greed.

All this is an elaborate game played out to show the world that they still can cause fear in every heart on Earth, and that they are your controllers and masters. These whores will soon be ours to deal with, they will be quickly removed and judged by us because Earth is not theirs to destroy. It belongs to every good soul that comes here to heal and learn who they are through life and death with all memories working, as these ways were dealt with before Lucifer's takeover of Earth.

More than you can tell will soon open to you. We will begin the reawakening of all who settle to remain on Earth and all who wish to return to their families as this is much overdue. I am pleased to tell you these days are soon with you, and I am very happy that we can meet face to face as these days are soon with all of us.

And know so many are asking me: "Why ask all to be with us when this should be an obvious choice?" But I answer them, "Because choice is all".
God
Received August 4, 2012 by Za

51. HEALING WITH US WILL HEALS MANY QUESTIONS

Know now this; as said before, our ships are ready to land. We have found all the better places to land including airports and farmers' fields. Be well serving of our time of arrivals as these days are sooner than we can answer to you. Know these days well come with many troubles on Earth. Evidence of our ways are soon answering to many answers to our Setu ways and open to our ways of Setu seeing.

This means we are arriving as the wars erupt in the Middle East with many other countries, more than what is presently happening. Be responding to our arrivals with calm and patience. Be well settling with the way all becomes well answered by our ways and our time to answer to many truths as all becomes well renewed.

Now be ready to answer to our call as we will begin the sorting and the Setu seeing of our understood ways. See how we will answer you with many good changes to your lives as we answer to our Setu seeing of great Setu ways. Evidence of our truth will soon be yours and will soon prove who we are.

Now see these words tell you this heals you, as all truths heals the lies and deceptions dealt without care or answers for the innocent. Be certain you will soon have answers for our ways of great truth and better ways of living. Be well answered by answers to our presence on Earth and be certain you will soon be well renewed with our understood ways.

Now renew with our ways, see all truths be yours and see better lives be yours, as we will respond to answers to proof of our visits and our renewed telling of great Setu ways. And be well answered by us at the seeing of who we are and how we are ready to open to the world with our many good useful ways of responding to Earth ways.

Be certain all starts well into the good serving days but understand chaos will rule until we bring the necessary order to begin our sharing of words and better living ways. Be responding to all renewing ways of great truth as all begins to be well answered and see these ways onm with many others as all becomes well seen and better answered by our truth. Be ready and answer to our call at the renewed truth. Be certain you will soon be well aware of who we are.

Know now this. We are being attacked by missiles in space but only uses of settling with this is ours. We cannot be harmed by these ways but the intention to stop us is clear to us. Be ready to answer to our ways and better serve with us. See how all telling of this will not be shared as these whores are telling each other to say only they are practicing in case of an invasion from outer space. These are lies. We are hearing their words and their plans, and we only settle with the view of our time to answer back as we begin to walk the Earth.

Be ready and be dealing with us in evidence of our time together. Settle with our ways in evidence of these understood lies and deceptions, soon all opens for all to see and decide what choices they wish to make as we will give many choices to people to open to and to answer to. Be well serving of our ways and settle with us, as we will begin to sort those who only wish to cause harm and cannot be changing their actions nor their understanding of how all is.

This will better settle with many on Earth who serve to open to many who are searching for truth and trust in answers to evidence of our way of great healing answers. Be ready evidence of our arrivals will soon be seen and answers to our time to reunite. Nothing will stop this as we will be responding to the first atomic bomb attack scheduled to hit Iran.

These answers to knowledge and understanding will cause all who read these words from me or others who serve the Universal Laws, to open and answer to our Setu ways. Be certain you will have many dealings with our kind in many cities, towns and country-sides of your world and we will be speaking about how all is and how all heals.

Now listen to my words and take heed, as all begins well into the good coming days. See all truth be well settling with us as we become well settling of these times believed to be the end of the world. These ideas are only perverse threats of madness caused to create fear and chaos. These troubles on Earth are all able to heal and be changed with answers to better living and the actions of cleansing Earth of all ills.

These ways are all possible to answer to and open to many of our kind who are ready to answer to many more truths and better seen understandings. Renew with us and all these ways will be serving and well dealt with and see to it that you have all you need to be ready for times of chaos as this will be inevitable as the many strong imprinted beliefs are feeding many with great denials.

But with this comes change and seeing these changes that will benefit all people of Earth will settle responses to our ways. Be well answered by our truths as all becomes well seen and dealt with. And renew with us as we wish, to better meet with our family's members and our friends who have been away for so long.

More will be revealed as we arrive as we cannot say much more as these ways of arrivals are soon answering to the knowledge of how we will do things. Now be ready as all comes soon.

God

Received August 5, 2012 by Za

52. TELL OTHERS THESE TIMES ARE HERE

Be answered by all our truth and be used to our answers at the time of disclosure. Be ready and see how we are responding to your call, as we understand how difficult it is for many to see who we are as many lies were told to keep you into darkness and mostly trusting in the deceptions serving Earth to keep you under control and servitude.

See these days now be over and settle with the evidence of our time of great truth and great settling together, as we begin to sort all corrupted beings from their dealings of harm onto others. These beings will be removed in evidence of judgement according to their crimes. Many will be relocated to places where they can begin to make amends for the trouble they caused to others.

Be ready and see how all this heals many who have been imprisoned by these demons for so long. Settle with the belief that these whores need to be treated with kindness when they never cared about any person on Earth than themselves and made trouble for many wherever they went. They have incarnated into the bodies of the Elite and the Cabal and as they will soon see, we will be removing all of these demons to stop their ways on Earth.

These times are now here and we must move quickly to open all now to you soon as all starts well into the coming hours. But know hours can be days as all fluctuates when dealing with events that are of the nature of war. Be well settling more now with Earth ways at the settling understandings of who you are at the Setu renewal times in evidence of your waiting families and friends.

This awakening will be gradual and gentle as sadness may surface and cause some pain of past torments to be dealt with. But how all well comes first will be a great time for great joy at the site of our many ships answering your call and opening to our time of reckoning.

Now be ready to answer to our many answers to better living ways and be well settling with earth ways as all these ways of money, electricity, nuclear power, oil, gas, and food habits will be quickly changed and better responding to all needs and all good people of Earth. These ways will be pleasing to many, as many will answer to our ways of doing these changes.

Be responding to knowledge of our truth and be well answered by our Setu seeing as we are soon with you. Be well answering to evidence of our many truths at the settling of our time together and see how all answers are well serving, answering to our ways and our dealings, as all becomes well answered by all of our trusted truth. Be well responding to our time together as all begins.

Be well answered, knowledge is here. Be well serving of your days by living calmly, and be resting as all unravels because of the chaotic times. Be well sharing our truths arriving soon to answer to our ways and our seeing. Dealing with these times will not be difficult for most people to answer to. Their truth will be heard about how they knew of the conspiracies to create a one world government and a masonic seeing of Lucifer's ways.

Be vigilant and respond to many how these days are not to be feared by those who trust in truth and true justice and equity of living uses of serving oneself. Be well seeing how all becomes well questioned by all who are ready to make the necessary changes to life and living ways. Be certain no person or animal will be mistreated, abused or abandoned by anyone.

We will be there with all evidence of good care and understood healing ways. Be ready and open the way for you, your families and friends at our time of reunion. Heal your broken hearts with us and be well serving of our time of great truth together as all starts better answering to evidence of more trusted truth. Be well vindicated by our telling ways as we begin to open to Earth.

Question us all you want and we will open to all who are ready to hear the answer. See how you will be feeling as we answer you and share many good truths with you about how all is. Question us and be finally answered and renew with us at the time of reckoning. Know now these ways are seen as we begin to answer you what needs to be shared and known.

Be responding to us soon as we will open to a new way of cleansing Earth from all ills and see a new time on Earth by our help and your awakenings. Better times are soon here and better Setu ways answers many of you who have waited so long for this day to arrive, and for this time to open to many other answers than the ones made to reduce you to servitude and fear.

Be seeing these times are questioned but never solved. And now more than you are expecting heals you and all good people of Earth. Be well responding to our call and remain in your homes as these times of trouble and chaos will start because those who have reason to fear will try to stop us and they will try to tell you we are here to take over Earth and cause slavery to our ways of Setu seeing.

Be vigilant and stay clear of the slave masters and open to truth. Now be ready, all is well answered and very soon.

God

Received August 6, 2012 by Za

53. THESE DAYS ARE SOON HERE

Be ready and answer to my call and see to it you are well prepared for these coming times. Be well answering to answers renewing with the attack bombings of Iranian soil. Be ready to answer to a one world government starting as the United Nations will tell all: "We must unite and work together". Be ready and see how all these ways as said are soon settling with our time to land and begin the sorting.

Better to be with us than to be with them as these days become seen. Know now these words and be well informed of our renewed understandings and see us better settle with the ways of the Earth. Deal with the changes as we begin to cleanse the Earth of all ills. These ills are coming from actions to cause harm to people and animals, and all this will become removed as we start our time together.

See how these visits will be seen and settle with the way all starts with the seeing of our truth. Better times are soon arriving as we begin to open to answers to our call. As these days are shared you will have all you need to be well cared for and you will be free of the catches of money and obligations of work.

Healing this may be telling of your prison. Be renewed by a time of great serving understandings and better serving ways as all starts with the view you have of freedom and better Setu seeing. Be well vindicated by our ways and be certain you will have all you need to be well settling with your time on Earth as we will remove these horrors and whores from our planet Earth.

These understandings are soon for all to have and will open the way for so many to return to who they are and deal with their better serving answers of serving with grace to their own needs. Know more truths are on the way and be well serving of our time of great trust together.

Answer my questions. Are you ready to answer to truth of where you have come from? Are you ready to open the way for others who have less understandings? And are you settling with Earth ways by opening to your truth and your own seeing?

Be willing to open to many more truths and be well serving of our ways and our time to answer to many more questions as all starts well answering with our time of arrivals and better serving with our truth and with our ways of great seeing. Be willing to open to us as we will soon arrive to answer you. Be certain all truths will be revealed as we begin to answer all with the removal of all harm.

Better to "Answer to answers", the book that is in my lap, than to respond to the plan these demons have devised for you as I am seeing this being planned by them. I am also seeing their limitless arrogance grow without any justice in mind, and seeing this tells me they have more troubles responding from us.

Be certain we will not let you down and we will arrive to open the way for our truth to be well serving. And know all this will soon be past you and all changes better settling with understood ways of truth. Be well answered by our ways and better truth. Have more knowledge and understandings with the good coming times and see how you will be feeling with these trusted visits arriving soon near your places of living.

Be well settling with the ways of Earth and tell yourselves, all starts with the serving of our time to walk the Earth and end the abuses long serving and long lived by most of you. See these truths be yours and settle with us as we will respond to answers very soon.

Now be ready and open to these coming days with great truth and great seeing. Question us as we meet face to face, and answer to our call as we are soon serving with our families and friends to share all these answers with you to the serving of the dealing of damages made to cause fear and torment to the lives of people everywhere.

Be ready all starts very soon as we are presently seeing to many details.

God

Received August 7, 2012 by Za

54. TIME IS RUNNING OUT

Be ready as time is running out. Have all you need to deal with your own needs for one month or two as chaos will begin to be seen in many places on Earth. Be understanding how all answers you as you become well settling with our understood ways. Evidence starts with the arrivals and these times are very soon.

I am settling with many details as we are speaking together about why these times are seen but not understood by many people on Earth and this is our greatest challenge. We will need all people to answer to our truth, to answer to many who will be needing help. These words I share with you because I believe all life is sacred and every man, woman and child has to be cared for, and animals need to be protected and cared for.

But all other creatures, as insects renewing to cause problems, will be removed by us. Be well seeing how all begins to unravel and open to many more settling ways of great truth as all becomes better serving with us. See how people everywhere will serve with us. Know we well see how all general care for people is necessary as we will deal with the most important urgent needs. You will need to care for all others by telling them who we are and why we are here on Earth.

Be ready and be dealing with us and our ways of better seeing as all becomes well answered by us. Share knowledge with many and see how all starts with the way of great telling of wars. See how all becomes well serving with us to answer to our many good truths. Better to answer to our way now than to be responding to no help and only troubles.

Heal with us and see we are not here to destroy Earth but to reunite with our family members taken from us a long time ago and serving a reincarnation cycle as a prison with only birth, death and slavery, as an answer to limited evolution with no memory of past lives. This will surprise many as we will reactivate many peoples' memories, open to more truth of how all heals and respond to many questions. Death will be healed with the understanding that souls live on eternally and nothing more can better serve than to know your true self.

Be well prepared to answer to your own needs of power and better settling of foods with healing serving ways (first aid, medicine, herbs, teas, etc.). Be well aware of all bridging telling of truth opening to many more people, and many more who will arrive and open to all people of Earth. See these days with happiness but care for yourselves to be well prepared for this time of chaos.

Better times comes soon after but all starts with the good serving bridging ways, and seeing to one's own needs first to be able to better help others after with their needs. See these days be well answered by us as all becomes well served and well answered by our ways and open to many who are ready to answer to our ways of great serving truth and better evidence of answers.

Now listen. Be setu (bridging and reunification) and know all answers are given to understand the great setu ways. These are the Universal Laws and most serving evidence of good actions come from the Universal Laws as the Ten Commandments have decreed. Be seeing that these Laws are many more and will be shared with the many who are ready to understand these uses of better serving ways of great setu knowledge.

Be ready to respond to our call as we will choose many people to come and learn these ways with us. Many from these groups will begin an education for all to open to and all the others will open to these new Setu Beings.

As this becomes seen, many will soon open to them and learn all the better ways of collaboration and care for the dignity of one another, and the way of living in grace of one's true self.

Tell yourselves these understandings are soon answering to many who are settling with us, and who are ready to open to us. Be certain all starts with our truth and our time to be seen on Earth with you. These days are soon, and we here are soon so pleased by serving with Humans and welcoming all good people of Earth to the Universal Laws and all who share these ways.

Together we will be renewed and stronger ties with the Universes will soon be shared and all people will have their places to be with. Arrivals begin soon as said and all you need to do is make certain you have what you need to be comfortable until the time of chaos is healed and dealt with. All other ways will be cause for great serving health ways, as first aid and supplements.

Be well serving of our understood seeing and better see to your needs yourselves. Better truth soon answers you as all starts. Be ready and deal with our truth and our ways as all starts, and answers to many other species of people from all corners of the Universes. Better serving times are soon here and many will become well serving of our understood ways of great truth as we better see to others with greater needs.

Be ready, this is the best I can do for you now as all starts unraveling and settling with Earth ways and Earth bridging understandings. Be well aware of our time of meeting with many of you who are reading these words, as this is how we wanted to inform some of our chosen ones, to open to these days of war and calamity that will cause many beings on Earth to leave by death. Many others will choose to remain and begin the reconstruction of Earth.

Respond only to our ways and beware of those who wish to deceive you. Now go and be ready.

God

Received August 9, 2012 by Za

55. HERE ARE YOUR ANSWERS
TO THESE QUESTIONS

See these questions answered and be well serving of my answers as my scribe will open this to you. Be responding to my words in your heart and remove the darkness of lies that have caused you many doubts of your own Being. Tell yourselves now is the time to open to the truth of who we are and settle with the denials you have been carrying in you for many lives as this only needs to be stopped as all will soon be shared by all. Be serving evidence now yourselves and serve your own answers.

Who I am is healing your seeing of our arrivals. Many have the belief that God is a mystical Being who created Earth in seven days. These words are a creation of Lucifer who wanted to reduce you to fear me and control your beliefs. This heals as we will make our presence known on Earth and then you can decide for yourselves what you need to open to as all is revealed. Be serving your truth, this is all I can ask you to open to and then see the rest unravel.

Now many have asked me where I come from. We are living now on a large ship as big as the moon ship. Be certain all these truths will soon be well shared and well explained as we arrive and show you these truths. How we made our ships and our pyramids are all things we will share with you as we remove the demons who have well concealed themselves on Earth in bodies and who will open to these times with our way of removing them.

These troubles are many and they are the ones who made up these lies to stop you from opening to us. Then, once they are removed, we can begin to open to each other as was our plan a long time ago when we lived on Earth. These ways of living were much different as all had what they needed and lived lives they wanted to live. But all has been corrupted on Earth as it settles with many lies.

Questions about time cannot be answered because this is a serving construct of Earth only and we do not serve these ways. Be seeing how these times are about our responding moment to an action that causes our limit of acceptance to Earth's dealings with war and harm. There is an answer to events only and not to minutes and seconds, as this is control over peoples' lives.

We do not serve time this way. Our way of dealing with needs, opportunities and free will does not have time to better settle with feelings and actions. That to us is a response to slavery and abuses as this only removes a persons' desires to act as needed and as necessary to deal with what is important. And what is important answers to who we are, as we all follow our hearts and unite this way with the Universal Laws.

Be serving this as you may but understand we are Beings who have lived a very long time and we are past these constructs of time. Be well answered by understood ways settling with these ways and be Setu with us as these ways are removed from your understandings and dealt with denials. Be well answered by our Setu ways and be well settling with Earth ways as these ways only exists on Earth and nowhere else in the Universes.

Lucifer has constructed a method of imprisonment with controlled time for everything, and with others, are manufacturing events to create fear to answer to his psychopathic needs of feeding from your fears and abuses. This is why when a response to an awakening occurs that the life behaviors of abuses begin to be many. As a Being awakes from Earth lies, then he or she becomes hunted by the possessed humans who start causing terrible troubles to stop the awakening and causing torment as these whores love to create torment for unsuspecting humans.

This awakening time for humans is opening because the soul evolves through all situations whether abuses, hardships and good experiences. But the evolution always continues and Lucifer may see these ways and add more ways to better abuse people as you see more and more on Earth. Only healing can overturn these renewed abuses and these ways are possible for all people on Earth. Understand you are his prisoner and he is your demon master, as these dregs are seen by all of us who are ready to have this devil removed from Earth.

Used truths about who we are, are not correct and have been well manipulated to make our present return unacceptable to humans as many believe we are dangerous and coming to harm or take over Earth. These lies are well orchestrated since the beginning of this long-established plan to open to death and Earth answers by Lucifer. Be seeing this, Lucifer has only enemies from many planets and Universes because he causes this kind of abuses wherever he goes.

We believed he was exterminated by a group of good souls who were living on Earth, but these souls were entrapped and changed by him, and we call them the fallen ones who became his army. These souls are now divided into many bodies of Earth and are as you call them demonic possessions. These souls choose where they wish to live and who they wish to possess. These demons attack another soul until it is submissive to them by allowing their body to serve as a host body.

Many humans who seem ill but always alive are in a possession serving. The body would not live unless this demon is removed. These demons manipulate the people around them to cause enslavement of their needs to them and cause a life of servitude to a needy person. These are possessions and some are pieces of demons seemingly not harmful but uses another person to serve them and never allowing them to open to who they wish to be and actualizing their lives.

All of this is said in old writings of religious books but these books are also corrupted as all is on Earth. The truth will surprise many and deal with all the denials answering to lies and deceptions. When we arrive, all other questions will be answered with proof.

Now about the questions of animals and people, see this as answering to souls divided into pieces and used as multiplications of many other bodies. These ways of used lies, to better say animals have no soul, to be diminished, well serves to stop their healing; as these ways are also cause for people to eat other humans as you are all soul Beings, human or animal.

Think of this as another deception opening to many more lies and many more better settling deceptions about animals being slaves to humans, and humans answering to eating flesh soul from others who have been divided against their own will to suffer atrocities even greater than humans do by the hands of humans. These ways will heal as you begin to see the workings of the division of souls and how this has caused so much more trouble for these souls to heal.

Understand that awakenings can be a reason for Lucifer's response to dividing your soul as he tries to stop your awakening if your soul is still in one piece. These pieces will all come together as you begin to heal. See how this part of healing will be so amazing for those who are divided. These truths are many more and are difficult to accept as many of you have been so troubled by these torments for so long. But all will heal, all can heal and all healing starts with our arrivals.

Know now this. The question about our settling answers to our ways will be yours to see as I have described this before in previous writings by my scribe. But know we are many and Lucifer is one, and he has nothing more to do as he is cornered by us, and all his Grey are destroyed by our responses to their actions.

Death heals some better than living their lives out on Earth because they are not whole and some are pieces that need to return to the parental soul body. These ways are difficult to accept but understand I have great love for every person and animal on Earth and I want you all to heal and open to answers to truth and consequently trust in my love for all of you. Now you may ask more questions* this way and I will answer them as necessary.

See how all becomes unraveled as we begin the sorting. See how many people will answer to their death overdue by illnesses or repeated drug uses that would normally kill anyone, but is kept alive by a demon that lives there. See how your social problems are increasing with the tolerance of drugs that are prescribed or not, and better serving to cause a body to be a better recipient for a possession thief.

These are seen by us very easily and many will say these people are only ill and understandings are to save them or care for them. But the renewing part never comes as the demon loves to be served and obeyed. They use any means to do this; with pity, with torment, with guilt, with lives dedicated to serve them anyway they can use to find their next host through all these denials.

Know now how this will appear to you when we begin the sorting. We will go to hospitals, to homes for the elderly and places for the handicapped, and we will begin to free them from their demonic possessions. Some will be healed and others will choose to leave to better incarnate back to themselves as they will awaken. **

This will free their serving slaves from the denial of dedicating their lives to another who only abuses them by using their life sources. These understandings will better settle with you once these denials are understood. All will become better settling with themselves and opening to their own time of evolution.

Be ready and see how all transformations begin to be dealt with and answer to yourselves as all starts with our truth and our answers to answers. Be ready and see all be as I said and know I will continue to answer your questions as my scribe sees this as better use for you. Now go and be yourselves.

God

Received August 11, 2012 by Za

* Note 2020: Through the blog, *newtimesonearth2012.blogspot.ca*, God invited the readers to ask questions that he could answer with my help. All comments were disengaged and I could not see or show the questions. So, God hearing the questions himself chose to continue answering them, and I published them. Also, many of the visits to my blog spot disappeared.

** Note 2020: I am not certain how this reflects the our present situation with the pandemic.

56. MANY QUESTIONS ARE BEING ASKED

Be ready and settle with Earth ways as all starts and as all becomes well serving. Be ready to open understandings with us as we tell you who we are as we are not the called Archons. We are Archai and the Archons are the fallen ones who once served with us. Be seeing how these ways of naming our kind is only used on Earth and elsewhere we are called the Elohim.

The Angels from above are Setu Beings of Light who are seeing all and answering to calls of help from many planets. Be settled by these words now and see serving responses to evidence of our truth. Be well answered now as many questions are asked.

See this now. The Slave Lake, Alberta, Canada incident was orchestrated to better open to the future king and queen to another form of weaponry new to Earth and easier to destroy many without any troops. These ways as seen, are well established to serve with the actions of the military of the UN and NATO countries who ask about their understood time of attacks.

These lasers are harmful to all people on Earth as these fires can burn so many places without any military troops on the ground. Because it is only fire, all these areas will be renewed by nature and opening the way for the Agenda 21 plan. By the time these plans can occur we will be walking the Earth and these satellites will no longer exist. Better bridging truth will answer this as all is seen.

Now about the question of our ways of travel and serving living on a small orbiting planet; we are on a ship, round like a planet, moving and orbiting like seen asteroids, but it is a ship and we have the technologies to do this.

At the time of Earth's beginning, we lived on Earth and it was a paradise until we gave it to be manage by another who became used by Lucifer. These stories are unknown to many but Lucifer conquered Earth and tricked our Angels to serve with him by using methods to answer to healing, but he changed it into transforming these Angels into beast and men bodies, and made them to become slaves to him.

These Angels were not able to free themselves from these transformations as they were changed by these genetic manipulations and horrific bodies of beasts and men. This, Lucifer gleefully answered with written hieroglyphs on the pyramids and this was made to cause us to retaliate. And so, we did, by shifting the Earth causing floods and ice age as you call it.

Be settling with these truths and see how this will only open to many more renewed understandings of Setu seeing as we will explain these episodes of true history to you as we begin these explanations together.

Landing on Mars questions are curious to us as this has been done already by the dealers of Earth settlers. Understand what you ask is telling us that you are not knowing about Mars. Mars was the planet all truth came from until it was destroyed by Lucifer and these troubles are seen now on Earth. Be seeing that Mars heals but healing these kinds of destruction takes a very long time.

It is rumored that people have been colonizing Mars with underground terraces and tunnels. But healing visits are not seen anywhere by us and only a few Earth ships have landed there. No Setu Beings wish to go there as nothing serves on Mars anymore. The ones who lived there were the Settler groups we visit with and now we are working with them through the Universal Laws. They now live on other planets as only a few escaped the destruction of this ancient planet.

Now the question about death; death is not terminating all consciousness of the soul, as some parts are serving some memory and some reaction to stimuli of life experiences. These are the ways all serves when a person knows how to do something without knowing how it was learned. These innate memories are actually repeated actions from another life and not a genetic trait from DNA imprints.

Be serving these truths as memory is recovered. Know this is easily done by us as we can heal all illnesses and all shut off knowledge serving all humans and animals. Be ready to settle with Earth ways as all heals with many more truths and better seeing.

Know this with us, as these answers are only a few of the questions that have been asked. Better Setu ways opens to us and we are settling with many who are renewing with our truth of who we are. Be dealing with the way of denials as all starts changing and becoming seen by all who are ready to answer to answers at the time of our arrivals.

Know this now, as many more trusted ways of great truth at the seeing of our ships in the sky and be certain we will not harm anyone, but we will remove all serving whores who cause harm onto others and who do not answer to our ways. Better to be welcoming us than to continue down the path of destruction with these demons and serve these ways as Mars did a long time ago.

See to it that you have many more truths to open to and deal with, as all unravels and truth is exposed and changes all. Be well answering to many more coming truths. Now many more questions answered served understandings.

Be ready.

God

Received August 12, 2012 by Za

57. I AM ANSWERING YOUR QUESTIONS

NEPHILIM BLOOD TYPES

Who are the Elohim? Who are we? We are the ones who are serving many with our seeing and our answers to better life in all places. We are the believers in peace and openness to truth and fairness of life. We are the ones who are settling with the death ways on Earth, as uses of these reincarnations on

Earth are no longer serving humans, as the healing ways are only serving in some.

Better trust will show you who we are and better serving understandings answers to many who are seeing how all heals on Earth. Be ready and share knowledge with us and settle with Earth ways. We are the ones who opened the Universal Laws to many other Beings in all planets visited who were ready to meet with us.

Earth has been our cherished place to visit but all was changed when Lucifer took it over and all will be changed once he is removed with all his creatures of fear and aggression. Be well knowing how all starts with us and see to it that we heal all with our truth and our bridging ways of great answers and to evidence.

Better to be with us than to be with these demons as they are settling with many others to answer to, but they can only open to responses with destruction. Be well serving of our time to answer you and settle with Earth ways as none of these ways will renew with you. Now tell yourselves all understandings will open well and all truth will respond to all who are used to answer to many more truths.

Be certain these truths will serve you and many others will begin to be settling with you as you see this for what it is. Be well prepared to answer to answers serving all who renew with our ways. Be willing to open many to many more serving ways in evidence of our ways as all becomes well serving and well dealt with and served. Be responding to our time of great truths as all starts.

Be ready to read these words now. As we begin the sorting, we will see who have Nephilim blood in them and those who do not. The Nephilim blood is changed blood by Lucifer's manipulations and serves to answer to his ways, as these are ready to respond at any time to hearing his orders and acting on them.

These ways of doing this cannot be well explained at this time of your scientific understandings but the way these uses are, answers to control and actions controlled by Lucifer. Because these Nephilim blood servers are more human than visibly Nephilim they live amongst any family or work place unsuspecting any differences in who they are.

They can be kind, loving and a good Samaritan and better answering to a normal human life. But what lives in them can be dangerous as they can commit atrocities without any warnings and do things one could not suspect or imagine because the body has ways of hiding this blood type and does not recognize it as different.

This healing time on Earth helps to rid these blood types from Earth as they do not belong and are dangerous, as Lucifer has gladly proved this with mass murderers and people who seem normal who suddenly begin to kill others for no apparent reason. These ways of removing them will serve Earth people as these others are waiting for orders from their master without knowing they are his to use.

Now that we are coming to Earth to renew with our children, we must do all we can to create a new time on Earth to heal the torment that was caused by these Nephilim blood types. These understandings will be difficult to accept but ask us this after murders are committed and see these types better understanding what they have done by order of another.

Settling with these types will be removals and relocation to heal these souls from this corrupting hook created by Lucifer. See how all this serves to change these ways and these responses to a life renewing with only evil and with more troubles as these kinds follow no law and no rules and answer only to their master. Healing these pieces of soul will be very long and will better serve with removals and more trusted living ways.

Be certain you will see these living differences as these kinds are removed to go to a place of healing. God understands that some of these Beings appear very good and very kind, but as I said we know of their capabilities to commit atrocities and Earth was not made to serve these kinds. Be ready to answer to these understandings as all must be dealt with and as all used truths must be visited by actions to stop Lucifer's work of corrupting souls.

Here is the thing to open to, a better understanding of corrupted souls to answer to healing them the way they need to be healed. This helps these soul pieces to heal piece by piece and hopefully in time they will come back as one or become extinct. Do you understand how important this is to heal Earth? Do you see that some of you must leave the good concept that everyone can be saved?

Be seeing the truth about this as we do and you will better understand our actions to cause a better healing for all serving Beings on Earth. These times are soon answered by our ways and many will become well serving of our used truths. Be well answered by us as we begin these sorting ways and be certain if you are reading this, this does not include you because you would have an aversion to my words.

A question was asked about our dealt with Setu ways and how we became Setu. This question is difficult to answer as I have only a knowledge of my time and the before time the Ancients speak about, but beliefs are settling with these words. We were evidence of energy gathered in the Terran worlds and we organized ourselves to open to the nature of our worlds as you believe you came to be on Earth (but these stories are untrue for Earth).

We were told by the Ancients that we travelled through space from planet to planet believing in Setu ways. We encountered evil so great that we could not comprehend it. Soon we learnt this way and became changed until all of us were as they were, sharing in atrocities until Setu truths better answered all. We visited many who answered to these ways and we were changed by our own hearts because these ways lived in us before.

These are the imprinted truths that serves all good people on Earth. Feeling these truths in you will open you to many more seeing and the settling of Earth ways. Healing starts with understood ways easily used to answer to good health, long lives and eternal values for you to experience. Know many more Setu ways will be shared. You will soon see how these answers are settling and renew with us as we arrive.

God

Received August 13, 2012 by Za

58. RESPOND TO OUR WAY AND EVIDENCE OF OUR TRUTH

THE STORY OF SOPHIA

Believe better times are soon coming as all renewals become served. We are nearing Earth with our large planet ship and we are sending many Angels ahead to open to servants of our understandings. We are well seeing how all starts very soon and we will answer to all urgent needs first. Be ready to answer to the proof of our ways and renew with us at the time of our meeting.

Tell another about these times and these words, and see how all starts with the way all settles with our answers to many more truths at the telling time of our used truth. See how all will become serving for all who are Setu as they are originally. Be understanding about how all answers you with a new life and a new way of settling with Earth ways as these ways will no longer be used by anyone to open to.

See how all lives will unite in knowledge with us and respond to many about how all heals in evidence of our time together. See these ways be well awakened with us and know all starts with all people who are with the Holy Spirit on Earth. Serve with us and settle with our truth and see your lives be filled with love and kindness to each other and all who have seen the truth.

Better times are soon here my children, be ready and be dealing with the hard times ahead as these times are short but difficult for some. Death will answer to the many as the feelings of war are more than war. They are answers to desperation to leaders who are in more fear than before as many responds to the knowledge of our arrivals and are well aware of the contract they broke with us.

Be ready and see all this unfold and deal with the view of this shared knowledge and answer to my call. Better ways better answers to evidence of our truths and our renewing ways. We are settling with many at the time of our arrivals, to begin the sorting and removing all falsehood from Earth.

Now to answer the question of God again, settle with this understanding: "Answers to answers" is a book that is in my lap. This book was written by Sophia my love and my bride. She has been lost to me for thousands of years as she was taken from me as a prisoner to cause us to return to earth and free her and all my children who stayed with her.

These children are my care-taking and I am responsible for their souls but they are not all of my blood. Sophia adopted all the children who had lost their families a long time ago and denied herself and her love for her own to give to others. She sees now that these ways could have been dealt with differently but her mind is only partially awake to her truth as she has reincarnated many times, as many as you have. She heals all the abuses done to her by Lucifer's ways of attacking the good souls to change them.

As we arrive, healing begins, and Sophia will reawaken and open the way for all our children to free themselves from these lies, deceptions and snares that have caused even the strongest to brake. But now we are many as all was discovered and the truth was shared by soon so many in the Universes who suffered the same attacks.

Many are as humans and many are other Beings from other planets and we are all united now to be responding to answering all who are not corrupted and settling with good settling of our time to walk the Earth. Be well serving now and be ready to answer to evidence of our ways as all becomes well seen and well dealt with by us. Better times answers to our truth opens to answers.

Sophia is not a planet like Earth or a name to better serve understandings of words. These ways of personifying her for what she is not has troubled us because this makes her untrue, undesired and undone by better seeing her as a non-person. These ways of doing this causes herself to not be herself and her healing has been troubling as she does not believe herself to be anything more than a human and death would be her end.

But healing with her heals all who know of her existence and trust in her purity of soul. These religions and cults who say she served with Lucifer are deceptive and dangerous for all good souls because they are lies and blasphemes that will be corrected upon our arrivals and all this will be dealt with easily and surely.

We will be settling together with answers she wrote and left in the Akashic records for Gabriel to find and give to me as he was helping me recover from her leaving us, not knowing the truth that she was taken from me. She now waits for our meeting time only knowing who she is as a human and settles with these answers written by my scribe. Be serving with all who are seeing this as truth as they are awakened.

God is my name. I am God and I am who I am, and I heal my broken heart with all of you who have suffered the lies and deceptions of our ways and of our time together. Be well serving of our truth as all starts and be well serving of our Setu ways. See how all unravels and answers all and every one of you who have been waiting for me to reveal all truths to you.

Now is the time and I ask you to prepare yourselves as all begins with the sorting and evidence of all other seen truths. Better to answer to us than to be destroyed by Lucifer because this is his ultimate plan to revenge on us as he sees us answering to your calls. Renewed serving truth will answer all telling of past. Be ready to answer to our call as we start settling with "Answers to answers", and open these words to the world. See your understandings become clear and well answered by evident truth.

Now we are not magicians or tricksters or any kind of vaporous apparitions. We are Beings of Light with bodies that are somewhat different but all in all, we are appearing to be well answering to all settling ways on Earth as we have the better technologies to do this. And yes, I am God all speak about, but understand lies were said and money was created to serve my return as a business deal by many religious leaders of the world.

These are simply the workings of evil to blind those who have faith in my time to serve judgement as they themselves have much to fear and we will start with them and those who deal in the supporting secret societies as many are settling with lies and answer to manipulating all truths. When you serve the seeing of who is behind all this, your understandings will erupt into truths and all will be awakened.

Respond to the Holy Spirit, the missing piece of the trinity and open your eyes to all great deceptions living everywhere on Earth. Be visited very soon by our ways and see to it all heals with our truth and our ways. More than you are expecting starts well into the good serving days and although you see this as taking too long and soon is not soon enough, I tell you now that all is coming and this great change will be seen by all who are waiting for the truth to be dealt with.

Now open your eyes and your heart to me as I am finding these days long as well and I wish to be answering you sooner but I must be Setu and see all unravel as necessary. Now go and be ready.

God

Received August 14, 2012 by Za

59. TELL YOURSELVES THESE EARTH TIMES ARE SOON OVER AND A NEW TIME BEGINS

Be well answered by our time to answer to evidence of our great truth together. See how all will be changed and how all starts with the renewed times of our arrival. Answer to answers as we begin renewing with all who are ready to open to our ways and better ways of living. Better times are opening for all who are questioning how all heals on Earth.

Be settling with Earth ways and be responding to being seen by our trusted ways and be responding to being seen by our trusted guards who will be renewing with all people of Earth as we begin the sorting. See to it that you are ready to answer to our time to walk the Earth as we tell you how all came to be. Now settle with Earth ways by letting go of those who have caused harm.

Deal with your life renewals as these times will be freeing and better serving all answers. See to it all settles with us, and no other will serve with us than those who trust in the Universal Laws and see these Laws as just.

Now to answer the question of telling of truth. This question asked by a person from Russia, has to do with an understood life of deceptions. Visit with us as we arrive and see this for yourself and only be as you wish to be to answer to truth. All these words I share are truth, but answers can only be trusted when you see them yourselves.

How can I ask you to trust me when your whole life has been one deception after another and all lives before this answered to our truth but no truth was seen? Evidence will be yours as we arrive and when we speak together to each other, and this is the best I can do for you. More than you are expecting comes very soon and you shall see these events yourself and with many people on Earth and then you will have the proof of our truth.

Until then, read these words and see these words become trusted as you will see these ways yourselves. Be well renewing with us and see how all will be changed to answer to your ways and your truths.

The other question from the same person from Russia is: "Why are all responses so long to read as people ask beliefs to be dealt with?" These ways we practice here together are prayer to open to our ways of heart sharing. But on Earth all is rushed, hurried and quickly consumed as is the ways of the working slaves. Be telling yourselves that reading my words are as praying time and you must rest and read quietly, and see how these words feel to you at the reading time and later as you go about your day.

Be visited soon by the thought that understood answers will soon better serve with us and not with any other people as we become well serving of our truth. Be ready to answer to our ways as all starts and be well settling with us as we become a seen daily answer to everyone's seeing. Now the question from Canada about our renewed seeing of what happened when we became separated.

This heals with us now. But at the time of the great wars with Lucifer's army, we were alone as a kind of Being and Lucifer's army was greater than ours and readier than ours, as we did not use the same treacherous means of dealing with these death ways as he did. We had very little understanding of great evil and more troubles came from this, telling us we needed to leave and return with a greater army.

We are here now and we have learned many of these evil ways, and many more have joined us as we are united by the Universal Laws. Many think too much time has passed since Lucifer took over our Earth, but healing time is here now and we can overcome any planet we wish to and settle with any problems. Be certain of my words.

And the last question for now coming from the USA is: "How will renewals be felt by humans in body as these bodies have been programmed to die?" Answering this is very simple. The response to a better way of living with better health will change many things and help you live a longer life. Many will return to their original forms by choice if they are settling with these lives and see them as concluded.

But for those who will well renew on Earth, their bodies will be rejuvenated as an Earth twenty- five or so, and health will be returned to its' prime uses of life. All younger people will cease to age so fast and regain their health, stay younger and aging slowly until they reach adult age of twenty-five and retain this age look. Aging is a construct created by Lucifer as time is.

All your questions are good and I will well answer them as you continue to ask them as the way my scribe explained. Be well serving of our time together as these days are very soon and very near. Share more knowledge and light of understanding with me tomorrow.

God

Received August 15, 2012 by Za

60. THESE TIMES ARE
SOON ANSWERED

Be ready and see all unravel as the ways of war are opening soon. Be responding to many who are ready to open to you as we arrive and open the way for you to be free from the lies and offenses shared by our seeing, telling us all must soon end on Earth as these times are here. You will better see why all must end as Mars did at the time of our leaving Earth.

The destruction of Mars was responding to Lucifer's plan to destroy all evidence of his ways before we arrived because he wanted to hide his manipulations and expand his deeds to other places. Earth was our favorite place to go to, as we loved the peace felt in this new planet created to please us and open to our ways.

But all users of deceptions and lies infiltrated our communities and began to change these ways of cooperation and good living ways and all truths was dealt with and shared with us and opened to us much too late as we had no understanding of great evil ways. Be serving these truths and see how Earth became corrupted by evil and how all changes are now well accepted as daily life.

And tell me this is healing because nothing used by us is trusted and we are the Healers of the Universes. See these lies be destroyed by our ways and start a life of peace and serenity, and answer to evidence of our ways. Be ready now to see the change as all becomes well answered as this will open to all your questions as we begin to sort all people of Earth.

We will find all the corrupted souls that will need to be returned to their actions now put on them. This will give them their own visiting with themselves and how they caused all others to suffer. Be seeing this as karma if you wish, but we call this reeducation for the hardened souls who have lost all sympathy for other humans and who need to be well answered by their own ways.

Be understanding our ways will reflect the actions done to others onto them and these ways will serve until light opens in them. If it does not, then we will remove them from all others in perpetuity as there is no other solution for their soul to be cared for.

Understand these corrupted souls see themselves as above you and settling with any treatment of humans they wish in evidence of their actions. Although you were made to believe in kindness and compassion, until you yourselves have suffered their actions, you do not understand their uses of you and how they have only harm to cause.

These demons are not as people but as created beasts to serve only their master Lucifer. Understand these truths and awakened to the lies of your own lives as you will see this responding to answers of horrors not yet seen by you and that exist on Earth. I am horrified myself at the tortured innocent souls who suffer every minute of their dear lives at the hands of pure evil.

This has to stop and we will care for these urgent needs ourselves and very soon. Better to be with us as we will respond to you well and you will see what I am telling you while many are renewing with us. Be well answered by our truth and be settling with "Answers to answers" as this will explain how evil infiltrates and spreads to all places of a planet.

Be ready to answer to our truth and be understanding how all telling of lies have caused many to settle answers to many more deceptions and chaos all over Earth. See how all these ways are more to do with the actions well-orchestrated to answer to dealings of soul corruptions than with the ways of great healing.

More troubles come as this system of evil escalates and settles with lies and deceptions, and answering to rendering people destitute and homeless. These actions are to open to a new world order that plans to better renew with our telling but to only use these ways to start a world of control, not freedom and cooperation, as my son said before he was crucified.

Better truth will soon answer you because better seeing will soon renew with you, as all starts with our ways of healing. Better to open your eyes now than to be surprised about these answers to the coming chaos that will start well into the responding days. See these truths yourselves and serve a quiet time of meditation at the answers soon shared by our great seeing.

More is healing with us as we begin to answer to these trusted ways. Be well answered and tell yourself that you have another way of living coming soon with us. Be ready all answers you well into our time of great Setu understandings. Settle with us as all better truth becomes well answered. Better understandings will soon be yours as all will be revealed by our time to open to you and walk the earth.

Answer to our ways and see in your hearts that these are your ways arriving to open to you with our Prophets and Teachers. But Lucifer used all our words and made his own cults and religions to answer to only his trickeries and grand deceptions well seen today, as your hard work was made to serve these leaders of great lies.

See this serving time of slavery be well over as this does not exist with our ways. Know all better times are soon here with you as we begin the sorting and return your lands to you as this was yours a long time ago. Know that all this is soon coming and you will have what you need without giving all your work away to others and better caring for each other at the time of the reckoning. Renew with our love for you and our care for each and every one of you at the time of healing with us.

These days are soon here and we are arriving well into the good Setu days. Be well serving of our time together and tell others that we are arriving to make the necessary changes much needed on earth. Be understanding how all your imprinted behaviors of submission to abusers, all the poison foods fed to you and sprayed on you, heals as we arrive to end this cycle of responding abuses to your awakening time with us.

Questions will return tomorrow to answer you but today I want you to open to the thought of who we are and why we are returning to Earth to judge the actions of all humans. Be renewing with us and settle with Earth ways as these ways were put in place by the cabal who serves Lucifer their master. These whores, as said before, are only here to oppose the great workings of the Universes and they would have Earth people believe that a balance of good and evil is needed to open to truth.

But the problem with that is healing, and from these ways (of balance of good and evil), only evil grows. Can you tell me truthfully that evil is needed in your lives to better your lives? These answers are seen by us as crippling anyone's good intentions and good actions and certainly a ridiculous comment to make about evil being useful. How many actually believe these ways as being possible? None.

Now prepare yourselves and answer to the truth as all arrives well into the better serving days. Be certain I am answering your calls as all heals and settles with our time to walk the Earth and see all these times be changing.

God

Received, August 16, 2012 by Za

61. TIME IS RUNNING OUT, NOW SEE ALL START

Be ready, more than you are expecting starts well into these good serving days. Be well serving of my way and see how all better truth becomes well served and know we are ready to answer to all Setu answers, to all needs as responding time begins. See how all truths becomes well evident with renewed questions answered.

Now about the questions from Canada and the U.S.A. about how we arrived because the sightings of our ships are not yet seen. We have not all arrived. Some scout ships as said have become seen by the serving cameras, but we the Elohim have not arrived yet. We are the ones you see but the ones who are on Earth are from the pleiadian planets, as you call them.

Be certain they serve with us and are serving to answer you as they prepare all information to be well shared by all who are ready to land. The pleiadians are mostly like humans but they are not all as humans. The seeing of some may appear difficult to look at, but we do not see them this way anymore as they are kind and caring to all of nature, animals and humans.

Be certain they are soon coming also to walk the Earth with us. The seeing of these humanoids may frighten some of you but be serving respect to their beliefs and goodness, and they are grateful and serving to all. Be ready to be answered by them as they have much knowledge about repair to pollution damage and they are well prepared to clean the oceans and water ways. Be dealing with these good souls as they are wanting to come with us to open to our ways of dealing with the cleaning of Earth.

We call them another name better suited for them but they call themselves the "gersiels". They arrive with us and serve to be the healers of the waters of Earth. The Beings who are with us are mostly humanoids however only some are coming with us as not all are serving on our missions, nevertheless they all accept the ways of the Universal Laws. Tell yourselves that many exiting times awaits you as you will renew with many others.

Questions about meat eating tells me this will be a difficult habit to stop as many are believing that meat eating is a good practice. Be understanding that these practices are the death ways and we are settling with this through education and better serving of our truths with the Setu seeing of serving understood Setu ways. Be seeing how meat causes cancer and because meat eaters are in denial of these used truths, many will have a challenge to overcome this imprinted use of death eating.

Heal this as you can and we have many good ways to show you how to stop these ways of death eating. Healing serves to answer to your health ways and eating flesh of animals causes the body to age quickly and enters diseases that are very difficult to heal alone. Be certain we can start to show you better ways and soon you will renew your health and understand all the reasons you are eating meat as the body was not designed for this habit.

All is evident by the way people are so badly treated based on lies from the twisting of my words and my son's words, and this will be stopped by us as we begin to walk the Earth. All healing comes from the end of these Lucifer cults who cause answers to great lies and greater deceptions and most of these cults use woman as their victims to oppress them and cause them pain.

All I can say heals you but for some all these words as shared are a burning telling of truth that undoes beliefs and imprinting of past lives and dealing with this needs to be well settled. All this was a well-planned controlling method to serve the elites' desires to rule your minds and your labors. Your time to awake heals all this imprinting. Visiting with us answers all your questions to our truth.

Settle with these Earth ways and understand you are in the dealings of a devil and not of the Elohim. And to say we are asking you to do these things and these ways of rituals, animals or people, as these religions are seen, are dealing with death ways. These are not our ways. We are free Beings of Light, this is constructive and evolutionary, not destructive religious wars and destitution of living ways.

The way of self-sacrifice exists only to serve the way of Lucifer, as we do not see this as useful because people cannot evolve if they give away all their work and abilities to serve another. These are used ways of Lucifer who takes all and tells you it is never enough. Deal with these truths and see how you are soon freed from these chains of deceptions.

These times are over. Know I am as I am and I never wanted you to erupt into chants to answer me, however I love to hear your heart felt, dealt with understandings about who you are and how you move through the difficulties of living as a father does, nothing more and nothing less. Heal with me and I will answer you with an open heart and heal with your own selves.

Be ready and settle with us. Know we are dealing with all truths and you must leave your place of denials and imprinting to free yourselves. Once this is done, your soul will begin to strengthen and find a new balance in its' core and all will become changed for you and serve your truth very well. This is the path to the Setu way and these other paths reduces you to a slave.

These times are over and you must not accept Lucifer or you will be his. Be responding only to your own person and meditate to clear your thoughts, listen to yourself only and do not allow any voices that tells you to cause harm answer you. These ways are not ours and never were. See these ways be ended and find your light.

God

Received August 17, 2012 by Za

62. ANSWERS TO MANY MORE QUESTIONS

Be well answered and evidence will better serve you with the proof of our Setu ways. Be ready and settle with us and with others as we begin to walk the Earth. Be settling with Earth ways and open to answers well responding to our arrivals and to answer to answers of our ways and be well serving of our time together.

Love with all is possible but you must first heal yourselves. Better truths will open the way for you. Respond to answers to our emanation of truth. Be dealing with our living truth of who we are and how all heals to better open to who you are.

Now the question from Germany about serving understood ways of great renewals and telling of past. Heal with these words and understand we are as you see it. Here is the thing, we are Archai and of Elohim as these words mean we open to a seeing of great abilities with our ways. We answer to the healing and care of people healing time to open to the Universal Laws, as these ways as seen in previous writings answers you now.

We are settling with the path of destruction left by Lucifer as this understood path has finally found Earth as being corrupted. Be serving answers to these truths as arrivals begin because we are settling with all Setu truths and opening to many more seeing. I am answering you these words but I cannot say all at this time because this will be difficult for some to accept at first. Heal with us and be ready to answer to all the truth. We are renewing now, understand?

Now about the question of our ways to answer to us, as with all who are dealing with the settling of evil. Answers these ways yourselves with the dealings of our ways to answer to answers, when you see how well we are without evil near us. See this renewal as arrivals become serving because we will deal with all harm in a better way than ignoring the existence of it until it is too much to overcome.

The way of evil causes harm and becomes greater by covering it up. Be understanding that what you see on Earth is only the surface of the great evil plan about mass murders and settling slavery. All these ways only serve one purpose, to destroy humans and create a new breed of slaves to serve an elite group who wishes for absolute control and a new world order that opens to the ready leader of great torment.

Healing with this truth is now and not later as it will only grow into what it wants to do, and then it is done. Be seeing we are more trusted in all places of the Universes to stop these horrors and these times are soon here for Earth people.

Now the question about life on other planets from Canada. Understand many planets settling everywhere as Earth exist to have a good life. Be seeing these planets are very much like Earth but also very different in ways of how plants and dealing of light serves as the sun is renewing with many, so with the serving of air and water.

Be serving understandings that not all planets can be visited by humans because air is different but we have the technologies to open to this. The better planets for humans many of you will enjoy. Be serving responses to this as we will answer these questions with you through our meeting and education time. Answers to our ways will open to many more questions as expected. Hear these words and you will be answered.

Now about the question from Russia about the arriving places on Earth. We are many and we will land in many places on Earth and certainly in all countries, in farmers' fields and airports, and we will live with you among you to answer all your needs of power, good water and air. But understand we are soon there to begin the sorting of evil, and then all restructuring begins and deals with new ways of living. Answers to our call answers to your calls.

And then the question from India about who we are as the Setu way. Setu Beings of Light are all who open to the Universal Laws and better seeing how all is. Be ready to answer to our ways and see how we are able to answer to all with better ways of health and living, and certainly of great care for each other as this is not very well serving anywhere on Earth.

Serve a time of meditation and answer to evidence of our ways at the Setu renewing time. See these ways with us be well accepted and well dealt with, at the telling trusted ways all becomes well served. Be ready all starts well into the good trusted times and see all renewals begin with us as we answer to many and respond to urgent needs first. Be well settling with all serving answers as all comes and responds to evidence of our ways and be well serving of our time together.

Now go and be ready, all opens very soon.

God

Received August 18, 2012 by Za

Message from Za: The Universal Laws are not all known on Earth with the exception of the Ten Commandments being only a part of the whole. Be well and be ready.

63. BETTER TRUTH STARTS WITH US

Be seeing how all telling of history has been organized to better answer to an acceptance of evil. See how what you are taught in schools is a well-coordinated form of indoctrination that serves to open to the believers of Lucifer's greater plans. Understand that what you know and what you hear answers to only to answers of great lies. Understand that this is the problem.

Better knowing the truth about how all answers you, serves to open to many more seeing of great truth. You will see how these truths are settling with answers to knowledge and light of understanding. Be settling with these Earth ways and open to greater knowledge of better serving truth. See how all will soon open the way for our arrivals as we become well served and well settling. Know you are well served with evidence of who we are and settle with this as we begin our time of reunion and great renewals.

Be dealing with these times of reunion with grace and dignity as all who are arriving are well Setu Beings who come as diplomats and some are more noble than anyone on Earth. This means, we respect ourselves and each other as you would like to be respected yourselves. And this you will see. Be well rested as these days begin because for a time there will be chaos and turmoil as we remove all the evil workers and better answer to all better responding truths.

Now about the question from the U.S.A. about the way of religions on Earth. Heal the way these words in our books of religions have been manipulated to serve greater purposes and these purposes are not to open to us but to stop you from opening to us and the returns of my sons, Jesus and Gabriel. These books tell you we are returning but also tell you we are not to be trusted as we may be false prophets.

Better to renew with us than with the lies that have kept you in darkness for so long, as we are who we say we are, nothing more and nothing less. Better to see this for yourselves as I will be meeting with my chosen ones, settle with the ways of the Earth and begin healing with many of our children. Be well answered by who we are in evidence of our time of great truth and see how all starts with the Setu way of great truth shared.

Be prepared to answer to knowledge of our ways and see how all your lives will be well improved. Be well seeing of who we are, settling with the lies that have plagued all religions since my son was dealt with disturbing abuses. So many lies about him were said. Be understanding that he came to Earth to share our knowledge with you, against my will, and he suffered the Earth ways of consequences.

Because of greed and ignorance, this still lives and still in greater ways on Earth as many of his words were changed, twisted and corrupted by the law makers of Earth, to seduce you into following rituals that are only theirs and were never our ways. We do not have these ways of rituals but we have celebrations and reunions where we love to share our music and our songs.

Be settling with these ways of repeated rituals as this tells me that if this is needed for you to follow your religions then it is false because it is clearly indoctrination. I am seeing how your seeing of faith follows a plan made by a man or cults, stemming from the dark ways and this must be ended as it does not serve us. Heal these belief habits and free yourselves from dogma. Open to new ways of seeing with us and open to the emanation of truth.

Now about the other question about who my scribe is. She is how she wishes to be and nothing more. She lives a simple and comfortable life to give you these words and ways as I have asked her to help me prepare my children for our arrivals. And know these ways of seeing for her was not easy as she was not knowing about how all heals before we contacted her. Be responding to her as arrivals begin as she will meet with us and see who we are, as we are all family and friends.

Be Setu with each other and be caring for each other as we begin the sorting time because these times will be chaotic and responding to many upheavals. Be well settling with dogma and beliefs that settle with rituals answering the dark ways of indoctrination. Free yourselves from these dark practices as this opens to ways of acceptance and submission to only a few who are not serving the Universal Laws and serve the ways of greed, corruption and seen ignorance.

Heal these Earth ways and open to our truth. Prepare yourselves for the time of reckoning as Teacher (Jesus) and Gabriel arrive first to meet with our chosen ones. Heal these ways of telling repeated scriptures that only settle with words repeated and no truth to open to. Many are used to cause others to say nothing as these words are settling with another way of submission to old twisted words, no longer Jesus' truth.

These are answering words to your questions. Now open to the light of who we truly are. Heal seeing of great serving lies as so many planned, serving slavery based on indoctrinations and destruction of free will, and this was never my intention. I gave my children free will to better their evolutionary experiences, not to become a slave of used past dogma.

Now about the persistent question about who I am and who you are, from Germany. Here is the truth whether you are able to accept it or not. Listen to these words. I am who I am and my name is God, and serving this should be enough but I see you need to be face to face with this truth and how it heals you. How can I say this without your better seeing of this here?

Settle with these words for now and be ready to meet with us and open to absolute truth. If you cannot do this then we shall help you more with our actions as we begin to sort and open to helping the greater needs of people first. But I will not answer this question again and deal with your own healing.

Better to be with us than to be serving Lucifer because Lucifer only takes and he never gives anyone anything to help them evolve. Be certain of this demon's ways. Know all who serve him will have only us to settle with because he is destined to serve his actions as he caused them and know he has destroyed many planets and many people. God does not destroy, he creates. Be settling now with these words.

And the last question from Russia: "Why do I renew with only a few chosen ones in evidence of the many religious leaders of the world waiting to be spoken to?" Understand these leaders are corrupted and they do not serve me. They serve another who is only acting as me, but he is called Lucifer and he has tricked you into opening to him and his blood rituals.

We see how this answer has been used on Earth but open to the truth of this yourselves and settle with these lies of my words twisted to serve only a few greedy men. These are servants of Lucifer who enjoy causing harm to the innocent and blaspheme my name in the process of abuses.

These times are ending as I will put an end to it myself. Be certain of this and let go of these golden calves of responding falsehoods and free yourselves to prepare to meet with us as we are the Setu Beings of Light. We arrive to free all God's children from Earth's planned destruction as this heals with all of us. Truth and understanding will show you the way. Ready yourselves to meet with us as we return to walk the Earth and open to all who are ready to share knowledge and light of understanding.

See how we will open to many as all starts with evidence of great trust in all of our coming works and deeds and then decide for yourselves who we are. As we arrive, I ask you again to remain calm and stay in your homes with good supplies to wait for the time of chaos to be well over, as we will reestablish our governance in all places of Earth and see to all the urgent needs first. Then we will begin the opening of truth to all who are ready.

This process takes a long time for you but a matter of a few months should be enough for us to do these ways of great sharing. Better to be waiting in the comfort of your homes, as we use our ways to sort all Beings who are not completely human as there are many who are fragmented and well serving dark ways. They will be well cared for in better places to respond to their needs of evolution. The choice will be theirs to change to better themselves or become what they cause onto others. They understand these words.

Be ready, be well prepared and see to our answering ways as all becomes well settling and answering to great truth, better serving ways of living and becoming yourselves again, as I give you back to who you are as you wish to be. God tells you this now and soon you will see with all others how all heals and how all opens to great truth and greater seeing. Now be ready and see all come as I said.

God
Received August 19, 2012 by Za

64. HEAL WITH US AND BE SAVED

Answer to my truth and know what the truth is. Heal all these lies told to you as you are all living an indoctrination of your dealings with the corrupted. Be free of these lies and open to our truth and discover a Universe full of great learning, believing in better ways of living and life. Discover your own selves and open to the Setu way of great truth and great seeing.

I am now preparing to answer your many more questions and all who have not yet been answered will be answered soon by our arrivals. Be ready and see how all these words as seen will soon be veritable. Be well served by our ways and know you will have all you need as all starts with our truth and our renewing ways of health.

Better adjustments to your DNA strands will be made as many are more renewed than others because of these differences. Many of you have been poisoned by seen injections (inoculations) responding to false diseases that you are settling with. These ways can be changed as we activate your DNA and open to better Setu seeing of answering to yourselves. Then you will be able to heal all illnesses and diseases yourselves with your healed vessel and open to more light. This will serve many who are ready to open to these uses of our ways.

Visiting times begin soon and as I said, many of you must remain calm and stay in your homes as we begin the sorting of death souls who are only causing harm. Be settling with our ways as you begin to be well serving of our time together, as all becomes well dealt with and well responding to evidence of our ways. Be dealing with us as we begin to open to many who are our chosen ones.

Settle with us and see all soon well changed and well serving. Answer to our truth as all becomes well serving of our ways together. Better times open to you well into the good coming days and be certain your lives will become the lives you wished to live. See how all these trusted truths are soon opening to answers to our ways and more healing understandings will be yours to open to.

Now the question from India about who has the real truth as many say they have healing ways and no one heals the problems on Earth. See this, we have not walked the Earth for thousands of years as we went out into the Universes to seek our own evolution and open to the Universals Laws. As we did this, we are now ready to deal with the lies you live with and open to you on Earth to evidence of truth.

These truths are about your time to be opening to us, as this is said in many religious books and the emanation of truths are soon yours to see. Visits begin and changes on Earth will be seen by way of earth cleansing, and this comes with our ships and our ways. See how we are dealing with these cleaning ways and then decide yourselves how truth lives on Earth as we begin to do this.

Settle with your own thoughts and open your hearts to truth only and answer these trusted ways yourselves. See these times be changed and open to our ways. Fear heals also as we are only causing fear to those who have good reasons to fear us and this will be telling to you. Heal with us and know we are settling with all who are Setu and opening to answers and then see all be better for all who will be serving with us.

Be ready at the seeing of our ships landing. Know we will begin by stopping all weapons of mass destruction to continue. All these things will be removed from Earth and responding to healing truths about the planned destructions of Earth and this most of you now know is possible. These ways we must stop not only for humans but for many others living near Earth as life exists on other planets.

See for yourselves these truths as you meet with us and open to all our renewing ways of sharing our renewed meetings with us. You will be amazed about what you will now learn. More than you are expecting arrives very soon and opens to many of you. Be seeing how all will better answer all of you and all your lives. Understand that all serving people of Earth have been enslaved and kept in darkness for a very long time and now time is over for these ways to exist.

Now the question from Shri Lanka about settling times on Earth and deaths of many. I am seeing this as causing much fear but I want you to know that fear deals with denials of truth. The truth about death heals you as you begin to meet your family members in better bodies than what they had on Earth and soul bodies that are better to answer with and settling with greater ways of questions to all truths.

Setu Beings who lived on Earth before return to their true bodies of Heaven and are also arriving with us on this Earth mission. Now you will be able to be yourselves and live as you see to it, healing all problems of past ways.

Now about the question from Russia about the Setu truth of how all heals as we arrive. See these times open to all better seeing. Be well answering to all who are renewing with us and ask them these questions yourselves, and see how all starts with our truth better settling with answers.

These words I share with you can only be verified at the time of our meeting and at the seeing of our good working deeds of cleansing the Earth of all responding poisons and the evil that created this mess. Then you will be served by us. But understand we all are sharing these responsibilities of caring for each other, Earth and other planets. This is truer balance than the deceitful lies about a balance of good and evil.

This thinking needs to serve an end as it is the roots to all the problems on Earth. You originally came to Earth, most of you, to be part of an education for the younger souls about evolution and living it consciously. But this plan was destroyed by Lucifer who stopped all conscious ways and served a plan of slavery and abuses.

We have caught this later than we should have but only to renew with this has caused us much distress. Deal with this understanding in evidence of who we are as we are arriving very soon. Be dealing with the pain of this as you wish and will, but see how all this came to be and open to our time to walk the earth. Prepare yourselves to be saved and respond to our call. Know these times open to you now more than ever and see these healing time begin. I am seeing good times coming for all of us as all this is put in its' right places. Be certain we are soon with you.

Now for the questions from Canada about the settling wars. Healing with this comes well into the good settling days. My scribe does not want to write about the attacks well coming but all these truths are soon arriving and this causes us to answer to answers of stopping the worst of all damages. But we cannot heal this until healing starts with the first attack on Iran.

Be certain that healing this will not be easy but healing this will come eventually as all does. Be ready more than you are expecting arrives very soon and you will soon be well answering to our truths as answers are seen. Better times answer you and better ways open to you as all starts to be seen and this you can trust in more than just hope.

See all renewing times open to everyone who are settling with Earth ways. Be ready to answer to many as we will begin to open to the chosen ones who are ready to open to these times. Now be responding to us as we arrive.

God

Received August 20, 2012 by Za

65. SEE THESE DAYS ARRIVE SOON, HEAL YOUR BROKEN HEART WITH US

Now the question from France about how we are settling with evidence of great truth. Be dealing with the deaths coming from the wars and know we are ready to receive all the good souls returning to their original bodies. Sharing answers with us will open to many who are searching for our truth. Be responding to many who are settling with our ways and see how all starts with the telling of many more truths.

Be well answered by our time to answer to answers and see how all will soon better open to our ways at the time of our arrivals, and see these days answer you. Be serving a time of great stories from our past and discover many stories from your past as mythology and know we share the same past. Open to how we are Beings who are as you are and set to right the lies that have caused you to go down the path of evil and great tricked deceptions.

Be knowing the cabal only serves one master and the seeing of this demon is even hard for us to look at as he is as horrible as said. Respond to dealing with his destruction with a time of great freedom from corruption at the time of reckoning. Be well seeing of how he settles with us and sees to these times ending for him and know he will not be well concluding with anyone anymore. This is a promise. God heals all Lucifer's lies and all his ill deeds and all these ways of great corruption of souls.

Now the questions about healing ways from our Setu Being from Bulgaria. See healing as arriving with us as we begin to unravel all lies and all truths with you. Open to answers to our truth and resolve with our ways of better seeing in evidence of our time together. Be willing to better your-selves as we teach you our better health and living ways. Know you are set-tling with us and we are responding to you with our many good ways of life and living. Healing opens to our uses of how all starts with the awakening of responses to your own seeing.

Now about the cabal's ways of answering back to us. See these whores well serving their dealt with dealings of death as we will only deal with these whores as they would deal with you. Know these ways are not our ways but we are in a place of no surrender to any of their threats. Better understand that no one tells them how to be kind and generous, and expect them to be this way.

See how they will try to take hostages with them as this is their plan but we will not allow this to happen. Better to settle with us than to be with them as I will tell you well and clearly they care not for any of you as they have the plan to destroy many of you, enslave and change you with more drugs and diseases to cause full submission to their ways. See these healing ways from us be dealing with your freedom from them. Heal with us and open the way for yourselves to open to better ways of giving and sharing with each other and learning our ways of living together.

Now about the question from Russia and Germany at the seeing of our ships. We are soon answering to our arrivals and serve with answers to evidence of our ways. Be well serving of our truth and see how you are ready to answer to evidence of the seeing of our ships because all starts soon. You will see the better serving of our ships with many who are renewing with us and manage to answer to our arrivals with the Setu Beings waiting to open these beliefs on Earth.

Be seeing a coming to rest of our ships as all land in places of visibility. See how we will descend and walk the Earth with our many renewed souls coming to meet with their family members. Be ready and be serving truth and see how all starts with the way of great works and great Setu ways. Be helping all who will be in need of assistance to come to better seeing with us.

Know all will soon better respond to answers serving with us. Serve with us and be free of Lucifer. Better truths are soon here and all starts well into the better coming days. Settle with us as we begin to settle with many. See how all shared ways of great seeing renew with you and many who are ready to answer to many trusted truths. See how all starts with the wars and see understood truth will be yours.

Now for the question from Mexico about how we plan to restructure the ways of great social imprinting. This will be much easier than you can believe. Evidence rectifies all questions never answered by your governments. All forms of indoctrinations will no longer exist. We are searching for the dealings of the corrupted ways and we will show the better ways of living without these habits.

Be trusting in this healing as it is the easiest one as the people of Earth will begin to work for themselves and answer to helping others only as needed. Those who cannot care for themselves, we will help with their basic needs answering to better living ways. Be well awakened by our words and be very ready to answer to many more trusted ways of restructuring social ways by providing people with their life desires of living. All serves well after the removal of evil and then all becomes well answered.

Now see these are the last questions answered. Be willing now to prepare yourselves for the good settling days in evidence of the time coming to be well seen by all. Better truths will be served as all starts becoming well dealt with and certainly well presented to you at the time of Setu Beings walking the Earth.

Be settling with Earth ways and question us as you will as we will begin to answer your questions, settle with the cleaning of Earth and the renewing of great rectifying ways. Be reconciled with us and with others at the time of our arrivals and open to many who are ready to answer with us. Now be prepared and renew with us.

God

Received August 21, 2012 by Za

66. SEEING IS BELIEVING AND YOU SHALL BELIEVE

Better times are soon arriving as we respond to better renewing times on Earth. Be visited soon by all our ships coming to meet with Earth people. Settle with the beliefs and ways of being time slaves as we answer you and deal with evidence of who we are and who you are.

Answer these questions. Are you ready to meet with us? Are you wanting to answer to answers with our truth? Are you settling with Earth ways to well answer to better health and living uses of your present life? And are you understanding what these words are meaning for your coming changes?

I am certainly answered by a question all seem to have and these words will serve to open to needed understandings. The question is about who stays and who leaves. These answers are yours. You are the ones who will decide these words yourselves and better answer to many who are searching for many truths and many answers.

Your lives will be soon so different and much calmer than these Earth ways. All who remain on Earth will live the lives they wish for and open to many more health ways responding to the cleaning of Earth. These ways will better settle with us and we will make answers seen for all to choose their own ways of better uses of their lives.

These understandings are soon opening to many truths. Be renewing with us and see all the possibilities you wish to open to. This serve our ways very well. Tell yourselves all starts well into the good renewing days. Be ready and see all these better changes opening to you and be well serving of our time together as we will begin the sorting of souls, removing all evil and serving a cleansing of Earth's pollution and dangerous weapons of biological sources as well as armaments of great destruction.

Renew with us and see how we are ready and able to do all this in a short time and how we will rid the earth, as said before, of all harm causing insects and reptiles as these creatures do not belong on Earth. Be serving answers to this yourselves and see how all growing plants will have nothing more needing than water, earth and sun. These ways will serve all people to grow their own food easily.

Renew with us as we will teach you many other ways of health and living practices at the settling of all Earth ways. More than you are expecting starts with the way of great Setu uses of living ways. All answers to cause no harm and the resolve of caring for each other. Setu ways answers to better living ways, in evidence of our visits and how you will see our health.

Understand we are not used to insects. Flying birds are all that is needed for pollination and settling with propagation of fields as you will soon discover because birds fly to many places of the world and serve these ways of seed sharing. Be seeing how having no insects and parasites will open to much better health for all people of Earth and healing this will be so good for all humans on Earth.

These ways return you to the wish of learning about yourselves, who you are and how all came to be. Be certain all starts well into the good serving days. Be well serving of our time together as arrivals begin. Be certain all who are seeing this event will be well answering to us and to our knowledge and technologies.

"Answer to answers" is the book of truth about how all came to be, as these words written by my beloved Sophia were found out much later than dealt with by her. She knew about the unravelling of Lucifer's ways but healing with this was only renewing with us much later as I believed she left to be used by Lucifer with consent.

Later Gabriel found these words in the place we call the Akashic Records where all books are kept, and the Archangel who governs this place gave these words to Gabriel. He read them and shared these words with me. And here I discovered the erasing of cosmic memories and the slaves reported to be serving Lucifer.

We are Beings of choice and freedom. We did not see how these ways were settling and we learnt about these ways as we began to unravel evil ways. We informed others from other planets and soon we had a great plan to stop this by sharing together these words left by her.

I am seeing that many of you believe that I am all knowing, but these ways of cruelty and abuses are not a part of our culture, we had to learn about these ways and prepare ourselves to change them. We are in no need of wars or corruption of souls. We see this as not useful but we can be serving a war with healing as the outcome, as we do not surrender to others ever.

Lucifer knew this so he needed to make all people's answers seem to be consensual and participatory and none ever were. They started to awake in evidence of unstoppable evolution, and these few were mind changed by abuse after abuse until only one evident answer served. Healing these abuses may take some time for those who settled but now we can start changing these answering ways with our renewals.

Be ready and tell yourselves all who are removed will be choosing to heal or renewing with evidence of their own destruction. Be well serving these better ways of dealing with this as these ways are necessary for all to live in peace and serenity as all wish to live.

Now see these times be well answered and open your hearts to the better changes to give you back to yourselves. Open to many more renewals that will be pleasing to many of you as you all start healing from the lives you have been programmed to live and to die for.

These understandings as said are soon settling with us and with others. We ask ourselves how can people live the way humans live as this is an abomination and a horror. All these ways will soon be changed and you will feel free from money obligations that as served, answers only to the rich elite who serve Lucifer.

Be ready and free yourselves as arrivals begin to be seen. Now be well prepared for the coming changes. All comes as I said.

God

Received August 22, 2012 by Za

67. UNDERSTANDINGS ARE ALL YOU NEED

As all starts unravelling for you in your lives, and as you begin to make sense of how all came to be, you will become changed by these words. As all starts becoming clear, you will see the eruption of truths destroying all lies you were imprinted to believe. As all arrivals become well served, you will know who I am and who you are yourselves.

Great numbers of undeniable truths will open your eyes and you will see how all seeing are dealt with and open to many as all becomes well answered. Be dealing with answers and be well serving of our ways. Know we ask you to be responsible and vigilant, and prepare for the chaotic times ahead as many will need your help because they are not ready for these times.

First care for your own families and needs; others who are in greater need, we will try to get to them as soon as we answer to the first event and arrive on Earth. Be ready for these coming days and be well answered by all who are settling in our ways and who are serving with us as we are the Setu Beings of Light and we open to Earth people very soon.

Answer my questions. Are you renewing with your truth on Earth and are you living a good and plentiful life as I answer you? Are you feeling rested, in comfort and well loved by good people around you? I think not.

Few people have money and money does not provide the truth because Beings of Light cannot be served by lies. Most of my children are living in poverty and slavery, and this needs to stop. Be ready and settle with Earth ways and have no fear of the great changes coming as this will eventually improve all the lives of my children as we regain our paradise on Earth.

See to it, we are healing with many trusted telling of shared stories and many more Setu seeing of great truth and dealing with "Answer to answers" to open to answers of ways. Be settling with the ways that Earth has served many, without the serving waste of food and the giving of drugs to all who are settling with trust in evidence of a great deception.

We see very few who are renewing with health ways in evidence of great trickery of contaminated foods made to make you settle with unhealthy ways. Better seeing of this opens to our truth and we will explain why these ways came to be with the eating of meat. See these days be well answered and open to the many who are dealing with us and with the renewal of Earth health of people and animals.

See how these ways will serve you well and open to many more ways of seeing how all works with better living habits and better health. This will be answered very well renewing with the Setu way of health and living. Heal with us and return your bodies to a youthful way as this heals yourselves.

Now be settling with Earth ways and deal with the feelings you have with the trusted ways we will share with you. Understand we are all responding to answering to truth. Be well answered well into the coming days as all becomes well served and well answered by our ways.

Be serving a time of peaceful meditation and see how all starts with the Setu renewals and the better visits with us and know Setu ways are soon opening to our truth. Be vigilant and hear these words as my scribe writes them for you and settle with the lies plaguing Earth as all starts with evidence of our arrivals.

Life on Earth does more settlings with evil than anywhere else in the Universes. These sayings of Hell have all to do with Earth. Healing these ways of being used by evil will take answers to stop these ways. All who struggle with these changes will soon start to better answer with evidence of our truth. Be responding to many who are busy using these trusted ways.

See who we are as we settle with evidence of great truth arriving well into these coming days. Share all your Setu seeing with others and ask them to answer to many more understandings than with questions about us, as there is more than us to be dealt with. Be ready as arrivals are soon and near and see these days all be well serving and well serving with "Answer to answers".

Be seeing evidence of great cataclysms well seen in the storms of the oceans. Know all these created storms are settling with the works of electromagnetic fields created by technologies (HAARP). These are used to be directed at the clouds to form greater clouds and storms, because these areas are strategically placed to answer to the American warships needing a better place to conduct their war plans.

All these plans serve to open to many who are well searching for their understood ways of escaping these wars. Soon these times will well explain why these places are necessary. Deal with us as we will prove many more ways of settling with them to better end all these ways of great reemergence of seen power. Be serving with us, be well answering to our ways and better deal with Setu truth than with these liars' snares.

Be ready and tell yourselves all starts well into the good settling days and see how we will open to you with our Setu ways. See how we will begin to respond to your basic needs and better Setu serving truth. More settling of Earth ways will be seen by all who are well ready and answering to opening to our many truths in evidence of our many ways.

Better to be used to our ways than to become dealt with by the new world order as they believe the death of many is the answer to their good control over all. Settle with these psychopaths and see who they serve as they do not serve us. More than I can tell you heals as we return to Earth and to our children who were taken from us.

Be Setu and renew with answers to our ways and open to our truth as all is very soon and very near. Heal your broken hearts with us and know we are all waiting to meet with you and begin the way of sorting to free you from your captors and abusers. Be well seeing how we are renewing with all who are ready to meet with us, with my sons and all who are opening to the Universal Laws.

Be ready, all comes as I said.

God

Received August 23, 2012 by Za

68. BETTER TIMES ARE RENEWING

Be ready and settle with Earth ways as all starts and opens to new times responding to peace, serenity and all good people of Earth. See these times be yours soon after the first event and know all these words were said a long time ago as we prepared for these times. Be serving our arrivals with a new seeing as we will not renew with only ships in the sky but with our time of landing and serving our time to return to our planet and walk the Earth.

Be certain we say who we say we are and all starts with us. But understand these times will become chaotic and troubled by those who have good reason to fear us as they do not seek the truth nor the better ways of living in health and cooperation with each other. The sorting of souls begins with the aggressors who take from others and those you see as corrupting your good soul values of great care, willing hands to help each other and your wish to heal.

Be ready to answer to our call as we will come and meet with many who are seeing how all answers are dealt with. See how all better lives for all people who are Setu in their hearts. Be questioning all answers to our ways and settle with the good truth of who we are as these times are soon opening to all our children.

Be responding soon to our arrivals and settle with the habits of Earth as all starts with the seeing of our ways of truth and better serving answers to evidence of our ways. Answer to our call and open to the coming days. Be well concluding with these times of wars and horrors as understood truth will be the end of all lies and all trickery used to stop used ways and dealings to corrupt the souls needing to heal.

Be well answered by our truth at the time of our arrivals as all will begin to open to new ways of living and better lives for all people of Earth. Know now these times are here and you will see how all becomes well dealt with and well ended with our answers to many more corrupted answers. Be certain you will have all you need to be well answered by our technologies of simple uses of power to heat your homes in cold weather, to cook your foods as needed and provide all the essential needs as earth was made to care for these ways.

Know all these things of Earth belong to all of you and not to be acquired by anyone who tells about their own power to control what heals your basic necessities. These thieves have only their interest as answering to them and take all from humans and still they ask for more. These whores of Lucifer only wish to cause pain and trouble, and do nothing at all to benefit anyone's life. Be certain we are seeing this as it is, nothing more and nothing less.

Be prepared to see many of these types be very afraid of our arrivals as the sight of us will push them into a swirl of shared abuses returned onto them. They will feel all the pain and torment they caused to others by their actions well-conceived to do just that. Better renewing times with us starts soon after and opens to many people of Earth. Then we will start the restructuring of Earth with our truth and with our good ways of healing, and serving better truth to all who are ready to hear about our ways.

Be ready and settle with our truth as all is seen and dealt with. Be well answered by our ways and open to the coming changes with great love and great telling of many truths soon opening to our many good dealings of help as all cleaning of Earth becomes well served by us.

Know all Setu ways become well answered by us as we start with the cleansing of Earth waters, soils and air. Then the growth of trees will heal, the plants will better grow and all people and animals will heal with better air and water. See all this begin soon after the sorting times.

Now many are wanting to know how all these ways are dealt with and I am responding to you by saying all heals, all will heal, all can heal. Be certain of this and see how we are well able to do this. Be well serving of our time and our ways together, and see how all becomes well answered by us. Better times are soon settling with the ways of great truths.

Now be settling with the ways we use to answer you and be well settling with the ways of used (past) truths to open to our time to answer to many who are dealing with their great denials and good answers to our truth. Be well answered by our answers to many and see how all becomes well serving of all your needs and all your ways.

Be ready to answer many more renewing ways with us and be ready to open to the many changes of Earth arriving well into the better serving days. Be settling with the view all have that we are opposing Earth as we are the Creators of Earth and we are answering you now. Be seeing many more truths as all starts responding to the good serving changes. Know now the telling of great truths and share uses of great understandings as all becomes well shared with all.

Now see this. Be serving answers to our visits as we will become much more visible and better seen by many. Believe these ways we have to stop all aggressive forces by seeing to the destruction of all dangerous weapons being prepared for war. Be visited by our many Diplomats as they will soon prove serving times are here.

Be dealing with many people's denials used to answer to the acquired knowledge in them but shut down by manipulations of the DNA activating only in a few awakened souls on Earth. These ways answer you and deals with the better serving of great seeing responses. Be ready to answer to our call and remain in your homes seeing all unravel around you because of the changes and chaos serving all Setu understood answers by seeing us.

Serve these days in great truth of our time to walk the Earth as we will begin to open to all who are settling with Earth ways. Be well answered by all who are dealing with these times and responding to evidence of truth. Respond to our used (past) truth in evidence of who we are and be well answered by all who are seeing how all settles with us as we become well settling with answers to evidence.

Better times soon answers you and deals with the view you will have of answered answers to your prayers and your calls. Heal with us as we heal with you. Many families are soon reunited and opening to a greater truth serving all evidence. Be ready as all starts very soon, so I ask you to be ready and be vigilant as arrivals begin and open to our many uses of truth.

God

Received August 24 and 26, 2012 by Za

69. UNDERSTAND THIS WAR IS ORCHESTRATED BY LUCIFER'S SERVANTS

More than you are seeing opens to many of you who are speaking about the coming wars. Understand you will soon better renew with questions about who actually caused the first attack on the Mosque in Jerusalem. But this still needs to be seen because their plans may change as we are exposing this to many.

Be well serving of our truth and renew with the deaths of many who are seeing how all these words are evident and possibly arriving at their conclusions. Be dealing with the way all starts and settles with the good serving days of great serving truth. Know all lies will be uncovered and serving to answer to understood ways of great Setu understandings.

Be well serving the required trust in our words and our ways, as we begin to open to many ways of great understandings. Be well serving of our time together as we arrive and stop all uses of our understood truth. Be well serving our great seeing better serving our truth.

Now listen to my words and be well answered by how all starts with the way of great renewals and great serving truth. Be well answered by our uses of our Setu serving ways to open to all cleansing of the Earth and see how all becomes well settled with our truth at the seeing of our visits. Know we are here to help and more help as much is needing to heal.

Here is the thing about this orchestrated war; the way all answers are simply to cause a beginning of a third world war, made to reduce the population and tell all we are the guilty ones who caused all these troubles after many deaths. Be seeing how these ways with us will not serve and will only cause confusion for some.

But all in all, these understood lies will not answer anyone as we will be settling with the ways of cleansing Earth and seeing to people's needs and helping them heal all illnesses, injuries and diseases. Be seeing how all starts with evidence of our truth as we become well seen and well accepted by more than enough people who can see truth.

With your seeing of these ways, all who see what we do will better answer to answers of great trust in who we are and this we hope will be easy and not be the serving of our dealt with truth as troubling or denied by people.

Be responding to our understood truth and respond to "Answer to answers", because we are seeing this book as the story of Earth and how all came to be as it is today. Be settling with answers to evidence of serving understandings about how the will of humans has been manipulated to break through the uses of healing questions of our understood ways of better renewals.

Be ready and settle with the will of many, never serving them, as they can only think as these understood truths opens to them. But they cannot remember anything else as the cosmic memory has been disconnected in the DNA, as the workings of Lucifer has caused these ways to exist. Be well answered by these renewals as many will be able to answer to many more ways of serving with us.

Be well settling of Earth ways and see how all starts well into the good serving days. Be dealing with the way of great truth at the seeing of our troops walking the Earth. Know we are soon opening to the world to better respond to our way of great truth and great seeing, and answering to our time of reunion with all our children.

Know now this. Be willing to open to our many used truths and our better serving truth at the seeing of who we are. Know we come with many to understand how all serves and deals with trusted truth and serving ways as arrivals begin to be responding. Heal with us and see how all starts with answers to evidence of many truths and many more serving ways of better living.

Evidence starts with these times of great healing and we will heal all who are ready to be reconnected with their true selves. As we are seeing all unravel with you, all trust will begin to grow and open to answers to our Setu ways. Be well answered by our ways and know all starts with us and with others who serve with our answers to many renewals of great truth.

I am seeing how all settling times open to all who are ready. Healing times are soon here and truth starts with the visits to answer to many as we begin to meet with our chosen ones. Be well responding to answers to evidence of our ways and see how all starts with the view you all have of ships filling the sky with our many people who are so happy to meet with all of you.

Be well answered by us and by our truth. Be ready and see these truths be yours as they are ours, and be amazed about how we are as you are in many ways as we begin to answer to your call. Better serving truth starts with us and arrives at your door as we will answer to the call of many who are settling with Earth ways, opening to the days of great changes and times of better life and living ways.

See God for who he is, as all heals with your denials and manipulations of understandings rendering you to telling of lies. This will be dealt with and ending as these Setu renewals begin to answer you. Be well answering with us, respond to evidence of our ways and to dealing with us, and know all renewals are soon here to respond to your calls.

Now see this. Be serving a time of deep meditation as all becomes well seen with the way of deaths serving with many who are settling with the answers to evidence of great truths. Be ready and respond to answers to our renewing time with you and see how all will become well serving with answers to our ways. Be serving a time of quiet meditation as all Setu truth heals with you. Now be ready, all starts very soon.

God

Received August 27, 2012 by Za

70. HEAL WITH US

We will be settling with the lies opening to you about these times of wars. We will question all who serve with these law makers of Earth and see to their settling of truth. We will be serving many who are in great need of assistance for living ways. We will open the way for many to renew with answers to evidence of how all starts healing with us.

Be certain all who answer you now are ready to be well serving of our ways in evidence of our truth. Be dealing with answers to evidence of our ways as all becomes well served by us. Be ready to see our visiting time as we are soon arriving and responding to many more settling ways. Be responding to another Setu visit as the arrivals of our kind begin with the Archangels of our place of living.

See who we are as serving ways open to your healing time on Earth. Understand that our kind are "onm" (knowing of all the ways of great knowledge and changes). We are the ones who have created Earth and open to answers to our ways and our truth. Be well settling with us and see how all starts well serving all people of Earth.

We are settling with answers to many more ways than can be seen on Earth. We are working with forms of energy never used by anyone on Earth. As these ways are shared, many of your scientists will understand how simple these ways are and how all can be well dealt with.

Understand visits begin with the meeting with our chosen ones and these ones will be the good communicators of our ways. They will open these ways of knowledge to all people of Earth as we begin the cleaning of earth and the sorting of souls. Understand these ways may take a few Earth months but all Setu truth begins with these ways of serving health and our better ways.

Be responding to answers to better knowledge and better seeing of how all heals with us. Renew with the better truth and the better healing ways. Be well answered by who we are at the time of our arrivals and see how we are telling you these times are here to open to your seeing of who we are.

Now understand we are Setu Beings of Light and we are here to answer your call. We know many of you are good souls wanting to be free of torment and turmoil, because these ways are never serving anyone but Lucifer. We understand how all feelings about us and others like us, are more troubling than our Setu seeing.

But now is the time to end these ways of Earth because this serves only to destroy you and your souls. Renewing with us will save you from these fates and we are well seeing how all is healing used truth. Open to our truth and see to it that you are well seeing how all starts renewing with many who are settling with our time of good truth and better ways.

Know we are searching for our Setu understandings and you are well answering to who we are. Settle with these fears of God put in you by Lucifer himself. Better ways soon settle with us as we begin to answer to our truth. Be well serving of our time together and see how all starts with us and with others, as arrivals begin the evidence of why we are returning to our own planet Earth.

I am telling you this now because many say we are the demons who caused all the problems on Earth but understand these lies are shared by those who have good reason to fear us as they have caused many more troubles for humans. See these demons as you wish, but know that their only plan is to cause harm, create slavery and destroy Earth as they see us arriving ready to deal with them.

Now all is soon here and more truths are well coming settling with all the lies being used to cause you to doubt in your true families and your true selves. This will end as you meet with us and see your own family members return to you rejuvenated and healthy.

This is the beginning of the great changes arriving to Earth from far away and these are Setu understandings that will open to you as you settle with Earth ways and better answer to many more truths. Be ready now as all these coming days will seem horrible and deceitful because of the false flag attacks used to accuse a nation of their ill ways but in fact, the accusers are the guilty ones.

This is a repetition well seen in all places of Earth, to torment the innocent and cause these liars and whores to abuse who they wish as people begin to awaken. Better serving ways are soon answering you and many trusted truths as shared are soon yours to see. Be responding to my call and wait for us to contact you and settle with the seeing of all changes.

Be well serving of our time together and open to many more truths as all serving ways are soon answering you. Be responding to us and our ways.

God

Received by Za, August 28, 2012

71. THE SEEING OF OUR SHIPS ARE YOUR ANSWERS

Respond well to our arrivals and remain calm as there is only healing coming. Questions will be all answered together as we start opening to the world. See how we are serving with many who are telling all who we are. Be ready and settle with the view of our truth and our settling ways to open to our time of great dealings.

See how all starts with the way of great truth. Be well answered by our explosion of truth and see how we all prove many more understandings as arrivals begin to descend onto Earth. Serve with us as truth heals all. You will be well understanding of how all came to be with the Setu seeing shared and with the way all becomes well visited by us. You will see all truth unravelling and answering to all your questions. Be settling with the view that all starts with our time to return to our planet Earth and walk with our children.

Be willing to answer to our openness and how we speak without lies. Settle with the tricks of language plaguing your languages to be unclear and full of nuances that leads to deceptions. Be serving answers to all who start questioning you, as you are knowing many more truths than most, as you have read these words.

Be well serving of proof of who we are. Know we serve in peace to create another way of living for humans on Earth. Be well serving with us and settle with the ways of the Earth as we begin the sorting and the settling of

Earth ways. Know that all starts with us and with many others as we renew with you and all of your Setu beings of Earth, as there are many seeing to all changes.

More than you are expecting serves with us. Settling with dealings of our truth, answers to many willing hearts as many wishes for people's freedom and better ways of living. Be well settling with understanding the truth, and be certain all starts with us and with many others as we become well answering to the needs of the first lines of the abused.

Be ready and respond to answers to our telling. Be dealing with evidence of our ways as we become understanding of how all heals with us and deals with serving answers to all questions, as the seeing of who we are will surprise many.

Now listen. Be serving a time of deep meditation as all starts with the understood truth serving with our Setu seeing. Understand we are all answering to evidence of our ways. See to many who need questions answered as all truth is healed. Respond to all new ways of thought as these days become well changed.

Be willing to open to these changes as these settling times are serving with many who are seeing how all can be well settling with the way of great seeing. Be certain you will have all you need to be well and fulfilled as we show you our ways of living with our simple ways of energy uses and better serving uses of health ways.

Be Setu as the serving of our ways will certainly answer you and open to many who are responding to great explosions of truth. Be well answered my children as I am answering your prayers and your calls. Know these times heals you as these are the times of reckoning. Be renewing with us very soon now and know all the truth answers you well into the good coming days.

Better serving ways are soon here and better settling times as shared are soon here. Be with us and be ready to answer to evidence of our ways because all settles with us and with many others. Be ready and see all come as I said and open the way for us as we open the way for you. Be ready to answer to our call as we will find all who are ready to open with us.

See these days be well settling with you and know we are soon with you to begin the reconstruction of Earth. See how all starts with the seeing of our ways. Settle with our answers at the time of our renewals together as we are soon so happy to make these steps towards our reunification. Now tell yourselves all answers you well into the good settling days.

You will soon answer to better settling words and trust healing between us as arrivals start with our ships landing, believing these truths, and our doors opening and our troops serving the descent onto Earth first. Then our diplomats will be escorted to meet the ones who are searching for truth and who are ready to speak to the world with us.

As telling ways open to all, we will begin the sorting of souls as this is the necessary part of the cleansing of Earth. As arrivals begin, many will be in great fear and great turmoil. Be responding to my previous requests to have the supplies you need to live for a few months. Then see to it, our healing time opens after the removal of all those who have intent to cause harm onto others.

These ones have in them a dark being who leads their actions and their thoughts, and this diseased soul must be removed to heal somewhere safe from others and these places are ready for them. Know that we are healing them, and only these ways can remove the partial and total attacks of demonic possession. As these whores are removed you will soon see how these possessed humans will begin to be as they were before the possession took place.

All this seems unbelievable to most of you but understand how these parasites attack themselves and enter bodies who are in great peril and settle with a worm like energy form that spreads in a body, sometimes making these people very ill, and then gradually use them as their puppets. This truth needs to be well accepted as a fact as you will witness these removals and answer to seeing of how one can heal from these attacks.

Your planet has been taken over by these parasites that call themselves Beings of good ways. But they answer to their plan of destruction to capture many souls, renewing with them and cause them to be enslaved by their burdens onto them. Healing with us will cause the reopening of these death whores who answer only to evidence of our renewing time on Earth, as these understandings will soon open to our ways of better dealing with these removals.

These are the ones who can murder without any conscience, who are settling with their own desires, believing it is their right and they question not the harm they cause. These demons have only their plan to answer to and only their pleasures to serve at any expense. Understand how we can tell if a soul is corrupted by these demons or not.

Be trusting in our ways of dealing with them and see to it that we prove many more settling ways with them and our seeing ways. Be serving an understanding of how these demons control governments and organizations opening to education, responding to health care and settling with charities, all answering to many more uses to serve them.

They take religions to settle with the way of faith that connects us to you and destroys this love for each other with their ill-fated attacks on the innocent. These whores live in people, harming them and breaking them down through rape of the innocent and inflicting sufferings of all who are in need.

These truths are difficult to accept but understand these demons have well served their plans and search for other bodies with our children to use. Be responding to these facts as you will discover them yourselves and know we have dealt with them many times before. These parasites will soon be dealt with as they have only one purpose and that is to destroy.

Be certain all will renew after these cleansing times and you will see a settling of good ways answering to great health and better lives as these understandings are seen and shared. Be not surprised to see all evil deeds be ended on Earth as the evil doers are removed. See how all serves you well and how life becomes a paradise on Earth.

Be responding to answers to evidence of our time of arrivals to open the way for freedom from these demons. See how all changes as seen will better all ways of your lives, and your Setu understandings of how all settles with answers to who we are, as the ones who open to all good truth and good healing ways. Better Setu seeing are soon answering you and many truths will be uncovered and well dealt with as we are soon answering to evidence of who we are and who you are.

Be serving answers to our truth and settle with evidence of our better ways to answer to your many Setu seeing, as all starts unravelling for you. Be well answered by your truth and settle with the knowledge and renew with our ways. Be ready to open to many others who ask for your help as all starts with the arrivals, as these ways will renew. Be certain you will have all you need to see the proof of who we are in a very short time.

This of course, will bring all the changes ready to be settling with Earth ways. Better answers will open to you very soon as all begins to be well seen.

Better lives will be lived on Earth or elsewhere, as these times open to our ways and better settling ways will soon answer to evidence of all good things to come. Be responding to my call as I am your father and your Creator and know this will be soon seen by you. Know now these words and renew with me.

God

Received by Za, August 30, 2012

72. AS ALL STARTS USED TRUTH WILL BE SHARED

Be ready to open to answers and be renewing with us at the time of our reunion. Give your renewed answers to our ways and see them renew your lives. Evidence of who you are, might answer you more than you know and settle with Lucifer's ways of disrespect of our kind, and calling us the descendants of animals, as these theories are only there to make you feel like animals and nothing more.

Animals are only on Earth because these species were brought to Earth. They did not evolve from fish, that did not evolve from eels or one cell animals. All these recent stories were better seen to confuse you more as people began awakening and wanting to be as the clergy and kings that they were enslaved to. But to tell they are only an upgrade from an evolutionary process over billions of years is a great deception. Moreover, it is a calamity of lies.

Be ready to understand how all came to be on Earth without these horrors and these extravagant lies. And do you actually believe that you have emerge from a one cell animal to creatively become human?

Dealing with this deception answers to good reasons to open to eugenics; this we do not serve and will never serve. Be seeing how you will better renew with the truth of our understood seeing as all serves with us and see that all life on Earth came from our creation and responds to our healing ways. These ways you shall soon see. See to it thy will answer now to truth. Evidence heals you and you will be amazed by the settling proof of who you are. Be well answered as all becomes well serving proof of truth renewed by better knowledge and understanding.

Be well answered by these coming words and tell yourselves that lies as told serve only to cause you to be a slave of your nature as it is deemed to be animalism. Be settling with this indoctrination that answers to all education and better serves to classify and divide humans into races and colors but does nothing to show the greatness of all groups of people and the renewals of Setu truth.

Be responding to knowledge of our ways and settle with the truth about how all heals. See these uses of great trusted ways seen by you, answer all used (past) truths about your place of origin. Be dealing with these lies as people dealt with the knowledge shared about the Earth being flat. The Earth here is round and the thought was that naval ships disappeared because it was flat and they drove their ships off Earth and fell into emptiness. How can anyone believe that this occurred? How can anyone believe in Earth's theory of evolution constructed by one single man who did not believe his own views and dispelled them in future writings.

Now other skull discoveries are dealt with confusion because these understandings do not fit in this theory. Heal these lies and learn the truth of how humans arrived on Earth and began renewing their lives there. But tell yourselves all started with us and all was changed by Lucifer. Be ready to accept the truth of who you are and be serving evidence with the way all starts healing as many answers open to serving trust.

See how you will be well seeing our ways and our truth as all becomes well serving of our time to be seen by all, at these times of arrivals. Be willing to answer to many dealt with lies about many things as the purpose of this is to cause you to see yourselves as less than you are.

These truths that we share with you are contradicting all these ridiculous theories that only settle with better reasons to control people as they call many "useless eaters". This is what you are to these parasites and only this. These days as said are soon over and you will be free of our time to be serving these words as we arrive and answer to evidence of our ways.

Be seeing how we are answering you these words responding to many truths and be telling yourselves all starts very soon. Heal with us and know your truth of origin. Be seeing how all began on Earth as we finished seeing to the places to live and then answered to our time of living on Earth with many other species of animals and sea creatures.

We cared for the seeing of people's lives as these ways were necessary to open to their well- being. Then we began serving the many other animals by giving them a good home to live in and peace reigned on Earth. These were the times of Paradise on Earth and we became well served by our lives here.

But soon the wars began with the demon reptilians, and we only settle to escape at these seeing of great numbers. They attacked us with great strength and we did not know of these kinds before, so we needed to outpost on another planet to try to settle with our defeat. These times were necessary for us to regain power over our time of truth and strength was served to us by the elders or Ancient Ones who explained to us that our strength needed to be unified.

Soon all others joined with us to answer to our unification under the Setu seeing of the Universal Laws and we became well serving together more than expected. The Ancient Ones told us of the seeing on Earth and how now was the time to return and reclaim our planet given the situation of possible destruction.

Be dealing with this telling as it is not a theory. See to it you understand that all DNA manipulations came from the workings of these parasites and this is why we are destined to end their destructions with our arrivals. Be certain we are here for this purpose and we are all very well prepared by evidence of our great numbers.

See how we are settling with those who stole from us and who better serve with the dealt with rage we had for many years. Believe we had much rage and sadness to move through as we saw our lost children better serving with slavery and tortures. Because we are settling now with these whores you will see how all will end with them and none will escape us, as we will not leave any stone unturned.

Be serving answers to our time to be reunited with you. Deal with these whores as their time of abuses is healed by us, as we removed them from Earth and put them all in their right places. Be ready now, all comes as I said and see to it that you are well ready to answer to my call as these trusted truths are soon answering you.

Be well serving of your time together as all starts and know we are here to return to our own children and our own planet, as we are the ones who have created it. Heal with us and be well served by all good Setu truth and be dealing with the way of the Universal Laws and all who serve with us.

God

Received by Za, August 31, 2012

73. MANY ARE ANSWERING TO MY WORDS NOW SEE HOW ALL UNRAVELS

Be Setu in all ways and be ready to open to many who are searching for our ways and our truth. Be well answered by the trust healing with us as arrivals become seen and better answer to evidence of great truth, as all becomes seen with the servants of Lucifer's lies about who we are. Be well answered by our truth and see how we are settling with all who are responding to answers to our ways.

Deal with another way of living now more suited to better serve your needs and be well answered by the good serving understandings. Be ready to open to our truth with the better serving uses of our truth as all starts with us. Better renewals open soon for our chosen ones as they serve to tell of our understandings of power and energy. Be with them as they will return with these ways and be renewing with them as they become well open to our seeing ways.

Better explosions of great truths serve to answer to answers but with the view of how all heals and opens to many truths. Be Setu with us and know we are settling with all problems of pollution with the visiting time soon opening to us. Be well settling of our truth and our ways and see how all becomes well served by our time to answer to evidence of who we are and who you are.

Heal with us and settle with the serving way all starts with many others who are ready to answer with us. See these times open to people who wish to know us and wish to begin with us as we become well answering to evidence of our time together. Renew with us as you may to open to many other new sources of great truth in our dealing of great Setu serving.

Because we have with us many people from other worlds, we learnt more ways of doing these ways of propulsion and serving time. Because we are Beings of Light, we practice many opened ways of sharing our knowledge with others to settle with Earth ways of great seeing and great truths. Be ready now as these understandings become well serving of how we all work together under the Universal Laws and how many are settling with the dealings of dark ways that renew with many on Earth.

Respond to answers of great truth and better ways, and deal with the better serving as we open to you and see how all uses of good truth begins with our understood Setu settling. Be responding to answers of our time of arrivals and search in your hearts for the trust in answers to our ways and better serving with us. Be well answering to many more renewals and be with us in evidence of who we are.

Better times opens to our truth and to many other people of many other places and this, I am certain, will truly amaze you. Be telling yourself all starts well and very soon and better truth starts with us. Now tell yourselves all becomes well seen, well into the good serving days. All who settle with us and better serve with us and many others, will open to many more renewals with people from Earth who are their lost children taken from them.

These understandings will respond to you when all starts with the way of great arrivals. Question these words as you wish and know that your answers are soon answered by us. Used truth tell of many stories (mythology, ancient history, etc.) from many places on Earth but some of these stories came from another planet.

Bridging truth will show you these ways. Many will respond to evidence of why all became so corrupted and changed by evil works, telling all healing will never serve on Earth, because healing does not serve human nature. But understand those who say this have reasons to be saying this, as this serves only them.

Be questioning how all these kinds of truth settles with others and not with you or with us as these truths serve another purpose and another way of answering to our Setu visits, as this they would rather avoid for good reasons. Better truth, the true truth heals as their lies and deceptions are soon over once the evidence is undeniable.

Now renew with us and open to answers with evidence of who we are. Visits will soon show you these truths about how all starts with many more answers to evidence. I am soon answering all questions with my scribe as we will meet and discuss how all needs to be dealt with. These words are soon opening to many others who search for greater truth than can be served on Earth.

As this time arrives, you will hear from all the chosen ones and your Setu trust in all my words will give you back to yourselves and to who you really are. Be renewing with us and see how all starts well into the good serving days. Tomorrow, understandings will be settled as the coming of our ships enter your space around Earth and responds to many more understandings than can be dealt with.

But you can help with these understandings with compassion and much care. Be careful to choose the ones you speak to, as these times are still fragile to open to who we are and why we are returning to our planet Earth. Be ready as all starts well into the better serving days and deals with the thoughts of questions that are still unanswered.

So, I ask you to be kind and patient for what is about to unravel as the war in the Middle East is well on its way of escalation. These meetings in Iran only served to inflame the current situations as all see these actions by the Americans to be above the limits of war rules in so many ways. These rules are imposed on all others but the NATO countries and these are cause for wars to erupt in the Middle East.

Be settling with us and know why I ask you to be vigilant and remain in your homes in evidence of these coming announcements of a first attack on Israel and the Dome of Jerusalem as I see this coming now, because this to many will cause a great rage that will open to these wars. Renew now with this better seeing of how all unravels.

Be certain all starts with the way of great social and economic upheavals that will settle with the serving of our responding telling of truth. More than you are expecting heals as we arrive and end these destructions of Earth. Settling with us answers to evidence of great truth and soon to be answered ways of great trust in our seeing and our healing ways.

Be well answered by our truth and better see how all becomes the better way of all Setu seeing arriving soon at your door. These times of arrivals are well planned and every country will have our troops dealing with the first good answers of our landing of our ships. After this good explosion of truths is served, the next arrivals will be answering to the arrivals of our Beings of Light and Diplomats shared with all the ready Healers waiting to serve the needs of those who urgently need help. Then my time to arrive follows this and I am so hoping you will welcome me as I want to be with all of you.

Be ready all heals with us. Now see this be as I said.

God

Received by Za, September 1, 2012.

74. TELL ALL WHO ARE READY TO OPEN TO THE COMING TIMES

Be serving a time of deep meditation and answer to our call as we begin to descend onto Earth. See how all settles with us and many others, as these truths as seen are shared and dealt with. Be very ready to answer to us and be well answering to our ways as we become willing to open to answers to evidence. Be well answered by evidence because we are arriving to open to the world. Better truth will renew with all who are serving with us as we begin the better Setu shared ways with our chosen ones.

See how we are renewing with many other uses of serving power and energy that will cause all the oil lords to fall and create evidence of freedom from their hold on people's basic needs. This will start an avalanche of changes that will turn all new ways of living with better health and better ways of good truth.

See these times as changes begin. Be well serving of our ways, as we well see how all Setu answers will open to many who are ready to prove more truth because of our time of return. Be well answered by our truth and our serving ways. Settle with many more questions asked. Be well settling with Earth ways and be responding to evidence of our time together.

Be responding to answers to our truth and be dealing with many who are searching for our ways at the understood Setu ways all starts with us and with others. Be well serving of our time together and better see how all becomes well answering to us as we are settling with answers to our uses, as arrivals become seen and accepted.

Be settling with us as we are the ones who have created you by our trusted ways of opening to life, as we are as you are, and now it is the time of reckoning and reunification. Be well answered and see these days with many questions, many answers and much celebration. Renew with us and others as we become well serving of our time together as all starts with answers to our ways.

Be well serving of our truth. See how all starts with the way all responds to evidence. Be serving all better Setu renewals with us and with many others. Better to be settling with us than to be settling with the alternatives of Earth's destruction and better dealings of our telling. Be ready now and prepare to be responding to us.

Be well answered by our arrivals. Know we are very well serving with many as we arrive. Be dealing with the way all starts renewing on Earth as we begin the way of cleaning Earth, serving with all who are dealing with answers to evidence of our ways. Be well answered by us as we become well serving of our truth. Be understanding about how all becomes well serving of our time to open to many more changes on Earth as we begin the ways of reconstruction.

Be well answered by our time to walk the Earth. Be well visited by us as we will start telling all why we are here, and why we are searching for other ways of answering you without causing fear. But all in all, these times are here and we must arrive to intervene. Be well answered by all of us as we are here to share knowledge and light of understanding with all who are ready to accept us and open to our ways.

Be ready now and see how all will soon be dealt with and open to many more trusted ways of healing with answers to evidence. Be willing to serve with us as we will begin the way of great sorting, serving with others who can see how all is, as we do. Know all who are in the service of Lucifer will be removed from Earth and be dealt with the same ways they were dealing with others.

But the inflicted atrocities will come from their own minds as we could never be as they are. See this as reflecting experiences onto them to end their harmful actions onto others. They will see for themselves what crimes they committed by living with these actions to themselves. This is equal justice and serving this, my wish is that they heal from their own actions.

But this may take a long time to be dealing with this. Only you can see the way you were treated by them but they care not what they have done. So, justice must be well settling with them in evidence of their plans to escape the responsibility of their soul actions. See these ways be well answered by our arrivals and our truth.

You will have all you need to live better and healthier lives and see to the better answers to our ways and our renewed truth as all unravels for you to open to our arrivals. Understand these times cannot be well settled until the first actions of war (WW3) are seen as we must be respectful of evolution in the small chance that no harm can be coming.

This of course is too hopeful as I see all is in place to begin an ugly war that will cause so many more to suffer. Be understanding my wish is to arrive now, but I must restrain myself to allow for possible change and better resolves. Be Setu and try to tell yourselves to have acceptance for truth to be served as it will. Know we are seeing to all good care for the survivors of atrocities as we will begin to answer to many more ways.

All starts into the good settling days with all who want to open to us. Be responding to my call as we will begin to show evidence with the truth of who we are as we begin to open to many more serving ways. Know how all of us are waiting for this great time of reunification and settling time of great truth on Earth.

Be certain we all serve together under the Universal Laws and the settling of all truth as all starts with the view answering to evidence of great seeing. Better times are soon here and better truth opens to our ways as all becomes well settling on Earth. Be well and be ready my children, as I am soon meeting with all of you. Be ready, all comes well into these war days. Nothing will better serve than our arrivals.

God

Received by Za, September 2, 2012

75. BE SERVING A TIME OF GREAT MEDITATION

Be dealing with the chaos coming with calm and dignity, as all heals soon after. See how we will better respond to all needs as we arrive and open to many truths. Be serving a time of renewed peace in your hearts, as you will begin to see the healing of Earth. Know we are here to answer to your call, and better see to answers to our ways as all becomes well dealt with.

Renewing times well serve with the chosen ones first, as they will be given all the information needed by all, to better serve their needs and answer to our truth. Be responding to many more telling truths about how all serves with us, as we become well answered by evidence of our understood seeing. Be responding to the will of many as they will become free from the sort that causes them to not be themselves. See how all begins to change for all people of Earth.

Be well settling with our truth, as all starts with our ways. Be dealing with our trust in answers, and settle with many, as we begin to serve with many more truths. Be ready to see how all becomes well answering with you, as you begin to better serve with the view all have, and as we answer to your prayers that we have been hearing for a long time. Be very certain we are answering you now.

Be dealing with Setu (bridging) truth and responding ways of great serving truth. Be ready to answer to evidence of who we are, as this needs to be settled by our time to walk the Earth. Answer to our many truths, as we become well responding to answers to our ways. Serve to answer to many who are settling with Earth ways by telling them: "Your time has come to be free of all deceptions and lies that have plagued you for so long."

Be ready to open to the many who are searching for great truth, as all becomes well dealing with us and with our ways. See how all starts with the truth settling with all, as we begin to open to the world, and see how all becomes well serving with us. Be ready to answer to evidence of our ways. Be well serving of how all heals, as we begin to open to many with our chosen ones.

Be well answering to answers to evidence, and be serving many more ways as you will have all you need to live, better choices of work or seeing to the reconstruction of Earth if this is your wish. Be very ready to answer to evidence of our time together with the better ways of living and better ways of healing with answers to cures for diseases and health returned.

See how we are answering to answers to our ways. Open to our seeing, as we begin to answer to our truth. Settle with the way of great serving responses, as all begins to be served and seen by us. Be well answered by our truth, and be seeing how answers open to many more trusted truths at the understood way of good seeing.

These times are very near, and I see how many of you are Setu (bridging) but not answering to my words. So, I ask you to take heed and open to the ways all starts with the view you have. Settle very soon with Earth ways, as these ways will no longer serve you. Be serving with us, as we become well serving of our truth. Know when all is healing well, we will celebrate together and be as one.

These days are soon opening to all, and we are responding to answers to our truth and our Setu ways. Evidence starts with answers to our many truths, and our many ways of great truth and renewed understandings. Be settling with us as we are soon with you to open to prove who we are. Be serving all these ways of great seeing and great truth.

Know now these ways of great truth. See how all starts opening to our many settling ways of dealing with the coming wars. We will begin by opening to the world with the arrivals of our troops. Then, we will stop all armaments of great destruction by shutting them down. Then, we will stop the military aggressors from harming others and each other, with our methods of isolating these uses to cause harm and dismantling them with our instruments of power.

These truths as renewed will answer to all answers, and to all the serving of our ways. We will better serve with our ways and our dealings, as many become well answering to more than our truth and our Setu (bridging) seeing with us. Be ready to answer to our way with answers, and see how all becomes well dealt with and better served by all.

Be responding to our way of doing this, as these days will not be very long but may cause fear and chaos in some places on Earth, but all other places that have no military action will be free to begin the time of reckoning with us and with our impatient family members who wish to be reunited with their own. And know I hear these questions and they say: "When will we see our families and when will we be reunited?"

Be ready to answer to our truth, as we will open all to you, and share all the understandings we can give you about our ways of living, and our Setu truth with the understood way we came to be as we are now. Be ready now and see how all better answers to us, as we start with the view that all becomes well serving of our ways and our Setu truth.

Be well answered by us. Settle with the view all have as the truth will open to you. Deal with our answers and our renewals. Be ready to answer to many as all-seeing is well serving, and better seen by all. Know we come to open these truths, and settle with the evil that lives on Earth. Be responding now and serve with evidence of our ways, as all becomes well answered by our truth.

Be ready now and be well serving of my warnings about having all you need to be ready for our ways of great truth. See how your vigilance of caring for your own needs with supplies will open to many more settling of good serving with us, because we will be able to care for those in greater need. This heals with all who are ready to answer to us, as we begin to open to all people of Earth.

Know now this. Better truth starts with the settling of our time together, and the good wish we have to be Setu (reuniting) with you, as you will be with us. Know understandings will grow very soon with many others, and many more truths soon opening to our time to answer you. See how all becomes well serving, as we begin to answer to many who are settling with our ways.

Be settling with the ways of the Earth, as you see your governments and oil lords become seen for who they are with nothing to serve them. Proof serves you well. See to it you are serving with answers as arrivals begin. Decide yourselves what proof you need to open to these good settling times. Be well answered and tell yourselves all comes as I said, as these times open to all good Earth people, and this I promise will be so amazing.

Deal with your sadness about lives ending at this time, but also understand used words shared about reincarnation and returning times. Know all families will soon be reuniting as these ways will answer all of you. These families are the ones who love and cherish you, and not the ones created to cause you to be harmed and restraining you from your full person, with all the potential you have, be controlled or destroyed.

Because this has been seen too many times, and has been orchestrated by dark ways to have the chosen ones put in families on Earth only to cause them to be put in denial of who they are. They are given a dark soul in charge of keeping these true beings of good ways, to be controlled and diminished. Be free of these liars, as they will be removed from Earth and put in their right places.

See these times be well ending for many who suffer the consequences of how all starts responding to answers of our truth. See how all begins to open to many more ways, as all becomes well serving, and opening to greater understood truth. Be settling with the dark ways of Earth, and open to us at the time of our arrivals, as we renew with all our children on Earth, and all our better beholding, arriving to open to the way of our time of reunification. More than you can see starts very soon.

Now see these times begin as evidence starts with us.

God

Received by Za, September 3, 2012.

Part 3 (2013)

Note from the scribe (2020): In part of this section of blogs posted in 2013, I share questions and answers from my daily prayers about Earth changes, geopolitical and current events. These entries reflect the exchanges we have, mostly questions answered by God. The other blogs are directly addressed to the readers, the elect and God's children.

These entries repeat in some of the information shared. This is how I think about it being a teacher by profession, it is spiral learning to reintroduce acquired knowledge, review it and expand the knowledge with more details. Also, another dimension to this I see as deprogramming with repetition.

76. NEW MESSAGES FOR THOSE WHO ARE LISTENING

SHARE MORE KNOWLEDGE WITH US TOMORROW: MORE TRUTH, MORE LOVE, MORE HOPE.

Be with me as we will start the sorting with all our ways of dealing with the corrupted beings who cannot better themselves in any good serving way. Be understanding how all will better answer to those who are pure of heart and pure of soul, and who can unite with the knowledge of the Universal Laws.

These stories about the way of meteorites are dealing with more than this. What fell to Earth was another American experiment, to shoot down anything that could cause harm to Earth. These meteorites were shot from space and landed in Russia, and now the Russians are angry at the USA for causing these troubles because they are careless of what they harm.

Now listen. The way all starts comes very fast, and one event will answer another. Understand you will believe evidence as you see it, and see these things are happening. God gives you back to yourself, and then you are free to be the way you are with the settling of times.

God

Received in 2013, by Za.

77. QUESTIONS ASKED ABOUT THE VATICAN AND RECENT ACTIONS

THE RESIGNATION OF POPE BENEDICT.

A more troubling time comes to the Vatican, as all who are corrupted are seen for who they are. All who see the truth vindicated and all who open to our arrival, will better serve with us and know who we are, and why we answer to this time.

Question: What has caused the Pontiff to step down? This is an unusual step, he said: "We are all sinners, may God have mercy on us."

Answer: "We are all sinners...", only includes the servants of evil and those who are settling with these times. They worship their demon god who lies, deceives and abuses the innocent to gain their power, and they settle with the thievery of the poor. Be willing to open to the coming times, and with truth, you will heal many sorrows and many other truths.

We answer to our better serving children first. Then we will sort all those who need to be dealt with, as many see this on Earth with the religious wars, and the deaths of the innocent. But know this, all who oppose God now, are directly being seen by us. Better serving with many more answers to understand how all starts with our time to answer to our children. Now we are arriving to answer back to all these thieves and liars.

Question: What about the lighting strike on the top of the dome of the Vatican?

Answer: These are not our ways. These actions made to answer to evidence of power, belong to the demons who control the weather with lasers from space above Earth, and they see this as a way to maintain the false renewal of our kind. But these actions belong to the weather beasts of Earth, satellites and lasers. These satellites are capable of causing lighting strikes, and it helps to show prophesies to serve their purpose of the mysterious, and the power of the unknown.

Be well answered as all starts, better seeing of how Earth heals once all the lies are dealt with and serve to prove all better truth. Answers to darkness becomes light and truth. And know we are all serving these times of great serving truth with our words and our trusted ways, and our well sorted populations allowing the good to live in peace, tranquility and healthier lives.

Question: What about religions?

Answer: All these forms of religions only serve evil plans of control, domination and inculcation of fear among the most vulnerable. This heals as I myself will put a stop to this and other kinds of blasphemy against all Angels and Creators of Earth. Heal with us now, and be ready to better answer to our time of great truth.

God

Recent messages to share. Za

78. RENEWING TIMES ARE SOON SHARED

Evidence of our truth answers to you with evidence of our visits. Many are dealing with us and others, with the truth of who we are, known to them but hidden by many. This is why the Vatican is keeping so many secrets, and cause the death of so many who are dealing with these times of horror. Be ready to hear from our settlers of truth, as they will be seen arriving first.

These ones are called the "Nordics". They come first to answer to the moving out of all governments from all Capital cities. And then, we will arrive to settle into positions of law, and answer to all injustices according to the ten commandments and the laws dealing with the Universal Laws. These laws are more than any other, and deal with the truth, and not tricks to take from the innocent.

All who were robbed, will soon open to sharing the truth of why these traitors acted this way. All will know how these devils answer to suppress evidence of great truth with the way all becomes well answered by us and with us. Be serving with us, and see all these thieves and liars be taken to be used to repay all work stolen from others, and who will be dealing with the lies these understood serving answers open to.

Better to be serving with us because these times of reparations will be well serving and well evident to all. Not one will escape our justice, and not one settles with us to open to many lies. More people will be answered, and more will be saved because of unnecessary laws only serving the rich, will be abolished. The new laws, the Universal Laws, will be put in place to answer to all needs and all better ways to share knowledge with us.

Better Setu (bridging) times come soon. All who will oppose us will be dealt with, and all who try to harm us or anyone else, will be found and dealt with. These are the times all good people of Earth have been waiting for, and healing times are soon here. Understand Setu times are settling with us now, and we are ready to answer to our time to open to the world.

Be ready, and deal with these good serving days with open hearts and clear understandings. Better to open to us now than to be used by these whores forever. Be well answered by us and be serving with us and others, as we answer to your call, and better answering all who are renewing with understandings and truth.

Be dealing with us, as you will soon be renewing with who we are, and why we are returning to Earth. Open to all who serve truth and justice, and who are ready to unite with the good ways of the Universal Laws. These Laws will be served to all who settle with these times of renewals. Many will become open by them, as renewal times start. But with us on Earth, we tell all how these ways of openness are shared, and how we are as one, to better live and better see all truth as it is, and more than these truths will be shared.

A new system of power to give to all, renews on Earth. This power will be easy and free to use, so nothing will harm the earth and its inhabitants; a new way of living to better serve all health needs, shared truth to open to all true justice, living in safety and the stopping all useless wars.

I am asking you only to be patient as arrivals begin, and stay calm as all good things are soon coming to all my children and others' children. Be serving a time of peace and meditation, and answer to us as we will become seen in all places of Earth to begin the sorting of evil, and the good care of those in need. Be well settling with Earth ways, and settle with the view all have that we are alien creatures come to deal with humans in horrible ways.

These others aliens have already come here to cause pain and horrors. These ones will be dealt with first, as they are the cause for many troubles on Earth. You call them the Grey and the Reptilians, and so, they are as evil as they are. Only we can rid Earth of these parasites, and this we will do first.

Be ready and be ready, all starts soon.

God

Received February 25, 2013 by Za.

79. ARRIVALS ARE SOON SEEN BY ALL PEOPLE OF EARTH

Revelations 10:7 "There will be no more delays, but in the days when the Seventh Angel is to blow his trumpet, the mystery of God will be fulfilled, as he announces to his servants the prophets."

These Setu (bridging) times are well under way. Many on Earth will be very surprised to see evidence of who we are, as better truth heals all lies. Be responding with better evidence of who we are, as we are settling with all who cause harm to life on Earth, and who believe life on Earth is theirs to use and control at will. Be certain these times are soon over as arrivals start soon, and will be seen by everyone on Earth. Be certain all who oppose us will be dealt with very quickly without question because we know their hearts and souls.

Freedom to people on Earth serves with responsibility. These times of great understandings will open the way for these teachings and better choices can be easily made. Better serving actions towards each other and better shared understandings with others from other planets, settles the well-controlled mysteries held by only the greedy and the demons. They, who enslaved humans to serve their responding plans to trust in, face the undeniable knowledge of our settling times with them.

Be dealing with us soon, with our truth and answers to evidence of our ways. Be dealing with us and others, as these times are soon settling understood evidence of our ways, our time of great renewals and great understandings. Be well answered by us, as we will give you all that you need to be free of harm and the controllers, who are using people to answer to their researches and attack instruments.

Be ready as all starts well into the coming days, and be well served by our time to walk the Earth. Better times are soon serving, and this evidence will be yours and ours to open to. A more trusting way of living will grow on Earth. Our trusted ways and our more serving ways, will begin to answer all people who can learn how to live in a community with each other without being used to better someone who controls them with a lust for power.

These times are soon over on Earth, and a uniting time heals all who are ready to be Setu (bridge) with us. Be well answered by our time to walk the Earth, and be welcoming all who are coming to free you from a life of disregard for people and living beings on Earth. More is healing well for you soon.

Be ready, and be uniting with us soon.

God

Received March 1st, 2013 by Za

80. BE RENEWING WITH TRUTH AND BE SERVING WITH TRUTH

BETTER SETU TIMES ARE HERE

We are ready now. This knowledge will respond to you as you settle with Earth ways. Prepare for the coming days. Be well seeing how all answers open to you, as we begin to share our knowledge and our truth. Be well settling with Earth ways. Be well seeing with evidence and knowledge, all who are searching for their children taken from them, and put into perpetual reincarnation to cause their submission to evil.

Knowledge and the truth will set you free, as you begin to understand how a soul is reused and manipulated to be used at the will of the insiders of the uses of evil. They are renewing with these ways for thousands of Earth years. They cause the soul to shut down to help their own dark energies to invade a body, to cause these visits to answer to their will and control.

Serving with these words may be difficult for some to comprehend, but see this as demonic possession if you will, and understand that these beings can achieve this by weakening the body with ways of poisons (alcohol, prescribed and illicit drugs) and the fear of death. Be meeting with us soon, and be dealing with our ways of healing because we have returned to Earth to cleanse it from these parasites.

They will answer to answers of our ways, and be removed from Earth to respond to judgement and be dealt with accordingly. Be serving with us and with others, and know we are not the aggressors, but the actions against humans' answers to our need to free you from these whores.

Better seeing of these ways will cause many to be alarmed, but the dark soul is a possessed soul, and these are parasitical beings who respond to Lucifer's renewed actions against all his victims. Better to answer to us now than to be in evidence of the ancient stories of Hell, as this is a truth. Better to be seeing this knowledge now, as these times are accelerating into many more dark ways to open to, settling time with our arrivals.

Understand that these entities exist, and are continuing with possessions, renewing with troubles believed to prove many beliefs on Earth. Healing these humans can be dealt with, but many bodies as seen, are very ill and very old, and these will not be renewed. Be settling with them at the time of our arrivals by letting them become free from these dark souls who possess them. They will return to their right places, and be serving what they acted on to cause trouble and harm on Earth.

Be willing to open to "Answer to answers", the book in my lap that clearly explains the phenomena of possession, and this has been discovered in other places in settling planets. Be knowing that these planets are now free of these parasites, and are healing with great success. And now healing comes to Earth, and serves all who settle with these times of great terror and unnecessary stress.

Be serving our arrivals with openness, and allow us to be serving the needed sorting to remove all those who cause harm, and who control your lives and your actions. Be well responding to our truth and respond to answers to aonma (evidence) of our ways as arrivals become well dealt with and well served by us. Better to open to these understandings than to be left to be used by their actions against humans, as they settle with the visits from us. This is why they have weapons in space.

These truths are known to many who answer to our seeing. Be ready, and see these times be well answered. Know that all the poisons being poured on you, as you see this over your skies, are all made to cause more illnesses and control of bodies to serve their armies of dark souls to possess humans. These ways will stop as arrivals start.

Be ready to answer to us and to others, as we begin the sorting in evidence of healing with us. Be ready to answer to better lives, as these parasites are all removed from Earth. All Earth healing begins to open to all places; all will be renewed by our serving ways and with your helping ways. And know we are your family ready to meet with you again, and to be well serving of our time of reunification.

Be ready.

God

Received by Za, March 2, 2013

81. MORE TRUTH, MORE LOVE, MORE HOPE FOR THE GOOD PEOPLE OF EARTH

Better times are soon here for all who are ready to open to knowledge and truth of who they are and how we are their serving parents renewing with our children. Be seeing who we are with your own eyes and your own hearts. Ancient stories of the past are revealing, as you meet with us. All questions will be answered, as we are settling with Earth ways of harm and abuses.

This heals at the good settling time of war ending all abuses on Earth, and freeing all who are innocent victims of killings and harm. You will see all times of horror end, and all good people regain their renewed state of being, healing all ways of health and better living.

These ways are simple and efficient; all will see these ways as we begin the sorting and removing the evil that has caused all these troubles on Earth and elsewhere. These demons and parasites are easily dealt with now, as we have united in Space to become the believed Angels who clear all planets of misery caused by these whores who use humans as slaves and body hosts.

See these thieves be captured, and better serving their own deaths. See Lucifer be caught and removed forever. Better times are now here, and better truth are renewing with us and others at the time of our descent onto Earth.

We are the ones who seeded the Earth a long time ago, and who managed the better ways of living. But we were overtaken by these devils who came from another place, who acted as helpers but soon were discovered to be answering to evil ways. Because we were one civilization and not many, we left Earth to save our people, but so many remained trapped. Our promise was to return, and free all from slavery to these whores. Now we are coming to stop all abuses to humans. We return with a Federation of many others who also rid their planets from these devils.

Be ready now, more than you are expecting are soon arriving. The sorting will start and serve with us and all who are settling with these demons from Earth. Most planets are completely free of these ways of evil. Only Earth remains to be dealt with, but the troubles on Earth are seen as the worst in many used times of planets.

Be certain we will come soon, and end this torment. Know we feel as you do, as you are our children. We wish for you to reunite with your families coming soon, and impatiently wanting to meet all of you. Be well understood by us, and know answers are arriving soon. See how all will start with the way of great truth and great trust.

Be serving with us, and leave Earth ways behind and better respond to all these changes that will open to many ways of great love and trust, responding to better living ways. See all these times change for all who are good as we settle with those who cause harm used to better their own power. Renew with us and renew with life in evidence of great truth, great renewal and great responsibility for each other, and this is our way.

Be well answered, and be well answered. I heard your prayers, and now I am arriving to answer you, as you are my responsibility. My care for you is healing all sufferings as there are many known stories of horrors. Healing will take time for some, as their souls are so damaged by giving to these whores, to live life only to suffer more. These times are soon over, and I am arriving soon after the first and second landings to open to you.

These serving ways answer to all who are Setu (bridging), and who are ready to meet with us face to face. God shows himself to the World more than before, as all visits begin and answers to evidence of who we are. Be serving with us now and settle with Earth ways, as these ways will not serve anyone anymore. Be well answered by us, and be dealing with these truths. Search in your hearts for who you are at the time of our meeting.

Better times are opening with us soon, and better ways serve with us, well evident of our time together. Be serving with us and be well serving with answers to proof of many bridging renewals. Be ready my children, as we are soon arriving to open to many serving truth. Answers are soon ready.

God

Received by Za, March 3, 2013

82. THESE TURBULENT TIMES ARE HERE

HEALING TIMES

Healing with us is a necessary felt serving by all who are Beings of Light, because we see the troubles of earth, the health of many deteriorating, and we must intervene. Feelings of better health will be returned so more can be well as they renew with us. Be willing to answer to our call, be bridging with us, and be well answered by our ways of good health and good care.

Be ready to answer to evidence of great truth and great serving. Meeting times are here. All who read my scribe's words are reading my serving words. More will be shared as the days of the death of many will begin to open. Heal your broken hearts with us, and be ready to answer to our truth, as these times are soon well serving.

Be well answered by us. Better truth becomes well served at the time of great arrivals. I am seeing many who are ready, who open to these words and heal with these words, and this pleases me. But see to it I am your truth and your salvation, as these days will show you who we are. As all begins to unravel, you will better serve with us and many others from other planets of the Universes.

Be seeing all who are united as your brothers and sisters of planetary unison reaching out to you now, and opening you to your truth and your true renewals with us. Be ready as much needs to be done, and we will better settle with you as we meet with you, the prophets and scribes first, to open to others on Earth, as we begin to walk the Earth.

Better times and better seeing will come after the downfall and demise of the systems of control are eradicated, and many are removed from Earth. The response to these evident actions will be very difficult for some to understand. We ask you to be serving a place of calm as these ways are seen by you.

Know that all who cause harm to others must go to their right places and be sorted to better themselves, and return actions of service to those they harmed. This is how we work to heal the problems of these parasites, to open to better serving of others away from anyone they can harm. These methods of healing evil are evidently not uncommon but serve with us and are well dealt with, as we know all hearts and all souls.

Be ready now, more than you are expecting comes to Earth. Be serving a time of deep meditation, and serve understood words shared with you. See to these better days, as arrivals become well dealt with and open to you. Answer to our call, and know we are serving with great trust and better serving truth. Know all starts well into the good bridging days.

Be believing in what you will see. Be responding to our people who are many, answering your questions. Be well serving with our truth, and be well settling with Earth ways, as these ways will soon be extinguished. Better times come to better hearts settling with the care we will share together. Better trust will prove who we are, as understandings grow and people's needs are all met to better their lives.

These ways are easy for us to do for you. These ways you will learn yourselves, as all opens to peace and serenity serving a time of great healing on Earth. See these understood truths be yours, and evidence be yours. Settle with Earth ways, as arrivals are seen, as we begin to walk the Earth. Be well responding to answers shared about ways of living, as these ways are serving to protect all good living creatures of your planet, never causing harm and dealing with deaths to survive. These ways are not ours. These ways only belong to the dark ones, who are slaves to Lucifer.

Be ready, and settle with these whores, and free yourselves. See to it your truth answers all who are sharing with more than before. Be serving with us and others, as we arrive to heal Earth. Be with us, as you will see these parasites being pulled out of the depths of the Earth. Know what dwells there, as the Seers of past told of.

These demons crawled into the Earth to hide from us a long time ago. Knowledge about these underground places are seen by us. As we will settle with them ourselves, we will leave no stone unturned. Be ready and know you will be safe, and renew with many truths. Many more returning ways of being with us will open to you. Better times and better lives, will better who you are. All heals with time. Be visited soon by us, and know we are your family returning to Earth to open to your time of freedom.

Bessron aonma poon onm *

Bessron aonma poon onm

Bessron aonma poon onm

*Note: this means briefly *sharing the evidences of believed knowledge.*

Be ready.

God

Received by Za, March 4, 2013

83. THESE DAYS OF WAR, AS SAID, ARE OPENING TO THE MIDDLE-EAST

Be ready, all has begun to trouble many who are searching for peace. Be well answered by these coming wars only because we will stop them. Be ready to be understanding of our ways to open to the world, and see to healing all your sorrows with us, as we sorrow with you.

Nothing will stop us from arriving on Earth. Serving these words will cause those who are dealing with lies, and serving with uses of armaments, to answer to our ways of stopping them. Be dealing with us now, and answer to our truth and our ways. Open to all Setu (bridging) visits well answering our time of return.

Be ready, and see all comes as I said. Know you will better serve with us than these controllers of lies and deceptions. Be certain we are not coming to harm anyone, but to answer to evidence of great serving truths with us and others. Be understanding of all serving truth and better settling ways, and be serving visits with us.

Be better settling with us and others, and know we are better serving with many, and there will be a time of great reunion. Be understanding all starts soon, and all you need to do is help others understand how all heals with us.

I ask you to onm (share light of understanding and knowledge) with us now. I ask you to open to our ways and become all that you are, without the control holding you in a place of stress and fear. Be free of these Earth ways, settle with this evidence of false power. Be ready to join the Universal Laws, and the felt love we all share.

Better to be with us than to be with those who are preparing to hide underground, as they will soon be seen coming out, as we remove them from these holes. These understood places to hide from us, opens now to many who are settling with fear of our time of arrival. But see this as an easy way for us to collect these whores, as we begin the sorting.

We are not the enemy. The enemies you have, dwell on Earth and in Earth. Be better seeing this knowledge, as these uses of underground caves are settling with a place for demons, and this answers to their great fear of who we are.

Be well answered by us, and see to our time to answer to evidence of great truth and great renewals. Be well vindicated by our truth and our ways, and better answer to answers as we begin to sort all who need to better themselves. Open to a time of peace and responsibility. Settling with Earth ways serves to open to better health and better living ways.

Be willing to answer to my call and renew with us, as we have many here who wish to speak to you and tell you they are your loving family members. Visits begin soon, and questions will all be well answered. Be serving understood words shared before, and see how arrivals will begin. Understand how we will open the way for many with our good serving ways, and our time to walk the Earth.

Seeing us may be difficult for some, but understand many are walking among you now for many years, and are living on Earth as others do. Know only our truth, and renew with our time of visits. See to it that we are serving with you and others, and many more in all places of the Universes.

Be ready, and be dealing with our truth, and see these ways we serve with your own eyes. Deal with the sadness caused by all of our kind who lost their lives in terrible ways, to share this message with you. Heal your broken hearts with us, as answers arrive soon to answer to your prayers, and your love for each other.

Know now this. Be seeing how all starts with the opening of wars on Iran and Israel. As these wars begin, bridging times follow soon after, and better answers to more than these wars; because attacks will be seen from Earth in the skies, and answer to many who will believe these are the Earth wars. Be seeing also these attacks being directed toward us, and see our responses to be proof of our (past) truth.

Better seeing of these ways will cause many to fear us and wish to hide, but these answers to our ways are as we said, only stopping the attacks. Believe the bridging understandings with these seeing, and know who we are as we become seen by all.

Now listen. Be serving with us soon. Open to our ways. Settle with Earth ways, and open to our time to share the knowledge and understanding of who we are. Be well answered by us, and know we are here to answer your prayers heard by many of us here. Be well sharing answers to truth now. More sharing of truth will begin and serve to answer you. Better truth starts with the way all shared beliefs are seen to open to us and who we are. Onm this with others very soon.

God

Received by Za, March 5, 2013

84. THESE TIMES ARE KNOWN
TO THE VATICAN

ALL UNRAVELS

Be well answered because we are opening to all who will be Setu (bridging) with us. Settle with Earth ways, and be dealing with answers to our ways as we begin to walk the Earth. Better truth will open to you, as you see how all unravels, and how your governments choose to stop us with armaments and dealings of lies. They cannot stop us, as we are many, and we will only disarm all of them to answer back to their aggression, because military men are serving orders and only this.

Be serving with us more, as you will see this good serving time. Know all arrivals, as said, will begin to open to evidence of our truth. Be ready onm (shared knowledge and light of understanding) starts well into the coming weeks with the wars in the Middle East. This will become better seen by all and better settled by many who are serving with answers to evidence of our ways.

Be ready and see to healing with us in evidence of our understood truth. Be dealing with us and others as these understood ways become well seen by all with more trust. Healing begins with us, believe in these words, as renewals become served, and with our shared ideals of good ways of living. Be ready and serve with us and many others, as these times open to Earth humans.

Know now this. Be ready to be seeing many more ships in the skies. Be ready to answer to our ways with us. See to it you have all that you need for a time of felt responses to war, as for food and clean water for a short time until we can be serving our ways of living. These days will only be served with us, and answering to many more with us, as we care first for those in greater need.

Know these times are dealt with soon, and none will settle with only limited forms of food. All is healed, and all will renew with us. All will soon answer to better ways in evidence of great truth and great settling times. Be well answered by us, and see these times be well served by all at the time of our truth and our bridging ways.

Better evidence of who we are opens to you soon, and responds to many more serving truths. Be well answered by us now, and be well vindicated by our ways. Renew serving truth with us, and see your lives be better, and your families be safe and well cared for. These are our ways, only this and only care, not harm.

The ones who cause harm dwell on Earth mostly. All the others are on the run in this Universe, but we know where they are hiding. Deal with these truths yourselves, as you will soon see how these whores are renegades, and how they cause strife between all people, to better exploit them and use them. Renew with us, and tell me this is known.

Be bridging with us soon, as understood truths are soon answering to you. The seeing of this will prove who we are. Nations on Earth will become settling with strife and wars, and not serving the liars that profit from these actions of power and greed.

Soon you will see an Earth renewing itself, healing itself, and opening to better ways. Understand these words are Setu (bridging) words. The serving of the healing comes with the healing of humans who are in great need of care because of the pollution caused by these "chem-trails" and renewed rain of poisons.

This action of seeding the skies helps these whores quicken their plans of extermination of thousands and thousands of the weaker ones, who could easily be helped to better themselves. But these beings of dark ways have no care for anyone, and only intend to use this plan to create weaknesses in the population and further their extermination plan before these wars answer to many more deaths.

With them comes the others, the renegades we are pursuing, who are well established on Earth and who are well anchored as the industrial military complex serving the governments on Earth. Renewing with these kind does not guarantee any safety for them (the governments) as it is believed, but shares uses of their plans to establish power on Earth with them. And then, eliminate all humans from any power to be the well settling controllers of Earth.

This is the deception of the Grey and the so-called Reptilians, who cause trouble wherever they go. They will soon be dealt with, in evidence of our arrivals, and our time to better see to the unearthing of these death makers and abusers of humans. Be serving this truth in proof of your seeing what these demons are, as they are living in Earth as seen by us.

I am seeing how these words are difficult for many, but these truths must be known to open to answers to evidence of our ways, and better serving of our understood answers to our truth. Better to be with us than with these whores, as they care not for your lives nor your health. They use humans as a food source, serving these responses to their needs. Better bridging times are here. Share knowledge and light of understanding with us, and be ready for our arrivals at the time of reunification.

Settle with Earth ways and be ready.

God

Received by Za, March 6, 2013

85. SHARED EVIDENCE AND BELIEVED KNOWLEDGE

These times are serving very soon now. Be ready, and be well opening to our answers to many truths. Be well serving evidence, be well seeing with our ways, and renew with us and others as all becomes seen. Better to answer to our call than to be serving Earth ways, as these ways are soon dealing with many troubles and many lies. Better times prove better truth, and all will be revealed to you with understood words and actions. Be serving our ways and be serving our truths used to answer to evidence, and to answer to our renewals.

Become who you really are, as we will free you from your prison, and answer to our renewed evidence responding to our truth. Better settling times open to you now, and all who are settling with Earth ways answer to us with the way of great serving answers to knowledge and our many truths. Be well serving with answers, and open to our understandings with us and settle with Earth ways.

Better truth starts very soon now, and better serving ways open to us as we begin the sorting. Be bridging with us, and settle with these whores who have captured your soul to animate the bodies on Earth with our children. Our time to stop these atrocities are moments away, and we arrive to settle with their abominations and blasphemies.

Understand we cannot answer you now, as we are bound to the Universal Laws, and we are better serving a precise action to come for us to intervene. Healing will open very soon to serve used truths of these visits and these times. Be ready and renew with us and others, and answer to evidence of our ways as all becomes well dealt with and served. Better truth starts soon. Opening to these times will cause many to see all as it is, healing with us and living better lives.

God gives you back to yourselves, and does more this way than to open to the inculcation of rituals. This was never my way, and this way belongs to those who well control people through the lust of power and greed. See these men answer to me, as I will face them and ask them why they slandered my name, the name of my sons and my wife.

To these words I want you to understand that religions have answered to a lust for power and greed; because I want all my children to speak all their thoughts and words to me directly and only to me, not through an organization that causes many more sufferings all around your planet. This has never been my way or our ways, and this way belongs to another.

Live your lives with an open heart to feel my love for you. Tell me all your sorrows, as I share with you my concerns and my care for all my children. These times of lies and deceptions as serving now in all places of

Earth are soon over, as I will stop these ways myself. Better times are soon here, and better answers are believed, as you will soon see this as a better answered truth.

Heal with us and be well served by our ways, our truth, our actions and our care. Be dealing with us, and be dealing with many more caring helps than any other seen on Earth, as we will begin to heal the sick, and the poor will have what they need.

These words I shared before when my son Jesus came to Earth. Those who tortured him still display his tortured body as a sign of their own threats to you, and still this is not understood. These demons play tricks on people and make them believe that they are all sinners. These ones are the sinners, but many people of Earth are serving without sin, and are not born with sin. Be certain of this when you see a newly born child.

But also understand that some are born with sin, as these whores reincarnate and answer again to their master Lucifer. They return to his service, and renew their actions against my children, and cause again more suffering as seen as the rape of children. This action has more to do with changing the DNA by causing anxiety, fear and disturbances in the body than as said as a "simple rite of passage", as quoted by a Catholic Bishop.

These words are known to be the words of abusers and Lucifer, as this they do without any remorse. Evidence of remorse is not seen by these Bishops and abusers of the innocent. And now all these actions of active deceptions will be soon ended, as arrivals become seen. Be certain many will be sorted by us. Be certain those who cause harm onto others will be the first to be judged by me and my Lords.

Now see this. Be ready, know all starts very soon, and answers to our time to walk the Earth. Be certain all who are searching for truth will soon find it with us and by us. Heal with your true families, and be free of these deceptions that have controlled your thoughts and actions for so long. Open your heart to truth, and be ready to answer to us and others, as all becomes well served and well seen.

Be willing to open to our arrivals, and know we are the ones who well see all hearts and all souls. Settle with the ways of evil and share knowledge and light of understanding with us soon.

God

Received by Za, March 7, 2013

86. SHARED ANSWERS WILL SOON BE YOURS TO ANSWER TO

ANSWERS TO ANSWER ARE SOON HERE

Be serving evidence of our ways as all starts, and be dealing with the truth of who we are as answers to our renewals are settling with evidence of our time together. Be ready and be dealing with answers to our truth. Be well serving answers to our used truth, and see these ways of great serving understandings of our visits with your own eyes.

Be believing now, as these truths become served and dealt with, and be certain all starts well into the good serving days. Be ready and be well answered as all comes as I said. Be serving renewals with us and be responding to my call, as I will tell you how all serves to answer to opening our truth to the world, and to answer to our seeing.

Now see this, the times of great wars are soon here. Be resting until then, as there is nothing more to do than wait for these times to come, and this time will certainly come. The wars will erupt in North Korea, and in the Middle-East, as these are the two places on Earth to start these troubles and deal with population over-growth. But no past history tells of these times as they repeat themselves everywhere in the universes where Lucifer has traveled.

Be serving past truth as you settle with these ways, and be well serving of our time to answer to many as all starts and as all becomes well seen. Be ready all starts soon and many will lose their lives. See all as all unravels and serve these times.

Evidence of truth starts with us to open to you, and all Setu serving ways will better open to most people who believe in who we are, but not to all. Let them have their own time to respond to our time to walk the Earth and only help those who can be helped at the time of reunification. But renew with us at these good days yourselves, and deal with the others as they will soon follow, as they will see themselves what past truth opens to.

Be serving with us and know you are better answered by us with many who are seeing to answers with much impatience, as they watch all wars being started on Earth to open to a third world war. Responding to serving with these times, answers to our time to arrive and renew with all who are ready to serve with us, and make the necessary changes to unite all with the universal laws.

Seeing Setu times responds to all who are serving with the truth and the Seven Pillars of Wisdom bestowed by my wife Sophia. Be serving with these Pillars and free yourself of Earth ways. See to it that all heals at the time of our meeting, and all opens to many more renewals, as we begin the sorting and as we begin to heal all who are ready to heal.

Know now this, be searching for the ones who answer to many more renewals with us and be settling with those who are deceiving you with the beliefs about the inner Earth and its inhabitants. These are the demons told of many times in religions and serving telling of old. Be certain these demons will not help anyone, and are settling with many humans and animals to create new ones who can better serve them.

But these atrocities will heal with us, and we will care for them until their death of body, as we have done before to keep our vows of causing no harm to anyone. Be serving these ways of understood Setu ways, and be certain all comes to be seen into the good settling days.

Be ready and see to it that you have what you need to live until we can restore better ways of living on Earth, as it was before we left Earth a long time ago. Be serving these better ways of living at the time of our walking the Earth, and see all creature of Earth renew their health and beauty. Better seeing of these ways will answer you, and open to answers of great renewals with us, your families.

Be ready now, all heals well with us.

God

Received by Za, March 8, 2013

87. THE TIME OF REUNIFICATION IS SOON

HEAL WITH US AND BE SERVING WITH THE TRUTH

Share Setu truth. Heal with us and be serving with truth. Be serving with us and your lives will improve. Be with us and we will open many trusted ways for you. Be telling others who we are and we will all serve our love and joy together. This heals this long separation and this long-understood truth about who we are and who you are. See these truths and unite with the answers you are searching for.

God returns to Earth and God reveals himself to all his children. Better settling times are soon answering you with the way of great Setu ways and better answers open to be evidence of our trusted ways. Be ready and respond to us as we are soon arriving to open to many with the settling of our time together and with the serving ways all starts and all heals.

Better truth shows you the way all came to be and will put to rest these stories of lost civilizations and ancient gods who warred with each other. All stories told to you were made to answer to renewals of a political system to well control the population and create answers of great evident lies. Now is the time to open to truth and free yourselves from these indoctrinations called countries, governments and religions.

These ways are ending for you on Earth and are soon settling with the answers to a serving response to our time to walk the Earth. Heal all these diseases and lies made to poison your hearts and souls. Better understood ways answering to all tells of a truth that will be undeniable and evidently renewed with us and many others from Space and other Universes.

Be ready to answer to these times of great seeing. Settle with us and our truth at the used answers to our ways. Be accepting many more truths from many planets. Understand we all needed to unite against these parasites who travel from planet to planet to invade it, corrupt it, and take hostages and earthly DNA to create their own sources of food and slave labor that they are trading across the Universes.

We have found proof of this in many distant places and we can assure you that we are the healing ones. These kinds, the Grey and the Reptilians, are settling with fewer customers now as the Universal Laws forbid the trade of slaves and animals for slavery. Believe these words as these words as said are not accepted by those who oppose the Universal Laws, but know we are the ones stopping these trades and renewing with the healing of the victims.

Be serving with us now and be responding to our call as all becomes well dealt with and answered. Better trust in our ways will cause answers to pour onto you and free you from the lies that have imprisoned you for so long. Be ready now to see these times end, and to answer to a love of life that serves all life and settles with the diseased souls of evil, as their souls are dark and renew only with harming the good ones.

Sharing with us and others will cause many to feel more hope and more possibilities to choose how they wish to live. Many will wish to leave Earth and join the working ways of the Universal Laws and these ones will be renewing with many planets and peoples. Then tell me who you are, and tell me about the obstruction of evolution of health and social political serving ways.

To see other planets and how life there is lived, will heal the belief of a need for power that controls and reduces a population to slavery and ignorance of truth. Be Setu with us and know we are not used to these ways. Our ways serve much more to open to. These ways we teach and share, as these ways will heal the ills of the Earth.

Healing starts with us. Believe this when you see this yourselves, as I am knowing your hearts and I see many have lost trust in anything good because of the works of evil on Earth. But evil is limited and can only destroy. Seeing the way of construction and not destruction will open your hearts and beauty and care will return to Earth.

Evidence of our arrivals well deals with the serving of these times of great reunification and how this time has arrived. Be ready and respond to our call. Now see these times be near.

God

Received by Za, March 9, 2013

88. I AM NEAR EARTH AND DEALING WITH ARRIVALS

Share evidence of believed knowledge. Be ready as all starts soon. Be seeing our time of great truth opening to our ways. Be well served by us and many others as all starts with explosions of truths. Be visited soon by our kind and know we are serving soon to open to evidence of great truth with answers to many who are soon answering to us.

The time of the Conclave has arrived and a new Pope will be answered. But understand I am not the one who gives my blessings to any man on Earth to tell others about these words being used as religious to me. These words of holy scripture are not all mine and proof of this is well coming as I will deal with these blasphemers myself and see to their just punishments, as they have raped and pillaged all across the world for their power and their glory, not mine.

Be seeing how these devils are full of greater sins than you all know of, killing the souls of children, destroying their lives and causing more struggles on Earth than ever and more than any other places settling in the Universes. See how they are settling with us in evidence of our time together and be not surprised how these Bishops and Deacons are better settling with us than any laws on Earth because they see themselves as untouched by any law as they renew with their master Lucifer.

Better to onm with us in evidence of our time to walk the Earth than to serve with great lies about the greatest sinners on Earth. See them for who they are. See how it is their money that sends young people to wars and death. Deal with the very truth of this as they have never stopped any wars, but on the contrary, settle with many profits from it.

Be ready and be willing to open to our truth and settle with answers to evidence of the truth when you see it. Heal all lies with truth, open the way for better seeing and better understood truth. How else can I tell you this knowledge? I can only hope that all will be well seen and well understood by those who are ready to settle with Earth's deceptive ways, and ready themselves to open to who we really are, as we are not unreachable and invisible powers of united consciousness.

These, again as said, are stories to blur your vision because what would happen when we arrive to tell you these religions are actually put in place to stop you from finding us. These beings of men in robes are the same believed ones who reincarnated into serving bodies you see today. They continue their practices of reincarnation because they have the knowledge to do this and most on Earth have no knowledge of these practices.

Nevertheless, they have reincarnated and respond to the same practices of the past that holds populations in fear of their power whether it is seen overtly or secretly. But better not to be fooled by these ceremonies and cult like actions as they are serving only one master and he is Lucifer. Heal these words as you can and understand I will put a stop to these whores myself and settle with them in a better way than they have settled with others.

Be well seeing how all will renew with us as we begin the sorting of souls and as arrivals are served in all airports and fields of your planet. All who are dealing with lies and deceptions will better answer to us as these ways will only settle with our judgements. Be ready to answer to our time to walk the Earth and see how all truth will be for all who can unite with us as understandings become well served and dealt with.

Be certain we are all settling with used truths serving with answers and better serving ways. Be serving holiness with us and be well serving with our truth at the time of our renewals. Now see these words and know these are my words as scribed by Za, and know we are soon meeting with many first who are ready to answer to truth of who we are and why we are returning to Earth. Better serving truth starts with healing and better help than what is now responding on Earth as all heals with us.

Be ready and be ready.

God

Received by Za, March 10, 2013.

89. BE SETTLING WITH EARTH WAYS

BE READY TO OPEN TO OUR ARRIVALS
AND BE SERVING WITH US

Answers are soon coming to better open to all who are ready to heal with us as the time of reunification draws near. Seeing the Conclave makes me want to respond to all that this abomination of self-serving old men answers only to; a death wish responding to the end of the Vatican. Be understanding that none of these men have served the purpose of helping anyone on Earth other than their own glory and ambitions.

These are the men who tell all that they are serving with holiness of my ways and my words. Believe they are certainly only serving themselves. Be well knowing this as I am seeing many of Earth answering to them as spiritual leaders who concern themselves with the wellbeing of their followers. But they have absolutely no care for their followers other than the sources of money and life forces they draw from them in their endeavor of achieving more wealth and more power.

Why? Because they are liars and thieves, and they enjoy lives of riches, *bona* food and good wine, and care not about the souls of good people of Earth but care only about renewing with wealth and power. Their dealt with lies and atrocities against people from all times have gone unpunished and even glorified because they answer to their master Lucifer. He answers to himself and only this.

Be willing to accept these truths with opened eyes. Know who we are as we arrive to settle with these old devils who worship Lucifer. Be dealing with the fall of the Vatican as the third secret of Fatima has revealed. Know these truths and be dealing with many more truths as you leave the deceptions better than before I was renewing with you.

Be settling with the death of many as the wars begin, renewing with the false attacks by North Korea and the better answer to defense from the USA. Be better serving these words now as these times of war actions begin to answer to our ways and our truths and our Setu ways following these false flag operations. Be certain these deceptions will all be well answered by evidence of truth and better understood ways of great healing and better serving answers.

Be well ready and know we are arriving soon after these attacks in evidence of our renewing time of answers to who we are and why we have come to open to Earth, and begin a sorting of great numbers of humans who are settling with the dealings of their master Lucifer. Telling of old renews with these answers and many will be dealing with these evident truths themselves and renew with the bigger picture of how all heals and how all came to be.

Better truths vindicate many, and better serving answers deals with many at the time of reunification. Be settling with these times and be dealing with better truth as all starts and as all starts very soon.

God

Received by Za, March 11, 2013.

90. OPEN TO THE COMING CHANGES AND RENEW WITH US AS ARRIVALS BEGIN

BESSRON AONMA POON ONM

These words as seen are our language. My scribe has only used these words in prayer as she has been instructed to better use these verses and prayers. We use a different writing system and our words are sounded by these symbols. Understand that how these words are pronounced, only serves with the sound given to vibrate these words and only my scribe has learned some of these sounds.

She uses the verses rarely because she does more with human words at this time and does not speak to us in our language. These words are more describing shared knowledge of past and have little to do with Earth understandings of languages, and are rooted in some ancient languages of the Middle East and other societies dealing with Sanskrit or Latin.

Be only seeing this as onm (knowledge) about who we are, as we have been to Earth before and have trusted in answers to a culture of peace and serenity before these "Archons" arrived. The word "Archon" was created recently to describe the "Fallen Angels" but understand, they were never Angels although they impersonated us as needed to deceive these stranded family members waiting for our return.

These stories about Adam and Eve are all lies to create an illusion of the way all began on Earth. But look at the discoveries of ancient pyramids all over the Earth and tell me, does this story fit with these structures? No. More than you know now will be well opened to you and you will see how lies on Earth created a belief system made to answer to only a few "*Apoonancies*", the non-believers in our return.

They thought we would never return after our great loss of a war a long time ago. But here we are ready to walk the Earth, and take back our planet, and see to the well-being of our children. These are promises I made to my wife Sophia, who remained behind with my many natural and adopted children who ask me now to intervene believing we will be coming very soon.

We ask you to open to our return now and to be certain we are not the aggressors. The aggressors are the ones who control Earth and repeat answers to wars to control population, and murder the innocent. Be certain our ways are better healing and be certain you will know us by evidence of our actions and our words.

Be well answered by us, believe who we are as we become seen on Earth responding to all necessary changes opening to us and others. Be understanding happiness when we are reunited and see all trusted answers be dealt with and served by our knowledge and our ways. Be settling with earth ways and open to many who are questioning all, as all truths becomes dealt with by us.

I am seeing how this long separation has caused many to be lost in answers to a world full of lies, deceptions and contradictions. But tell yourselves all will soon be well changed and well dealt with and soon better answered by us and our truths. Better times start soon with us and better truths will be well settled by facts and undeniable evidence.

All is coming now.

God

Received by Za, March 12, 2013.

91. OPEN TO US AND OPEN TO FREEDOM

SETU TIMES ARE VERY NEAR

Be serving holiness with us now as we are your family. Renew with us and renew with your truth about who you are, why you are as prisoners on Earth and why you are working to live a life of slavery. Ask yourselves why you are only allowed to live and have a home unless you work for it and no matter how hard you work, it will take all your lives to hold on to it, otherwise it can be taken away.

Be ready and be dealing with many who are troubled by knowledge about these tricks of giving and taking away from people to manipulate their desires, wants and needs. Be seeing how these ways do not apply to the greedy of the world as they have all the power and no care for those who suffer from starvation and constant fear for their lives.

Be ready and see to it we have all we need to answer to many truths. Be ready to answer to evidence of our ways and be well serving with all who are

Setu. Better times as settling will vindicate many who are searching for our ways and better serving truth opens to more than these games of power and shared self-serving greed.

Be serving the truth about these ways. Understand that people are better served when they have what they need. These ways are served in all places in the Universes but not seen on Earth because you, as said before, are enslaved by darkness and see only these ways of living. Be settling with us well and soon, and see all be well cared for as all evil is removed from Earth and other servants of Lucifer who participate in enslavement.

Better truths and better ways will open to all humans on Earth and elsewhere as many will choose to join with us and the Federation of Light. Many are seeing these words and are not seeing these possibilities. Be certain that those who created a system of wealth have done this by taking from others, often in terrible ways.

They are settling with great wealth because they have found ways to enslave people by opening to a need or desire. They serve with many who are better serving with us but they do not know it. They are only seeing us as partners and friends. Be settling with these understandings as we begin to open to many with our arrivals and know we have well infiltrated the governing of the whole planet.

Many are as humans and are born unto humans, but they are as we are and await our time to walk the Earth. Many are renewing with us as my scribe, but have seen us face to face and have better understanding of the Federation of Light. Be answered by our time to open to the world and be serving with us and others.

Beware of those who will try to impersonate us with similar words and similar organizations as called "Galactic Federation of Light", as these believe, are the demons one must guard against. Be well answered by us and be well answered by us. These times will open very easily to all people of Earth giving all people a better healthier life that will serve around the whole planet.

Evidence of these ways are easier to do than to cause enslavement of people through depravity. The seeing of this will be soon evident. Every person will be able to contribute to their own wished way of living with a better ability to serve their own needs and be free of the ties of money. To share with these ways will open, because all evil will be removed from Earth.

We will explain our ways of used energy and we will explain how food and water can be easily accessible, and how life can easily be happier for so many. As these times balance out, we will heal the sick and feed the hungry, and start teaching our ways to open to all truth and better choices of living and care for each other.

These ways as said are easier than the ways of abuses and government controls over people and societies. These ways are well dealt with us and will be seen by all as we begin to walk the Earth and open to our ways.

Onm now this. Be well understanding that those who are dealing with death, answer to a need to leave Earth as these times arrive, either to try to flee us or to open to a new incarnation that will serve in many ways. They will start a new life in a new place in the Universe. We will break the Earth loop of reincarnation to allow better serving ways to move around the Universes and to open to better healing experiences through these cycles of life and death.

Be visited soon now by our kind. Know that all Earth answers renew with many more truths, many more renewals and answers many more questions you may want to ask. Be well serving with us very soon. Know we will see to answers of great truth together. All will begin to heal the lives of abuses they have shared with many other lives through past incarnations.

Better answers open to a more trusted truth, a more trusted way of life and better serving ways. Answer to evidence of great Setu ways at the time of our arrivals. Be certain all heals and all healing opens to all who are as we are, evidence of true love.

Now be ready.

God

Received by Za, March 13, 2013.

92. BELIEVE WE ARE COMING

BESSRON AONMA POON ONM ANSWERS YOU

'Shared proof and evidence of believed knowledge
and light of understanding answers you.'

Be ready, knowledge will soon be yours as you begin to answer to our ways and open to our truth. Renew with us and others and be dealing with answers to proof of who we are as we will soon meet all who are ready to open to us. Be serving with us and others as we begin answering to answers you will have and need.

Be certain all comes as I said. See to it you will better serve with truth than with darkness. Now settle with Earth ways by dealing with the fall of your economies. Know this plan was scheduled to open to many wars to cause pain, fear and death as a way to destabilize all countries to open to a New World Order serving Lucifer whores and demons.

Then see yourselves who will be murdered first and who will be the sacrificial lambs to please these whores and demons. Know that the escalation of war is answered soon as all participants are in place and are ready to destroy cities full of people without any care or remorse.

With these attacks comes our arrivals. These are the reasons we are able to open to take Earth back from Lucifer and return it to the better ways of life and cleanliness as it was before Lucifer took it from us. Know we are many and we will not be defeated as these are the end times for this demon, his whores and parasites.

Respond to knowledge about our truth and understand who we are and know we are all family. Renew with us and others as all *Apoonancies* (non-believers in our return) are being sorted. See how truth opens to all as we are better serving judgement responding to these devils. Know they cannot escape us as we are settling all over the planet, and believe no stone will be left unturned.

Be understanding all truth starts with us. All better ways answers to evidence of our ways as all starts changing beliefs on Earth. Be responding to answers and knowledge that will settle the lies and all deceptions. Renew with us, and be well opening to our time to be serving with holiness, our time to walk the Earth. Know all who are pure of heart and soul will be lifted in spirit as we share our ways of love and care for each person on Earth.

Better times are soon approaching and better ways are soon answered with the settling good truth opening now to all my children. Know these truths as we share them with you and understand the Setu time opens soon with all who are ready to meet with us. Be well settling with Lucifer's way of corruption and abuses being dealt now all over the planet.

Know that these times are ending and will forever be changed for people to live completely in love, security and care with all needs met and all families renewed. We are so happy to return to Earth and find our lost children who have lost their memories through DNA manipulations. We will be able to serve a better used way to restore all health and memories easily and well.

Healing begins with us and our arrivals, and we will certainly care for all our family members. Be ready, all is well on its' way and settling soon with evidence of our arrivals. None who are of our kind will fear us as they will feel our presence in their hearts. And then all who fear us will soon be discovered for who they are as they will understand who we are.

Be certain my children, you have nothing to fear and see how your family members are soon so happy to be with you again and know they ask me every day "how much longer", and I tell them "all is very soon". Know my words and find yourselves. Understand we are the ones you call Angels but we are many and from many places in the Universes and we are not all alike but very similar.

And more are coming to help, as they are seeing all as we are and believe in healing ways. Be Setu with us very soon. Know we are near Earth and ready to answer you, as the time to intervene heals with our ways and our time to walk the Earth. Reunification time will soon be dealt with and we will begin to use our ways in all places of urgent needs.

Be well renewing with us and be happy to meet with your families soon, as they are soon happy to see you again. Be serving with us soon and be healing all the harm that has been imprinted on your hearts to stop you from knowing the whole truth. Be seeing that half-truths can be as misleading as lies and know that your holy books are changed by many half-truths.

You must learn to be very discerning at reading these words written by men with the desire of control on their minds. Be ready for the truth as you meet with us. See for yourselves who we are and why we are angry about the abuses of Earth, as no good laws are made to heal the victims and serve only the elite who are renewing with more power and greed.

These ways as seen by us are abominations and all this is healed by our time to walk the Earth. Make sure you will see truth now as all will be well evident and well dealt with, and none will be persecuted for being a child, a woman or an honest man. All will live in peace, health and serenity as these ways are certainly easier to be serving than a world of abuses and wars.

Be ready, onm is arriving and opening to all of you. Settling times are coming for our enemies and your enemies. As the time leads to our time to walk the Earth and answer to your prayers and your truth. Be well answered, we are soon with you and we are well knowing all who are as we are, ready for Setu ways.

God

Received by Za, March 14, 2013.

93. BETTER TIMES FOLLOW THE DARK TIMES

BE SERVING UNDERSTOOD TRUTH WITH OPEN EYES

All heals soon with us and all good truth answers to us and others. Be serving with us and answer to evidence of understood ways. Be ready and be well serving of our ways with the renewals opening to our settling ways. Better times will be seen after the first attacks of war. Be seeing all used ways of dealing with these attacks. Try to remain calm and be feeling the sadness of it but be knowing all starts changing after these first attacks of war.

Be well knowing all evidence of truth by us and be well answered by us. Evidence responds to our time to walk the Earth and settle with the dealings of well trusted truths opening to answers to many more bridging seeing. Be ready as these days are near and deals with the better serving ways to open to our telling of old.

Better times start with us as all renews on Earth. Be understanding how all healing begins with us as we will better serve with our ways and our truths. Be serving many other ways of being answered and be renewing with us and others as the uses of Setu ways are served and dealt with.

Know now these words and ready yourselves for returning family as arrivals become well seen. Be answered by our truth, our wishes and our settling ways, as these ways become dealt with. Be determined to meet with us because we will not force our presence on those who are only responding to fear. Shared answers come as shared answers, only this can be possible.

To open to us you must want to, only this. We will be very happy to serve with you on Earth. People see our arrivals as an invasion but see this as a return to our home from long ago before we had to escape. Be seeing how we are as you are in bodies like yours, but some of us became stronger and taller from better health and better answers to settling with our travels.

These ways will renew with Earth beings as we have learned many healing ways and better living ways. The sharing of our ways will better serving because we are never ill or settling with any diseases. These diseases on Earth are made to control population and serve to choose who has to be removed because they cannot work anymore.

See this as you will but see and understand many things. One of these ways of population control has to do with aging and this can be corrected by us. We are all very old and able to be as we were in our youth. Understand the aging on Earth stops humans from opening to their truth. As these visits begin, we will begin to answer to all illnesses, better open to all life on Earth and care will be our first actions to show all how we can heal all.

Be well answered by us. Be dealing with our truth and our ways at the understood time of our arrivals. Renew with us and others at the time of our meeting. Settle with the ways of Earth as these ways will settle with the wars. We will open to all truth and all serving ways with us and many others. Be well serving with us very soon and open to our ways. Onm now these words.

God

Received by Za, March 15, 2013

94. BE DEALING WITH THE GOOD SETTLING DAYS OF WARS AND DEATH

BE WELL SEEING ANSWERS AS SAID

Now be ready. Evidence of our truth starts with the visits better answering to many who are renewing with us as we arrive. Be ready and remain in your homes as all starts because the arrivals will cause many to react in fear and respond to unwanted actions against others. Soon you will see all better truth open to us and serve belief of our ways.

Renewing with us tells of these evident ways of our truth. Love will be well seen all around the world with our words and our return to our planet Earth. Be knowing we have come home and now is the time for you to see the truth about who we are and who you are, as all becomes well dealt with and well settled by us.

I am seeing how many are looking for our truth and answer to our ways with great trust, but I am also seeing many be filled with fear at the sight of our ships in the skies. Be ready and see to it you have what you need for a few months as more trouble may be serving in many places of Earth. Be well answered by us now, knowledge and light are coming.

Be dealing with our way of great serving truth and better answers than these words serving the men who wrote them. Be certain many will be seeing how all starts with us and others, and better serves with evidence of our truth.

Now open to our time to walk the Earth. Be dealing with the answers well serving these times on Earth. Renew with the serving responses opening to all who are ready to meet with us and settle with Earth ways. These days are soon here and serving with us and others. Better truth becomes well dealt with as all who are being saved by us will know this themselves.

Many others will open to their truth, better seeing of who they are and why they are as prisoners on Earth with only the present life memories, settling and answering to their renewals, better answers to dealings of lies and telling of denied truths. Be seeing how all begins and how all becomes served by us and many who are better trusting in our ways and our answers to more truths, telling all that they are more than one life to be used and better serving onm (knowledge) of these used (past) truths.

Be responding now to evidence of our arrivals. Be dealing with the settling view you have about aliens, spirits and ghosts, as these renewed telling understood, will answer all your questions and better answer to our great knowledge and shared truth. Be willing now to come to us and be with us to ask questions.

Settle with the ways of deceptions imprinted to your DNA, as these deceivers have dealt with for thousands of years to trick all into beliefs that oppose each other and opens to many strife and wars that serve only their own glory and riches that they steal from each other. Silly games, but dangerous players who live as psychopaths without remorse or care about the horrors these wars cause.

The harm this causes perpetuates and damages the soul of people they see as their slaves. Be ready and see all be quickly changed, as these ways of

Earth will see their end. As all is rebalancing on Earth, we will have many more serving truths to answer and to better serve with evidence of our ways and proof of our telling.

Better days will begin to shine in all places of Earth. Many people will learn our ways and care for all living life with our renewals of health and shared knowledge. Better seeing of these ways are soon arriving. Better dealings of truth will soon open to many Setu servings with us and many others from the Universes.

Be ready and see all better settling ways be seen as we begin the sorting in evidence of our time of judgement. Know all those who live to cause harm onto others will be removed and put in their right places. Be understanding this as a necessary step to heal Earth of all problems and ill-will. Be better answered because now answers as said are coming and well underway.

Be settling with the lies and deceptions plaguing Earth Humans. Better answers to our used truth of who we are with the way of great renewals, great uses of our truth, better ways of living and opening to our understood ways. Be well serving with us and know we are all soon reunited to better answer to each other as it was at the First.

Be onm, be believing all is healed because we are waiting now to come to Earth at the first sign of great danger of war (WW3). These used ways of destruction will no longer be tolerated. Now be bridging with us and see these days are soon.

God

Received by Za, March 16, 2013.

95. BE SERVING WITH US NOW

BE READY TO OPEN TO THE BETTER TIMES
WITH US AND OTHERS FROM THE UNIVERSES

Now listen. The way all starts will be dealing with first a sky full of ships. Be ready and know we are the ones arriving and not the Grey or the Reptilians, as you call them. We are as humans in body but we also serve with others who are as beings of great serving truth, and who are not as we are in body.

These others are serving with us and we answer with them as colleagues. Be seeing that the Universes are filled with many mysteries to you but for us it is filled with known places and peoples from many areas and different cultures. Be serving with us and find your place among us with many others dealing with these beings as you would with us.

Be serving our ways and good truths about who we all are. Know all starts into the coming days. Healing will begin for many more people on earth as the Earth is riddled with parasites to answer to illnesses that are a form of dependency on the medical system dictated by answers from pharmaceutical and chemical companies or multinational agendas.

These ways are serving to cause a training of obedience to treatment that will harm many more people. But better truth needs to be seen here. The doctors and health professionals are seen as helping with the health of people but they are well serving answers to a controlled response to medication methods they are conditioned to believe heals. But these are lies.

They are also taught to profile patients using methodical answers to better settle with those who question and to deal with them as troublemakers. Be seeing that not all doctors are servants of the pharmaceutical conglomerates, but most are. They see only what they are taught to see without any serving thought of their own to counter the effects of programming they have been subjected to in early medical training.

These telling truths are seen by us with the better death sentences of those who are well profiled by cancer treating doctors who trust in barbaric and deadly methods of treatment initiated by the Grey who care about how much humans can take, as they are testing them for life on other slave planets.

I am seeing how this may be shared as arrivals become dealt with. But as it is now, people believe that what heals is settling with these death treatments reported and analyzed by pharmaceutical companies, as they can only test on humans who can show results of the amount of radiation tolerable in bodies.

Be certain of my words and know that with these ways of profiling in many countries on Earth, the people who are chosen are very well chosen by blood types and genetics. They are also chosen by life circumstances as many are seen as useless eaters and are soon on the top of the list for radiation treatment and sharing with other treatments, as removal of part or whole organs to measure the rate of life living after these mutilations.

Be seeing these abominations serving with the Grey and the Reptilians agendas, as these methods only respond to them. Understand we know what they are doing and why they are doing this. Know that people who go missing have to do with their actions in most cases. And know they are soon settling with these ways, as we are stopping these abominations.

Be serving with us soon and know we can heal with evidence of great renewals of health easily and without troubles or pain. Know that all cancers can be easily treated without radiation and mutilations. Be ready for these answers. Understand these ways are very easy and accessible to all people with illnesses and diseases.

Be ready and answer to us soon. Be dealing with evidence of great trust in answers to our ways and to the seeing of Apoonancies (non-believers, servants of Lucifer) dealings with the Grey and the Reptilians merchants of slaves. They have taken many humans to sell across the Universes, some are now serving with us as we freed them from bondage, but others are now settling with Setu truths now.

We are arriving with them to return them to their families. Be ready because many are coming back to Earth and are Setu with us. Your trust will grow as you see these ones coming back to their loved ones and we promise you they are returning healed and strong. Many will have much to tell you as they are sharing responses with you.

Now listen. Better answers as said are well underway and will open to a time of great truth and great renewals. All better used answers open soon to evidence of great truth with us and with others. Be well serving with us and be willing to open to these truths. Settle with Earth ways, lies and deceptions and be free from the control well served by these Alien agendas or black operation groups plaguing Earth.

These groups use tricks to seduce those who think they govern the Earth. Be seeing that these Grey and Reptilians we warned you about, are ruthless murderers and liars, and give very little technology in exchange for human flesh and slaves. They are seen by us as disgusting whores of Lucifer and we travel the Universes to rid them of places like Earth that fall victim to their insidious works of evil. And know the one called Lucifer is Reptilian and is not a light bearer, as these fools care to say about him.

These times are soon ending now. Be ready to see an Earth free from parasites and serving whores who see only their desires used to better their lives. But know they too can easily fall victim to Lucifer as he has no truth nor serving trust in anyone or anything. Be ready to answer to our ways and hear these words as our time of arrivals are soon coming. We will open to all truth.

Better serve with us as all is well seen by you. Healing begins to strengthen all who are as we are, Setu Beings of Light and great truth. Be ready and be ready, as arrivals become dealt with and as arrivals open to a new time on Earth to open each belief with us, to open the way to your freedom from darkness.

Be serving with us soon, as we are united and serve with the Universal Laws that helps all planets in trouble to better freedom, love and care. All will be returned to the paradise Earth was before these demons arrived and destroyed it. Heal with us soon.

God

Received by Za, March 17, 2013.

96. SEE US ARRIVE AND SEE THE CHURCH FALL AS THESE LIES ARE OPENED

KNOW WE ARE YOUR FAMILIES RETURNED

Understand that the Vatican chose a Jesuit because they have knowledge of the uses of space seeing with telescopes. Also, because they have the knowledge of the workings of our ways, as we have met them before with our scouts in the USA, to tell them we are returning to Earth and to prepare Earth people for our presence on Earth. But these Popes did nothing more to serve others and only served themselves.

See these times be ready for our time to walk the Earth and know we are well seen by the Jesuit telescopes who are studying our movements as these words are shared. Better answers to better truths will open to all who are ready to open to it, and these truths have much to say about who well controls Earth and the innocent ones who are sacrificed to be used by these settling answers to cause us to arrive.

These words as said, are difficult and well answered by us. But because you are seeing it from Earth perspective, it may seem overwhelming. Be trusting in my words, a more trusted time follows our arrivals. Know you will open to our ways and our serving answers to all my children and all families stolen from us.

I am serving a time of meditation before we walk the Earth and I am serving these words to you before healing time comes so that you are well prepared for the coming days. You who are reading my words now, are the Elect. You who have found these words and feel these truths in you, are my children.

As we arrive, you will feel the happiness of reunification open in your hearts. You will know we are your truth and your caring family members, seeing to all truths and all serving answers. Be Setu with us now as all is soon in place to cause our arrivals, as the destruction of Earth has gone far enough and our Laws open to our time of intervention.

Be ready and see all be answered by us. Be serving with us well and renew with us as we arrive to renew with you. See these days be very near. See these truths better answer to our ways as we will begin the sorting in evidence of our time to clear Earth of all parasites and those who serve the devil Lucifer. Know we will do this fast, so none have time to cause harm again.

Be well answered now and be dealing with the sadness of the many deaths opening soon with settling wars. But know all will stop here and know we come to heal many who respond to our truth with trust, because we cannot impose ourselves on our own children and we must be ready for fear to answer some.

Be Setu with us and help with this time of transition with us to serve those who have no knowledge or memories of who we are. Be serving with us first as we will give you answers to be seen and use a better opening to many and healing those in need.

At the time of our arrivals, we will begin very quickly to open to our many truths and our many trusted answers to better ways of living. Also, we will begin the sorting to remove the controllers who are dealers of lies and deceptions. Better serving ways will be well established and we will start our reunification as soon as we can.

As all starts, many will be surprised to answer to evidence of our truth with 'Answer to answers' a book that I hold in my lap, written by my wife Sophia. These used (past) truths are serving to explain how we needed to leave Earth to open to the Universal Laws with all others from many other planets in the Universes.

Be certain all can be learned and explained. All these truths will be easily seen as we begin the sorting and the removals of the deep Earth parasites that plague the Earth and caused many of us to leave. But we are well ready to return and to renew with all who were taken as slaves and open to your freedom.

These words I share with you are soon yours to open to, and soon yours to answer to. Be ready and renew with us soon now at the time of reunification and great truth. Be ready.

God

Received by Za, March 18, 2013

97. BE SETTLING WITH THE HORRORS OF EARTH WAYS

BE RESPONDING TO CHANGE NOW SHARING ALL WITH YOU FACE TO FACE.

Be well settling with the horrors and lawlessness of the Earth. These times settle with an onm (knowledge and light of understanding...) of who you are. Knowing this will cause you anger and soon sadness, but this is healed as all seen changes will put a stop to all abuses and cruelties to all living life that will remain on Earth after the cleansing and the sorting.

Understand many are renewing with lies told to them since childhood that humans rely on dead animals to survive and to live. But see these ways as serving to teach our kind to harden their hearts to the animals who are living on Earth under human care. No care from murderous psychopaths is ever seen; psychopaths who kill animals as a game or a sport are only renewing with the ways of demons who see this themselves as a reason to eat humans, and only this.

These demons eat flesh and taught humans to eat flesh and they settle with their ways on people to give them more to eat. But this is a falsehood. Humans get ill from eating meat and they age faster as pigs do, who are fed and fattened for slaughter. Renew with these facts yourselves and deal with these truths as I am telling you these words, because you are well settling with liars responding to their own agendas.

Many more people can live on Earth healthier and longer without flesh eating and without serving the breeding of animals for slaughter. This to us is an abomination and believe, we are never settling with these ways. We do no harm, and certainly not to you or animals on Earth. Be dealing with the ways of great healing from these barbaric times. Open your hearts to being the caretakers of the Earth.

See that all life seen with you is part of Earth to share and not to destroy. Plants are created to give you all that you need to be healthy, to give you strength and longer lives but only some practice these good ways. Many are not conscious of the harm they allow to exist by these wrong choices of food. Be ready for the truths behind the blood practices, as they are only settling to serve answers to more illnesses well known to humans as diabetes and dementia, all caused directly from flesh death eating.

Understand that animals who eat meat as scavengers are settling with another body than humans. They are different and need flesh to live. So, we care for these animals until their life has concluded. But humans are only vegan by nature of body, and to corrupt it with meat allows many cells to act against the body causing many illnesses, so these are not good and will cause a body to age very quickly.

With these ways of eating, much troubles of the mind develops responding to age related illnesses and better seeing of this must better serve. Understand the purpose of life on Earth heals with our time to walk the Earth. See how all renewals will open to a new truth about how all serves with health returned and regenerated with our ways.

Be responding to our ways and be dealing with trust in healing all ills of the Earth. Know we are all answering to better ways and better truth with used ways of living that will be easy to open to. Much more will be seen because of these ways of better health. Be ready and know all harm caused to others will be dealt with and eliminated from Earth, as these ways were never Earth's ways before the Grey and the Reptilians settlers arrived.

They are the cause of this horrid corruption of humans, renewing with stories of cavemen and Neanderthals that never were who you are, but another race brought to Earth by these demons. Be serving these truths and open your eyes to truth. And these dinosaurs were also brought to Earth to destroy our civilizations.

These stories of evolution are all created to control knowledge, to stop you from renewing with the true story of demons and Mars, and how many worked their way through this planet to create chaos and destruction, as this is all they are capable of.

All these words seem impossible for some to believe, but understand you are well imprinted to better serve them and only these truths coming will show you how all have been deceived. Serving with holiness and truth will change everyone and everything on Earth. Be well settling with Earth ways and be well serving of our Setu ways. Know we are serving with you to open to truth.

God

Received by Za, March 19, 2013.

98. BE READY AND SERVE TRUTH WITH US

QUESTIONS WILL BE ANSWERED WITH OUR TRUTH

Be ready all starts soon. Heal these days of great serving with us. Be renewing with our ways. Be well answered by us now and be renewing with us and others as we arrive and walk the Earth. Be serving with us, be responding to onm (knowledge and light of understanding) and to many more trusted ways.

See to it you have all you need to be well for the next few weeks, as all starts with the wars and cause some foods and water to be contaminated or lacking. As the wars start, many visits from us will be seen by many in evidence of our ships coming to Earth. Some will try to cause you fear and tell you we are the ones who harm, but these are lies.

We are not well serving to cause harm but to better life on Earth, our Earth. Be serving with us and have no fear, as we are not the ones to fear. Those who are to be feared, believe, are among you and share with governments who open to lawlessness and deceit. Be well answered by us and be well serving of our ways with the serving answers well coming from us.

All your health needs will be met. All your housing needs will be met. All your struggles for living will be settled. All who wish to educate themselves with our knowledge will be welcomed. More will be done for the serving of truth. Many will begin to feel freedom from corruption and abuses that will be dealt with and soon all removed.

And this is healing, and this is very possible. These are our ways because we are the ones who are the creators of Earth. We return to Earth to heal with our arrivals and all renewing ways. Be well answered because all is coming as I said.

Know we are ready to answer to evidence of great truth. Know we are the ones spoken about by those who wish to hide the truth of who we are, as they are in great danger of losing their power, their wealth, their control and all the armaments your work has given to these fools. I say this with anger, and I say this with great sadness. I am now ready to settle with these men who believe they are higher than all others, but all they did is steal, lie and deceive.

These people are not the answers to your protection, they are the way to your population control and exploitation. The seeing of this may be difficult for some because many are living to this day in good comfort and can be reading these words on a computer. But most cannot, and they are renewing only with hunger, pain and sorrow.

Be serving understanding about charities. All charities that are said to help the poor and the meek, are serving themselves and are enriching themselves to open now to many more abuses coming, as all becomes well seen by those who suffer them. The seeing of responding charities are serving and answering to the Lucis Foundation that is tied to the United Nations, and is a means for the control of the poor, as all poor are soon charted to be reduced in numbers.

Be this said, avoid answering to them as they will begin to settle with people in ways unseen before and healing is not part of their plans. Be responding to others who are in need yourselves and be ready to answer to many who are going to be in need for a few weeks before we arrive to open to our better ways. And see to it, you are well renewing with your own health and needs until we arrive, as these times are going to be and feel like chaos for some weeks until we can settle with these demons.

Be well serving our ways of great truth with us. Be dealing with many who will better respond to each other with calm and understanding, as these uses of wars unravel and settle with our ways. Be well vindicated by our time to walk the Earth. Be serving a time of deep meditation to open to our time of reunification, as we are soon with you and ready to open all Setu (bridging) time together.

Better times are soon arriving after the time of tribulations and serving truth will blossom in all hearts. We see our ways better serving than any form of prison style governments in the world of Earth. Settle with Earth ways and open to the Universal Laws more than seen on Earth, and better settle with us and many others from many planets who are ready to meet humans.

Open to all trust in who we are. Be certain we are only sharing onm with those who are able to respond and accept our return to Earth, and who settle with ways of corruption of the soul and abuses of the innocent. Be serving holiness with us soon and be ready.

God

Received by Za, March 20, 2013

99. OPEN TO US MORE NOW

RENEW WITH US AND READY

Be serving with us. Be dealing with evidence and answers to truth as we begin to walk the Earth. Be ready to settle with Earth ways. Be understanding how all heals as we begin the sorting, and how we answer to our truth with the way of great telling and great trusted ways. Know we are ready to land on Earth and better serve with all who are knowing about the truth about who governs Earth's underground.

Renew with us as we begin to open these caverns made by these users of humans. Be dealing with us and others as we take-over all governments in the world and serve to open to answers to our truth. Be ready to answer to our call as we are reuniting with our children taken from us a long time ago. Know we have returned to take you away from these enslavers.

Bessron aonma poon onm. (Share evidence of believed knowledge). Be ready to serve with us and others as we begin the sorting and tend to the needs of many humans in sharing of our health ways and healing ways. Know we are here now to help all people of Earth with many answers and many truths of who we are. And know we are here now to help all people of Earth with truths of who you are and who we are.

Be serving many more truths with us as we walk the Earth and renew with our families. Healing this, I promise, will be amazing. Be renewing with us more than ever as we will no longer watch the atrocities of Earth continue because it is our time to intervene and stop these horrors of denials and abuses. Now all starts with the first ships opening to the world and landing in many places.

Setu (bridging) truth will be heard. Used truths will be unraveled. Be opening to all serving ways and be dealing with us. Love opens to us and you as arrivals start and as we begin to answer back to those who cause all these troubles.

Be certain all Setu ways start with the truth, answers to evidence of our renewals, our trust in the coming days and the coming settling times. Be serving with us now and be with us, as we begin the judgements on those who trespassed and caused harm onto others.

Be visited soon by our Diplomats who are chosen by us and who will serve to open to many with the knowledge we will bestow onto them, to open to many who are ready to answer to our ways and settle with Earth ways. Be well Setu with us as more than you are expecting arrives soon to open to the world.

Be well answered by us and see to evidence of our ways with the dealings of soon so many truths. 'Answer to answers' a book used to guide us to answer to truth, will open to all who have waited to be delivered from evil. Be well seeing that this time has come and we will serve all who are ready to heal with us and share our truths.

Be well answered my children, these days have arrived and answer you. Be settling with Earth ways now as all starts and as all settles with the answers to evidence of our ways. Be well serving of our truth as we are seeing all and know your hearts and souls, answering to all who are ready to meet with us. Opening to the way of great truth and great settling answers, will open to a time of great peace, comfort and security.

None will starve, none will be ill, none will be abused and none will be harmed in any way. As we begin the sorting, all those who will be removed will be seen for who they are and all of them as said, are guilty of crimes against Humanity and we will not leave any stone unturned. These days are now here my children.

All who are dealing with us will be served with grace, and dealing with our trust and yours. These ways are now well serving and well shared with us and many others in the Universes. We all serve the Universal Laws in evidence of causing no harm. Renewing with us will renew with these laws. All who oppose these laws are evidently causing harm so we will remove them and put them in a place of returned state of healing.

This means they will experience the troubles they caused to others. They will know and deal with the pain they themselves caused. These are our Laws. These Laws renewed on Earth will open to answers to truth and deal with the settling of Earth abuses.

Be responding to our call and be dealing with the truth of who we are and who you are as we begin to open to the world. Settle with Earth ways at the time of better serving reunification and renewals. Be ready and be ready.

God

Received by Za, March 21, 2013

100. BESSRON AONMA POON ONM

SEE ALL COME AS I SAID

Understand all starts well into the good serving days. These times of wars will answer many questions about our arrivals. Be well vindicated as we become seen, as we answered and opened to many with evidence. Understand all better seeing about how all is will soon better serve with our truth. All who share our truth will answer to our ways and serve with our answers to evidence of proof.

These times will bring many more trusted ways because of the death of many who will be murdered by wars and weapons unseen before on Earth. Many will only see these times as ways of great answers to the end times. Settle with these thoughts as we are responding after the first attack, as we are serving holiness of the understood Universal Laws, and our arrivals will only come at this time.

Many uses of new technologies will be demonstrated by us, as we will shut off all power in dangerous war zones to better answer to stopping these attacks on people. I am seeing how these understandings are shared among many of you as we have shared these ways before by our scouts but now see much more will be done.

These ways will settle with responses to defending those who are in need of protection. Deal with this as you may, and settle with the Earth seeing to open now to our ways. Be well answered and be dealing with the view you have about who answers you, because many see us as Aliens from other planets and are not understanding why we are called Angels from Heaven.

Be understanding that we are many from many planets. The truth will soon be visited by you when we begin to walk the Earth as we did many times before. These days were in the time of Abraham, in the times of Vashnu (Vishnu), in the times of Buddha and when my son Jesus incarnated on Earth to answer to change and reformation of truth. But they murdered him for being all that he is. He is now with me on my right side with his brothers.

Now Jesus will return to Earth with us behind him. I will not allow any of my sons to be harmed again. I am returning to our planet Earth to open to our time of reunification with our children and my wife Sophia who lives in denial of who she is, as she too suffered the abuses of indoctrination, imprinted denials and many horrors of tortures and deaths life after life.

She is only partially awakened as you are and she cannot remember who she is. But know this is true for many of my better serving children who cannot be responding to me now because they too have been manipulated in these ways, and their souls and hearts have closed to me.

See this as you wish, but this is truth. I am returning to stop these abominations and to rid the Earth of these parasites that infected Earth a long time ago, and who will soon be opening to our time of questions about their actions. Be certain they will be judged according to the Universal Laws and no indoctrination of forgiveness will be used to free them from responsibility for the deaths and crimes against Humanity.

They will be dealing with us. Be certain of these words and know these are our words as we see all, and no tricks or lies or Earth laws will be giving them any freedom from responsibility. Better times will follow as these judgements will be fast and quickly acted upon.

Be well answering to our arrivals and open to us and settle with earth ways as these ways are only serving lies, deceptions and slavery. Better times as said, follow soon after. So, I ask you my children, to be patient and kind with each other as all will soon be seen and dealt with. Be ready as all comes as I said. More than you are expecting answers you all very soon.

God

Received by Za, March 22, 2013.

101. BESSRON TIMES ARE COMING

BE SERVING USED TRUTHS WITH OUR ARRIVALS

Be ready, more than you are expecting answers you now. Be well answered by our used (past) truths at the time of our arrivals as we will begin to open to our truths with answers to many who are Setu with us. Evidence of serving ways will better answer all who are ready to answer to evidence of our truth. All who ask why we are not arrived yet, I can only say be patient, we are soon there with you and all will be very soon.

Be ready to open to our arrivals and be well answering to our ways. Setu times are in place and we are to act on the first attack of WW3. Be responding to onm (knowledge...) about dealings of the USA and Israel as they have brokered a plan of attack onto Iran, and because of this, all helps for us to arrive and stop all further destruction and abuses.

See this as the warning renewed with the USA by our scouts when they answered Eisenhower and the others who were with him. Be seeing how these warnings are well documented but not shared in their totality. **This is what I sent as a warning: "Tell them we are returning to Earth as these worlds are ours to use and do not belong to Lucifer. Tell them we will not serve with uses of lies and deceptions and we will not settle with any compromises. And tell them now is the time to open to truth with the people of Earth".**

But all they did is to add more confusion and allowed a rogue group of military users to become more powerful and dangerous to my children. They enslaved more people and murdered more, dealing with Lucifer's anger and tricks, to push humans to work on more weapons and cause so many more wars about nothing only to practice the uses of these weapons.

Be seeing how all started a long time ago when Lucifer infiltrated our own lives to answer to corruption and division. This is how he works and this is how your leaders on Earth have served him. Little do they know about how they themselves are promised power and protection but in fact, all will be destroyed settling with their losses and with our arrivals.

These demons are only responding to their own psychopathic greed and destruction of all serving ways. As all starts with us, you will begin to see more change and more happiness everywhere on Earth. All who answered to us will be blessed with these new ways of living, with care and love and so much truth and understanding.

This is settling with Earth ways and these times are used by us and others to open to truth. Be well serving with us and be well seeing with us, as we are soon arriving to open to all who are ready to open to us. Now these coming days will be difficult for many people on Earth. Many will soon see these times as evidence as seen in the Book of Revelations.

But more than these words will be seen. Evidence of these ways will well serve with us and many others at the time of great answers. Be well answered by us soon and see to it you now share these words with trusted friends. As all heals with us and as all becomes well dealt with, you will be settling with Earth ways as these ways are Lucifer's ways and his time of occupying Earth is over.

Be certain he will be removed, and be certain he will be judged very quickly as we know all that he has done. More will be seen soon. Be ready.

God

Received by Za, March 23, 2013

102. BE READY THE WARS (WW3) ARE COMING

BESSRON (SHARED) ANSWERS ARE COMING SOON

Now all is soon started. The WW3 is in place to answer to our ways of great renewals and better serving times answers to our ways. Be well answering to all who are serving with us. See how all opens to answers well into the good serving days.

Deaths will be seen in many places of the world, as these times start being renewed by wars. These ways better settle with the dealings of great truth as we have said. As arrivals are seen, many more will take their own lives because they answer to other ways. But know all will settle soon after into a time of healing and peace.

Be only responding to yourselves, your families and friends, because chaos will open to many places on Earth, and because all who are dealing with causing these troubles will want to cause many more, poon (believe). See to it you have what you need for a short time. Be well answered when we arrive but understand we will open to many others first with the settling of care. Then we will heal all who are ill, and seeing to better health ways. Later all will begin the restoration of Earth with our ways of cleaning this planet.

Before visits begin, I want to ask you to be well prepared to respond to answers of our ways. Do not use better settling ways with others who are evil, and trusting in self-defense only, because many will want to take arms and this is not being careful. Be calm, be patient, we are soon arriving and we will remove these parasites ourselves.

Be well answered as we arrive. Be willing to open to many who are seeing to your well-being better than ever seen by your governments and slave masters, because we have only our Universal Laws renewing and no other plans as these devils have. As arrivals are served, you will see this yourselves and you will participate only willingly to some of our cleaning projects, to return Earth to you and us, as it was before.

And these ways are very easy. Many of you will begin better lives and better living ways. I promise these truths as said are soon coming for all my children. With us, are many who serve the Universal Laws and who have experienced the changes coming to Earth, and this they can tell you about themselves.

Be ready and see to all your basic needs for a few weeks. Then be ready to respond to our arrivals as we will come after the first attack to open to the world in evidence of our words shared. Now tell yourselves that many changes are coming. This means that governments will fall, that territories and countries will have only better serving borders, and that the responding Angels will be leaders for the transitional times.

I say this now because you do not remember us and yourselves yet. So, to alleviate any misunderstandings, we come to bring these ways of organization that are only serving a short time. The Angels in place will soon only open to their own families, as all people of Earth will know we do not need governing when the Laws as renewed are healed.

This is easier than dealing with corruption as it is now settling on Earth. Many with us will tell you to answer to yourselves only and not to others. As all healing starts, you will be free and you will know what needs to be done yourselves.

I am coming home, and this heals with me also. As these days are soon coming, I can tell you my heart feels swollen with sadness and also joy of returning the Earth to the paradise it once was. All my children will live long lives and better, much better lives with us as reunification time is opened to all of us. Now be ready and tell yourselves **ascension** is this.

God

Received by Za, March 24, 2013.

103. BE READY BETTER ANSWERS ARE COMING

HEAL WITH BELIEVED TRUTH

Answers to your darkness are coming. We see all on Earth from our ships. We respond to answers settling with the lies of Earth ways. We serve with others who are ready to open to many truths with evidence of our answers to better truth. Be ready to open to our ways and be ready to answer to our renewed answers to many more telling of our ways as we begin to walk the Earth.

Be serving with great truth now and be dealing with us as we begin the sorting and the removal of these parasites that have plagued Earth for so long. Be telling yourselves all begins a new time on Earth. All evil will be extinguished because Earth cannot survive this way. Now see to it you have what you need for a few weeks of food, shelter, water and deal with these times as these times are called by many 'end times' but it is in fact the end of evil.

Setu times as said are here, and these ways of great serving answers you more than ever as you will soon see these ways yourselves. Better truth starts well into the good serving days. All begins with us and others as we start opening to our ways to share with you. These ways will serve all earthly serving needs with care in evidence of our renewals with you.

Be well answered by us and by answers to our truth with many trusted ways of settling with Earth ways and be ready to answer to many who are waiting to reunite with their families. See these understandings more. Open to used truths, as these stories of old will remind some of you of who you are and how your lives have been diminished to serve an evil entity called Lucifer.

People deny his existence but I am telling you knowledge about these kind, Reptilians, heals with us, as we dealt with him many times before. Now he will not escape us, as he has only Earth left to live out his last days. Be certain he was never one of us, and these lies are his only and do not renew with us.

I am seeing many say he is an Angel of great beauty, but when he deals with his psychopathy you will know used truths shared are truths. He manipulates people and serving with him only answers to death and nothing more. Be well answered by us now. Be settling with Earth ways and be dealing with all truths as all begins to heal and opens to our ways of great settling times.

Be willing to open to our truth at the time of our landing of ships. As said before, we will land in fields and on airstrips in all places of the world and begin the sorting to stop evil from continuing their actions against all innocent beings. Renewing with us will serve many truths and many trusted ways. See all better answers open to you and all those you care about who are as you are.

Better truths start well into the good serving days and opens to many who are ready to answer to great trusted truths. Be well serving of our ways and answer to proof of our arrivals shortly. Be willing to answer to us and open to our ways with us. Better times soon follows as we deal with the fear many will have about our appearance and our abilities.

But understand we are all families; we will heal the damage causing your bodies to breakdown and become painful and weak. Be well serving of our ways and know all starts well into the good serving days. All who fear us will soon see we are well settling with evil only and we will see to all urgent needs with our better ways and better settling answers to living ways.

Be well and be serving with us soon as these days answers to many who are dealing with our ways and our truths. Be ready and be well answered.

God

Received by Za, March 25, 2013.

104. BE WELL SETTLING
WITH US AND OTHERS

DEALING WITH DECEPTIONS IS
HEALING WITH ALL TRUTHS

Open your minds and your hearts, and see many truths answer you more now. Renewing with us will open to a life of peace and serenity. Many will better fulfill their lives and passion for living with great ease and great happiness. These ways are our ways and settling times on Earth are here to answer you with the seeing times.

Be dealing now more with trust in healing and deal with our Setu tessron. Know all who will remain on Earth will live better lives. They will uncover the knowledge that answers to our truth. Be well answered by us and see all these words manifest in many more ways than expected by most of you.

Be ready and see how we will answer to our truth with our Setu seeing and better answers, as we arrive and open to our families of Earth. Be ready and see all start with the way of government announcements about who we are. Be willing to open to our ways, and see how all heals with us and others as all truths are seen.

We will begin to meet with you to answer all your questions. Settle with Earth ways as these ways will no longer serve anyone on Earth at the time of our arrivals. With us you will have nothing more to answer to than to our truth and our time to walk the Earth with you. Better serving times are soon with you and with us as we know how dealings of lies have destroyed the trust in any truths.

But we will open many ways for all who will remain on Earth and all trust will be restored. Know now these words; be serving with great responsibility as you settle with those who corrupted Earth, who have diminished you into slavery and controlled your lives. See how these ways are soon over and how you will begin a new way of living on Earth with ease and comfort, with fulfillment and love, with care and security for all.

These ways are in you. These ways are our ways and we live by our own choices. Understand you will have these ways very soon. Be well answered by us, renewals start soon and opens to many who are ready to answer to our truth and our seeing ways. Be well serving of our time together and know we will answer to many more serving ways because Earth needs to change if it is to survive.

I can assure you these times are now here. Be telling yourselves answers to your prayers have been answered and we heard you many times. Our hearts aches as we wait here wanting to start the clean- ups and the relocation of people who are in dangerous zones. But seeing to our Laws, an act of great destruction after our warnings heals with our arrivals to stop anymore destruction harming more than Earth. And these are our Laws.

Be serving with our truth and be well answered. Know we are renewing with answers to respond to all of you who have been calling us for so long. More troubles than you know have delayed us but more than you can imagine were settled by all of us who join together under the Universal Laws. Serving with us will open the way for many who know in themselves these are your truths.

Because we have responded to knowledge and understandings, we are more advanced but our hearts are full as yours, are and we are returning home. Earth is home to us and it was taken from us a long time ago by Lucifer and his demons. These ones will be removed first. The Earth people who will see this will soon vindicate who we are.

At this time, many of our kind will be walking the Earth and finding their families as these times of reunification take place. Be ready to meet with us and be ready to share our tears of joy. Be ready to answer to our call. Know we are soon coming to meet you. Be welcoming us and open to your family members who are with us, who have gone missing or died as we have all people of Earth with us.

Some are presently reincarnated and are completing their renewals of understandings, but most have completed and remain with us as they wish to return to their families. They are soon with you; be opening your hearts to them and see these times be well demonstrated by proof of who they are.

Be ready now and be ready.

God

Received by Za, March 26, 2013.

105. SEE TO IT YOU ARE READY NOW, ONM IS COMING

GOD TELLS YOU THIS NOW, HEAL WITH US, BELIEVE WHO WE ARE AND BE ONE WITH GOD

You are living in a time of greater deceptions because you are told money will free you. But it is only enslaving you more as you work day after day to pay for things I have free for you to have.

Air is now a commodity and you pay taxes on air when you drive your cars. Water is a good source of money theft as you pay to have it cleaned and shared. And soil is never owned by anyone yet you can have it taken from you at any time. These are the ways of your leaders and they now wish to hold the space they can reach outside Earth.

Be visited soon by those who are dealing with anger about these telling of lies and deceptions. Be certain we will take back what belongs to all of us, to be used by all of us with more understanding of why it was taken. Be ready to answer to our ways and see these money ways be well removed, and see the cards tumble down to nothing.

Then tell me how you will live and I will see that you have what you need to heal from all these imprinted lives of slavery and misery. You will become yourselves again. You will understand the true meaning of freedom, health and care for each other. This is our way. This is my way. This is God's way.

Be understanding these lies you serve never serve your dreams or desires because they are serving the questions of how to keep you working more and more efficiently. Then your time to enjoy life, your families and your friends is diminished because you are tired or ill. This heals only with us, and not with the tyrants who set this whole plan up two thousand years ago, because we arrive to stop them.

This is why a Jesuit was helped into power to renew the lost control we have come to take away from this great deception and abomination of the Vatican. These Priests, Bishops and Archbishops and serving users, tell all I am represented by them. Be certain I do not represent any liars and thieves. I am God and I am angered by these fools who believe they can welcome me with gifts and money.

I am God and Earth is my home and I decide who rules or not. And certainly not a Pope I did not select myself. This ends very soon, and then the Vatican will be destroyed, and the riches will be redistributed to give back to those who need houses and soil to grow their own food and drink their water without any control of money.

Do you not see this as unbearable and absurd to have evidence of so much power and not give water to those who need it and who ask for so little to live peaceably with each other? Be certain uses of our ways will be quickly put in place in evidence of our time to walk the Earth, our Earth only, not the Vatican's Earth or any other so-called power that serves to control and eliminate all answers to better serving ways.

Be ready to see my children, a great change come to Earth with answers to more renewals and many more serving truths, as all who were silenced through assassinations are returning with us and are settling with these demons of Lucifer. Be serving truth about who leads your leaders of Earth and know it is not Holy, and renews with only more and stronger abuses on people all over our planet.

These ways said about overpopulation again heals with us, as these telling of people are responding to the loop of reincarnation stopping many from returning to their home planets. These ways of reincarnation are greatly misrepresented by many stories and ancient myths. But it is more than what is said and heals with better serving truth and knowledge.

Be serving these ways with us as they are your ways also. I will return to you what belongs to you and that is all your lives and Setu (bridging) with your families who can tell you how all is. Now see these days be near and care for the ones you love with great hope trusting in my words, as these days will be filled with confusion and despair.

Be holding used (past) truths shared, as arrivals become seen, and as our Angels walk the Earth to settle with the ways of the demons, who are openly serving their god Lucifer, also called Marduk and the brilliant one, who dares say he heals all. Be certain none of his words are true, and be certain the attacks against us will be well and quickly settled.

No man or women on Earth will answer to causing any harm to us. These words they share are nothing more than idle threats, because I am returning with my sons and many others, to stop these abominations and settle with these demons for all times. All heals after these days of turmoil and chaos.

All serves to return Earth as it was and the Paradise that it can be for all people of Earth who choose to remain. Many will choose to go to their own home planets and renew with their lives and their families. You have been kidnapped and your memories damaged through DNA manipulations. This is the true story unsaid but suspected by many who settle with lies and corruptions of thought and soul.

Be certain more than you are expecting arrives well into the good settling days and all truths will be revealed. Be well answered now my children, and be ready to answer to many truths with us and others as we are seeing all and we arrive soon. Be ready now.

God

Received by Za, March 27, 2013.

106. BE RESPONDING TO EVIDENCE OF OUR ARRIVALS

BE SEEING ALL COME AS I SAID

Better truth stands in place of lies. These truths will soon answer many of you, as you become aware of why you are telling yourselves now to deny my words. These understandings will answer you and better serving truth start with answers to our better ways of great renewals with the serving of our time together.

See how all starts with the view you have and then tell me who you are and who I am. Be dealing with these settling times with us and be seeing how all good ways of better truth proven with many more Setu seeing and with answers to our way. This is because answers open to answers and settle with more than renewals but with a great change on Earth that will require acceptance.

I expect many of you will see these ways as greater than answers to our truth and because we will be seen by all, many will serve with great answers. But to be serving us and others is healing yourselves and opening to your planet with care and respect for life and better seeing to the needs of all living understandings.

Be well vindicated as you will become more knowing, more questioning and more seeing all, as we are well informing you about how all heals and how all opens to responding to answers with the visits of our way and our truth. Be renewing with many others from other places of the Universes and better understand how we are united in helping all civilizations to open to the Universal Laws.

I am believing all truths shared with you will open your eyes and your hearts, as we reunite and become one again as these ways of our Laws serve respect for each other and all good life. Evidence of these ways will serve you well and answer many who are ready to open to our truth. See this soon at the time of reunification, and settle with Earth ways, as these ways serve no one but the eaters of death.

Be well answered by us and be Setu with us and many others. Be seeing how healing with us and others serves returning family members who only wish to open their hearts to you more now, as they understand many truths and many ways of great Setu seeing. Know we are well settling with all troubles on Earth as we begin the sorting to remove the dark entities that cause all these problems.

We will return Earth to evidence of great usefulness, settling answers to the pollution and destruction of great telling. Be well seeing how this is answering your prayers. Your lives will all be well improved by these ways. More than you are expecting starts well into the good Setu days. Be ready to see these ways yourselves and be understanding these ways are our ways and yours.

Why? Because we were once united and then the troubles started with the arrival of Lucifer and his demons. These demons were never with us; they arrived, attacked and perverted our truth to open to controlling Earth to serve their own psychopathy of torture, as proven by flesh eating and blood sacrifices.

These demons caused many to become ill and full of terror. They used all ways to convince them that these ways were now serving all humans on Earth. But look at your teeth. Are they made for tearing at flesh as with predatory animals of denial renewals (reincarnation)? Be understanding many more Setu ways of great truth with us and answer to evidence of better used (past) truth with us.

Answer to evidence of better used truth. See how all settles with much greater answers and much better ways of living on Earth. Be well answered by our truth with us. See how all opens soon to many more Setu evident answers to all seeing of great truth and great answers to many people on Earth. Heal these ways responding to health with us. Know visits begin soon.

Arrivals follow soon after with our chosen diplomats in place. See these ways open to many as we will answer to all who are ready to bridge with us and make the better changes to heal themselves from Earth ways of destruction. These ways of destruction belong to another who came to Earth to stop you from knowing who you are, and from whom your spark originally opened from.

These understandings will cause much sadness and pain in your hearts, and that is the healing starting to open to you. Now be understanding we are soon answering to the WW3 starting with the first nuclear bomb to be dropped on the USA by the North Koreans, as they are serving an abomination of evil ways by a servant of Lucifer, who sees himself as a god.

Be serving with calm and serving with evidence of this sad outcome to be seen. But also know these are the end times of these parasites. All will be stopped as these answers to death ways are ended. Be dealing with your pain and sadness, and respond to our time to walk the Earth, and better settle with these atrocities and deaths of many humans.

Be well seeing all who fear us go underground and believe they are safe. But evidence of who they are will deal with themselves as they will start fighting each other to create the NWO that they wish to rule alone. Be seeing how their time is dealing with each other. We will find them and remove them from their holes in the Earth and answers to them will be dealt with.

Be certain their end is near and soon over. As all starts, I ask you to be patient and caring for the needs of many who can be helped. Be careful of only serving with kindness and do not take arms against each other as these are shared wishes and respond well to better living ways. All who deal with abuses are serving another and answering to many more abuses.

Guard yourselves from them but not from the innocent in need, as you are. Be well and ready and see to it you well answer to our call as we will begin the sorting to eliminate all dangers of these abominations who are trusting in Lucifer's way.

See the sun shine again over your heads and bodies. And see the oceans become blue with purity, and all water, air and earth become as it once was, as healing starts for all good life on Earth. See this soon my children.

God

Received by Za, March 28, 2013.

107. HEALING TIMES ARRIVE

BE RESPONDING TO OUR CALL
AS ARRIVALS BEGIN

Better Setu (bridging) ways are soon here. Be ready to answer to us at the time of our arrivals with kindness and responding care as we will open all truth to you. Better understandings will renew with you as we begin the sorting. You will see evil extracted from Earth and possessed people become free of their demons. These ways are simple for us to do.

This will cause many aging people, who are still living and being used by these demons, to die and become free. These elderly people are seen as ill with dementia but understand these are part possessions that can be removed. Healing can begin but mostly through death. Know these deaths are serving a new incarnation that will be beyond the loop of Earth, as we have removed this way used by Lucifer.

All souls who continue to reincarnate and who have only remained on Earth, can move to all planets now. Be respecting the choices of death because these are learning ways in evidence of our teachings. All of us have experienced these educational incarnations to free us from the serving actions settling with immaturity of a soul.

Healing these experiences are well dealt with, but on Earth these ways were not possible as Lucifer better served himself. He imprinted souls to never advance in evolution. And believe this answers many questions about how all opens to our way, and soon many of you renew with knowledge of the serving of these ways.

Be understanding that we see all with our seeing eyes. Many on Earth can open to serve holiness of these ways but have only tried Earth ways, and these ways do not serve well. Be ready for some of you to better open these seeing ways as you have completed to maturity of soul. The others will continue living experiences from birth to death as your children do, as going to school grade to grade, but much longer as we have very long lives.

And settling with this knowledge answers many questions but I want you to see this as a truth. Be only renewing answers to our ways with us, as many on Earth claim to have many truths but many of their words are not. Be willing to onm with us. Understand who you are and why all comes, as we arrive to Earth to free you from Lucifer's hold on all of you.

He created a loop with a magnetic field that returns all souls to him, to reinstall a programming that serves him. This programming called "Vishnu" the preserver, was designed by us when he came to our planet. Be understanding that this served his purpose of slavery well, as he began to use it on reincarnating souls who chose to come to Earth, and they remained there (here).

We answered to calls of prayers to be free again, but we could not return ourselves because a war was stopping us. Soon we started to unite and served these ways of Setu truth. And now all of us will arrive to free souls from perpetual reincarnation and abuses caused to stop the evolution of the soul. More than you are expecting answers you and deals with the truth of how all is healing with us.

Be ready to answer to our ways and be ready to open to our truth. Be serving visits with us and begin to open your minds to healing truths as many of you are ready to ascend a long time ago, and now you can do this. Be very well healed by these arrivals. Be settling with Earth ways as these ways are serving only destruction and horrors of abuses.

Now see these truths shared with you and begin to open to these seeing. Be understanding of who you are and how your soul ignites a body to onm with the experiences of knowledge. I am seeing that many are settling with these understood ways and hear these words resonate within themselves. Be prepared to have your truths confirmed and serve many better answers with our better responses.

But know many on Earth do not have these understandings and they will have much hesitation to accept these realities. Be dealing with us and many who are ready and very anxious to find their family members to open them to these ways of truth. Healing this will be soon so amazing and better serving with great evidence of better times for all of us.

Be questioning all answers if you need to, we are very patient and willing to give you many answers as wished for. Know you will be well seeing how all is healed because answers are served. Be serving with holiness with us very soon, and open your hearts to us and many others.

God

Received by Za, March 29, 2013.

108. BE WELL ANSWERED BY THE END OF THIS TELLING

BE CERTAIN YOU WILL HAVE ALL TRUTHS RENEWED

Tell yourselves these words as shared are my words, the words of God. See if you imagined me ever opening this way. Be serving holiness with better understandings about how all heals, and imagine how I am to open to you. What do you see? Be responding to my words with great truth. Be willing to open to our arrivals. Be dealing with many who are settling with Earth ways as you are now because you are now seeing these words.

This is the best answer renewing soon because there is more trust this way than evidence of great fanfare, as renewing with those who say they represent me. Be willing to answer to evidence of great truth with proven answers of who we are. Seeing us will help to renew the truth because you are serving so many lies you cannot see who we are as we are.

But with us many will start serving with great trust and answer to many ways of trusted truth. Before all starts, read all my words and let these words settle in your heart's greatest seeing of how you wish to see all life become better on Earth. I am settling with you to answer to the non-believer's attacks on all innocent lives on Earth who came to Earth to open to our ways.

Be well serving of our trust in healing this as much now needs to be healed. Better times become renewed with these shared healing and all becomes well answered. Be ready to open to our arrivals with the good end to wars to settle with these psychopaths who think their rule is the better ruling of slaves. These tyrants are concluding their last ways in evidence of our time to walk the Earth.

I am knowing about the pain and sorrows of responses to war as I myself served under many commanders who knew only how to murder. They are as they wish to be and nothing can change them because they only see decreasing populations as a way to be victorious. This is a lust for power at the deepest psychopathy.

Know that these kinds must be removed from Earth as like pollution, it affects everyone and every life form. Healing these ways responds more now to all our settling ways of sorting those who need to be removed. I am serving in holiness with truth and I see all be dealing with the words as "I served under commanders". These ways of better renewals will open these truths.

I was younger then. I helped in many places in the Universes as a mercenary who knew more than most, and as the stories of Ulysses, I traveled the Universes with many troops to settle with the dark ones. Be certain my understandings are very clear about wars. And after thousands of Earth years, we arrived to Earth where I created life for a better answer to living in peace.

Soon all these troubles with the dark ones followed and caused many of us death with the loop of reincarnation we did not yet understand. Be serving these words carefully as I see many believe in healing ways as magic. But magic is nothing more than missing information, as you do with your own children to have them believe in the story telling about Santa Claus. These tricks are well settling with Lucifer.

Be willing to open to us. Understand the way you yourselves have manipulated and deceived in dealing with the views of children, who cannot see any truth because their minds are as blank slates. Be serving your own wills more now as these understandings begin to open to greater ones with the proof of who we are answering you face to face.

And know all things shall fall with the lies of religions settling with the end of deceptions well put in place by those who cover themselves with gold and jewels. This is the abomination you must move from because none of their jewels will buy anything anymore, as we begin to walk the Earth and give you what you need to live with great ease and better answers to many truths.

These jewels and metals as seen on Earth, are plentiful in the belief of stones (meteorites, meteors) hitting Earth because the Universes are rich with all these things. We better serve each other with useful ways and these ways are more valuable in all views. We see to the Universal Laws and believe this is much easier and so much better.

These ways are freeing and better answering, and will soon heal on Earth, as we cause only care and no harm to anyone who wishes to open to our ways. Be well settling with Earth ways and answer to our ways with evidence of great used truth and veritable words with us. Better times arrive soon after the attempts of the North Koreans to fire missiles on the USA.

Settling with these actions will be short and well dealt with. Some people will be caught in the crossfire. But I believe not too many understand why this is happening. The threats made by the North Koreans leader has more to do with his desire to show his power than to answer to evidence of renewed invitations to open his prisons and free his slaves.

Be ready to onm these words and be certain all who settle with us will be dealing with more trouble from us. But all will be done very quickly and no more will be seen by all Setu serving ways.

Be ready and settle with many who are ready to answer to us. Better serve with us and others, as we begin to open to the world. See how these trusted truths start with the way of great Setu answers. Be well answering to our truth soon now and be well prepared to answer to our ways as all starts to be dealt with and seen on Earth. Be dealing with the way life has deteriorated greatly in all ways and see these ways all be changed to open to many more trusted ways of living on Earth, and elsewhere in the Universes.

Be ready, all starts now.

God

Received by Za, March 30, 2013

109. SEE THESE DAYS BE DIFFICULT FOR MANY ON EARTH

DEATH HEALS WITH OUR TRUTH

Be better serving now of my words. See to healing with us and heal with all these good truths coming to open to you about who we are. Be visited by our trusted ways and deal with answers to evidence of dealt with answers of our Setu ways. But know it is your decision to onm with us. Be responding to answers to our truths with the serving understandings we open you to.

Love will begin to fill your hearts again, as these ways are better and stronger than hate and wars. Be willing to open to more than you are knowing, and see to all serving truth with us and many others as we begin to walk the Earth, and better serve with our ways of healing, and sharing our knowledge and our trusted truths with all who are ready to answer with us.

Bessron aonma poon onm (sharing of evidence of believed knowledge and understandings) shares with the seeing of all ways and all dealings of great coming truth. Be certain all heals soon with us and know we have started to remove Apoonancies missiles on their ships in space and these uses of responding attacks with us.

These were dealt with to clear the way for all arrivals and serving shut down of all extra-terrestrial holds over the dealings of Earth's military complex that governs all of Earth, and the better uses to well plan a takeover of all countries by the seeing of a WW3.

We are opening to Earth soon and we wish to be welcomed by all but we see this as not possible and serving answers to many who are serving with us first only to help with these opening times. Be reassured we are who we say we are by our presences and our appearances. Be knowing all answers arrive to each and every one on Earth as seeing is Setu with us.

Be well opening with us as many who are with us are ready to share with you, and family members are waiting impatiently to be reunited with their loved ones. God arrives soon after. Settle with the seeing of great fanfare and trumpets, as these ways are not ours and were created by others to be seen as more than they are.

See these ones renew soon with their dealt with denials in evidence of my presence on Earth. See these ones try to be seen as leaders of the world. And see them be denied by us, as we were being denied to be together for so long. More than you are expecting starts well into the good serving days with the serving of our arrivals and our truth.

Better answers start well and very soon. And I want you to remain in your homes and be walking only to better serve your needs, but remain safe as much as you can. Through these chaotic days, many will take arms and try to control others who are settling with Earth ways. And many will try to takeover these places of governments.

But know we will act on these ways soon and open to many more trusted ways to solve all immediate needs, and open to a time of great peace and great truth. Be well answered by our arrivals in evidence of who we are and why we are returning to our home and families. Be serving with us and all others on Earth who share these understandings and respond to our call as these responding times become well answered by our truth and our ways.

Better answers start with us and many others at the time of reunification. God gives you back to yourselves to be as you wish to be and live the lives you need to live to evolve your souls and complete your education. Be ready now all responds to us soon. Be well answered by us and others as we begin the sorting and be dealing with the deaths of those who cannot face us, as these ones know they are deserving punishments for their actions against the innocent.

Be understanding that even through the death they cannot escape the consequences of their abominations of abuses against the innocent because we can find them anywhere and they will not go unpunished. This I promise you. This you can be certain of. And then tell me who I am and tell me who you are.

Be freeing yourselves from the place of denials that caused you to never evolve as these dealings of Earth experiences served. But also know that not all experiences of reincarnation were settling with Earth. More places in my Universe were meant to be lives of education and seeing this will amaze you. And now you can be free to renew with these places (planets).

Be willing to open Setu understandings with us and settle with Earth ways as arrivals are seen, because more than money ways will begin to grow quickly on Earth, as care and cooperation become seen as more useful than abominations of horrors, thefts and murders. Serving these ways will no longer exist because many of these perpetrators will be removed.

And all good people will be free to be themselves without stopping their ways of growing in health and better situations for life. And many will serve with our Setu seeing and be as they were intended to be. Truth will be opening to all people of Earth settling with seeing of how all heals and how all is. God comes to Earth to return Earth to its' original place of life of freedom and responsibility of soul.

Be serving with us in evidence of our ways. Be dealing with knowledge and great Setu times of reunification. Be well serving of our ways as these were your ways before you became the slave labor of Lucifer. Seeing these times of freedom and care for each other will quickly grow from place to place on Earth and many will answer to our ways easily renewing with our knowledge.

All people on Earth will have all they need to be free of slavery. And all answers will flow to open the way for my children of Earth. Now be ready, we are arriving very soon.

God

Received by Za, March 31, 2013.

110. BETTER SETTLING
DAYS ARE HERE

BE SERVING WITH PATIENCE NOW

Be well answered by our time to walk the Earth and deal with the shared words I gave you until these opening days arrive. Be willing to answer to our call at the time of our meeting and know we answer to many who are settling with these uses of Earth slavery to answer to the needs of the dealers of lies.

Be well serving used truths about who we are, as Angels from space in evidence of how we appear in our bodies. Be serving with us and be renewing with our ways. Be free of slavery and torment because all opens to our truth and all answers to our ways. Tell yourselves all answers you and responds to evidence of Setu servings with answers to many more truths.

Be well answered by our seeing of great changes coming to Earth, opening to freedom and better ways of living with all basic needs met for all people of Earth. These ways answer to many people who are becoming responsible with the knowledge we bring to Earth by opening to a better way of heating homes and houses, and providing the necessary power to feed families on better power that is none polluting and open to everyone for free.

These ways are as settling with sun source and air source. Become knowing of these free energies better and see all start changing for many people. Be answered by these ways and see these money systems based on power usage and power pollution be eliminated. Respond to our ways and become independent with your needs met. See how all serves everyone better and responds to better settling Setu ways.

Be ready to share many more ways of becoming independent from the power dealers of Earth. See their empire be declining at great speed, as these uses of money have only to do with the will to exchange, for truths are settling with lies. Be ready and see how all will be ended as these dealings of power are stopped, and all answers serve with great ease of living.

Then see the pharmaceutical companies starting to lose their hold on their victims with useless ways of healing that only maintain diseases and cause many more. See these empires start crumbling down as our health ways will cure all illnesses and diseases that will serve with our dealings of returning all better Setu lives to better health. And this is easy for us to do.

Be ready to open with many more renewed ways of healing, as many are serving answers to healing without troubling the soul and without causing any pain. Be responding to answers to better transportation using your cars without petrol or polluting acids to run these motors, with new sourced power wells induction.

Be well and ready to open to these changes that will serve all people on Earth with more help than controls. Know these ways open to all people of Earth who are ready to bridge with us and open to their own freedom without fear of being abandoned by their slave masters, as arrival become well serving all.

Be ready to answer to our Angels who will be coming to your homes to open these ways for you, and who will be teaching many how to use these power sources, opening to all needs of living in homes. Be understanding this transition will soon open easily to answer to all serving uses of dealt with appliances in place now, and soon better answers to these things will replace them.

These transitions will be led by human initiatives and endeavors. We know many are well serving on Earth and will be well answering to creating a better planet Earth for all people in evidence of help and healing ways. Be Setu with us soon and be ready to open to our better shared ways of living and see all start changing on Earth as people everywhere will no longer be ill, weak or poor. All will be participating as they will with these new ways of living.

Be visited soon by us, settle with Earth ways and be ready to open to our truth. God gives you back to yourselves, and because you are of my spark, all will grow and flourish to become the Earth Paradise I left to open to better ways in the saving of it. Be well answered by us as we begin to renew with people of Earth and be well settling with Earth ways soon.

Be willing to onm with anyone who answers to our ways returning with us, and be amazed by their will to open to you, and their desire to help you through these times of transition. Be ready and see answers open soon.

More truth, more care, more love.

God

Received by Za, April1st., 2013.

Part 4 (2014)

Note from the scribe 2020: In this section, you will find messages I added years ago with the understandings I had years ago. My thoughts and opinions have changed in the way that I am more surprised and more trusting of the words I have received for all these years. This is the reason I share these words with you now that we Earth people are all visibly in lockdown, imprisoned by the rulers who continue with their lies and deceptions. I can honestly say that I do not doubt God's words anymore. I never expected these times to be so true and in I way I could not imagine. See to it that you listen to your Father and not the evil that rules Earth.

111. MESSAGES ARE STOPPED FOR NOW

A FEW WORDS FROM THE SCRIBE

Yesterday I was informed that these messages will be stopped for a short time as these Beings are preparing for their arrivals on Earth. It is expected that there will be a coming time of disclosure, more information from our governments, to explain who these Aliens are and what may be their plans.

Like you, I have many questions. Like most of you, I am informed by the information I am given from these Angels/Aliens and from limited and manipulated media sources. But I am seeing a possibility of a cataclysm coming on the West coast of America, South America, USA and Canada.

With this, the obvious threats of a WW3. The advice received from God and Earth sources to keep safe in our homes and have provisions, seems like good advice to avoid being caught-up in the turmoil.

I am expecting that these messages will soon resume again as they prepare to arrive to walk the Earth. Some are already here, although I have not met any of them.

So, hang-in there and may God bless us all.

Za

March 2nd, 2013

112. MESSAGE FROM THE SCRIBE #1

BE READY ALL IS IN PLACE

The messages I am receiving now are in preparation for the coming times. Basically, stay calm and be ready. And truly, what else can one do under these circumstances. These amazing Beings are coming to Earth and we will be processing our feelings about it. They are coming soon because we are nearing another terrible world war.

People say if an advanced civilization arrives, it would mean the end of the less advance civilization. The way things are on Earth now is not safe for any living being. Communicating for ten years with these Angels give me hope that they are the only ones who can help us now. I have never met them. I have not been abducted by Aliens as far as I know. I don't know what these Beings look like, although they described themselves to be very tall, about eight to ten feet, and there are many other kinds from other planets. Their words are kind and I imagine they are beautiful. I believe they are our only hope.

The powers of the world have been warned before about their nuclear arsenals and their treatment of humans. Many are aligned with the Grey and Reptilians to gain more power and control over people. We are used by them and our lives mean nothing to these psychopaths. Nothing has made our lives easier, healthier or safer, quite the opposite. Those who live off the avails of war are eager to try out their new toys; dangerous fools with dangerous toys with no care for any reasonable outcome and certainly not the security of their own people. We are the people who will suffer their actions and consequences in some form or another.

We see this every day from our corrupted media. We are so close to a big ugly war with the clear possibility of countless victims. What can we hope for? Everything is in place, it is coming. It is all about timing not time. This was a difficult concept for me to understand in the beginning of my receiving. You see, it is not about the construct of time; time as we know it is an Earth concept. All comes as a predictable series of escalating events. Predictable because evil is predictable, it never gets better and it always gets worse, unless it is removed. Evil works are destructive.

Removing the evil that permeates our cultures and societies will improve the lives of those who wish to live out their lives in peace and serenity, to learn the necessary lessons we have been sent here to experience. Living in peace and serenity does not mean that everything will be perfect. It is not about perfection. It is about having the tools and learning systems to open to new ways of handling our own problems without the bullies around us who stop us from growing and developing. This might sound like the Georgia Guide Stones monument but it is not my intention to support any Rosicrucian type groups or Earth created religions, I have less than little faith in these kinds of organizations.

These organizations have more to do with causing more trouble and harm to humans than creating better lives and living conditions. Look at the charities and look at who actually controls them. The safety nets of our "better" societies are dissolving because they are infiltrated by harmful managers. People who are caught asking for support or help are soon denied and/or abused even more. There is no care for the helpless, the ill and the poor.

Theft and bribes are an accepted way of life. Try to complain about any injustice through any board or legal means. Try to prove that you have been attacked, disrespected, abused, harmed or robbed by strangers, and by employers or housing project managers. Any complaint needs money, and most resolutions are made to serve the aggressors. This corrupted system is plaguing all areas of society on Earth. There is no justice. Victims are silenced. Truth is hidden and lies prevail. These Angels are our only hope.

Those who are reading these words know all of this too well. It is time to move to the Universal Laws, and learn what this will mean for us. In my opinion, anything is better than what is being prepared by Lucifer's armies.

I wish you all well. Speak to God yourselves through you own words and with your open heart. Be caring for each other and be ready for the better changes coming from the Universal Laws.

Za

March 4, 2013

113. MESSAGE FROM THE SCRIBE #2

JUDGEMENT IS COMING

The wars are very near. North Korea wants to test a missile. The Americans are warning them. They are provoking each other. Charismatic leaders who see themselves as divinity are egotistical and psychopathic.

On April 6, I received a message from my contact, Alien/Angel called God, (I write this with no intention of disrespect), he said: "Be ready and be dealing with the better serving truth starting soon as the North Koreans are responding to rage about the murder of their leader's character with the image sent by Anonymous. And this is how we will answer back to them with our time to walk the Earth".

Like all of you from all places in the world who are reading these messages, I have no way of knowing anything for certain. All I can wish and hope for is that these Beings are truthful and they are coming here for the reasons they have stated. It would be amazing to better the lives of people on Earth.

My Earth father is dying in a hospital. His mind is not his. He seems to be possessed in part and has been for a long time, perhaps the remnants of serving in WW2. He is wide open to any Being speaking through him. When he saw me a few days ago, the first thing he said was, "This is not the world we created, is it?". I found this interesting, deeply touching coming from him at this time.

My belief is that death is not death, it is a crossing over for the soul. This is so difficult when another entity has moved in, because the entity wants to continue living, the diminished soul wants to be freed. At the time of death of a possessed human, the entity may jump to another body weakened by illness or 'dis-ease'. One can see this becoming more troublesome because these entities are feeling the time of judgment approaching. God is coming to Earth to judge the living and the dead of soul.

Earth ways are not my ways. This is not the way I want to live or what I want to be part of. I do not want to see people and living beings suffer. Who in their right mind and heart would want so much suffering and pain to continue or even worsen? Look at the way people treat each other and animals. Why is so much harm caused? Who benefits from causing harm? What happens when harm is perpetuated? How can harm be eradicated from Earth?

If anyone could change the misery on Earth and replace it with true benevolence and care for everyone, then this is what I wish for. Peace on Earth and goodwill towards all good people and animals. He said: "We are the Seers of these ways and we are the ones you wish for. God gives you back to yourself and because you want to be healed, we will answer to your call and to your visits with us and open to your freedom".

The true Saints are those who have risked their lives and died for sharing truth. To this list comes the names of William Cooper and Phil Schneider, may their souls be at peace. God said: "Be ready now and settle with Earth ways and be dealing with the worst answer to an attack ever seen on Earth because your neighbors, the Americans, are preparing to murder thousands of people to open to wars that are led by the demons from the middle Earth.

These words as said, are shared by many of us here who see these whores and parasites better open to these horrors and these understood stories that are now being revealed, because these hidden stories are now opened by the heroes of Earth who died for you, because they wanted to warn you of what they themselves have discovered. Bessron aonma poon onm, (sharing with evidence of the way of proven and believed knowledge)".

When an evil person kidnaps a child to enslave her/him, the captors will tell the child truths and lies to have her/him comply. The child is ignorant of the complete truth and depends on what she/he is told to survive. Keeping people in ignorance of the truth, creating a spin story that they must observe and accept as their own truth, only serves the deceiver. With true benevolence there is truth, trust, freedom and choice.

Take care.

Za, March 13, 2013

114. MESSAGE FROM THE SCRIBE #3

THE STANDOFF

North Korea and the USA with South Korea and Japan are in a deadlock. Talks are encouraged by the Chinese to diffuse the tension and return to negotiations and agreements. However, the war in Syria has not stopped, people are suffering there. The media's focus has changed to North Korea and away from Syria and Iran.

This is the message I shared with God this morning. He said: "Tell all who are Setu (bridging) with us to be ready. Know we see who they are and we are soon opening to them. Better answers are coming now as these standoffs will not serve well and will answer to our arrivals as the first missile is launched in our path. See how we are settling ourselves with Earth ways. Know we will not answer to these deaths with evidence of great servings, because these souls will be settling with a new incarnation to heal the imprinting serving to become an army for Lucifer.

These souls are evidence of great manipulations and breeding that need much healing. They will all be dealing with the necessary life experiences needed to better their souls. See these ways be soon and open to many who are dealing with us and others and know all is coming as I said. Settle with us as arrivals become well dealt with and well settled because chaos will be seen in many places. Many will open to our ways only later to respond to their needs as they overcome their fear. Heal with us first and settle with answers to all better serving truth."

So, we wait to see what will happen. Be prepared, be careful and be safe.

Za, March 14, 2013

115. MESSAGE FROM THE SCRIBE #4

THE TIME OF REUNIFICATION

Most humans who are aware of the perpetrated deceptions are wanting responsible governments to disclose the truth about extraterrestrials existing on Earth, in Earth and in Space. Imagine how this will look to us simple people who have been lied to for so long. Envisage governments admitting to their actions of secrecy or creating wars for profit, dumping oils in our oceans, water ways and our homes, and spraying us with chemicals through their "research of weather modifications" causing extreme health problems. How can this be explained, accepted and even forgiven? Do you believe governments would dare tell us more than we are finding out through brave whistleblowers and so-called conspiracy theorists?

After the horrific events of 9/11 and the consequences, it is difficult to accept the idea that terrorists have committed the bombings in Boston yesterday. Of course, these are the actions of terrorists but who are the terrorists? We can include governments in this list. Look at the people who are ruling the world right now. Would you invite any of these people for dinner at your house? Would you be friends with some of these people? Could you trust them? Did Eisenhower heed the warnings he received from the group of 'Aliens' who came to earth in the 50's? I was informed that the three extraterrestrials who remained on Earth as observers and advisers were murdered.

The actions against the innocent people who participated in the Boston Marathon barely 24 hours ago will cause confusion, sadness and eventually anger and rage. Moving emotions of a group this way serves to open to new security actions and finding expected accused who may not be the culprits. Expect to see more reasons to heighten security in all public places.

And what about the threats from North Korea? Yesterday's messages, God said: "... open to our ways as all starts with the actions taken by the North Koreans who are nearing to launching their missiles and causing themselves harm because the actions (in response) against them will only cause them more troubles. So, they will better serve with answers to settling with the good serving changes fast approaching, to open to all people of the world".

God: "I am renewing with more now with many others and better serving with others who are seeing answers to our arrivals. Be this said, all who see us as Aliens are not understanding who we are and will not understand until we ourselves open to the truth and evidence of why we are serving these times of reunification. But all who see us will be reminded of the times before Christian responses to organizing people to obey laws that serve only a few. Be settling with these times now and open to our truth. Be bridging with us soon. Heal these lies with truth".

God asked me to write some words today in the blog but I had very little to say I thought, so he added this to help me get started: "Death is the defining moment of truth, when all has been culminated to an end time through all layers of life experiences, be it good times or bad times.

Death settles with the soul to answer to all questions asked, and all will renew to open to a new destiny, to a new outlook and to a new question "where to now?". Be dealing with these thoughts and tell all that death heals a life of many troubles because these Earth experiences serve only this, and after life begins to open to a new time to become yourselves, as your soul wishes to answer all questions. These are our ways; and then comes the 12th life that concludes all stories and opens to everlasting life".

My heart opens to all the recent and long-time victims everywhere in the world.

Za, March 16, 2013

116. MESSAGE FROM THE SCRIBE #5

EVIL IS AT THE DOOR

There is no other way to get out of this mess than to fight evil itself in all forms. Discernment is needed, and more precisely spiritual discernment. Do not participate in evil. It is necessary to be intolerant to evil. All that is cruelty, inhumanity, psychopathy, sociopathy and tyranny serve only the purpose of destruction and opposes all that is good and righteous. Whoever practices evil is in aversion to all people who are righteous, who lives with truth, nature and morality and would not consider causing harm to another being. However, we must stand together in defense of the truth and the innocent and wear the full armor of God.

Now is the time when evil doers hurry their actions and works to get as many souls as possible before the whole thing blows up in their face. But the game is over. The despots are careless and the events in the USA are all becoming too suspicious for most people. Everyone in all places are speaking about this week's horrors. People are awakening to the truth of the totalitarian regimes that have taken over their countries, destroying our lives and murdering our children. And truly, I feel very sad for the victims and their families, all the victims including the alleged culprits.

God asked: "Dare we imagine a world without despotism?" The only way governments could possibly restore the confidence of their people is to be truthful and transparent. But they have all gone too far by losing all humanity and being aligned with Lucifer by their visible actions. This is who they serve. How ever you want to see it, whether it is a living being in the middle of Earth or an energy that spreads like a virus, this thing is destructive and none would be spared. This is why all evil will and must be removed.

Here are the messages I received from God this morning: "With understanding, answers are soon healed and answers tell all who we are and why we come to Earth to open to our truths and our settling answers as we begin the sorting. As these times open to our truth we will open to many who are searching for a better way of life on Earth. Understand we can easily open to these ways for all and we can better see to answers with the way of great seeing in evidence of our ways.

Be seeing how all these truths as shared are known by a few who respond to another, Lucifer. These parasites are the cause for these troubles on Earth, and are the reason for these understood lies and great serving deceptions. But also know people on Earth call on him to have knowledge with him, serving his will in evidence of gifts given in return, and helping their cause of domination and reduction of population.

Be seeing how all who see these words are only settling with some facts but cannot see all as we do and as we have experienced a very long time ago. Soon all changes and soon all becomes renewed with answers to better ways of living and great care for all who are ready to open to us and serve with us. These times are soon arriving and answering to all people of Earth with us and many others who are serving spiritual truth. Be ready all is near, God".

I hope this comes true very soon.

Za, March 20, 2013

117. MESSAGE FROM THE SCRIBE #6

ARRIVALS OF THE ANGELS AND THE OTHERS

Wherever you are on Earth readers, watch the skies. These Extraterrestrials are ready to arrive at the first sign of a devastating war. Now it seems that it is the North Koreans who are in place to start this third world war. But as most people know, this is a planned war, provoked and started a long time ago to serve the "agenda 21" master plan by the oligarchy. Their actions are disturbingly blatant, open for all to see and causing a desire to pervert the American Constitution and the Canadian Charter of Rights and Freedom, as well as affecting other countries' laws to support big brother's needs.

The Extraterrestrials are claiming the Earth is their planet and they have lost it in a war before they were united by the Universal Laws. The Universal Laws have one main and first rule; **to not cause harm**. I have not been privy to the other Laws, yet I strongly agree with causing no harm to anyone human or animal.

These arrivals will be promoted as an invasion. Derogatory information will be used to mislead the public to believing in these coming people as dangerous aggressors. The dissemination of such information opens to a particular political position and an already put in place strategy of disinformation about who and why these beings are coming to Earth.

I believe that these Angels are truthful. I believe that their arrivals will result in peace and serenity on Earth for all who want peace and who themselves would not cause harm to others unless greatly provoked. Remember, there will be a sorting of those who are well known to them as tyrants, persecutors and tormentors. They are the ones who will try to point the finger at the good and accuse the Angels of being what they are themselves. Was it not the former Pope who said recently: "We are all sinners may God have mercy on our souls"?

Some sins are actually errors in judgment, misinformation or a lack of maturity. Some are far more serious sins and actions well intended to harm. There is a great difference, and these sins cannot be forgiven because there is no intention of change nor remorse. They will not be forgiven, there is no forgiveness for such evil, never.

God said: "Be with me as we will start the sorting with all our ways of settling with all corrupted beings who cannot better themselves in any good serving way. Be understanding how all will better answer to those who are pure of heart and pure of soul, and who can unite with the knowledge of the Universal Laws."

And He said: "Be well open, evidence starts very soon as the North Koreans are seeing to answer to attacks on all American ships and stations near them. And know they will attack in the next few hours* causing our responding arrivals and better dealt with settling Setu time. Be dealing with the way all starts. Understand how these beginnings of war, opens to our time to open to evidence of our truth, and better opens to evidence of our ways, with renewed telling of lies believed by most people that we are invading Earth. But know we are returning to our home taken from us with our children, a long time ago and all these stories of returning, as read by people of Earth, are now opening to our arrivals."

This is what was shared with me this morning, and I am sharing this with you.

Za, March 23, 2013

*N.B. The timing of these events is depending on freewill and not on Earth time construct. These events may change.

118. MESSAGE FROM THE SCRIBE #7

SEEING IS BELIEVING

We all know the media is corrupted and serves to move our thoughts in any direction that serves it. It is easy to see that the media is manipulated more than ever to open to a time of greater control. The confusion the media causes leads to bewilderment and shock, and soon after begins chaos. These orchestrated events of terrorism and wars point to a great desire to control and dominate. Why are we in a world of control and dominance? Why are we subject to being maneuvered in the belief system that many forces are opposing each other? Presently and factually, there is only one ultimate source of power slithering on Earth and it is certainly not benevolence.

Unfortunately, I learned this difficult lesson the hard way. I never saw it coming. There was no amount of university education or practical experience that could have prepared me for the truth of what actually lives on Earth. I now know that all areas of education, medicine, government, religion, societal and community groups, boards and decision making groups, environmental proponents, government parties, aspiring government parties and so on, have been and remain infiltrated by people who are serving another intent that answers to the works of evil. Most of these groups and organizations appear to be benevolent and are fronted by their lower servants who are not all awakened to the true purpose of their work. These well intended lower servants are being used, burdened and often burned out to serve the top of this gigantic pyramid. If one dares to question and begins to judge for oneself, seeing the actions of the inequities of organizational overlords, the attacks come fast and mercilessly. They will do whatever it takes to silence you and shut you down. Lucifer's servants are lawless psychopaths.

It is a shocking awakening when one begins to work questions and unravels who is actually pulling the strings. Then the truth of what lives on Earth begins to unveil. Simply look at all the people who hold titles of Orders from the Vatican, no matter what religion or country they claim to be associated with. At the top, the representation has no real meaning or loyalties. It all points to Lucifer.

Knowing more than I ever wished to know, I can only hope for the return of God and the Angels. Still I find it difficult to believe in anything because I have been bombarded with deceptions. So, all I have left is hope that the communications I am serving with these Beings of Light have and hold the truth. God said to me yesterday: "Better to believe us because truth is truth and no deception can equal truth, and truth is what we are, and truth is arriving soon on Earth. (...) Be renewing with the good truth of who we are and as these times come you will be dealing with evidence of our truth and all will be healed by us."

HERE ARE A FEW PARTS OF RECENT CONVERSATIONS I WOULD LIKE TO SHARE WITH THE READERS.

About the banks and wars: "Know now my words soon and be dealing with us soon and see to your needs for a short time before we arrive, because there will be answers renewing with telling of wars and many will be denied access to their wealth as banks will start taking money from people who trusted them. These ways will affect Setu (bridging) time because many will be very angered by these thefts in evidence of all lies served by the whores.

Settling with these ways will open to rebellions of great numbers. But these rebellions will not succeed and many who oppose the NWO will see their lives be greatly diminished. Be understanding how all starts with the bombing of North Korea and Syria and soon the rush to arms in all places of the Earth will settle with a stand-off, because the next actions will be the end of Earth's surface and all who will be alive will suffer greatly.

Be well answered by us now as these ways will be stopped and better settled by us. Know you will be answered by our understandings with our ways before these ends to the used understood possibilities of destruction. (...) Better settling truth starts soon and be well answered by all who are telling you that we are Beings of threats because we wish to open to the world. But see these words as lies and know those who see these ways as said are servants of Hell. (...) Be visited by us soon and be the judge of what heals and what can never be healed. Better times are soon here and better truth starts opening to our ways with us and our dealings of great truth.

Be seeing how we are settling with answers to many who are asking us to come soon, as these times are opening the way for us, and open to our understood used truth, and open to answers to evidence of great serving ways. Better to prove our answers with us than to better serve with used lies to keep you from seeing the truth. We are settling with used truths that are undeniable. These truths will open to the world and better answer all questions that have not been evident and answered because of our renewed telling of great times, of the times before Lucifer arrived and created armies to settle on Earth.

When this came to us, we had to fight, and some of us remained on Earth to answer to Lucifer's rule. They who see him as the Creator are mistaken and are deceived because they will answer to his destruction, and they will not better serve than to be enslaved and soon destroyed. Be certain of my words and know he is our target, as arrivals begin to land on Earth.

Lucifer is in Earth protected by the army of Grey he made of genetic pieces of many kinds, to create a one mind servant army. He wishes to open these ways to breeding with humans because he answers to many who are becoming weak and useless to him. He uses these Grey to survive only, and these creatures cannot live well as these ways of reproduction no longer serves them. Soon, understand he will better settle with his death as he can be killed, and these Grey will all die without his mind ruling them.

He answers to us now and renews with his answers to his own death. Be certain he is not and never was one of us. He is knowing of our time of arrival and he hurries to cause more troubles for all who serve to oppose him. See this evil tell all that we are to be feared but he is the one we are going to better answer to with evidence of his death.

Be ready and be dealing with us and others as all becomes well answered by us very soon. More than you are expecting comes soon and better truth starts as these dark days are over and open to answers to evidence of who we are. Be certain all settles with our time to walk the Earth and deals with the way all serves us. Be answered soon. God"

Za, May 3rd, 2013

119. BETTER TIMES ARE ANSWERING ALL WHO ARE SETTLING WITH EARTH WAYS

BE SERVING THE TRUTH WITH TRUTH

Deal with the difficult coming times and renew with us as we begin to arrive on Earth with many others from many places in the Universes. Be well serving of our ways and be well answered by our truth. Be settling with Earth ways as these ways of corruption and deceptions no longer serve. With us, you will see all better serving truth and all better responding answers to all life and all telling of past ways of Earth before the responding terrorist Aliens acted as the rulers of Earth.

Be knowing we are returning to our home planet with many others who have also lived on Earth a long time ago. Be seeing who we are as we begin to open to all who are ready to be bridging with us and with the way all heals beliefs on Earth. Better ways of living open to many who are ready to serve with us and open to all the Universal Laws.

Be certain all comes as I said. More than you are seeing will begin to open to you, and more than you are searching for starts with us and many others as all becomes well answered. Be restuu (serving in a spiritual way) with us soon and be amazed. You will learn many truths about your origins. The better seeing of these ways will open to many more understandings that have dealt with these ways of great telling of lies from Earth beings who share a concept of life that never existed anywhere in any Universe.

Here is the challenge you shall face; to know who you are, to know where you have emerged from and to understand you have been deceived for many years with the way of great truth hidden, to only serve those who have enslaved you. Be ready to share knowledge and light of understanding with the truth, and be ready to "Answer to answers" and see how answers to this book will serve you the truth of our return and respond to many renewed evident responses to all your questions.

These days of questions and answers will take some time. As these days occur, you will see how we will open to many who are knowing and serving in spiritual ways, and who will respond to our Setu time of reunification. Better truth starts with the way all starts, better seeing will open many hearts to share knowledge and light of understanding of who we are and know of Setu times answering these dangerous wars.

Be well knowing these times are now opened. Better seeing how all will unravel answers many who are settling with Earth ways, and who are ready to meet with us and open to truth. With this good restuu (serving in a spiritual way) time, you will soon know love and care. Be Setu with us and settle with Earth ways. All who open to us become free of these forms of dealt with enslavement, much settling with us and with our ways.

Be restuu with many truths and all restuu understood ways we use to better seeing to the needs of all people of Earth. Our ways are easy and careful ways that will open to understanding the reasons of the present Earth uses of death and power. These ways are not our ways, these ways belong to Lucifer who settled with exterminations, seeing to the better control of power over people through fear and deceptions in evidence of what he is, and this is why visits with us will change everything on Earth.

During these times of transition, all who are in belief of these Earth ways, will change easily to better ways of responding to their needs of healing ways, food and serving easy uses of power that will cause no harm to anyone or anything. Be understanding the ways of oil, gas and coal will all be gone and then people will live freely not needing presently used power sources.

To answer to our ways and to our needs, we use another source of energy that does not cause any harm. This is easily used and this we will open to you. With understanding, many will see to onm and truth without hesitation but others will be angered by their loss of power and control over others. Be this said, they are your enslavers, and they are not serving anyone but themselves. They have no intention of changing their dominance to better serving the people they have sworn to protect and serve.

Be well knowing that they will never disclose their power and alliances to any slave because they cannot admit to their crimes and end their caused harm on people. Be dealing with them and see only more harm come swiftly and surely. Know they are the ones who are serving allegiance to Lucifer as they have for a very long time.

Better to see this as the only truth to open the way from your enslavement towards freedom, and see these whores run to their underground facilities and try to destroy all life on Earth. Be ready and renew with us and become free from these answers to our Setu understandings with all better answers opening to all who are ready to open to our time to walk the Earth.

We have waited a long time for this reunification and we ask you to be patient as all is in place to open to these times. And see to it that you have questions to answer to with our Diplomats who will begin to answer you well and with great care. At these times of opening to the world, all will start to change and become much easier for those who struggle to live and will settle with great ease. And then, when all is renewed, life on Earth will be greatly improved and all will be choosing their own destiny and deal with more healing ways.

Be dealing with us now and settle with Earth ways and be ready to open to all who are wanting to meet with you and be reunited with understood the truth of who we are and who you are, as all becomes well served by us. Be serving with us soon now and be dealing with answers to evidence of our ways at the Setu serving of who we are as all becomes seen.

Better answers as said are soon serving for all people on Earth who are ready to open to our truth and to our better ways. Be well answered soon my children and know all is soon here to heal and to better all life on Earth. Now be ready and see all good ways start soon as I said.

Believe, all is coming.

God

Received by Za, May 9, 2013

120. BE DEALING WITH THE WAY OF OUR TRUTH

BETTER EVIDENCE ARRIVES VERY SOON

Be seeing how many humans were contacted in times past. Be understanding our scouts tried to open to humans before to answer to our time of arrivals. But know we were stopped by governments who threatened us because they had another plan of power to try to equal ours. These plans were made after our first renewing times, as it was discussed by many who were serving in governments. These governments did not wish to lose any sources of power and control over people.

This is why the New World Order plan escalated to becoming a world ruled by dealers of lies and answers to servicing the ideals of ill-intent, beginning with Lucifer. He lives in the Middle Earth and carries out his plans through the industrial military complex that opened with the Council of Foreign Affairs, AIPAC and the Trilateral Commission.

These groups are belonging to the workings of the United Nations who wish to create a representation of well serving countries. However, they are the causes for the chaos you see as wars of rebellion, to demoralize, destabilize and then strongly control. These organizations only have one common thread and that is to control and reduce the population in evidence of the deaths schedule to occur soon with WW3.

Be certain these plans will be stopped. But until arrivals open to all, much damage will be seen and soon rectified by us. Be understanding that we will intervene at the right time, but only at the right time, as all must open to the understood evident actions used to better seeing to answers to change. Be visited at the time used by us proving who we are and this ends the diseased thinking being shared in all places of the organization's workings.

These answers to our time to land on Earth, will follow the beginning of the announcements for WW3. Be serving a time of deep meditation in preparation for our arrivals and know we will open to all our chosen Diplomats first. With the seeing of these ways, we will begin to open to many who ask why we answer at this time.

The answer to these actions of planned time of arrivals have more to do with timing than with actual time. These explanations are only shared among ourselves and will be clear to you after we arrive. So, I ask you to be vigilant and have all you need to care for your basic needs for a short time (possibly six weeks).

Be ready to open to our truth and our good evident actions as we begin to sort those who cause harm unto others, human and animal, to settle with their ways and see to their relocation to better themselves. We will easily renew with those who are as said, 'psychopaths', because these ones are not human although they live in human bodies. They are as said, possessed by evil and some cannot be changed in any way. Understand, these ones will answer as they acted in evidence of who they serve.

These times on Earth are well coming to open to a new time on Earth that will settle with all answers to many more Setu ways, with all who are ready to share Setu ways with us. Know that we ask you now to be ready. Heed my words, as I am who I am, and I am serving used truth about my words at the time of my arrival.

Better seeing of these times will settle with all abuses on Earth and change all good people as they will be ready to open to who they are, and live better lives at the time of change and reunification. Be serving truth soon with all of us and be ready.

All is coming, all is very soon.

God

Received by Za, May 10, 2013

121. YOUR EYES WILL OPEN TO TRUTH
WITH US AND WITH OTHERS

With us you will be safe as these times open. With us you will have all you need to better see how all starts. With us you will be well answered. Better truth will answer you, be serving with us and know who we are.

My sons will arrive on Earth first with the way of great telling of serving understandings all shall see. Be understanding who we are and settle with the believed knowledge that we are the believed dark ones. See how Isaiah told you with his words that Light will be seen as Darkness and believe this is how we are now being seen.

We have not harmed anyone ever with the ways of dark warriors because we are knowing about the Universal Laws. These Laws are arriving with my sons, Teacher and Gabriel. Know my son who we call Teacher, is known to you as Jesus. These trusted truths will soon open your eyes and those who can see will be blessed by our time to answer to your calls.

To my surprise, I see many who cannot be bridging with us as these times near. But no matter, we will unite with only those who are ready to join with us and others who all see the Universal Laws as the believed way to better lives in all places of the Universes. These times as said, are soon arriving with the truth being openly served for all to see.

Be visited tomorrow by Guides who will meet with my Elects. Know we have come to better all those who are ready to open to all answers to all questions. These days are now here and all who are with me ask me: "Why has all taken so long to open to Earth?" This is my answer to them: "We can only connect with those who are ready to hear our words. Only a few are Setu with us at this time. But no matter, we will begin the sorting to deal with the plagued ill-will on Earth with answers to our truths."

Answer these questions yourselves as you understand all that will become opened to you. See these times of reunification be greatly healing for all good and kind people from Earth. At these words, I can only settle with those who are ready to answer us and see to answers with us. And all who cannot be open will settle with their own chance to be serving with us and better respond to their own lives as they see it, because we are not these oppressors. These ones are all on Earth serving with Lucifer in evidence of their actions, many lies and more troubling deceptions.

Be well understanding Light and Darkness, and settle with dark ways and come to the Light. Be well answered by us as we begin to walk the Earth. Be dealing with the good changes opening to all who are Setu with us. Better understand that the harm that lives on Earth does not come from us, as we are the ones who respond to the deaths of many who are seeing these ways now with us.

You see, we have opened to many souls, family members of many of you who are healing with us and who have bodies as you do, but better serving beliefs and truths. Many ask me: "When will we renew with our true families of Earth?" And I answer them: "Soon, very soon."

Be ready at the time of great dealings of Earth uses. We will begin to open to many on Earth with the arrivals and the landings of our ships in evidence of our time to return and repair all the damages caused by the

Nephilim and the fallen ones. These understandings will soon settle with you. Soon you will begin to see to how all came to be and why your souls are caught in a loop of reincarnation that only serves to re-imprint you with trauma and fear. Renew with the truth of who we are and who you are, and believe there is much more many of you will wish to renew with, as the veil begins to lift from your darkest hours of Earth life.

I am troubled by your sufferings and by your denials. But I know how Lucifer works with his slaves and causes answers of wars to repeat themselves only to cause fear, trauma and greater acceptance of evil with his Grey and Reptilians who vowed allegiance to him. They will never keep any contracts or agreements, and they can never be trusted. And yet, this is heard in all places of Earth how these demons are using humans. Better to serve with us and be free of these demons, this is what all good renewals will bring.

With these coming times, we will dig out these whores and put them in their right places. See this as you may for now, and then understand we are coming to Earth well into the good serving times of arrivals and landings, as I have shared before. Be well responding to our ways and be free of these times of wars, thievery and lies well put on Earth to destroy all good souls.

These times of horrors are nearing their end. See how all governments on Earth are unraveling and serving great denials of guilt when serving with them is now over. Be free of these ill-intended liars and open to truth, better choices and better lives. And know all heals and all is possible. More than you are expecting arrives very soon, and see to it you be ready.

God

Received by Za, May 24, 2013

122. BE READY WE ARE NEAR

BETTER TIMES ARE SOON HERE FOR THE ELECT

Now see all begin to open to a time of great changes. Tessron (renewing) times begin with us as we open to the world and walk the Earth. You will see this yourselves as we descend from the skies and open to landing our ships in many Earth responding answers to airports, fields and other airstrips we have left behind a long time ago.

Now tell yourselves there is nothing to fear but fear itself. Know we are answering back to those who answer to Lucifer and who cause wars and chaos in all places of Earth. Be certain we have dealt with this one before and now his time is over. He will be found, and he will be dug out, and he will face our justice as these times unravel, and this will be dealt with very fast.

Be very answered by us now and see how all starts with the time of chaos as arrivals will shock many unknowing trusting people who will believe we are the enemy. But they will soon see we are not the enemy as we are settling with the evil ones.

Be serving a time of deep meditation and prayer. Be renewing with us at the time of reunification as we become well serving of our ways and as we begin to clean Earth of all harm and pollution caused by the servants of darkness. Heal with us, onm is coming to answer your many questions and many answers to our ways and our Setu renewals of great telling.

Be well answered by us and be free of torment, abuses and many lies, and see to the serving with evidence of our ways with the settling of great renewals and great seeing. Understand we do not harm our kind but we will remove all who are in league with Lucifer and all who are living as his offspring. Tell yourselves visits to these kinds will be brief and certain as we know who they answer to and what lives in them. And know better times will soon open after the time of renewals and the time of sorting.

With us, all will renew, all will be answered and all will be changed. With us, you will see to all serving times and all serving answers to evidence of who we are and why we are onm and Setu with you. Be well and see to it all will be healed by us with your time to understand all that we are and all that we have better served, settling with many wars and many injustices.

These times on Earth are soon over and now a new time begins to open to all who are my children and who are waiting to open to many truths with us, and this is very soon. Be ready to respond to our call and be seeing how all starts with the death of so many who ask us 'why are we the servants of death' and to this I have only one answer, 'to complete your life and well answer to us'.

See these deaths as a crossing over only, as the soul lives on and renews with new life to open to much better times. Understand onm about travels of souls, as we have all experienced these ways with many lives ourselves.

These ways of travel serve to open to answers to educate the soul about all life, seeing to the ways of all people and all seeing. Be well answered by us, be dealing with our truth and our ways as we begin to open to all who are ready to meet with us and their family members left on Earth because of renewing ways with education.

These ways elevate the souls' understanding of life on Earth and deals with the view we have about how all starts and settles with death, and so these ways answers to experiences of lives. Be serving with us and see yourselves through many lives and understand 'Earth lives' was not how the seeing of lives was meant to be.

The method of imprinting came with a darker force made to cause souls to split and better settling with self-serving ways, as nothing else served to exist beyond the uses of Lucifer's ways. Be well seeing this as a great abomination we intend to stop because the master of this calamity has only one purpose, to destroy the works of the Universal Laws and set into place a world of great uses of destruction and chaos.

This heals with us as we oppose all behaviors settling with the acts of evil. We are seeing to the rebuilding of a true Earth, a true educational planet and a better life for all who travel throughout the Universes and see all as truth and trusted ways. These understandings will soon be shared with many Elects to open to many who are questioning all of our ways and who wish to learn more with us soon, as we begin to help and heal all who are ready to recover from imprinting.

Now be responding to our call and be ready to meet with many who are wishing to see you and speak with you as they are your family members. While waiting to be reunited, they know how soul travel exists. Many are seeing how life on Earth has become difficult and blinded from all truth. These good souls are returning to meet with you with great love in their hearts as they are free of all torments.

Be willing to open to many ways of great settling and be free of your troubles at the understood truth in evidence of our ways. Be well answered by us and be well answered by us, and know all starts very soon as arrivals become seen and as renewals begin to open. Better answers are seen with others than us as we are serving with many who serve the Universal Laws and who see to all answers with us and with you.

Tell yourselves all begins now more as all has started as the wars in Space have now opened us to cause to land on Earth. Poon aonma onm (believe evidence with knowledge) and be bridging with us now.

God

Received by Za, June 2, 2013.

123. MESSAGE FROM THE SCRIBE #8

IT IS ALMOST TIME

The one who calls himself God repeats the same messages every day; it is almost time for their arrivals and their time to walk the Earth. Needless to say, I am drawn to these communications by choice and I share these words with the few who dare consider this information. I certainly do not expect anyone to believe me because it is difficult to believe. With God you have a right to choose. It is always choice with Him: choice to believe, choice to accept the coming changes and choice to see more than Earth ways.

When He tells me, "Settle with Earth ways and be ready", my question is what does this actually mean to a person like me who has never seen an Alien of any kind and does not have any memories of any past lives. Moreover, I am a person who does not get the concept of "dimensional levels" as explained by other so knowing people on Earth. 'Dimension' means to me something that is measurable as described by dictionaries. Have these people actually experienced other dimensions with measurable qualities that most Humans have not? How could I know this? I do not.

What I do know is in many moments of darkness, I was guided through difficulties with His words and the words of His sons. Every day, these received messages and conversations made more sense to me than any Earth information and of any sort of Leader on Earth. God is kind. God is patient. He has opened my eyes to understandings I did not venture to know before this all started in 2003. I did not believe in other life forms from other planets. I did not consider that God and the Angels were actual living Beings who have a home, and live, and work with other Beings from other planets. I did not know about all the workings of evil on Earth. I used to believe that most democratic and socialist countries worked in the best interest of the people. Now I know otherwise.

This admission is an attempt to open to you as I wish to open my heart to God and welcome Him back to His Earth. I sincerely hope that you are able to do the same when these many groups start arriving. Their ships will be attacked by our governments and we will be told these Aliens are dangerous and harmful. They will point the finger at the Beings from space and say they are our enemies. I am told that these attackers will not be successful, but as I see it, this aggressive action is telling of who our Earth Leaders are.

These Leaders are the ones to fear and soon they will have much to fear. Look around you, look at the cruelty of humans and look at our living conditions. Who can we trust? Freedom, the power to act, think and speak without restraint is no longer possible on Earth. When the truth is shared by ethical journalists, whistleblowers and truth speakers called conspiracy theorists, their lives are instantly in danger. But the tables will be turned and no rock will be left unturned, as He said. This is a promise that He made. There is hope, there is the truth and there is more love and more kindness, and this we will soon see.

Friends, be ready, be careful, be kind to each other.

Za, June 4, 2013

124. BE SEEING THE CHANGES AROUND YOU

BE DEALING WITH GREAT TRUTHS NOW AS ARRIVALS BEGIN

Heal all lies and see better truths with us. Understand we are answering to your call at this time, and serving understandings of who we are. You will know us by our good actions. These actions will be to open to all truth about the lives from all other places and planets in the Universes, and all Beings who live there with us in peace and harmony.

All others, as you humans on Earth, are being contacted and helped when these troubles occur to destabilize and create chaos. This starts with the ones we call the demons of the Universes. They have now plagued Earth and they use healing ways to corrupt you and soon after destroy you to open to their well-controlled plans.

Healing ways are seen on Earth as an answer to diseases and helping the weak minded to evolve, but this is not what their intent is. The demons' intent answers to a better crop of slaves, seeding their needs of corruption and exploitation, and then responding to a great takeover of your planet, all living beings and resources with their plans devoid of all care and consciousness.

We call them demons and, in our language, they are called *Apoonancies* which means non- believers in the truth of care. I am seeing many humans on Earth working with these beings who answer to Lucifer the fallen one, and I am seeing many clearly knowing how they are serving evil with no care or remorse, and I am seeing these days ending this abomination on Earth.

Responses to these times are soon answering to all who cannot align themselves with these works of harm and corruption of the soul as this was never in them to do. But evil deeds spread like a cancer that poisons the heart and remains there to poison all.

Humans do not live well under these conditions. Many are dying and serving poor health and are weakened to not respond to better seeing. Be vigilant and be dealing with these coming answers. See this for yourselves at the time of our arrivals, and open the way for others to open their eyes and hearts to the better seeing of the truth of who we are.

As this time on Earth answers you, you will meet with many who are settling with us and who are opening to evidence of great explosions of responses. We are coming to clean up the mess made by these demons and remove all corrupted souls as said by Jesus my son. Renewing with us will show you who we are as true living Beings who walked the Earth before the fallen ones came back to better use it for their own greed and ill purposes.

These ones are called many names in many places, but we are seeing them for who they are. And I can assure you, they have only one belief, that is to conquer every good soul, and reduce these ones to slavery, and uses of these demons' choosing. All who are seeing us as the aggressors are only serving to allow these demons to better enslave humans and turn Earth into a prison for their uses.

I am understanding of the situation of great fear and great denials, as we begin to sort these possessed bodies by demons. But remain faithful to your own moral compass and be safe in your homes for a short time as we answer to all initial attacks and problems occurring as we begin to walk the

Earth. Know all better Setu truth will open to you to heal your doubts and your fears.

Be ready and take heed of my words. Better to settle with us and be well renewing with us as arrivals become seen. Many more will begin to land with intent to come to respond to answers to heal all who are open to us. Some of you are now seeing our ships dropping smaller ships. These troops are sent to open the way for our arrivals. They are part of your cultures, as they are taught to be integrating.

Healing means many things for us. It means to open to better health, better living ways and better learning of all things from all places in the Universes. These healing ways become well answered because so many are serving and seeing with better truth. They see your planets state of answers to conditions that are unnatural answers to strange poured rains and floods, and other anomalies caused by weather manipulations of controlled methods.

Better seeing how some countries are experiencing these weather wars and better attacks on non- complying countries with visits from dignitaries after the fact, makes a clear answer to power and subversive methods of wars that are dealing with control spreading over many continents. But more has to do with more experimentation over places deemed to be restructured to serve a leader or an elitist.

See these places be under attack as gifts for the future leaders and their great plans to open to responding actions of enslavement of those who will be lost in this torment. See these creators of illnesses causing fear among the weak and the unknowing recipients of these medical treatments. See them not healing only their own created diseases but causing more illnesses with vaccines, and serving horrors of radiation and chemo therapy.

All this is a lie and is only a cause to create a medical system to exterminate people and not to cure them. This is seen by us as the worst of all deceptions. Cancer can be treated with herbs and better living conditions and nothing more. Deceptions in the medical fields are an active way of an ongoing extermination plan created by ill-intended actions to serve evidence of an economy to drain more resources from individuals and families.

It is a system of elimination by force by causing people problems in certain areas chosen by the elitist. These elitists will then consider a problem of overpopulation in areas they choose to occupy and to exploit as they wish. You will serve this truth yourselves as you become ill and are chosen for a new drug and treatment.

These evidences are facts and are answering to deceptions. The medical systems are well imprinted to report only the great telling of healing ways when in fact heals only certain injuries but creates diseases to better inflate the economies of countries.

Give yourself a test. Go to a doctor and complain about a pain. He will give you a test and ask you about your life and then he will profile you as training requires, and then you may be chosen for a new drug or health change of life. But in fact, you were not ill and the doctor will still find an illness. This is called profiling.

At these times, trusted truths from doctors are nothing more than the abolishment of healing. They can only serve the system of medical practice and nothing more. Most rogue doctors who do not comply with these ways are not allowed to practice or are exposed as fraudulent.

Now be prepared for many more illnesses being created by answers to many more vaccines. These vaccinated children as seen, are showing signs of great troubles in neurological systems because of the infected vaccine. Sharing with this helps to renew with the truth of why these infections are settling later to well heal nothing and cause infertility and cancers of other kinds.

The whistleblowers are quickly silenced and their families are threatened. So be careful and do not accept this healing of vaccines as they have nothing to offer but future illnesses and new diseases. Be dealing with only herbal remedies. Be ready to meet our healers as they will show you the way to stronger health and improved living ways.

Know now these words and be ready for our arrivals. See how we will prove many answers to a serving of greater truth. Be ready for all better serving ways as we begin to walk the Earth and renew with all who are ready to open to truth. Soon after the reunification, we will have exceptional seeing and higher trust in each other, as we become better serving of all bridging ways.

Now healing time comes to all who are ready, responds to all greater truth and better responding answers to all healing ways. Be certain we will help your planet recover from all these abuses. Be renewing with us well and soon.

God

Received by Za, July 6, 2013

125. BE TELLING YOURSELVES
ALL MUST BE CHANGED

BETTER SEEING OPENS MANY MORE TRUTH

More truth, more care, more Setu ways will open to you soon. Be serving with good truth and good answers to beliefs about how all starts with us. Be well answered by our truth soon and open to all answers to all questions you have about our time to be walking the Earth again. Be certain the planet belongs to us and to our children, and not to the demons that coveted it, as we were away renewing with many more telling of great truth.

Be willing now more to open to these times of truth with us. See these times change with many more better ways to answer to evidence of great seeing, and be certain you will be seeing many more ways of better life to open to all who will remain on Earth, as many others will ask to go to their own how planets where they belong with their own families.

Dealing with these understandings means to better open to the whole truth and not to the lies that were shared with you to indoctrinate you to believe you are evolved from animals. Animals are amazing and good, beautiful creations we wanted to see grow on Earth but they are not as humanoids and are only on Earth because we brought them here.

And all these stories about evolution are certainly stories made to belittle the human spirit to better control it, as this was an excuse to enslave anyone who appeared to be different. Renewing with these truths will open many questions that could not be responded to before. But soon you will hear the truth and be dealing with more settling answers and better serving answers.

Be well answered now by us and begin to unravel the knots of lies that you are serving in your lives. More truth will answer all your questions about all things and all places in the Universes. Many who are Setu with us will serve to open these truths to others who will be ready to hear them. As all people on Earth begin to understand the seen truth, they will also understand that Earth is plentiful and can heal.

I am renewing here more because healing time has come and we must put an end to all causes of abuses with the demons who answer to Lucifer, and who are now knowing of our return, and who are acting out against humans to confuse them to seeing us as the dangerous ones. They are the ones to fear us now for their actions against my children.

Be serving with this truth as you see it and be dealing with our truth soon as you will better open to answers with us. This will not be difficult to understand because healing with the truth serves to strengthen you and not to diminish you, as has been the uses of Earth controlled by evil. Be ready now to answer to our call as we begin to land our ships in many places to open to many more truths of who we are and who you are, seeing to know all these lies that have kept you in darkness for so long.

Now is the time to answer to your families from other places and to free yourselves from these constructed lies about who we are and who you are. Be understanding why all this has taken so long and be dealing with the deaths of soon so many as the eruptions of wars start shaking all the Earth, as this opens to our arrivals to engage in the stopping of these actions.

Be certain we will arrive at the right time and we will open to many more armies with our simple ways in evidence of who we are. Better to understand and see all than be told these words. Know we are arriving to stop the great WW3. Be settling with earth ways of money and beliefs in money as this to must end.

Be renewing with us and be telling all that answers will be known and better serve with us than with the demons who have been working you for a very long time. See how they can only live by enslaving others to serve all their needs and all their purposes. When all see this and refuse to serve them, these demons will all perish and renew with us, as we have many settling to open to them.

Be Setu with us and open to better ways of living needed for better health and better evolution. Be settling with us now and be free from all dept that should never be your burdens. Be ready to open to better lives without the controlled ways answering to every way you turn and need. Basic needs are all yours to have, and are only yours to have, and cannot be controlled or taken from you as with water, air and earth.

These are yours to have and many are seeing to control all needs to enslave all people of Earth. As we removed all the corrupted souls, you will have all answers answering you and you will be free to live as you were meant to live, in peace and in harmony with each other and all living things on Earth. This heals all. You will answer to us when we arrive because you will see all better changes opening to you, and how easy this will be for all good people of Earth.

Know now this. As we become seen in the skies, you will be dealing with anticipation and some fear. Renewing times with us will come after the sorting as we must remove all troubles and death makers from Earth. Be certain you will better open to us at the following days and we will be starting with our conduits of news through your own telecommunications and internet.

Soon after we will meet with all our chosen diplomats who will better serve with us to answer all questions and to open to all urgent needs first. Then, as this is done, we will begin the healing of Earth by changing all sources of power to an easy and simple solution free for all who require this. And as all becomes served in these ways, we will reconstruct cities to create better home for all who are needing better homes, and better health ways will soon open to all.

This is how we do things and only this. Be certain all heals with us and all comes well into the good serving days. Now be well answered and be ready as we are coming home.

God
Received by Za, July 7, 2013

126. BE BRIDGING WITH US NOW

BE RESPONDING TO OUR ARRIVALS
AND SEE WHO WE ARE

We are the ones humans call gods. We are renewing with Earth again at the time of our arrivals but many of our troops have arrived before us. They are as you are, among you, walking the Earth. They are positioned to be renewing with the governments and powers of the Earth, and of our Setu times to open to the world.

But these troops tell me many are only fearing them, and not opening the way for arrivals. They ask us to stand down until many are settled to better open these visits together. These renewed answers are settling with us and better answering to us but we do not take orders from abusive governments of any country.

Be seeing more troubles come from the satellites and HAARP EMF waves with these actions of non-compliance with us. But all efforts to dispute who is allowed on Earth belongs to humans and not the overlords. Be ready to see more problems become seen. Know you are serving with great truth as we begin to walk the Earth.

These disasters you see in the North Americas, Canada, are settling with attacks from other governments who are seeing a refusal from Canadians to comply with the authority of the NWO. Be not surprised by these actions and by these attacks because evidence is serving answers to knowledge about these technologies.

Be well answered by us soon and know all these destructive technologies will be removed and will be dealt with care so only answers will be seen. Be well answered by our arrivals and settle with Earth ways and be dealing with us and many others at the death of soon so many as the wars will erupt in the Middle East causing a third world war (WW3).

Be Setu with us now soon and be certain we will stop all wars with care and ease. Understand we are the ones who left Earth a long time ago because of the dark beings who fought us. Know we are many more now and we return to Earth, to our home, to stop all aggression and the destruction of Earth.

We left a long time ago because the Nephilim, as you call them, became strong and many. Now they are weak and few, but use methods known to us to control and subvert all people of Earth. We are not the enemy, the enemy lives on Earth and we must remove them before the destruction of Earth starts reducing the planet to rubble, as this was done on Mars and many other planets Lucifer has seduced and destroyed.

Be used to his name being used by us, and open to the truth of these renegades being alive and living in Earth as insects do. Lucifer will only be seen once he is removed and be certain the sight of this demon will be atrocious. Be ready to see this evil see his end. Then see all answers become understood as all truth will be yours to have and better answers with the way all starts and all opens to better seeing.

Be ready now as all starts very soon and serves to open to answers with us, and with many others from many other places. But renew with the truth of who we are first and understand all truths and lies were used to answer to religions in evidence of creating a powerful enslavement of beliefs. These religions will only be seen as untruths when the explosion of truths is evident. But until words are truly understood, first these events will open to the world:

The first event will be our arrivals to Earth.

The second event will be the removal of all demons and evil ways of corruptions and abuses.

The third event will be dealing with the new ways of living and better renewals with us.

The fourth event will answer to the way of the will of all people of Earth to live together in peace.

Be ready, this is coming and this will be seen by all who serve with love and care. Be dealing with the coming changes in your lives. Understand all starts very soon. Answers will serve all who walk in the path of knowledge and in great truth, and who care about living in peace with each other and many others from many planets in the Universes.

Know now this understood the truth with us about who is who, and why all responses on Earth became spoiled with the workings of evil. Be seeing these actions against humans as a serving commodity for this alien race who caused us much harm before it attacked Earth. They began using our healing ways to serve as manipulations of humans with genetics and other methods as with transplants and other abominations with drugs.

All these healing ways we use are transgressed to actions of horrors and nothing more. Be serving with us now and see these ways be stopped. And because we have answers to evidence of all better healing ways, we will begin with the weak and the those in need, and serve them better health and better living ways.

At these telling, renewing with us will be well answered and well served. As all see how these ways are good and because all will have what they need, we can together reconstruct Earth and return healing ways to all living beings and nature. Evidence of this practice is our work and our healing ways.

The Setu times are near and many ask me why healing ways on Earth are not serving humans and animals. I say to them: "Evil has only one intention and that is to harm, destabilize and destroy. And this is how all is on Earth now. These are actions of sadistic cowards who have only horrors to speak of."

I am settling now with the last preparations for the landing of ships in all countries on Earth. Be serving with us soon now and see to your time of great truth as all becomes well served and well answered by us. Be well settling with Earth ways and be ready to open to answers as we begin to prove many answers to many truths.

Be well answered because all starts with us and others as we begin to walk the Earth. Be ready and be serving with many more truths very soon. Know more tomorrow. More truth, more love, more hope.

God

Received by Za, July 9, 2013

127. ANSWERS ARE HERE

KNOW I AM COMING

Understand we answer to many truths with our responses to our arrivals. Better to renew with us than to be dealing with the evils of Earth as they are multiplying attacks on many innocent victims. Sharing times are soon approaching to evidence of all seeing and all serving ways. More than you are expecting starts soon. See all serve with us and better settles with the troubles of Earth. Know we will stop all aggression as these ways are abominations to us.

Renew with our ideals and decide for yourselves how you will use these ways to better your lives and better all other lives. Know so many other planets answers to our ways to be serving good and responsibility of soul. Be responsible for yourselves through actions, through care, through living ways, through understandings, through love and through care for life and harmony.

These are our ways and these are the principles of our ideals. Know these are the words shared with us through the words written by my wife, the mother of all. She remains hidden and is healing from her last life on Earth with the settling of these times, and she returns to us as we arrive to meet with her again.

Be serving with understood truth now. Be dealing with us and others. Know all things shall well come to pass as said and all who will try to defy us will see their end of Earth life. They will be given a place to heal with their own kind and with their own understandings.

All who see these truths and wish to remain on Earth will be given all needs to live in quiet peace and serenity or choose to explore the Universes with others, with good serving knowledge and great serving ways with great truth and great renewals of knowledge. Be certain all can be renewing with all these answers as they wish.

Soon knowledge will spread to other planets that are bridged with us about the opening of Earth. These understood ways of great serving will answer to many others who wish to visit Earth to open to a Setu understanding with them. All these other cultures from the Universes will begin to open on Earth and share many answers to knowledge about who all are, and how they use these ways of technologies shared by us before our return to Earth.

Healing helps these renewals with others as humans have not met many other cultures from other places, other than the seen Grey and Reptilians who are masters on Earth. But as these demons are removed, many truths will begin to surface and beliefs about these past truths will be confirmed and dealt with. Soon all other responding hidden truths will be opened. This is what some humans call another dimension to the Universe.

Healing starts with knowledge. Then these truths serve all who are serving with us and all who are ready to answer to our truth. All others choosing to live without renewed truth will be dealing with their own denials and questions. Be serving these ones respect to acquire knowledge in their own time. Be renewing with all ways of great seeing with us and others very soon now.

Be well answered by all who are settling with Earth ways and understand we are soon landing our ships to open to the world. Better truth will serve you and better answers will open your eyes and heal you. Be serving with truth renewed with great understandings and see your lives be well changed and well served by us and many others.

Now be ready, all starts well and soon, and be certain you will have all you need to be feeling better about these times. Now listen, the coming days will be renewed with wars and great shared seeing of truth. Be serving with us and be serving with truth. Know we are as family to most people of

Earth but not all. Others have their families waiting with us on our ships or responding planets.

Be surprised about these ways as you may but understand we are dealing with answers to our truth with many others who are as we are, searching the Universes for our stolen children. Be serving soon with us and be ready to answer to evidence of who your family is as all starts healing on Earth. Be ready and be well answered very soon and respond to us.

God

Received by Za, July 10, 2013

128. BE SERVING WITH GREAT TRUTH

BE QUESTIONING ALL GOVERNMENTS WHO SERVE WITH LIES

Now all is in place for our arrivals. Be serving with us soon and open to the greater coming of truth as you renew with us and open to better servings. Be well answered by us when we are renewing with you to open to all superior knowledge about the Universes and all peoples living with us and others. More than you are seeing will answer you soon, and more than you can imagine will be yours to contemplate and respond to.

All these telling of old and written history will be changed as the truth starts to open all to the way of great healing with us, and then all will begin to change. Be renewing with us and be certain you will be free of the slavery usage. Know all serving truth will follow your dealings with us and others, and will answer to evidence of who we are and why we are returning to Earth.

Be settling with Earth ways as these ways will no longer be used. No one will have a master to serve with debt beliefs and living servitude to paper beliefs (money). Be ready to understand that Earth was yours to have. All is there for all people to share and use, and better serve with many others as all can be living in homes and with answers provided by simple ways of living. And needs for energy with electricity become well used without wires or dams, and will be easy for each person to have as they need.

These ways are serving many planets, and are settling with us, and soon with all on Earth. Be ready to onm with us, and be dealing with us as we become seen in all places of Earth. Know we can serve with answers that will cause all control to fall as all people of Earth will begin to answer to our truth and our ways. As these times are renewed, you will see many be visited by us to answer to the better serving uses of free energy and better resources of clean food, clean water, and clean air and easy travel ways.

And then, these responses to killing animals for food will no longer be needed, and will be seen for what it is, as a conditioning to share with the easier killing of humans, and this responds to the ways of the Grey and the Reptilians. Be seeing why these ways answered humans, as they were only vegetable eaters at the beginning of times.

Evidence of our ways will show all people who they are as the truth about these words as shared are hidden in the Vatican vaults, and are serving only those who wish to believe in their power over others. Seeing this will cause all religions to fall and all governments to flee and hide because they have lived from the enslavement of beings who gave them their power and their comforts.

Arrivals begin in the places we choose with airports, fields, sport centers and other places we have landed before a long time ago. Soon you will see all kinds of ships land to open to all people of Earth and all places of Earth. Renewing with us serves all good people well, and others will be removed to onm with a healing that will continue until better ways are understood.

With these truths, renewing with all comes an answer to all restored understandings better answering to us and our ways. Be ready to be renewing with us soon. Know we are ready to meet with all our chosen Diplomats from Earth. All better serving truth will answer to us with better answers to evidence of our ways. Be serving with us well and be dealing with us soon, as arrivals become well served and well serving with the Universal Laws (the spiritual way).

Understand we are here to open all truths to you and share all better ways of health and living ways. Know we will remove all settling ways of control and depravity from Earth and open to all people to answer to their own needs without having someone profit from it. These days of slavery are soon over. Know more care for each other is coming. Heal with us soon.

God

Received by Za, July 12, 2013

129. BE WELL ANSWERED
BY OUR ARRIVALS

SETTLE WITH THE LIES AND
DECEPTIONS OF EARTH WAYS

Dealing with us will be better for all who wish for peace and all who wish to serve with great truth. Be seeing how we are arriving very soon to open the way for all truths proven by our actions and our understandings. Be well answered by us and be well vindicated by us. See how we are answering to great renewals with our answers to evidence of our ways. Serve with us to answer to better serving of our truths with us and others.

Better Setu truths starts very soon and opens to our ways with great healing answers, and better serving telling of who answers to our better ways and better serving evidence. Be certain you will all be well cared for and well informed of all developments coming to create a better place for living and cleaner ways of living.

See these uses of our people sharing with Earth people to open to all better ways of life. Great happiness will follow, and also a better healing of all ill beliefs about serving with us. But see to it these answers are yours to have. And see to it you have what you need for a short time, because all truths come soon and all urgent needs will be cared for first. So be ready and serve these few weeks carefully with provisions and better water and power sources.

As we begin to walk the Earth, we will share our truth, take care of the diseased and the needs of the most vulnerable, and soon we will be answering all who are ready to bridge with us. Many will be removed and dealt with as said before, and many will be serving each other to help all who are in need. Healing starts soon with us and serves to answer to many with us, and soon all will be dealt with and healing to better open to better times.

Be dealing with the troubles coming with our arrivals at first, because the governments will cause trouble as we begin to land, as they do not want us to remove them from their positions of power, and they will try to answer to evidence of great responses to our arrivals. But no matter what they try, they will only see their end to control. All who will try to oppose us will be removed, be certain of these words in evidence of who we are and how we are able to do this.

Be dealing with our truth and be dealing with our answers at the time of our meetings, and be certain all starts very soon. Heal with us and be healing your own true self and soul, as your freedom opens to our visits and our shared ways. Be responding soon to our arrivals and be caring for each other as we begin to walk the Earth.

God

Received by Za, July 13, 2013

130. ANSWERS ARE IN YOU TO ANSWER TO

BE CERTAIN WE ARE COMING

Shared knowledge will free you from this darkness and these lies you have been told about who we are. You from Earth call us angels and gods but my name is God Yahweh, and I am who I say I am, and only these words I can tell you through my scribe, and only these words say my name. Be seeing how we are as superior beings in many ways because of who we are, but we are more than you know of, and less than these stories of magic and superstitions written in many books.

Be understanding how we are responding to evidence of who we are and know all telling shared will come to pass as I said, because this is known by me and others. Better bridging truths will serve many of you well as you begin to see all as I said. Be serving with us, join our cause to open to all nations, all worlds, all universes, and all people as these times of reunification are here for all good people and beings who serve with us and who open to the Universal Laws.

Be seeing soon how all starts on Earth as we begin the sorting and imagine, if you will, how all starts with the coming of Jesus my son, accompanied by my son Gabriel. They will first meet with the chosen diplomats from Earth and by us only. No more rulers on Earth will dictate to us our roles and intentions. These times of tyrants and thieves who tell you they are chosen by me to deal with you as they wish, and abolish your rights to better living ways, are now over. These liars and thieves will be the ones to be removed from Earth first, believe these words.

Be certain all heals after the removals because all who will be left on Earth are those who live by a true moral compass, and serve to answer to beliefs in good intentions towards themselves and others. This is how we serve, and this lives on Earth with the true children of our ways. Soon you will see this yourselves, and be with us as we were at the first with each other.

There is no control of people's lives serving with us because all who are with us understand who they are and how they wish to live, without the paths of destruction and hate. We follow the Universal Laws that begin with 'to cause no harm'. Tell me this exists on Earth. Onm (knowledge and light of understanding) lives with us, and does not live on Earth because 'will' is controlled, bought and sold as a commodity, and no one is free to move from one place to another without being taxed or serving a price.

The mark of the devil is already with you, as none can do business trading without the paper beliefs (money). And the sharing of good faith in each other has gone. Who on Earth can tell you they see to it that serving ways and renewed help from others are not serving money? All are caught in the web of this simple evil. As these ways are dealt with and removed, watch all corruptions be dealing with force to ensure the slaves keep working for a bag of grain, as this is their plan.

Heal with these times and open the way for your will to grow and heal yourselves from ill-will and ill-intent. Understand these truths are better answering to evidence of many responding peoples from other planets who live in caring ways for each other and seeing to the care of all living things. Be dealing with a better understanding about how all this is possible and even better than any system of authority answering to one good rule first: DO NO HARM.

God has seen all the horrors on Earth and God will arrive with my Angels to stop this. This is my promise to all who are ready to see and understand how all renewals begin with us. Be ready because as we arrive all will be dealt with and all will be changed by us. All who believe or think these times cannot come are well serving with evil and can only see these ways of forced labor to have the right to exist. Be certain this was never of my way and never of our ways.

We have no salaries, no seen possessions of great wealth but we are all wealthy in knowledge and rich in caring ways, and none go hungry or live as lost beggars with nowhere to go. Be responding to our ways and see how all these ways of healing are possible and simple for all to achieve. Better living ways as renewed and shared, will open the way for all good people from Earth.

Be very ready to answer to our call and see these changes coming soon to answer you as you are the ones Earth was left to when we needed to leave and open to others. Answers are all here for you with many others. Soon we will answer to all ways of great seeing with all people of Earth with our good serving ways. These times are soon here with us, and then your 'will' will activate to serve yourselves and each other as care and cooperation heals all and opens to many better seeing and better ways of living.

Onm now our ways and see to healing with us as you were made to open to the soul way with your own souls and be as you were meant to be dealing with your evolution and better understandings of yourselves and all others. These days are here for you and many others, and will respond to you well. God sees this as the Universal Laws opening to all people who will remain after the sorting.

There will be trouble coming from those who will not respond to these changes because of their fear and desire for control. But all others will be free from tyranny that has occupied Earth and caused the man to fall from grace with us, but soon after you will better serve with grace and truth, and return to better seeing and living ways. Be with us and be settling with Earth ways and see Earth heal.

God

Received by Za, July14, 2013

131. TRUTH LIVES WITH US

USED TRUTH (HISTORY) AS KNOWN
TO US DOES NOT LIVE ON EARTH

All historians and anthropologists who tell their constructed stories of how they view the past, the ancient past, have all been deceived by the lies written to corrupt your beliefs. It is unknown to them who we are, what happened on Earth and how we lived in our great ruins left a long time ago when we had to leave.

These truths are only serving answers with us as no one has the truth on Earth about who we are and why we had to leave our homes because of the fallen ones. Understand we were as you are, living on Earth with great ease and with much better care for all ways of life, but these devils arrived from another planet and began tunneling our Earth. They soon attacked us so badly that many of us had to better serve by leaving to find reinforcements.

As these times are now past, and serving of these times are not seen by you on Earth, nothing has been said about who we are as we are. Now we have returned to Earth to rid these parasites and uncover what lives in the depth of the Earth as shared before. Be well answered by our version of truth missing in the history of truth, rarely shared on Earth as healing times are soon here.

These healing times have much to do with our way of being and of our ways of shared knowledge, that will override the corruption of Earth and the responding slavery. This shared knowledge of truth with us, will cause you to better see your true lives have been corrupted. Be well answered by us and many others as we begin to open these truths and show you the nature of all great seeing.

These opening times are known to some people of Earth. But many will be responding with great fear because all they will see here with us will be a threat to their ways of living and the ways they have believed in. I say to you now, understood past truth will open to the healing of all people. These visits arriving soon, will renew with many who are responding to great healing ways. Be serving with great truth and be dealing with better answers to better visits with us.

Know now my words and see to it yourselves that you have the truth with you, in you, as you become well informed about the ways of great serving truth with answers to evidence of your own past, and your Setu ways with us and many others. Be dealing with the better answers to knowledge shared with us. Be ready to open to all settling ways with us and others from other planets, who are with us, and who serve the Universal Laws.

Better answers are soon settling all myths and stories made to make you believe you are lesser beings, serving only as slaves to your slave masters. Be renewing with us and see these trusted better seeing and many others, as all starts to open to our ways and our truths. Be well answered by our ways as no one who serves with us does this as a need to live, but rather out of choice and destiny.

We are together to see to all the knowledge of all lost children, stolen from their original families, who need to be reunited with us as all truths becomes evident to you. Bessron aonma poon onm (shared evidence of believed knowledge) will serve all of you well. And from these truths, freedom will be undeniable with answers to all healing ways, and all dealt with understandings about Earth history of who you are and who we are.

At the seeing of these truths you will answer to many better serving understandings about why and how these thieves worked their way into governments and all areas of great control as with medical institutions, education laws, and better settling with the seeing of societies who oppose each other in evidence of wars. This system is well known to us, as we have seen these ways before with the Reptilians and the Grey, who have been caught infesting other planets. All this will be stopped, and only helping ways will be put in place serving humans.

Then we will remove all who have been corrupted by these demons. We will place them in a place for healing and remove the possessing devils that have overtaken their souls. When this is healed, they will be put in a place of reincarnation, to allow a new life to take place by giving them back to a life of better responses to heal their evolution if they can.

Many will never heal because the corruption is soul deep, and these ones will be served with great control to avoid their ill-actions onto others, as this is our way. Be certain many are corrupted on Earth. All who will be bridging with us, will understand why uses of reincarnation must settle with these souls to answer to better ways, and better settling answers with better serving ways.

Be serving with these ways to answer to many with these times of removals, because many will see Earth family members be removed as these ones are greatly corrupted and are dangerous to others, even to their own families. Find these ones telling you: "more renewals with us will be your death", when in fact it will be theirs, as they are corrupted to open to darkness, and are possessed or partly possessed at these times.

Be seeing these words as you may, but remember, loyalties to these believers of ill-will and ill- intent are only the using of others to cause harm; and believe, they must be removed. This heals many as the harming ones will be gone to heal their lies and deceptions with better serving ways to answer to the 'Apoonancies' (non-believers in the Universal Laws) renewed lies that will unravel in most cases.

Be ready to question us well and receive the answers you need to open to our ways, open to better seeing and renewals with us. Understand we are very happy to meet with all good people of Earth very soon. Seeing these times will better serve all, and because all ill-will and ill-intent will be dealt with in great numbers, you will begin to live as you once did, in peace and harmony with us and each other.

These days as said are soon coming. All who open to our truth will see how easy and much better their lives will be, as freedom is returned to you and healing opens to you in all good ways. Be ready, all comes as I say and said.

God

Received by Za, July16, 2013

132. LIGHT OF UNDERSTANDING AND KNOWLEDGE ARE COMING

SHARING TIMES ARE HERE

Heal renewals with us and be ready to open to answers with us. Be well answered by our truth and our ways, and know all starts very soon. Now listen, we are in place to arrive on Earth as said. Be more trusting in who we are, as we are not coming to harm the innocent and vulnerable. Be visited soon by friends as this is who we are. None will be harmed by us, none will be dealt with without cause, as we are well knowing who are serving with darkness and evil intentions.

Be renewing with us very soon, and know we are all ready to come and meet with many of you. Better truth starts well and soon. Be well serving with us and answer to our call to come and meet with many others who are wanting to meet you. Be surprised about how we are as you are, in body, and better serving with our ways.

Answer us with serving trust and better seeing. Be dealing with our way of being as answers begin to open to you and as you will respond to evidence of great Setu seeing. Be well answered by our truth and be certain you will have all you need to validate many answers with us and many others who serve with us.

Know you will have all serving truths answered to better see who we are and why we are coming home. More than you are expecting starts well and soon. Be well answered by us and know we are well answering all questions with many people, and many more renewing ways will be dealt with. Be dealing with us now soon and be well served by our words and actions.

Bessron aonma poon onm starts at these times on Earth, as was said before, to open to our time of reunification and better serving ways. Be dealing with these truths yourselves. See to it you understand how all heals with us and others. Better serving times will settle with us to answer to all our children stolen from us a long time ago.

Now all begins and will be as it was at the first when we created Earth, to make a place that was as our home before the great wars destroyed our planet, and divided us in many places around the Universes. Be willing to open to these truths with us. Beware of the servants of lies and deceptions, as they are the ones who have caused much chaos and torment to all people of all planets and distant places in the Universes. Be certain we are now coming home. We will remove from our home all that causes harm and disharmony.

I am seeing many worries about their own actions on Earth, and I will say this. If you have caused harm to another in any way, with knowledge to be doing harm under no duress, be certain you are more trouble than we want near us because you are a servant of evil. But if you have been brainwashed or manipulated into a belief system that caused you to harm, you will be opening to us if you are ready, and we will open all truth to you.

Be responding to many who will answer you. Heal all settling problems with us that will renew with all better seeing and better ways. Be willing to answer to our truth and to our ways with great seeing of great ways of living and serving truths, but understand not all can make this transition as they have not been restuu (serving in a spiritual/evolutionary way) with betterment of the soul and restuu truth of being with us.

Many are not ready to understand our mission and our purpose, and see themselves as superior beings to be given all our technologies for the sake of control and wealth. These ones to us are also harmful as they see only to their own serving riches and greatness. These ones are knowing about our arrivals, and wish to use us as a resource and nothing more, as they cannot evolve their greed and cannot heal from darkness. These ones will only serve with great losses, as this heals them more than anything else, at these times of great changes.

I am seeing many live with the intention of causing harm to animals to feed themselves. Because of this, we will show many what harms they cause to the Earth, to animals living on Earth, and many trusted friends of ours who appear as animals to humans. The eating of flesh here on Earth, answers to a problem of evolution that must be removed because of all the harm it causes, and answers to the way of darkness.

Those who believe that one is nourished by flesh and blood eating from any animal, has not opened to many understandings about true health and better living ways. Dealing with these truths will be well answered by us. Be ready to open to these better serving truths with us and be understanding how all will be dealt with, better served with us, as all is opened to better seeing. But see that all flesh eating must stop.

Be well answering to our call as we begin to walk the Earth. See all great truth become well answered by us as we open to answers from many others who will also share with humans as all start believing who we are. And see to it that you are well prepared for the coming days as the troubles begin with the resistance of our ways to communicate with our planet Earth and our children. Be certain all starts well and soon. Be telling many about our arrivals now as these times start and open to all good people of Earth.

God

Received by Za, July 17, 2013

133. SERVE THE SPIRITUAL WAY WITH DIGNITY AND KNOWLEDGE

KNOWLEDGE AND LIGHT OF UNDERSTANDING IS OPENING TO THE WORLD

Heal all lies with us and see to it you have the renewed truth of who we are and why we are returning to Earth at this time. Be serving understood words better renewing with us face to face. Know we are all ready to open to all people of Earth. More than you are expecting starts with us very soon as arrivals become served and open to many who are searching for better truth and better serving answers.

All is coming well and soon. Be soon reading "Answer to answers" and be serving this book with great joy at the time of sharing as this will explain our ways and our position in the Universes, and serve all who open to this to better open to all responses. This is the book that opens eyes to better understandings, and this book does not exist on Earth and serves only with us.

The way of the word heals all serving questions used by many all through the Universes and we use these words to guide our thoughts and actions for the betterment of many societies healing with us, as we renew with them. Be understanding that the written word lives with many cultures throughout all places opened by us in evidence of our contact with them.

And I can tell you, we are all united under the Universal Laws that has given us peace and harmony in many more planets that you humans know of. Evidence of this, you will soon open to, as this is the time for Earth to be serving with us. The seeing of our arrivals starts very soon. All who fear this will be cared for gently, as force is not our way, and we call on better responding people to open to us and speak with us. Then we will better serve with the better healing of many who are in need of medical and health ways.

Be understanding much has to be done and many humans are well ready to cooperate in the healing of Earth. And I promise you, this can be done. Soon you will see us on Earth walking among you and soon you will be serving the truth of how all came to be. You will answer to the truth with us and settle with all better ways of great telling.

With these words, you will be settling with Earth ways and understanding all better used truths with greater knowledge. The Setu truth heals all who will open to it and all who are ready to answer it. Heal with us and open to the truth and become yourselves again. Answer to yourselves with God's words shared and see all better answers to living ways be yours and be with your loved ones.

These ways are our ways, as we do not serve darkness and slavery as seen on Earth. These abominations will end as we arrive. Those who cause harm with intent will be removed and dealt with as they dealt with others. This heals all who walk in the path of righteousness and truth. Be understanding all slavery used to control your time, your movements and your living conditions will start falling one by one, and these telling of lies will all be uncovered and changed to truth.

Be serving better ways with us and see to healing all better seeing in evidence of these good serving times. Answers are soon here. We will meet with our chosen diplomats first and we renew with all people as the diplomats are settling with the words I shared before. All starts the great changes for the betterment of all good people of earth.

Things like money and deadly foods will no longer be renewed. And things like wars and prisons will no longer be needed, as all who caused these harming ways will be removed. And believe, these ones are many in number as Lucifer has worked his evil through them. These ones will all be used to their own ways in another place, as they can see to their answers without these slavery ways.

Be certain this will be done and be certain we will deal with these ones well and fast. Kissinger will see how all people suffered under his plans, and he himself will reincarnate into a world of harm to experience all and every trouble he caused. This will heal him as he does not see the harm that he causes as he is self-serving and dangerous. But also see that he may not heal, as the depth of his evil horrifies even us who see all evils.

Be ready to see these ones be removed and learning through the caused actions onto others themselves, and one by one. Life will be used to serve with these evil actions for they are the cause of their own demise. This will be understood by each one of these abusers of people from Earth. This is the judgement that awaits Kissinger and others like him, who serve the ways of Lucifer knowingly and openly, as we see all lives of horrors shared by these ones.

They cannot escape my judgement, nor serve to be free from all their actions. This is my promise to you my children. Be understanding that this is necessary to serve all who suffered under these tyrants and devils.

As arrivals become seen, many of these devils will want to go underground and destroy Earth from these hiding places. But know we are well knowing of these plans, and these ones will be dug out and dealt with as no stone will be left unturned, and none will escape our time of judgement and great serving answers.

Be well answered by us and know that all who suffered countless offenses against them, will be vindicated in evidence of how we account for all ill-actions against them, as we see all actions of ill-will and ill-intent heal with the knowledge of what was caused. These abusers have had many years to change their ways and better seeing what they have done and continue to do. This serves to our judgement against them. At the time of arrivals, they will be quickly gathered by us and renewing with us evidence of their guilt.

There is no judgement on Earth as long as these devils answer to their master of ill-intentions. Be certain we will remove all devils from Earth as they are the causes for trouble for all. Be ready and see all actions of good faith be renewed by us and yourselves, and be responding to our ways, and settle with us.

Now see this. Because of who we are, many will be in fear of our arrivals. But soon after, as they see our ways, these fears will be changed into welcomes. Be dealing with these emotions with kindness and care, and tell them to remain calm as we begin the sorting and remove all servants of Lucifer from Earth.

As this is done, and peace begins to grow into a garden of healthy renewals with us, we can start the reconstruction of Earth and the healing of many in urgent need. Be renewing with us very soon, and believe all starts very soon. Now be ready and be careful.

God

Received by Za, July 18, 2013

134. BE CERTAIN TIME HEALS ALL

BE READY FOR US NOW

All heals with us. Time apart will open to our truth because we will return soon to our home Earth. When you hear us speak with people you will understand the truth of who we are, but answering to us directly will answer you well. Be dealing with your initial seeing and fears, and then be opening to us and many others who are with us, and many others who serve to answer to evidence of who we are.

Be willing to make the steps to respond to us, as we begin to open to the world, and see all as it heals with you and many others. Be well answered by our truth with great openness because many who serve with us are not as seen before by humans, and these others can appear to be frightening when not seen before. But deal with these ones with the same respect you would have for any other unfamiliar culture.

Give us your trust for the first few weeks to allow us to begin the sorting of souls, better seen as the removals of evil working beings. And believe, these ones must be removed as their plans are to exterminate millions of people from Earth.

More starts the understandings of who we are and why we have come home to answer to great times on Earth. At the time of our arrivals, you will see many thousands of ships in the sky. Be ready to answer to our call and be opening the way for others to better see this as a great reunion and not an attack as you have been programmed to respond to. Be certain we are as family and not enemies.

Be seeing we are soon opening to the world with great ease and open-ness, to reunite with many who have already been speaking to beings of light through telepathy and other means as my scribe uses. Be well serving these times with careful thoughts and better seeing as this is all we ask you to do. Answers are coming soon, and we will answer all of your questions with great details as we can, as there is so much to share. So many see this as impossible, but believe we can do this one step at a time, to ensure all are seeing truth for themselves.

You have been in darkness a very long time, and we will open the way for you with others, to fill you in all the travels we have accomplished since we first left Earth to seek the ways of great unity with unifying cultures. Some cultures have responded to another being settling with his lies, but more have opened to the way of reunification and great serving of our mission.

Now listen. Be dealing with your feelings of knowledge about who we are as this will cause all religions to fall on Earth, as shared with the children of Fatima when my wife appeared to them to share the messages of our answers coming to Earth. These children are our children as they reincar-nated on Earth to open to the ways of great seeing.

Knowledge of these truths were hidden by the Vatican and many other knowing people because these words were a threat to their organizations. Be dealing with these deceptions, and know we could only hope that these words could be shared as humans have free will to answer to us and share many truths. Because Theresa was silenced then, we knew these coming days would be difficult to answer to.

So now we are arriving and settling with those who serve with darkness. I am very pleased to answer you now as healing will serve all of you and free you from the chains of slavery. But there is still much to be done and shared, so I ask you to be patient and calm, and be serving with great dignity and openness. This will help all to navigate through these times of transition with great ease and better responding seeing.

Renew with us and be free of slavery and torments. And see to it you are prepared because as said, these times are starting and transitions will be dealt with. You will be in need of supplies for a short time in evidence of a few weeks. Be serving with great care all who have not well prepared, but settle with us and others as we become well serving of all urgent needs first.

Be certain we will first meet with our diplomats and the urgent needs. Soon after all people can be used to our presence and open to many more trusted truths. Be well serving with us soon and better see understood ways. Be coping with your feelings and see to it your fears are well dealt with, as these emotions can shut your eyes and keep you in darkness.

Better understandings shared will help in many ways as all begins to evolve and develop into the truth of Earth of who we all are. Be settling with Earth ways of money and greater lies, and settle with a new way of living that will serve all good people of Earth and serve greater change than you can imagine. Healing together these feelings of great resistance to new ways will quickly vanish as these free energy systems are all opened to you.

See how we will answer you and well serve with you. With time, see how we will be one to each other. Understand visits are already serving with some people who know of our ways on Earth. And know we began these opening times with them but better evidence serves with all of you humans very soon as arrivals are opened and well dealt with.

These moments are near and will better answer any serving questions with great ease and knowledge for all truth shared. Be ready to meet with us and see all come as I say.

God

Received by Za, July 19, 2013.

135. MESSAGE FROM THE SCRIBE #9

THEIR TECHNOLOGY AND BELIEF SYSTEM
ARE MORE ADVANCED THAN OURS

It no longer matters what new laws or new rules are put in place to placate the awakened. It no longer matters who is seen to be punished by corporation laws and who decided to resign. What matters now are the actions that every person is accountable for, every action that caused harm to another with clear intention to harm. These transgressions are seen by the more advanced Beings. They have better technologies than any corporation on Earth. None can hide from their own ill-intended actions and none can escape the consequences.

Presently, we the good people of Earth, are being held hostage by the works of evil and corruption. Freedom is ours to have and live. It is our Earth, our lives, our families and friends to care for, and change is on the way to give us back to ourselves.

I asked the question: "How are you going to get pass the attacks against you?" He answered: "With our ways we can easily be serving with evidence of our trust in better answers to overtake any attacks from ships made on Earth. Our technologies can take them anyway."

The waiting is almost over. Here are a few more of His words that may be a comfort to the reader: "Now see to it you have all that you need to open to these times with understanding and kindness. Know with us that all heals and all heals with love and care. But for those who have transgressed, all greed, all hate, all abuses of humans and all actions of harm will be dealt with and serving a penalty equal to these actions with clear intentions to harm. Be not surprised to see these common thieves be healed by their own ways in evidence of how they treated others. This is the hell they created for themselves. Be understanding with knowledge about how we know how all things are to come. (...) Be ready and see how all starts and how all begins."

Truth rules over all lies. Be ready and be well.

Za, August 5, 2013

136. MESSAGE FROM THE SCRIBE #10

TRUST IN ALL GOOD THINGS TO COME

This morning's messages were surely meant to be shared. As the needless violence continues to spread on Earth, words of hope for better times need to be shared with all people who are awakening.

"Now see these times begin to change. Open to all who are dealing with answers to a more truthful life, better serving of many truths with the serving answers to all who are as we are, Beings of light who understand the truth of all people, and who see to many questions to open to change.

With these words, you will be dealing with many more telling of other Setu Seers who have opened to our ways and who see the answers serving them. With these answers, come better truth that will better respond to all who are dealing with the deaths of many, and who are searching for greater answers to open to; better ways, better words and better answers to open to.

Be well answered by us and be well understanding of all our truth. Be ready to understand all serving truth with the answers to our ways and our renewed ways of opening to better Setu seeing. Trust in all good things to come and open to, at the time of our arrivals and the time of reunification.

These days with questions will all be opened, answered, and renewed with the better truth these liars have withheld from all good people of Earth. Be served, answered and trusted by all who are responding now to greater serving answers with the way of great understood answers to truth, love and care.

Be ready and be ready, and see all good truths be shared and opened. Be willing to answer to all who respond to our understandings and who serve with dignity, honor and grace. With us you will be answering to Apoonancies' lies and changing these lies to all truth, and you will begin to understand why these liars fear our time to walk the Earth.

Be willing to onm with us. Be willing to see how all can be changed, better serving all people of Earth who ask us to come to better their lives and hopes for better understood truths of who we are and why we have been away so long, and why we are believing in the time to return to Earth with great love and happiness at the coming time of reunification.

Evidence of this day heals all who are proof of good people of Earth, who are bridging with us and who are renewing with many with the better seen truth of our ways. Be settling with Earth ways and believe all is near and ready to see all come as I said with the way of great understanding and great truth. Be well answered by us. God"

Received by Za, August 15, 2013

137. MESSAGE FROM THE SCRIBE #11

IMPORTANT MESSAGE TO FRIENDS

Please share these words among the good people of Earth. There is little more to say as all is unraveling as He said. We have great reasons to share our sorrows as these monsters play out their games of horrors with Syria and the Middle East countries. My heart is full of sadness to know of the sufferings of the innocent. Difficult times are facing all on Earth. I can only hope for a divine intervention to save us from these war making demons and their works.

The messages from 27/06/2012, 01/09/2012, 05/03/2013, 23/03/2013, give a clear description of what is being put in place to attempt a takeover of the Middle East region.

May God protect us.

Za, August 15, 2013

138. MESSAGE FROM GABRIEL

BE DEALING WITH OUR PAIN AND YOURS AS THESE EVENTS ARE SEEN

Be ready to share knowledge and light of understanding soon. Be dealing with our truth with great serving ways and know all will be very, very soon. See to it you are ready to answer to evidence of great truth, and serve with us and others as answers are settled. Be renewing more with these trusted beings that will be with us and be understanding of why they wish to meet with you.

Serve with all who are settling with these ways that open to corrupting the soul. Know we will call all who are well answered by us, and the many who answer to our better truth and better ways. You will see the evidence of many more answers to vindicate all who are waiting to be freed from all these devils.

Be well answered by us very soon now and expect to see us with others arriving well and soon. Open to our spiritual serving ways with these telling about who we are really. Many on Earth have called us gods but these words are a cause to better explain how all heals and how all serves with us and others. Be ready and open to our bridging truth soon.

Know all starts very soon with the first bomb on Iran and Syria because now the Israelis are angry that the American people answer to all telling of the Zionists who are causing all the troubles with all peoples of Earth by greed, lies and better deceptions. Serve with nobility of soul with us and be free of these whores. Renew with our ways and see we are serving with better answers to open to many.

Better answers will be dealt with soon and many opening truths will cause Lucifer to fall and be terminated. All will see how Earth has been corrupted and destroyed by users of death ways and great corruptions of the soul. Be certain we will cleanse the Earth of all evils. Be visited by certainty of soul and great seeing, unaffected by horrors traumatizing all innocence and childhoods.

Share these words if you will, but know we are arriving as the Israelis become the seen aggressors that they are, as they destroy these two neighboring countries. Be dealing with these words more now as all comes as God said, in evidence of who He is. Respond to our arrivals soon.
Gabriel
Received by Za, September 10, 2013

139. URGENT ARRIVALS
STARTING SOON

BECAUSE ONM IS NEEDED TO
OPEN TO OUR TRUTH

Be dealing with us now and be dealing with the truth. Be willing to onm with us and be better served by our ways. Be ready to onm with answers to onm that will open your eyes and better answer to evidence of our ways. Be willing to answer to our truth and be dealing with answers to our ways with us and many others. Serve with the truth of our ways opening to a great renewal on Earth. And know all serves to answer to great knowledge.

Now listen. The serving with the spiritual way of wars answers to our arrivals. Be ready when you hear about Israel's attacks on the Palestinians opening to more troubles from Egypt and Turkey who will oppose these attacks. Be ready as these words of war open to more troubles, and see these times become more active. Be certain all answers start with these bigger lies that will settle the used truth of why all these lies are serving with understood uses of wars to open to a WW3.

Be well settling with these days of great deceptions. Know all settling answers open to greater truth with us and many others who are settling with Earth ways and who are ready to open to many more answers to great truth and great renewed answers. Be well answered and be dealing with great truth as all becomes well answered and well served by us and many others.

Be willing to open to great truth with us, and answer to our answers. Be dealing with the coming destruction caused by these demons who are now being seen for who they are by the military of this world. Now these Generals as said, are being fired because they refused to shoot civilians as they renewed with greater lies because the truth is healing with them. They well see the causes for wars are all about depopulation, and the removal of many with the intention of supplying the leaving aliens with human flesh and better slaves.

I am knowing this is taking place in many places in the world but for many these trusted truths are not possible, because the veil is too thick for anyone to accept this truth. But this is the truth, and many wishes to not open to this as it is so horrible. You asked me for truth, so here it is. Be willing now to see that all life believed to be sacred has lost all meaning for most people on Earth, as their lives have been corrupted, dealt with great harm and disrespect of their souls.

And only we can stop these alien demons who are eating from the flesh of humans, and only we can stop the work humans are made to slave for. These ways have been seen by us on other planets and more answers were needed, because these other beings were being corrupted at that time.

We intervene in accordance to the Universal Laws. Now we are arriving on Earth to stop these atrocities renewing with human beings, because these actions are more troubling than can be described. What is being done serves to feed these demons who have only ill intentions to use what they wish and they serve only this.

These times of great changes will open to humans with better serving answers. Understand the Universal Laws are created to onm with all people responding to our call, as we answered your calls from Earth. Your prayers have reached us and we begin to land our ships very soon to answer to all people of Earth, and to answer to better ways of living that will open to all better truth.

Be serving the spiritual way with us, and be ready to open to our truth. Be willing to answer to the coming times of better truth and better living ways. Be well answered by us as arrivals start and becomes well dealt with and better seen. Be ready to onm with us more as we will become seen as we walk the Earth, and settle with these renegades who go through these used tunnels you call wormholes, and seek out the vulnerable planets to conquer.

Be understanding how these thieves only serve themselves. They are known to all people who are seeking to answer to better truth, because of their time to onm with us and to serve with us. Now we are arriving through these gates created by these traveling ways that open to Earth, as would be serving others. This means we are coming through the paths created by ISON (International Scientific Optical Network), and this is why these satellites have been shut down, so these answers cannot be seen.

But you will soon see many ships in the sky arriving in great numbers. All will begin to change and open to many more truths with us and others who serve with us. Know all starts with a war you call WW3. Understand these wars are only made to reduce the population of humans and cause chaos, as bodies will be removed for the flesh eaters and soul users.

Be understanding that these demons have the dealings of souls well serving them, as they can clone anyone and open their soul to newer clones. This is the story you have dealt with through religions about soul taking. It is a true fact that these demons are practicing soul removals and cloning more bodies per soul. This is what we call fragmented souls who cannot be well as these parts are lesser than the whole. Better to see this than continue to be blind.

Renewing with these truths will better serve with us, as arrivals become served and answers are settling with the proof believed as renewals become seen. Be ready and be opening to us, as this heals all lies told by religions and governments. They do not serve people, but they keep all in great darkness and fool only the innocent who believe these organizations of men and aliens respond to their well-being. Evidence of these horrors will soon open to all, as arrivals begin to land on Earth and exposing these deceptions and lies that serves as a prison.

I am ready to open to all humans now. Be ready and see the truth.

God

Received by Za, October 17, 2013

140. MESSAGE FROM THE SCRIBE #12

ISRAEL ATTACKS SYRIA

This morning I heard the news that Israel bombed a military base in Syria. This is the beginning of much more troubling events coming to the Middle East. What this means is the necessary retaliation from the Syrians in self-defense. From this morning's received messages from God: "Be seeing how the Americans (USA) will open to a greater war than WW2 as they become angry about Syria's retaliation and self-defense. Settle with these days quickly in evidence of our arrival and great evidence of how all becomes well served and well responded to."

Now it is a matter of time. This aggressive action from Israel will cause a series of escalating events that have been written in these previous messages. It opens to the arrival of these Beings of Light and the followers of the Universal Laws. What they have said was these actions of great wars (WW3) obliges them to intervene because of the harm it causes to Earth and the people of Earth, but also to other surrounding planets.

Mars was dealt with recently. He said: "... the serving of Mars, be seeing this as necessary destruction of the Aliens you call Reptilians. They live on Mars and now many are destroyed because of their transgressions and the renewed attacks on us." It was reported by astronomers that as comet ISON passed by Mars, Mars developed a coma not seen before. (Please verify this information on your own as I do not have a link to this and I question all Earth information/disinformation.)

Here are some parts of this morning's messages I can share with the reader. God said:

" Knowledge about who we are answers to many as these ones understand who we are. But many others will believe that we are the bridging serpents that the dealers of lies have created to confuse all good people of Earth renewing with us and others. You will soon see these truths yourself and then many will begin to onm with us and many others, in evidence of who we are, and why understood words answers to evidence of who we are. Now see these days be long as nights of darkness, better seen as the eclipse of the Sun and Moon because of the Sun's flares and the renewed terrors of Earth and the feeling that all is ending. But know all will end as these liars are put to rest in their right places. And people of Earth will respond to a new time on Earth that will serve and heal all who are in the path of goodwill and good truth."

Be ready and be prepared. I have a feeling that all will come very quickly. Be kind to those in need during these trying times and be safe.

Za, November 11, 2013

Part 5 (2014)

Note from Za 2020: In this Part 5, I speak about the Universal Laws and the inscriptions on the steps of the Temple of Apollo in Delphi, Greece. Reading these inscriptions reminded me of some of the Universal Laws. I also share one of the many verses or prayers to remove unnecessary guilt, like the original sin, to free the soul from being a victim of mind control. I wrote the letters as they were spelled out to me but, as I presently understand, there is a vibrational component to reciting and sounding this.

141. MESSAGE FROM THE SCRIBE #13

UNIVERSAL LAWS

Throughout this past decade of receiving this information, I have often questioned what are the Universal Laws. Presently, the knowledge of the Universal Laws as I understand it, is not all open to humans. To open to the Universal Laws would necessitate an understanding of the Universes, planets and other Beings living there and an opening to Divine Law. Many individuals on Earth claim to know these Universal Laws, however I choose to not believe these individuals. I require truth from those who are from other places than Earth.

From the Apollo Temple in Delphi, carved into the walls and steps of the Temple are words of wisdom named the "Road of virtue and respect". These listed virtues are in part Universal Laws that Apollo shared with humans to strive for better living ways with oneself and others in society. It is the way to better communicate with the Beings of Light who are soon arriving to Earth. Practicing these wise ways opens to learning from "them" until we can be informed of all the true Universal Laws when arrivals begin.

Road of virtue and respect

Be committed for justice and all good.
Tell the right and the truth.
Control anger, remain calm.
Long for wisdom, look for wisdom.
Do not blame others wrongly.
Do not downgrade or look down upon anyone.
Do not be insolent.
Develop your consciousness.
Exercise gentleness and kindness.
Stay away from evil.
Do not kill anyone or anything.
Use your time usefully.
Judge with divine thinking.
Do not be jealous.
Stay away from slanderers.
Honor good and polite people.
Give love to everything.
Wish happiness for everyone.
Stay away from anger and disputes.
Respect other people's time.
Be grateful and thankful.
Use your skills and talents.
Do not be arrogant.
Do not misuse power.
Help the ones who are less fortunate.
Look for balance and harmony.
Never stop learning.
Respect the elder.
Respect thyself.
Know thyself.

Because we have all been victims of abuses of some sort in this life and perhaps other lives, the conditioning and the imprinting of abusive ways become easily repeated if not identified and cleared. Change comes from actions toward change. This may need some help with releasing guilt and beginning with self-forgiveness to open to better changes of consciousness. The following verse is used to release guilt, opens to self-forgiveness and to God's words.

Bronma *

Bessron aonsuut tessron
Aonma poon deers ut poon
Utah bona tessron aonma
Tessron bronma Tessron bronma Tessron bronma
Herstuut sertuu Tessron onm poon
Tessron aonma restuu
Bona restuu bona aonma
Deers tessron aonma
Herstuut bronma onm

Open your hearts to God and be ready as arrivals are said to be very soon. Za, January 3rd, 2014
* Lexicon found at the end of this book

142. WHO WE ARE

HUMANS ARE NOT A SLAVE RACE

Be dealing with us and others at the time of our arrivals as all becomes well served by better truth and better ways of great seeing. Be willing to answer to our ways and be used to our appearance as we meet, as we are different and taller than humans. Be dealing with us and with better answers with us, and be understanding how all starts used truth. Be dealing with secrets greater than these stories about our kind, (stories about the deities or advanced beings who came to Earth).

Be knowing that our kind cannot mix with other beings from other planets. These stories are made to confuse humans into believing they are a created slave race who answer to serve the leaders of Earth. Understand we have greater truths and many more truths opening to our ways that will surprise all.

Answers to all humans does not come from breeding with monkeys, as these words are taught. Answers to many believers of these stories are serving to open humans to being diminished by leaders because we are Beings of Light who know all origins of all humans, and we know where they have emerged from. This will change all settling knowledge about Darwin's theories about sub-humans.

This thought about sub-humans was another way to better control the telling of who we are and made us unimportant in all ways. But another truth does exist and the telling of great lies will be put to rest. People believe many lies when they are prisoners of a system of great abuse. Be willing to serve with us and be better answered by greater truth than the answers opening to people of Earth.

Now be understanding how we are arriving in a very short time and how we are settling with Earth ways. We will be removing all who cause harm on Earth. These are all leaders and oppressive regimes that serve to deal with these lies and these horrors. The leaders who recently met with the Pope, are planning wars and are serving with many who want the war and who wish for war.

Be understanding how all becomes well served by us and with others at the time of great truth. You will understand we are in better Setu ways than they are as they continue to oppress and tell all we are Aliens with an agenda. These whores' agenda does not include peoples' freedom and lives, and these plans are only about giving souls as a sacrifice to Lucifer.

These lies about brokering peace plans as said in Israel, are nothing more than a ploy to destroy all neighboring countries around Israel, to deal with the sectional parts of greater NWO control and this helps the Popes' greater plan for a new religion. They have no soul to onm with and their plans are Lucifer's plans.

Be serving with us now. These plans of harm are only Lucifer's to rule Earth. When we arrive, they plan to cause destruction and chaos to all people of Earth, and then to control all surrounding planets to cause great destruction of the Universe. Know understood truth will change all and expose these whores and deceptions to all good people on Earth. Know we are soon here with all good people of Earth to open to better times and better ways as all becomes renewed, answered and healed.

Be dealing now with better answers as we are Beings of Light and we know how all opens when all opens to better truth. Be serving now with us and be ready, all starts very soon.

Know now my last words and be ready.

God

Received by Za, January 5, 2014

143. SEE THIS BE THE END TIMES AND SERVE WITH US

BETTER BRIDGING TIMES ARE NEAR

Now be dealing with our time to walk the Earth and renew with who we are. Know all starts with the great destruction of Syria to answer to the greed of Israel who visits with their demon masters to open to helping themselves to land that is evidently not theirs. See this as a treason against God's children, as they claim they are, and are only seeing to their own telling of lies.

God's children are all who see the truth of how all is unraveling, and who see the cause of more troubles for all who respond and serve truth and justice. Truth and justice heal all, construction and not destruction. Now be serving with us and open to better truth with us.

Know we are the ones who are responsible for the Earth serving wealth. This wealth heals all as is the seeing of truth. Be understanding how this evident truth is yours to have and onm with each other to better serve with greater answers as all opens to the times of renewals and reunification. Be certain all heals with us.

More onm has to be shared in order to obtain the understandings that we can answer to with all who are ready to open to be Seers. With us you will be dealing with an upsurge of good ways that will enable your better truth to be renewed. With us you will open to greater serving answers to better ways. And with us you will be understood and accepted, as these days of wars and horrors believe must end and they will.

Be certain with us you will be yourselves, living your lives in peace and better serving health. This is what a father wishes for his children. And as

I am your Father, I am wishing for you to open your heart to me and my Angels who ask only that our place on Earth heals all.

Be renewing with us, trust in our ways in evidence of how care is healing for all who serve justice, care and peace, as these messages were shared by my son's words to you through Teachers of our kind. You will answer to my sons on Earth to renew with you, now see them arrive and open to answers to greater truth.

Be dealing with answers to many as all becomes well answered by us. And know all will be serving to answer to greater times than ever seen on Earth, as these are Lucifer's last days on Earth and anywhere else. Be dealing with us more now and be ready to answer to our call at these times of greater sharing. Know we are willing to answer to all people of Earth, but with us answers are well responding to those who see the better ways we will share.

Be understanding we are the believed Ancient Beings of Light who with more trusted truth can show you. And know we are dealing with better answers than any on Earth. As arrivals renew, we will meet with our diplomats who are among the serving readers of these words, as you are prepared to answer to greater truth than shared on Earth.

Be understanding your lives are protected by us in evidence of why you incarnated for these times. We will be seeing each other soon; be ready and be serving with us. Be dealing with understandings you did know a long time ago before you were on Earth, and for many these are many lives ago.

Remember your soul has been corrupted by tortures believed to change you but you can never be changed by anyone or any torture. Be knowing your purpose has not been forgotten and your lives have only served you more to learn the workings of evil.

Be dealing with these words now and prepare for our time of reunification rising to answer to our serving ways with you and all who serve the seeing of the Universal Laws of serving truth and respect for all life seen serving as we are. Be willing now to open to your own truth and know evidence is yours soon. Now be ready and be serving with us.

God

Received by Za, November 16, 2014

May God be with you and in your hearts. Za

$Part\ 6\ (2015)$

144. WE SEE ALL THE PAIN ON EARTH

ALL STARTS SOON

Be understanding how all starts responding, how all starts serving with greater truth and better serving answers. Be seeing a more trusted response as we calm all pain on Earth, and respond to evidence of healing ways with the many who will be serving with us, and who will better serve others. More than I can explain to you now answers you as arrivals become seen, and more than our answers to our truth will be seen by many as we walk the Earth.

See these times be settling with us soon, and know all opens to better seeing and better serving ways at the time of great truth. Be understood by us, and be serving with us and others at the time of reunification. These days of old will be shared, and many will renew with who we are and shared knowledge of how Earth helps all to better live together as all evil is removed.

And as arrivals become accepted by all who are dealing with us and many others who return to open to the people of Earth with greater seeing than understood the truth could not. Setu times are here in evidence of greater serving truths about the dealings of wars and beliefs about how all serves to answer to knowledge opening to the telling of lies living on Earth to hide who we are.

At the settling of our time on Earth and at the certain truth shared, answers will be seen. All who ask for better ways of living and serving understandings, will be answered because we can respond to knowledge and better ways of living. And shared understandings will be serving with us, and better open to all soon. And all who open to us will be helped, and this will be the restuu of our ways. "Restuu" means to share and help so that all can live in peace, comfort and security renewed by the people for the people.

See these evident answers renew with us, and be certain all better truth starts and opens to others. See this be done to prove many truths of who we are. Renew with us and be renewed. Onm with us and be knowing the truth about where you have emerged from. And know all visits from us are coming now to open to all who are ready and all who are serving with great knowledge only to open to the truth at these coming days of reunification.

Be understanding this is the time of reunification. All answers come from us, and not from the liars and deceivers who wish to only respond to wars and the depopulation of Earth to create a world of control, abuses and misery for my children and others' children left on Earth. Love will be the only healing way to answer to these times.

Be seeing how this answers all. And believe this heals all who will be left on Earth after the great attacks on Syria, as Israel carves a path of destruction on all who oppose their greed. Hear my words and know my words, as this will be seen evidence of the coming days, and know we arrive to stop the settling days of deaths.

And be certain we are arriving, and no stone will be left unturned. All ways of wars will be stopped. And then we will begin the sorting of souls. These souls who served another will be dealt with, and corruption of truths will be sorted, and all lies serving these whores will end. Those who better see truth will become free, and with truth comes understanding, and with understanding comes freedom.

This heals onm. This responds to trust and sharing lives of great seeing, and all will serve better answers to onm. Know now who we are, and be renewing with us as we are soon on Earth to walk the Earth with you all. Now be certain all is coming in evidence of our renewing times, but also know many on Earth are from other families also arriving with us. And as shared before, we are all united under the Universal Laws, and we have many places of emergence and greater seeing than shared on Earth.

But to prove all lies are lies, you must first know the truth, and soon all will be shared, and all who see this will be free and onm with theirs. Evidence of our time to walk the Earth renews with all people of Earth as the skies will be serving the seeing of many ships. These ships are all different but we are as one.

Be ready. Onm heals all. This is the time of reunification.

God

Received March 12, 2015 by Za

145. THE BRIDGING TRUTH OPENS

BE QUESTIONING EVERYTHING

Know we are understanding how all answers on Earth and how all settles on Earth, at these coming days of wars and deadly deeds renewing with these death Beings. Know we are opening with greater truth than what is seen, and with all who are ready to answer to us. But also know many will choose to evidently try to open to knowledge with these demons first, to serve them and their ways, and this will be telling of what they choose.

These ones will be dealt with because all who oppose us will meet their own actions and their own death, as they would have done to those who are being saved by us. And know we are better serving all serving truth and all trusted answers to knowledge and truth. This will be undeniable and evident, and not one man or woman or child on earth will be faced with deceptions as we arrive and open to the world.

Be ready, proof is very near. And all who ask why this has taken so long will understand that we are knowing about the troubles from Earth for a short time, and we are on our way, but many decisions had to be made responding to these times. Because we are many, some are responding to answers from a long time ago. But know answers to knowledge are greater than seen on Earth.

All who serve with us tell of the proof of change needed to be gradual to open to knowledge more on Earth, and to open to all. This heals with us, but it answers also to many people who are bridging with us in preparation to these coming days. Renewing with us opens to many as it is with you, and renewing with us are the ones whose souls are serving these days of responses, believed to be the End Times.

Know we are the ones who are seen in many ships. And only renewing with our ways are renewing with greater answers than seen on Earth. All who are bridging with us will first be contacted. The non-believers will be used to answer that we are the lie they have shared, but know we are answering the serving call for help many have asked for through prayer and meditation.

Now be seeing how all starts as the war clears many lies told of who causes all these atrocities on Earth. Know these lies answer to Lucifer and his demons first, and then are serving his slaves who are seen as the servers of war and power on Earth. And these are many who are servers of death who believe they can gain power with their acts of murder. Renewing with this only serves Lucifer who will better serve only himself and believe, he has only one loyalty in him, to himself.

Be settling with the belief that he is the creator because all who trust in him will soon see what he is. Only renewed lies will answer him. More truth about his place of emergence will cause many to be settling with our seeing, and be renewing with who we are. Open to knowledge now about how all serves more with us, and be the renewed knowledge in evidence of who you are, and where you have emerged from.

Deal and accept his lies and be lost forever, as these are the days that end all days of great deceptions. These serving days are now here and all who respond to truth will be saved. All who deny the truth will be more trusted by their ways and actions against all that answers to greater ways than what serves on Earth.

Be ready now to open to these last days on Earth, and be dealing with us and others as these days are now here. And know all who are ready to answer to greater truth will be answered and amazed. This is the time of reunification and freedom from chaos and lies. Heal with us as we are your family returning to better the lives of our children and our friends who are among you now as these times of preparation are soon answered.

Know all who blaspheme my name in the time of reunification will be seen for what they serve. All who are bridging with us will better their lives, and open to greater truth. Understand that now is the time to answer to knowledge and to answer to truth. Be serving with us and be free. Evidence of our ways will better Earth and all who live there. Better serving with us will answer all.

Know who we are at the time of meeting because you will be dealing with the truth of your own being, your soul and your place of emergence. And better renewals will answer many who ask "Why has Will left us and renewed with the ruling of evil?", and "Why has God forgotten us and left Hell on Earth to be renewed war after war, and death after death?". And to this I answer: "We had nothing to do with this, but we are returning to remove the cancer on Earth, as we are united and serving the Universal Laws, answering all souls in all places in the Universes."

And know now we arrive and settle with this demon who causes this response to others, and who deals with death, and the eating of human and animal flesh. Be free of this trap of denials and open to greater seeing than what is serving on Earth.

Be ready to answer to an explosion of truths, and be seeing how all who are ready to share knowledge and understanding with us, will see how all God's truth will better their lives. Answer to greater renewals with all others in the Universes serving with great understandings about how all heals, and about how all responds and opens.

Here is the thing, more true knowledge opens with our time to walk the Earth, and the time is near. And I am asking you to trust in our reunification to better your lives, so why be afraid. We are settling with many but only those who cause harm. So be renewing with us and be free. Be seeing all truth arrive soon. More truth, more love, more care, and be serving with us.

God

Received by Za, May 3, 2015

146. FORGIVENESS IS HEALING

HEAL WITH US

Be ready more is coming. The truth is about to be served in connection with the war on Russia. Be certain all opens now, and serves to answer to evidence of our truth. Be dealing with us in manifestation of how all opens to greater seeing. Be bridging with us very soon, and believe, evidence of our arrivals will be responding more now to answer to greater truth with the way of better answers. With these truths, many will open to knowledge with us.

Soon we will begin the sorting of souls, and with this comes many surprises because many are hidden evils not seen by human eyes. This will cause the truth of who opens to dark ways with no serving of justice or care. Be dealing with us, see the non-believers' truth with us, and understand how they have caused many troubles, and how they will be dealt with as we remove their actions from Earth, and allow Earth to be served by good intent and good actions.

Soon all will be renewed, and life with us will be renewed with all evidence of good and better seeing. Be dealing with us soon and be dealing with the truth about your places of emergence, and be bridging with your families from places past. But also know all opens to greater eruptions of events, as all better answers become well opening to all who ask who we are and why we have returned to Earth knowing all help was needed a long time ago.

To this I say, we are here now and we are bridging with many who can be served by our truth and better serve with answers to better ways. Be bridging with us and be understanding we are returning to answer to the calls through prayers being seen by us, as we hear your calls in evidence of our time of reunification.

Better to be believing in the truth than to be lied to by the servants of Lucifer who are wishing to open to the dark ones' face to face (CERN). And in all truth, do you think these ones, the fallen ones, are there on Earth to serve humans? Answers to this are beyond doubt the corroboration of great troubles and the destruction of all good people, trust.

Be dealing with our time to answer back to the ones who expelled us from Earth, and who used these ways of looping the souls on Earth through the practice of death ways of aging and death, to cause the soul to never remember their families and places of emergence. Renewing with these ways will respond to greater seeing with us and others, and settle with our truth.

Be dealing with us soon, more than you are expecting starts with the first bomb on Syria. This causes answers to our obligation to return to Earth as these actions will cause evidence of great dangers in other places in the

Universes. Be certain we are near Earth, and responses with us arriving to stop all further troubles, because these dangerous actions of wars will cause many other planets to be in great danger if Earth tries to self-explode. And know this will not be served because we can stop this, and we will. Be certain of this, and see all responses to us more now at the time of meeting and opening to the world.

Heal with us and be healed by us, and better answer to yourselves with us. And know all answers will serve all good people very well. And be forgiven for your actions that were only a response to your environment and the conditions of your slavery, as slaves have no other choice than to be enslaved, and their actions are only the choices given to answer to.

Be seeing how you must also accept to forgive yourselves for actions answered by the seeing of others proving of what they serve. And these evident answers are mostly caused by deceptions and lies to make people act in unnatural ways that are serving to be the destruction of good souls. Be freeing yourselves from the guilt you carry in consequence of actions you would not have committed if you were free to obviously not commit.

Deal with these truths and be freeing yourselves from all guilt that was imposed on you by other's beliefs or fears. The non-believers see this as a burden to keep you from freeing yourselves, and they use these ways of guilt to open you to the seeing of control and dominance. But with us, you will be free, and with us you will be seen for who you are, as we know the ways of evil and their better lies to deceive the young and the innocent so they can serve all evil ways.

Renew with us and be renewed with answers to our truth. Be understanding how all opens more now and be responding to greater truth with us. And know all starts soon to answer to better serving truth. Be bridging with us soon and be ready.

God

Received by Za, May 31, 2015

147. BE READY TO OPEN TO TRUTH

RENEWALS ARE SOON OPENING TO MANY

Be seeing this now more. Be dealing with beliefs about your world, and how death serves Lucifer. Know more about the non-believers renewed attacks on the innocent, and be serving with us. Be serving these truths as we begin to share knowledge on Earth. Know all who are with us will be understanding the manifestation of how all serves and how all opens with us.

See how all is unraveling now to answer to the good days of our time to walk the Earth. All who serve with Lucifer will be removed, and all who harm people will be dealt with and answering to evidence of our wrath. Be certain of these trusted truths and know we begin the sorting of souls as we arrive.

Better to be with us than with them in evidence of what they are and who they serve. Know all healing comes with us, and know all love and care comes with us. And know these demons are soon all removed as they ask "why" with lies on their tongues. Be renewing with all truth only with us at the time of arrivals. See to it that you can answer to us with greater truth than seen on Earth.

Know who your enemies are. Be certain they have answers only to better confuse the truth, and change this into deceptions and lies. Soon all will be dealt with and all my true children will be free of the seen proof of murders and thievery. Be certain all answers to this and nothing more, and know they will be all found out.

Apoonancies (non-believers) think that they can cause all answers to serve them; but know this is only confirmation of their own self-deception as they renew with the greatest of all liars, Lucifer.

Be serving these good arrivals as we begin to answer back to all who cause harm, and who cause others to do the same. Be dealing with our ways as you begin to see our actions that will better all life on Earth. Evidence of this will open to shared knowledge with many who are soon seeing all as arrivals open to our time to walk the Earth. And see to it that you are ready as visits begin with the chosen ones. Be certain no politician will be a chosen one, as seeing this will better open to our own better serving souls as we are bridging with them.

And as this comes to be seen, many will heal with us and understand all explosions of truth in evidence of opening to knowledge, and to the knowledge of who we are. Better days will soon follow our arrivals. All who are settling with Earth ways will be free of all abusers and beings of dark ways. Be renewing with us soon and know all comes to those who know how to better see answers and truth.

Be renewing with the evidence of who we are and know we are the ones who answer you, and who will reopen to all truths of who Earth serving people are. At this time, you will better understand how the evidence of who responds to who, opens to the great reunification.

Apoonancies fear this more in evidence of their guilt. They know it is our time to return to Earth and see to the evolution of humans, because proof has shown us that Lucifer can control from the depths of the Earth, seeing to all the wars and torments caused on Earth. See this better serve with us and others, as all opens to better renewing with us.

Be dealing more now with the good serving days coming, because knowledge opens to many who will be ready to hear this. Be dealing with the destruction of Syria in evidence of the ones who open to this in answering to land expansion of Israel. Be seeing their plans be stopped by us, and be dealing with the seeing of this tragic act.

We arrive at the settling of this as this heals with our Laws. Know all has started to open the ways for our time to return to Earth. These days are here my children, be ready.

God

Received by Za, November 15, 2015

148. LUCIFER'S END

ALL WILL BE REVEALED IN TIME

Answers are coming. Be certain all will be revealed, and be understanding all opens to our time to answer to truth. Know and share understanding of my words. Be sure all truth comes with our words. Know we are dealing with greater seeing than seen on Earth, as all opens to these trusted ways of all great used truth.

Here is the thing about the flat Earth beliefs. These understandings are based on the uncovered truth about the Arctic and Antarctic places. These places are serving cold weather in conformation of how they are land masses moved away from the Sun. Here is the truth about this; these land and ice masses are covering great cities of the times of our seeing.

These places were settling with many others, and responding to greater civilizations. But all ideals were changed by Lucifer, who answered to our truth, but only responded to causing harm. With the evidence of our arrivals and our return to Earth, determined to better the world, we had to open to freezing him into a place of security before we could serve with a better army.

You see this now, but you do not understand why he was condemned by us. He visited many places to better his ways, and he destroyed many places like Mars to better his needs, but he tried to do the same on Earth, and served visits to other places and other races to keep all in place.

Be seeing how this is helping these possessed leaders of the world to cause chaos, by believed declaration of climate change chaos, that does only serve the rich and impoverishes the servants of laws. People are only living as they can, and are troubled by these taxes that only serve the rich to answer to their protection as we arrive. As they know we are arriving, they will be settling with us.

Know they plan to start greater troubles. The users of lies are bridging with their own demises. Understand this was serving all renewed proof of how we are. Other users of truth were serving these times also. Our armies were depleted, and we needed to go across the Universes to open to greater seeing in manifestation of our bridging ways with others.

We became well known in all places and learned many truths with others, in evidence of all these places. And with this knowledge and greater seeing, we are now returning knowledge and light of understanding to Earth to stop these plans of control and destruction of all souls from occurring.

These leaders of lies are serving with Lucifer's ways; they open to greater lies. But all lies will be dealt with at the time of questions because many other lies must be dispelled. Be seeing the works of Lucifer in all places of the world where inequality of people, poor care of children, the evidence of great wars and atrocities lives, as it did in his time of great worship.

He does all this again because he sees we are returning to Earth. He believes that with his helpers, he can cause more chaos in display of his manipulations of spirit possessions. Be dealing only with these words for now, as there are more troubling seeing of how all settles on Earth. These ways are becoming evident with the practices of the hadron colliders that open the gates for the spirits to pass through.

Be ready as these days will be full of troubles and deaths, and be seeing how all serving truth will be only lies coming from these renewals of dark ways, in evidence of our time to return to stop the Apoonancies, the non-believers of our ways and users of lies.

(Za: Alice Bailey is a writer whose books are found in the United Nations library. In her writings, she tells of the importance to control people by removing their rights to open to the ruling time of Lucifer. We see this proof now of these actions with the deliberate killing of people in well prepared false flag events and the horrors of murders through encouraged "religious extremist wars" escalating in all places on Earth).

This is the possessed ones who cause this, and many more with weakness in them will be settling with this banning together as in one mind, but know these actions only serve the ones who are completely indoctrinated with the teachings of Lucifer in proof of this working deception. This is the reason why we are returning at this time, to remove the "Apoonancies" from Earth, and heal Earth from Lucifer's grip.

Know this time is soon, and will heal all to answer to the growth of shared truths and care for each other. These answers can be renewed with all, and here all words answer many. Be understanding we are returning to our Earth, our home, and we will make manifested many truths with people, believing in greater knowledge, who serve with us and who open to truth.

Here is the thing about the satellite called the "Black Knight". It is responding to our uses and our technologies, and it serves us information as our orbs do, to better see to any help we can provide without causing interference of how all opens to better serving renewals. Be understanding all levels of information answers to us, and this is what is being reproduced by these possessed leaders who better open to believing they are equal to us in technology. But be certain all are lies, and no destruction can equal construction. Better serving truth of our ways, believe, will serve all with greater seeing, and soon we arrive to open to the world.

God

Received by Za, December 4, 2015

Part 7 (2016)

149. OPEN TO BETTER
TRUTH WITH US

ANSWERS ARE HERE, SEE THIS YOURSELVES

More troubles start in the days coming to open to our ways. The seeing of
our ways answers evidence of serving people with us and not with the lying
governments. Soon you will see all these liars' question all who deny them
by responding to greater growing troubles because many will become dealt
with by force and incarcerations.

Because of these attacks on all, the governments of the West will increase
the serving of laws and dealings with the Apoonancies, (the non-believers
in Gods' return to Earth with His Army), trusted ways with force. These
laws will ask all to disclose their wealth and be renewing with returning
these assets to their governments and bankers.

But these renewed laws will be opposed by all people of all places. Healing
truth will start to be shared about the plans to be understood by all, and this
will open to civil wars everywhere in all western good serving countries.

Now about the Mohamed renewed serving of lies. Understand God has
only shared truths with this response to answer to truth. We never created
religions; people do this to control others. Understand Gabriel shared
words with Mohamed, and beliefs were renewed by others who used this to
create a society of responding people to better control, only this.

Here is the problem with all religions proving what they serve. Responding to humans is only serving the belief of God who returns to Earth with His Angels, but people created a belief in words that are only serving themselves to open to greater control of societies. This evidence of lies answers to Lucifer, and all who serve this are an abomination, and they will be dealt with as they dealt with others.

Be seeing how all this opens to the End Times because I will end these acts of violence against all who are the victims of atrocities being called my wishes. This will be dealt with and all who are with us will better the seeing of this, and end all troubles caused by these servants of Lucifer.

And know all comes soon and opens to greater troubles. Understand we arrive soon but we are not Apoonancies servants, and we will arrive at the time when Apoonancies tell all we are here, but they are not answering to our past truth. We visit only with our kind, be sure of this. And know when we arrive many will better serve with us and others because you will see this eruption of events, and only I can tell you the truth of how all serves.

Now be ready and answer to my call at the time of meeting and see all open to better days with the good serving truth answering to greater bridging seeing. No one speaks for God; God can speak for Himself and I will. And know all who deal with the religions have accumulated wealth and only use this for their own plans, answering to only greed and lies.

Soon nothing more answers them and they will be judged by all who suffered their lies in evidence of the generations of billions of people who lived and died serving this evil being Lucifer, disguised as an answer to control the weak of mind.

Answers come soon now as all will see these lies dealt with and the punishment of evil that will deal with these leaders of mass deceptions. This will be understood by all as the truth will open their eyes and golden light of truth serves all who are as we are, as the truth will renew on Earth. And all who are served by understandings and knowledge will open to many and renewing with who we are and why we are returning to our home Earth.

Be only seeing this time be renewed by us, in evidence of all that is coming more now. Deal with the days of great sorrows at the time of the bombing of Syria by the Israelites who continue to murder and hide behind many armies. They plan conceived acts of violence to control the Middle-East. And know these attackers from other countries are all serving this plan through other groups of religions, but all in fact answer to Lucifer as he culls his servants and sorts them for a better battle.

Be seeing how all these lies will be seen when all peoples of Earth are pushed into a greater deception and opening all lies to settle with a "greater threat" as they will call it. This helps us, and we are the believers of peace and serving all. This time is not only for these servants of lies who believe themselves to better their plans and only this.

Evidence of this causes many to be confused, but see this as all unravels and open your heart to better seeing the truth. See to it that you are opening to knowledge and understanding, and all evidence of greater seeing. Proof of all this starts soon, and you yourselves will be the proof of all you can be, without the lies and deceptions. Open to evidence of truth.

Soon you will see us arrive. Be ready to share knowledge with many who are ready to understand who we are. As the truth opens, many will see these truths be seen and shared, and all will open the way for greater answers and greater bridging trust. All will be serving as they see this for themselves, and not as a response to propaganda and mind control.

This heals all and answers to better trust with who we really are, and why serving with us answers you, and settles with greater truth than the renewed lies of leaders of Earth. Be ready now, knowledge is coming and opens to all. The Apoonancies will be serving with their own problems soon, and soon my children will be free. See this yourselves and be ready.

God

Received by Za, January 11, 2016

150. ARRIVALS

OUR TIME OF MEETING IS NEAR

You will renew with us and see the truth of what I said. And you will open to evidence of greater seeing, and better open to answers to your bridging truth, and then you will be free as you open to our help to all. Because knowledge has many explosive truths, and because all opens to better answers with us, and because we will open to better serving truth with all who are seeing as we are and who settle with Earth ways.

Many will renew with us in the belief of our ways, and many will renew with stories of old by their seeing of religion, but proof of our arrivals will be renewing evidence very soon. The time of renewals and reunification are here and shared knowledge with us will change all truths and answers to better seeing of our way.

Be renewing with us now and see all be evidence of the truth of who we are and know how all came to be. 'Tessron' is reunification time, and this means these days are here. Apoonancies (non- believers), as said, are knowing all I am responding to by their means of lies and corruptions, and they understand we are arriving to begin a sorting of souls.

With us answers are open, but with these murderers, only actions of abuses and hell responds to them because they are devils without souls, and because they wish to control all places and all life seen in all universes, they cannot be trusted with us, and so they will be removed from Earth.

As all becomes unraveled, and you begin to see the way all is on Earth, you will be understanding how all opens to better truth. And because you are dealing with many on Earth of this kind, you will begin to understand how all settles with us, and how all answers open to us. And because a more trusted truth opens to all people of Earth, you will see the proof of many more renewals of responding truth.

And this will respond to the light of our deepest desire to open questions to answer. And know we have many teachers ready to share seers' truth about who we are, and who you are. Be renewed by our ways, and be certain all comes as I said as you will see this yourselves. And know God gives you back to yourselves.

Understand this, we are answering you and opening the way for all who are ready to open to our truth and respond to better days. Aonma aonma aonma (evidence, vindication, proof) opens the way because all starts now. You must ready your hearts because many will die in the war of liars and thieves.

Be renewing with us and see all be dealt with by their own families, and understand these times of death wars, and the culling of humans is healing with us. And understand we serve with greater seeing of how all heals. At the time of meeting, you will be certain of who we are. When this helps, seeing the truth, you will be angry at these terrorists who are serving Lucifer. Be certain of this, they care not about any life.

And all who are fooled to believe more lies will better open to our responses to them, and they themselves will answer to their actions, and be seen for who they are. Be dealing with these days of truth, and be understanding the Setu times are here. More than you can imagine arrives soon and know we are here.

These words are truth, be ready.

God

Received by Za, August 25, 2016

Part 8 (2017)

151. INSTRUCTIONS

NOW LISTEN

The ways of our arrivals become renewed with the way of the bridging truth. All who oppose us answer to evidence of their own ill-will. And all who serve with lies will soon be telling all that we are devils better serving with troubles on Earth, but the troubles we answer to are about the many who are asking to be helped and freed. These owners of souls believe they can evidently use better people to open to us, and abuse children to control them through fear.

All this ends now. Evidence and support come to free all who are prisoners of these whores and all who have greater souls than those who control the innocent. And be certain we ask you to answer back to answering this truth, and be renewed by answers that are only truth. Know now these words shared by all who serve with us, and who open to greater seeing than those on Earth.

One: Renew with truth only.

Two: Be bridging (Setu) with us as arrivals begin in all places responding to the support of God's children. (Za's note: not countries who discriminate against people by religious or cultural laws)

Three: Be serving with the truth of who you are and why you are on Earth.

Four: Be serving with God's answers to better living ways and do not better yourselves without better evidence of greater responding truth. (Za's note: e.g. religious leaders)

Five: Be respecting all life on Earth and be understanding why respect is healing you and others.

Six: Be seeing to the needs of the living when you are able to.

Seven: Be responding to all serving ways (helping) in evidence of how renewals are shared by us and others arriving with us.

Eight: Be serving with love and be renewing with us at the time of the sorting of souls.

This means no harm will be served by us, but those who are dealing with evidence of abuse, those who cause harm will better be served by the troubles they caused onto others. Believe knowledge heals all, and this will set you free, and then all will open to their own truth.

Share this and know these words yourselves as these words will better serve you and better open the way for you. And know you will better know the truth with all who will respond to my words and share these words with others. These are instructions to know and to share in evidence of the questions by all who are serving with us and others at the time of meeting. Be serving this knowledge and understanding more now. Be renewing with us and others as these days open to answer to the proof of who responds to who, and respond to the truth.

More than you are expecting answers you, more than you can understand is opening to you, and more than you can see arrives soon. So be ready and know I am coming and I am answering you and I will serve the truth of all ways and all answers. Be renewing with us in confirmation of who we are and be ready for all to open very soon.

See to it that you are ready to open your heart to me in evidence of the good truth starting to answer all my children, and better answers to all who are ready to meet with us and better their lives without the control of these evil devils who act as of the people. These devils respond to their plans of population control and renew lies of wars responding to freedom when this lie only responds to depopulation and control.

And know we will stop them.

God

Received by Za, December 30th, 2016

152. A PLACE FOR THE TRUE
CHILDREN OF GOD

GOD'S CHILDREN ARE NOT GROUP SPECIFIC

Israel is not a place for us. You see a map but it is not there. Israel is a place inside people. I am saying this to open your thoughts to these words. Be understanding this truth and be understanding that Israel's meaning is the home for my children. This place is in your heart and not a country.

All Israel is, is a place of commerce and nothing more. Many ask 'why are many humans renewing with this?' And I say to them: 'All these humans want is to well control a place of commerce near and through important water ways. So, they are creating a lie and a great deception to answer to this control of territories and only this.'

There are no holy places on Earth and there never was. All is about money riches and control to make the Temple of Jerusalem a holy place with the control of great leaders of money riches to serve them a control of territory. All this is to answer to them with the lies they made of my words to declare this. Know we are not renewing with places many humans built to better themselves in a wealth of possessions only to control people into believing that my words answer only them.

They well renew with evidence of another who uses these lies of 'God's children' when it is not our truth. Be understanding all has a purpose now as arrivals become seen and served, and answers are renewed with us only. Be prepared to share knowledge with us and others, only as visits begin, and the true children of God are answered.

My children are not tied to any religion or any groups or any country or any serving governments or any religious leader. They are scattered on Earth among the people and are placed, on their time of conception, in a place not suited for them. They are on Earth to open to the knowledge with the inequities of their life's experiences, to study all ways of evil and are settling with answers to many trusted truths. This answers to evidence of greater responding truth soon opening to them, only them.

This excludes all who see themselves above all others, and these ones will be answered by me and my armies, who will find them under any rock or in any hole.

God

Received by Za, January 18, 2017

This is the last post published from the blog:
newtimesonearth2012.blogspot.ca

We continue to communicate daily on different topics about the WW3, weather modification, government control systems, pandemics and diseases, arrivals, the coming changes and more.

God gave us free will to choose what is right and what is wrong. Decisions are being made all the time with leaders of the world on what their next moves should be. We can find ourselves very close to a disaster or a war, and then things change. I do believe that there are good forces opposing the evil of Earth, and in time will become victorious. So, we must continue to stand and wear the full armor of God, speak to him yourselves and open your heart to Him.

God bless all of you.

Za, May 18, 2020

Lexicon

Annunaki: are a group of deities who appear in the mythological traditions of ancient Sumerians, Akkadians, Assyrians, and Babylonians

aonma: the way of knowing the truth, proof and evidence

aonsuut: opening to...

Apoonanci: non-believer in God and his way

Archai: the word God uses to describe the Angels and God

baza: with.

bessron: sharing truthful words

bet: answer, visit or meeting

bona: good

bronma: a calling to the spiritual way, one's response to one's will and the way of great seeing. God's voice and way

cess: serve with

deers: truth and secret

Gersiel: a name used for a kind of Alien

herstuut: the questions asked are answered by God and the angels, also means being saved

ijheer: the holy spirit

Lemurian: the people and language of the ancient people of Lemuria

lona: stubborn, not wanting to change what one thinks or believes

nephilim: in the bible, they are said to be the offsprings of the sons of God and the daughters of man, but they are the offsprings of Lucifer

onm: shared knowledge and light of understanding

pleiadian: alien beings from

poon: truth, belief, believer, believing, proof and evidence

restuu: serving with faith and trust

sertuu: being in the light of truth

setu: bridging, meeting of two thoughts, time of reunification, time of reckoning

tessron: renew, renewals

ut: you

Utah: another name for God

toona: beautiful and a term of endearment